Military Departures, Homecomings and Death in Classical Athens

Also available from Bloomsbury

After the Crisis: Remembrance, Re-anchoring and Recovery in Ancient Greece and Rome, edited by Jacqueline Klooster and Inger NI Kuin
Military Leaders and Sacred Space in Classical Greek Warfare, Sonya Nevin
War as Spectacle, edited by Anastasia Bakogianni and Valerie M. Hope

Military Departures, Homecomings and Death in Classical Athens

Hoplite Transitions

Owen Rees

BLOOMSBURY ACADEMIC
LONDON • NEW YORK • OXFORD • NEW DELHI • SYDNEY

BLOOMSBURY ACADEMIC
Bloomsbury Publishing Plc
50 Bedford Square, London, WC1B 3DP, UK
1385 Broadway, New York, NY 10018, USA
29 Earlsfort Terrace, Dublin 2, Ireland

BLOOMSBURY, BLOOMSBURY ACADEMIC and the Diana logo
are trademarks of Bloomsbury Publishing Plc

First published in Great Britain 2022
Paperback edition published 2023

Cover image courtesy Antikensammlung, Staatliche Museen Zu Berlin – Preussischer
Kulturbesitz. F 2444. Photograph by Johannes Laurentius.

A catalogue record for this book is available from the British Library.

A catalog record for this book is available from the Library of Congress.

ISBN: HB: 978-1-3501-8864-8
         PB: 978-1-3501-8874-7
         ePDF: 978-1-3501-8865-5
         eBook: 978-1-3501-8866-2

Typeset by RefineCatch Limited, Bungay, Suffolk

To find out more about our authors and books visit www.bloomsbury.com
and sign up for our newsletters.

Contents

Figures, Tables and Maps   vii

Acknowledgements   ix

Abbreviations   x

1   Introduction   1
   1.1   The 'PTSD in history' debate   2
   1.2   The distinction between public and domestic   10
   1.3   Methodology and structure   14

2   The Warrior's Departure   17
   2.1   Methodological considerations   17
   2.2   Departure from the *oikos*   19

3   The Military Departure   35
   3.1   Joining the muster   35
   3.2   The army departs   52

4   Military Homecoming   63
   4.1   Arriving in Athens   64
   4.2   Dedications   75

5   The Warrior's Homecoming   81
   5.1   Homecoming arrivals on red-figure pottery?   81
   5.2   Homecoming arrivals in the literary evidence   90

6   Military Homecoming of the Dead   105
   6.1   Battlefield cremation   106
   6.2   *Patrios nomos*   113

7   The Domestic Reception of the War Dead   123
   7.1   The family and the funeral   123
   7.2   Experience of the *oikos*   137
   7.3   Return of the war dead   146

8   Conclusion   149

Contents

Notes   153
Bibliography   219
Index   245

Figures, Tables and Maps

Figures

2.1 Red figure *stamnos*, attributed to the Achilles Painter, London, British
Museum: E448.   21

2.2a White-ground *lekythos*, attributed to the Athens Painter, Berlin,
Antikensammlung: F2444.   23

2.2b Red-figure *hydria*, attributed to the 'Dwarf' Painter, Boston (MA),
Museum of Fine Arts: 03.798.   23

2.3 Red-figure amphora, attributed to the painter of the Berlin Hydria,
London, British Museum: E275.   25

5.1a Red-figure *pelike*, unattributed, Rome, Mus. Naz. Etrusco di Villa
Giulia: 46942.   83

5.1b Red-figure *pelike*, unattributed, Rome, Mus. Naz. Etrusco di Villa
Giulia: 46942.   83

5.2a Red-figure *pelike*, attributed to the Altmura Painter, New York (NY),
Metropolitan Museum: 56.171.44.   85

5.2b Red-figure *pelike*, attributed to the Altmura Painter, New York (NY),
Metropolitan Museum: 56.171.44.   86

5.3a Red-figure amphora, attributed to the Niobid Painter, Atlanta (GA),
Emory University, Michael C. Carlos Museum: 1984.12A.   97

5.3b Red-figure amphora, attributed to the Niobid Painter, Atlanta (GA),
Emory University, Michael C. Carlos Museum: 1984.12B.   98

7.1 White ground *lekythos*, attributed to the Vouni Painter, New York (NY),
Metropolitan Museum, 35.11.5.   130

7.2 Relief for the cenotaph of Dexileos, Athens, Kermaeikos
Museum: P1130.   133

7.3 Grave relief for Demokleides, Athens, National
Archaeological Museum: 752.   135

Tables

3.1 Athenian mustering figures   42
3.2 Athenian battle figures   43
4.1 Athenian musters and method of transportation   66

Maps

3.1 Map of possible mustering points in and around Athens   48

Acknowledgements

The idea for this book was formulated as a PhD thesis under the keen and critical eye of my supervisor and friend Jason Crowley. But the manuscript was put together and refined during the year 2020, which has, without a shadow of a doubt, been a s**t year all round. Because of this context, I will acknowledge here the most pivotal support I have received. First and foremost, my thanks go to the Bloomsbury team, in particular Lily Mac Mahon who has fielded no end of e-mails and queries and offered unwavering support throughout this process.

In this year of hell, my wife, Carly, has seen her time and attention forcibly split between the family and her work, through periods of isolation, lockdowns, my own period of unemployment and doing right by her parents. During it all, she continued to work when she could, worked her budgeting magic when the money looked to run dry and never once allowed me to give up on completing this manuscript – no matter how many times I tried. Together we faced the unknown together, evolving and regularly swapping roles as the world demanded more adaptations than either of us are usually comfortable with. As she took that great weight on her shoulders, my two research assistants Matilda and Henry put up with their dad's efforts to home-school them. Our time spent all working at the kitchen table is a memory that will be with me forever. You always let me work on my laptop while we all watched *Captain Underpants* or *Horrible Histories* and I am forever grateful. We have witnessed a very strange period, one with great sadness and loss, but what we were not, was ever lonely. I can say all this here, because I know you will never read it!

Of course, more generally, I am indebted to various scholars who have offered advice and their thoughts during the development of my ideas. In particular, my thanks go to Tim McNiven, Robin Osborne, Susan Deacy, Peter Liddel, Alexandra Wilding, Roel Konijnendijk, Cezary Kucewicz, and Sam Fernes. I am also extremely grateful for the help and patience offered by John Taylor and Costas Panayotakis who both had the thankless task of teaching me ancient Greek. I am also appreciative for all of those who have made that experience more sociable, particular thanks goes to my comrades in research Ian Bass, Tom McGrath, Jessica Purdy and Michala Hulme.

Abbreviations

Abbreviations of ancient sources follow the Oxford Classical Dictionary.

AIO   *Attic Inscriptions Online* [Online]. Available at: www.
             atticinscriptions.com/

ARV   Beazley, John. *Attic Red-Figure Vase-Painters,* 2nd edn Oxford:
             Clarendon Press, 1963.

BA   *Beazley Archive Pottery Database* [Online] Available at: www.
             beazley.ox.ac.uk/pottery/default.htm

CVA   *Corpus Vasorum Antiquorum (1925–)*

GHI²   Tod, Marcus N, ed. *A Selection of Greek Historical Inscriptions, vol
             II: From 403 to 323 BC* (1948).

IG   *Inscriptiones Graecae* (1873–)

LSCG Suppl. Sokolowski, Franciszek. *Lois Sacrees des Cites Grecques.
             Supplement.* Paris: E de Boccard, 1962.

LSJ   Liddell, Henry and Robert Scott. *Greek-English Lexicon,* 9th edn
             Oxford, Clarendon Press, 1925–1940.

PH   The Packard Humanities Institute *Searchable Greek Inscriptions:
             A Scholarly Tool in Progress.* [Online]. Available at: https://
             inscriptions.packhum.org/

SEG   *Supplementum epigraphicum Graecum (1923–)*

TrGF   Snell, Bruno, Richard Kannicht and Stefan L Radt, ed.
             Tragicorum Graecorum Fragmenta, 6 vols (1971–2004), vol. 1.
             Göttingen: Vandenhoeck and Ruprecht, 1986.

1

Introduction

The subject of homecoming in the classical Greek world seems, in many ways, hardwired into the disciplines of Classics and Ancient History. For many, one of our first encounters with these disciplines came through the *Nostoi* stories, most likely that of Odysseus. So, it is of little surprise that the idea of homecoming permeates through the literary studies, nor that ancient historians have become fascinated by the idea of the homecoming Greek warrior. How did he adapt to coming home? How hard did he find it to reconcile his experiences of war with the normality of domestic life? How had war affected him on a personal level?

This interest in homecoming as a literary concept and, in turn, as a psychological experience, has meant that one area has been neglected to date. The process of homecoming itself. While it is, of course, important to understand the warrior's experience after his demobilisation, this can only be understood after we have identified how a man transitioned from his domestic life to his military service and then how he transitioned back into his domestic life again. What was the process? What were the basic logistics involved? What rituals and customs took place? Who else shared these experiences with him? And, of course, is there any evidence for how these transitions were perceived by the warrior or by those around him?

Some of the questions asked within this book have never been satisfactorily answered and some seem to have been rarely asked. Yet, it is important to ask them so that we can begin to gauge the experience of transitions between the domestic and military duties. Like all such enquiries, our analysis is guided by insufficient evidence, thus not all these questions can be satisfactorily answered. But, by asking them, we can begin to pick away at our historical preconceptions and start to understand the homecoming transition within a diachronically sensitive framework.

1.1 The 'PTSD in history' debate

The most prevalent analysis on the experiences of the homecoming Greek warrior comes from the studies of post-traumatic stress disorder (PTSD) and its presence in the ancient world.[1] Proponents for the idea that PTSD existed in the ancient world base their work on universalist principles that accept all combat experience to be inherently the same and, because modern combat produces stress-related trauma, this must always be the case wherever and whenever there is, or has been, war.[2] Conversely, those scholars opposing this model do so on relativist principles, trusting in turn in the individual, the idiosyncratic nature of every culture and their style of warfare.[3]

Both viewpoints are strongly focused on the psychology of combat stress and the trauma it may create. Both schools of thought survey the evidence to examine how exposure to combat affected the behaviours of the combatants, how individuals are said to be feeling, whether there is evidence of addiction or depression or any other signifier stated in the American Psychiatric Association's *Diagnostic and Statistical Manual of Mental Disorders* (the DSM-IV, or DSM-V in its most up-to-date version). They look at the vulnerability, or strength, of the individual based upon their social integrations before and during combat, as a means of analysing whether it is possible for ancient warriors to have suffered trauma.

1.1.1 Universalist approach

The primary catalyst behind the examination of PTSD in ancient history is, without question, the revolutionary work of Dr Jonathan Shay, a former staff psychiatrist at the United States Department of Veteran Affairs Outpatient Clinic.[4] Within his two influential books, he showed how both the *Iliad* and the *Odyssey* could be used to aid in the rehabilitation of Vietnam War veterans. In so doing, Shay aligned the experiences of the heroes Achilles and Odysseus with those of modern veterans. With Achilles he offered a model of the combative military experience; with Odysseus he formed an allegorical homecoming narrative. While Shay was aware that his connections between the past and present experience could be strained, it was not his intention to analyse ancient mentalities or experiences. For instance, his work on Odysseus focuses on the modern diagnosis of PTSD but he is clear in stating that Odysseus did not have PTSD as the American Psychiatric Association defined it.[5] Yet, this did not prevent Shay from placing the hero on a hypothetical therapist's couch; historical credibility was not his primary concern nor should it be a factor by which his work should be judged.[6]

Unknown to Shay, his work tapped into a growing field of military history that was exploring the individual experience of military service. This approach was born from the seminal work of John Keegan who set down a model of research in his book *The Face of Battle*.[7] Keegan's revolutionary approach redirected the study of warfare, which was primarily based on tactics and strategy, to the examination of the individual soldier and his varied experiences. Keegan's work would strongly influence that of Victor Davis Hanson, who used Keegan's ethos to re-examine the lives and experiences of the combatants in ancient Greek warfare.[8] When Shay released his novel interpretation of the Homeric epic poems, he tapped into a growing field of both ancient and military history; but, more than that, he brought a plethora of outside knowledge and experience to allow for a completely new reading of well-trodden ground in classical literature.

Shay's first book was quickly picked up and qualified by Lawrence Tritle in his equally hard-hitting book *From Melos to My Lai*, which was an examination of the impact of war on the participants in Ancient Greece; often calling upon his own experiences as a veteran of the Vietnam War.[9] Where Shay's analysis was based within the realm of poetry, devoid of any wider cultural or historic context, Tritle attempted to qualify this analysis with an evidence-based review of historical narratives. *Melos to My Lai* was followed by *A New History of the Peloponnesian War*, a book in which Tritle attempted to employ the conclusions he drew in *Melos* to analyse the Peloponnesian War as a whole, with a particular focus on the socio-military aspects of the war, rather than the more conventional approach of political, and strategic analysis. His works have highlighted the potentially traumatic experiences that are evident in the histories but, more importantly, he has identified three direct, non-fictional examples from the written record which he believes express the symptoms of combat-induced trauma.[10] The first instance, according to Tritle, comes during the battle of Marathon with the strange case of Epizelus.[11] Epizelus fought in the frontline of battle and saw the man next to him killed by a large imposing Greek warrior fighting for the Persians. At that moment he went blind, although he was not touched by any sort of blade or projectile.[12] To Tritle, this is a clear case of trauma-induced blindness and his comparison with a similar phenomenon in Cambodia is used to cement this idea.[13] The second instance, according to Tritle, comes from the writing of the logographer Gorgias.[14] In his defence of Helen, Gorgias describes an incurable madness that can result from abject fear on the battlefield, something Tritle sees as a reflection of trauma.[15] Tritle's final example from the Greek historical record comes from Xenophon's mini-biography of the Spartan mercenary commander Clearchus. Tritle identifies Clearchus as a man deeply affected by war and whose personality bears a striking resemblance to the criteria of PTSD.[16]

The work of both scholars has become the lynchpin to the universalist position which has, for the past twenty years, been the most prevalent analysis. In 2011, Aislinn Melchior noted that the view that PTSD was present in the ancient world was 'fast becoming dogma'.[17] The work of these scholars popularised the study of trauma in the ancient world and has stimulated a large number of publications exploring the theme. The model of combat trauma has been used thus far to explore the characterisations of dramatic figures such as Medea, Heracles, Ajax and Philoctetes;[18] to examine Athenian theatre as a form of 'restoration';[19] to try and understand cases of military desertion;[20] to explore the military resilience of Socrates;[21] and to explain the character of Alexander the Great.[22] The work of Shay and Tritle has also become a springboard for scholars to examine combat trauma in different ancient societies, such as the Assyrians and the Romans.[23] More importantly, the universalist model has become influential outside the historical discipline.

Since the end of the First World War, the academic sciences have been interested in finding historical precedents to combat-induced psychological trauma. In September 1919, Dean A Worcester wrote a short letter to the editors of *Science*, published in the Notes and Comments section, in which he quoted Herodotus' story of Epizelus, followed by a simple question: 'Is this, perchance, the first account of "shell-shock"?'[24] The story of Epizelus appeared subsequently in a myriad of non-historical publications, assigning various labels and diagnoses such as war neuroses, battle hysteria, conversion disorder and, of course, PTSD.[25] Over time, he secured himself a place in many psychological textbooks, so, as Helen King so aptly describes, within the innocuous letter of Worcester 'the [new] phenomenon had been given its origin in myth'.[26]

It is not just Epizelus, but ancient history more generally which is so often drawn upon by the psychological sciences. Some scientific papers have tried to explore the ancient sources to offer psychological trauma a lineage and heritage that it is felt to be lacking.[27] Some studies have tried to push back the origins of PTSD from Herodotus to twelfth-century BC Mesopotamia;[28] another has gone one-step further, pushing it back to *c.* 5000 BC India.[29] Others have used ancient history as a starting point from which to explore modern trauma and even offer new forms of therapy.[30] As a result of this pervading truism, the *Encyclopedia of*

Trauma states that the themes of trauma are easily identified in ancient drama.[31] In both forms of study, ancient history is used to justify modern ideas and modern understanding without the necessary historical due diligence. The difficulty of using modern diagnoses in the study of the past has been acknowledged, but this does not stop many bold conclusions coming forward regarding the history of PTSD, the understanding of the ancient world and how the modern world could learn from it.[32] This is a natural repercussion of the universalist position.

1.1.2 Relativist approach

The relativist position is still in its early stages of development. Before 2011, there was no study which actively critiqued the models of Shay and Tritle; any such criticisms were tucked away in book reviews.[33] However, there has been work outside the historical discipline which challenges the universalist position surrounding the study of PTSD. The most forthright of these is by psychiatrist Prof Allan Young, who argues that PTSD is a historical product, not a universal diagnosis.[34] However, this scepticism of the universalist model did not enter the study of ancient history until the work of Aislinn Melchior. In her influential work, Melchior brought into question the method of using modern psychology to understand the ancient world, with specific regard to ancient Rome.[35] By identifying basic social differences between modern and ancient people, such as the mortality rate and therefore the personal exposure to death, Melchior suggested caution in the use of PTSD models.[36] However, Melchior never went so far as to dismiss the possibility of PTSD in the ancient world.

Melchior's analysis of the PTSD model influenced Korneel van Lommel, who followed an anthropologically inspired analysis of the Roman source material. Rather than transplant modern psychological and sociological theories, he explored the Roman accounts to identify their reactions to mental disorders in the Roman army.[37] He identifies evidence for an accepted distinction between physical and mental ailments in the Roman army but does not align these ailments with any modern diagnoses. Yet, much like Melchior before him, van Lommel does not go as far as to say that PTSD did not exist in the ancient world; indeed, he puts forward a case that the same psychological strains and impairment are present but does not think they should be called PTSD. The first and thus far only scholar to actually challenge the PTSD model head on and argue that it could not have existed in the ancient (Greek) world, was Jason Crowley.[38]

Crowley formulates his hard-lined relativist argument by comparing one form of modern soldier, the American infantryman, with one form of ancient warrior, the Athenian hoplite. To avoid arbitrarily unique characteristics between each form of warrior, Crowley's work focuses on four main elements: the core norms and values of each warrior; the social environment for the combatant; the tactical environment; and the technological environment.[39] After a close analysis of these four intersecting factors he identifies the modern infantryman to be more susceptible to PTSD, whereas the Athenian social and combative environment left him 'effectively immunised against the same risk'.[40] Thus, by identifying his historical anomaly, Crowley claims to have proven that the soldier is not universal.

Crowley's argument is enticing, not least for its historical relativism via its demand for contextualisation. However, the argument against universalism does not actually disprove the notion that the ancient world witnessed combat trauma. By engaging with the universalist model, Crowley moulds his argument around similar universalist principles. He assumes that the factors behind modern combat trauma would be the factors behind all historical forms of combat trauma. For instance, his engagement with the experience of death is relevant to disprove the universalist position, but he does not consider other factors which may have effected an Athenian more than a modern infantryman.[41] One prime example would be the social stigma and shame inherent in the discarding of one's shield, something Crowley identifies as a form of 'direct action' for the hoplite.[42] On the one hand, this direct action does alleviate the hoplite from the psychological stress of 'palliative action'. On the other hand, it does not alleviate the stress, social exclusion and legal ramifications that came with the discarding of one's shield.[43] This cuts to the heart of the matter: the perspective is taken through the eyes of the warrior from his position as a warrior. This builds on Crowley's earlier work evaluating the motivating factors being an Athenian's willingness to fight.[44] It assumes a seamless transition of ideals between the civic and domestic base in which an Athenian lived and the military service he was duty-bound to perform. However, an Athenian hoplite was not always a warrior, this was a role he entered and exited numerous times during his life.

What Crowley's thesis has revealed is the need to reassess the ancient PTSD model. It successfully brings into question the ability to simply look at the sources and try to identify features of combat trauma. It is now pivotal that any study investigating this theme does so with a diachronically sensitive approach. In addition to this, the flaw in Crowley's own argument highlights a second important factor in the future study of PTSD; the need to evaluate the wider sociological framework which not only produced the hoplite, but in which he also engaged outside his military capacity. To avoid the methodological weaknesses of both sides in this debate it is necessary first to identify a well-established factor in PTSD studies but examine it solely through the social context and ritual rubric of the historical culture.

1.1.3 Military homecomings

During the outbreak of the first Peloponnesian War (460–444 BC), a battle between the Corinthians and the Athenians was fought to a stalemate.[45] With no clear victor, the Corinthians departed from the field and went back to their city. But the Athenians, feeling that they had held the advantage during the battle, decided to erect a trophy and claim victory before similarly departing to nearby Megara. When the Corinthian army reached Corinth, the men underwent a torrent of abuse and taunting from the old men of the city. Out of shame, they left the city twelve days later and marched back to the battlefield to erect their own trophy. Unfortunately for them, the Athenians were aware of their expedition and staged an ambush inflicting heavy casualties upon the Corinthian army. This episode from classical Greece offers an extreme repercussion to a volatile military homecoming. The Corinthian army had returned home believing they had done their duty, only to be judged and scolded by men who had not fought and did not appreciate the circumstances of the battle. The judgement and abuse was a systematic torrent of social shame, driving the returned veterans to action. Thus, their annihilation was a direct consequence of their homecoming.[46]

The homecoming of soldiers has long been identified as an important post-military risk factor in the study of PTSD. According to numerous studies of veterans from the Vietnam War, the psychological isolation, the feelings of rejection and the lack of support or celebration that defined so many of their experiences, 'were the strongest predictors of frequency and intensity of their PTSD symptoms'.[47] A recent longitudinal study selected twenty-two pre-military, war zone and post-military variables to predict symptom severity in male veterans forty years after their period of service.[48] After their multivariable analysis, the authors identified a perceived poor homecoming reception as a robust predictor of PTSD.[49] The high prevalence of a perceived poor homecoming reception is not unique to Vietnam veterans, nor to American soldiers. Studies have made similar observations when studying the Israeli forces, Portuguese forces and British reservists.[50] Within the umbrella term of 'homecoming', one major factor that has been consistently linked with PTSD is a perceived lack of social support. This includes the support of family, of employers, of the military and of society in general.[51] From as early as 1985, a clear link was identified between veterans with PTSD and their reports of a decline in social support post-homecoming.[52]

The benefit of using homecoming as the primary factor for consideration in this research is its tangible and identifiable nature. A warrior returning home is as much a physical event as it is sociological or psychological. With regard to identifying it within ancient Greek sources, it is neither controversial nor subjective. What is more, the subject of homecoming has begun to appear in the universalist research outside the historical disciplines, making it a timely and important area for consideration. Case in point, research by Kamieński looks to the ancient world while examining the use of pharmacotherapy to help modern veterans with PTSD.[53] In his conclusion, he clearly states that there is a continuity in western warfare, and that the modern world must look to the ancient Greeks to learn.[54] As it is one of the only papers to articulate such a bold view so openly, it is necessary to quote it in full:

> By instrumentalizing war, the West deprived its homecoming soldiers of a social healing mechanism which over the centuries had helped warriors in their transition back to a civilian life. Traditional societies practiced special purification ceremonies because they understood that war affects society as a whole. These rituals were a way to tell the soldier that what he did was good, and that "his community of sane and normal men welcomed him back". This ceremonial cleansing helped warriors to deal with stress, guilt, and sorrow. Certainly, there were warriors suffering from what we call PTSD, but this condition 'was treated as a communal rather than an individual problem'.[55]

Karen O'Donnell has recently aired a similar hypothesis, but there is no suggestion from her referencing that Kamieński was an influence.[56] For O'Donnell, ancient cultures 'understood better than our modern culture does, the need to aid warrior [sic] in their homecomings'.[57] Both authors use the ancient world to make a modern observation: returning soldiers are not being communally reintegrated into society. However, their reliance on the ancient world is allowing them to over-generalise and combine sociological and ritualistic phenomena which have no right to be grouped together. Most concerning is O'Donnell's ability to move seamlessly between Homeric Greece, Imperial Rome and then the modern Maasai of east Africa.[58] What is perhaps more interesting about O'Donnell's observation is that her prime example of a troubled homecoming comes from the *Odyssey*, but the same poem cannot be used to show that the Greeks executed any form of purification ritual during a warrior's homecoming, the very argument that O'Donnell is trying to make.

This hypothesis that the ancient Greeks understood war and its effect on individuals and society as a whole is fundamentally based on assumptions. A relativist such as Crowley would argue that the classical Athenians would not need a purifying reintegration into society following military service. His psychosocial model is based on a seamless transition, a congruence of ideals and behaviours between domestic and military life.[59] For Crowley, the Athenian man was 'prepared, even conditioned, by his socio-political system to be ready ... to take his assigned place on the field of battle'.[60] By extension, this institutionalised preparation for war would require neither a process of resocialisation before combat, nor one before homecoming. However, Crowley's thesis is based primarily on sociological influences and neither examines the Athenian processes of going to war, nor returning from it.

Considering the important role that homecoming has in the understanding of PTSD, it is an appropriate psychosocial factor to analyse in the context of classical Greece. The work of Crowley has emphasised the importance of cultural specificity, thus it is necessary to examine the Greek warrior for which we have the most evidence, the Athenian hoplite. Remarkably, the logistical and ritualistic process of an Athenian hoplite returning home has neither been attempted nor analysed before, so it is important to establish the fundamental elements of the transition, without being guided by a search for trauma, or the absence of it. To that end, it is necessary to set aside one important factor in the modern studies of homecoming, reintegration.[61] Of course, any examination of homecoming will touch upon the issues of reintegration, but a full examination of the subject will only be possible once the basic framework of a homecoming can be established. To understand the reintegration of an Athenian hoplite, it would be necessary to draw upon a greater level of evidence than is available. Instead, there are areas of the homecoming transition that can be examined in detail.

As Crowley's argument focuses on the societal processes and pressures that prepared the Athenian man for the battlefield, it is first necessary to set down the process by which an Athenian man departed for war. This must include the departure from the home as an individual, as well as the departure from the city as part of an army. Following this, the homecoming of the hoplite can be examined: first as part of an army, then as an individual. Finally, the dead must also be afforded a homecoming, for the Athenians practiced repatriation for their war dead. Therefore, the process of bringing home the dead needs to be assessed, followed by how both the families and the *polis* memorialised their dead. What this line of enquiry offers to the PTSD debate is a sociological framework of military transitions based upon the available evidence, rather than a leading hypothesis. If there was a social tension involved in the performance of military service, it will be evident during these transitions. Similarly, if the Greeks did perform purification rituals for their hoplites as part of their homecoming, it will be present in the source material.

1.2 The distinction between public and domestic

This work will demonstrate that there is a clear distinction between domestic transitions (leaving and returning to the home) and military transitions (joining and departing with the army, returning and disbanding). Such an observation was born organically from the evidence and was not an original hypothesis of this work. However, such a distinction must be validated; not least, because it asserts a clear distinction between the domestic and military sphere. On its own, this may not be contentious, but when we consider that some of the military rituals and transitions that will be considered were, in fact, performed by citizens, doing their public duty, while inside the city walls, it is important to understand the parameters with which this research will confine itself.

A contrast between domestic and military spheres of activity will naturally attract a comparison between the *oikos/polis*, or the *idios/demosios* dichotomies that has been so influential in the study of ancient Greek life. However, neither paradigm is strictly appropriate for the subject at hand. *Oikos* may be appropriate to describe the social unit of the household, but *polis* encompasses much more than just the military. To define and describe the transitioning into and out of the *oikos* is made simple by the boundaries described in the sources. The *oikos* encompassed a ritual space that was distinct from the world beyond it. One manifestation of this boundary was the statue of Hermes that would stand outside the door of the home. In Vernant's paradigm, the symbolic boundary between *oikos* and *polis* was the herm;[62] this consisted of a carved head of the god Hermes, sat atop a square pillar, adorned with male genitals. As Thucydides relates, some Athenians kept these sculptures at the doorway to their private homes, and therefore this offered a clear threshold and distinction between the two spheres.[63] Of course, not all Athenian houses had such a physical marker of space, but it is clear from the evidence that the sacred space of the *oikos* was well understood; nowhere is this clearer than in the customs associated with *miasma*.[64] The topic of *miasma*, as pertaining to hoplites, is dealt with in section

5.2.2, for now it is important to establish that a household would become collectively polluted by events such as a death. This not only affected all the members of the household, but it also affected the physical space of the house (*oikia*).

The sacred space of an Athenian house was symbolised by its hearth. By the classical period, the hearth was as much an ideological construct as it was a physical thing.[65] The hearth was sometimes called upon to emphasise domestic relationships, such as when Xenophon described one of the social restrictions placed upon the *tresantes* (tremblers) in Sparta: 'he must sit by his hearth without a wife' (γυναικὸς δὲ κενὴν ἑστίαν οὐ περιοπτέον).[66] What this meant, in reality, is not clear; it may have amounted to the *tresas* being unable to marry, or maybe the wife being able to leave the home.[67] In any case, the identification of the empty hearth (κενὴν ἑστίαν) is a notable emotive ploy used by Xenophon to emphasise a sense of isolation that continued inside the *oikos*.[68] Domestic relationships are similarly reinforced within Attic drama, such as those between Tecmessa and Ajax, in Sophocles' *Ajax*, when Tecmessa calls upon Zeus of the hearth (ἐφεστίου Διὸς) and her wedding bed in her attempts to persuade Ajax not to take his own life, once again reinforcing the ties between the hearth and familial relationships.[69] Whereas Aeschylus emphasises the sacrilege of Clytemnestra's murder of Agamemnon when the king demands to be let through to pay his respects at the hearth, laying the emotive foundation for what would later become the scene of his murder.[70]

A second method of emphasising the *oikos* through the symbolism of the hearth was to make reference to the 'paternal hearth' (ἑστίας πατρός). Aeschylus has Orestes swear on his father's hearth that he was not lying to Electra, giving greater rhetorical weight to his words.[71] Similarly, in Euripides' *Alcestis*, Admetus underlines his foolish character when he claims he would have renounced his father's hearth in public if it had been deemed necessary.[72] While both examples here are in keeping with the overarching storylines – the siblings' revenge for their father's death and the sense of betrayal felt by Admetus that Pheres would not die for him – no similar observation can be levelled at Plato's *Laws*. Plato describes a person who is seen to defile the paternal hearth (πατρῷαν ἑστίαν) with unworthy pursuits as being deserving of a year-long imprisonment.[73] The crime described is following a trade in retail, any legislation for which, the Athenian acknowledges, would undermine the dignity of a freeman, so the only authority Plato's Athenian has to call upon is the father as head of the *oikos*.

The sacred role of the hearth went beyond an ideological function, it was often the ritual focal point of familial rites: whether it be the offering of libations and prayers, or the initiation of new born babies, new wives and new slaves.[74] In each instance the hearth was the symbolic centre of the *oikos*, whether it was the source from which the family could communicate with the gods, or as the focal point from which strangers were introduced.[75] Furthermore, in each instance, the hearth became a sacred space for the performance of ritual, requiring a state of cleansed purity before they began.[76] As a sacred space, the purified status of the hearth was of great importance; as Clytemnestra declares to the ill-fated Cassandra, she was chosen to share the holy water of Clytemnestra's house, making a direct reference to such a purification rite.[77] The Greek term here is χερνίβων, literally a water-basin, but in the wider context of Clytemnestra's intent to commit a sacrificial murder at the hearth, she is making reference to the water bowl used to purify the sacred space around the central hearth (ἑστίας μεσομφάλου).[78] This sacred space could not, from necessity, function like a temple with a full restriction of polluting acts such as death and birth, both of which generally occurred in the home.[79] However, there was a tradition of sexual restriction, whether by the refusal to have sex in the presence of the hearth, or alternatively not appearing before the sacred space in the aftermath of masturbation.[80] There is also the strong suggestion that the hearth was a sacred source of asylum, and to kill a man at your own hearth was a worse crime than simply murder.[81] In this regard, the hearth was not as much the physical construct of a fireplace, but the focalised ritual space within the *oikos*.

What made the hearth a unique sacred space was that suppliants could be immersed within that space while both they and the house were in a state of pollution.[82] The placing of the lustral water at the door, described as a standard custom by Euripides, allowed those who became polluted by entering the house, especially in the event of a death, to purify themselves on leaving,[83] an act that prevented the pollution infecting the wider community.[84] Nevertheless, the state of pollution that consumed the house could not stay forever, so the house itself was ritually cleansed and purified.[85] This is the clearest evidence available that the *oikos* was distinct from the world outside of it, epitomised by this ritualised boundary that was defined by the purification rite at the doorway which, in essence, determined that a state of pollution was allowed in one sphere but not the other.[86]

According to Vernant's paradigm, anything outside of the *oikos* is categorised as the *polis*, which was the public and political sphere. This distinction is problematic for it assumes two fundamental things: there was no crossover between the *oikos* and the *polis* and that everything outside of the *oikos* can be grouped together so simply. While the evidence clearly shows a separation between the sacred space of the *oikos* and that of the outside world, it does not preclude an interchange of actions, ideologies and behaviours. Simply put, the *oikos* and the *polis* were not as separate as scholars once believed. More importantly, by grouping together all of the other elements that made up the city under the banner of *polis*, the model ignores the complexity and individuality of the composite parts. This distinction has led scholars of ancient religion to identify religious activity as either *polis* religion or domestic religion. Most influentially, Christiane Sourvinou-Inwood has argued that there was only *polis* religion and that all domestic religion was 'perceived as part of the *polis* cult'.[87] This model has been instrumental to furthering academic understanding of Greek cults, but conversely limits our ability to evaluate the multifaceted elements of Greek society and, in turn, their relationship with cult and ritual activity.[88]

It is not pertinent to look at the *polis* as a whole, because the Athenian hoplite did not strictly depart and return to the *polis*. Walter Runciman defines the *polis* as a citizen-state, rather than a city-state, thus the *polis* is centred on the adult male citizens of Athens.[89] This definition ignores the urban space as an important defining feature of the city but does offer greater clarity to the ideological underpinning to the term *polis* than the more conventional translation of city-state.[90] The term *polis* can thus incorporate both the body politic and the urban space. As an Athenian hoplite never left his peers who were, by extension of Runciman's definition, a part of the *polis*, the hoplite could not therefore depart or return from the *polis*. Similarly, the notion that the *polis* was a city-state is problematic because it implies a formal structure and places an emphasis on the physical locale. Yet a hoplite could depart for military service, as part of military group, without leaving Attica, or indeed the walls of the city, especially in times of emergency.[91] Furthermore, this distinction of *polis*, by either definition, assumes in the case of this study that the political system of Athens was ideologically and ritually congruent with the military.

To avoid confusion and unnecessary qualifications, the two elements under review here are not *oikos* and *polis*, but rather the household and the military. Household and *oikos* will be used interchangeably, by which it is meant that the ideological and wider familial construct of the *oikos* will be combined with the domestic locale, that is the domestic space from which a hoplite departs and returns. The second category of 'military' avoids any ideological construction of *oikos* versus *polis*. The military system was the one the hoplite joined to enact his service and, once he was dismissed from his service, he could then return to his day-to-day life. It is not assumed that there was an absence of shared ritual activity, religious behaviour, or of ideology between these two spheres.

1.3 Methodology and structure

As previously mentioned, it is important for this book to be contextually and diachronically sensitive to the material. As such, a Panhellenic study would be too broad and would be forced to overlook many of the unique contexts of the various *poleis*. The choice of Athens requires little explanation, as the majority of the written sources and archaeological evidence come from Attica. This permits the avoidance of speculation regarding the adoption of Athenian ideology in other Greek regions. Similarly, as the majority of the available evidence about Athens dates from the fifth and fourth centuries BC, the book will focus within this timeframe.

The lack of scholarly discussion on the departure and homecoming of either individual hoplites or Athenian armies is, perhaps, indicative of the scarcity of evidence available. To piece together a template of a hoplite's transitions to and from military service, it has been necessary to draw from a wide range of evidentiary forms. Literary evidence forms the predominant basis of examination, but it is also necessary to analyse the orators, fragments of drama, ceramic art, sculpture, epigraphy and grave goods. Often the sources do not mention the transitions in any form of totality but offer brief insights that must be brought together with other scraps of evidence to form a coherent narrative. These variant forms of evidence raise numerous methodological issues which are discussed as and when they arise.

This book will follow the transitional experiences of the hoplite, with each transitional phase split into two distinct parts. By assessing both the domestic and military transitions side by side, it will be possible to highlight the variances of ideologies, ritual activity and individual participation. It is also possible to trace the relationship between the hoplite and his own personal, civilian identity, as he undergoes these transitions. In essence, it is possible to see the process by which the Athenian military system encouraged a state of de-individuation. While the general discussion on de-individuation focuses on the loss of personal moral identity within a group, our interest here is more specifically on that sense of personal identity and personal agency which is being lost, and examines how it is reclaimed during the homecoming. Only by understanding how the various transitions occurred and indeed varied, is it possible to understand the importance and influence of them on the individual. Chapters 2 and 3 focus on the departure of the hoplite from his home and then his departure as part of the military group. While our understanding of the domestic departure is fundamentally a ritualistic one, the military departure necessitates a greater understanding of its logistics. Once this understanding of the logistics of muster is understood, it is then possible to assess the rituals involved in the physical departure of the army, and the de-individuated state of the individual within this process.

Chapters 4 and 5 move to the end of the military campaign and thus follow the army back to Athens, before examining the hoplite's later return to his home. To understand the military homecoming, it is of fundamental importance to establish exactly how Athenian armies returned to Athens. As this is an area which academics have not fully examined, it is necessary to ask some basic, yet integral, questions: how did they travel home, did they come back as an army or as small groups, did they receive some form of parade or public reception? Chapter 4 follows the Athenian army to Piraeus – their primary entry point of Attica – and then looks at their reception having returned to the city. Having established the basic experience of the army's return to Athens, it is then prudent to examine the point at which a hoplite was actually released from his military duty. This naturally ends at the point where an army ceased to claim any mutual identity, the collective and individual commemorations for a particular period of service.[92] It is only at this stage that the return home of the individual hoplite can be constructed; this is analysed in Chapter 5. Much like Chapter 2, the domestic transition focuses predominantly on the ritual activity associated with the homecoming.

Chapter 6 acknowledges that not all homecomings are made by living people and that the Athenian process of repatriation did, in a very real way, offer the war dead a homecoming of their own. To align this section with the previous, it has been necessary to move beyond the rhetoric of the source material and analyse some basic, yet unestablished, forms of enquiry: How did they burn their war dead? What were the logistics involved in such a commitment? In what state were they brought back to Athens? From this logistical underpinning, it is then possible to try to reconstruct the practicalities behind the famous *patrios nomos*. The entire funeral process was one of de-individuation, the hoplite was stripped of all identity and joined a collective mass, the war dead, as a recipient of state honours and state memorialisation. Chapter 7 examines the familial reaction to this. For the family, the dead hoplite was made a hero of the state but equally he was stripped of all his links to his family, he was no longer theirs. In this final chapter, the subject of a domestic reception for the war dead can be approached, that is, how the family was able to reclaim the identity and memory of the individual lost to them by a public funeral.

2

The Warrior's Departure

The departing warrior has been a long-studied artistic motif of the classical Greek world. These iconic images, that adorn some of the most striking artistic works surviving from the late archaic to the mid-classical period, have been studied in isolation, revealing important elements of Greek socio-military history.[1] However, the lack of extensive literary evidence has meant that the historical topic of the departure has been rather neglected. This chapter shall rectify this by supplementing the pictorial evidence with the few examples of literary departures and will build upon the existing scholarship and extend the analysis into three key areas: (i) the possible ideological undertones that these images reflect within their domestic settings and strong focus upon the *oikos*; (ii) the 'real-life' version of these artistic, and ideological, portrayals – how did a Greek warrior actually depart from his home, who else was involved, what rituals were performed, and what was the overarching emotional framework for the rite? And (iii) the experience of the family during this departure.

2.1 Methodological considerations

Regarding the theme of a warrior's departure, it is immediately apparent that the ceramic evidence is the most abundant, with over 1,126 vases (330 red-figure) having been identified, or tentatively labelled as, depicting a departing warrior.[2] The use of this evidence herein will essentially follow the direction that classical scholarship has taken in the past twenty-five years, that is, to move away from an iconographical approach and toward an iconological one.[3] Following from Mary Beard, the emphasis within this study is not on artistic motif, but an exploration of what these scenes can tell us about classical Greek attitudes to men departing for war, from the perspective of the viewer not the painter.[4] However, it is necessary to exercise due caution with this form of visual evidence. These images cannot be read as perfect representations of the reality of their subject matter, these are not photographs that have taken a snapshot of time which can then be analysed.[5] As François Lissarrague observed, each painting is, in fact, a construction, a product of the painter's own interpretation of the real world around him.[6] Yet, Patricia Hannah, following Tonio Hölscher, argues that these vases were seen every day, maybe even used every day, by someone somewhere in the classical Greek world and could thus play a role in 'the dissemination of the community's ideas and values'.[7] Furthermore, Hölscher separately argues that the use of art as an outlet for a visual–mental construction of a society's experience of war makes it an invaluable form of historical source, quite apart from literary or epigraphical sources.[8] Thus, it cannot be assumed that what is portrayed on a vase is a mirrored reflection of practice; however, the ideological constructions that they continue to project are of intrinsic value to this study. Having now established the fundamental, methodological concern surrounding the use of vase paintings as cultural evidence, there are further problems that arise from the warrior-departure motif in particular.

Through the predominance of art as an evidential form for the 'ubiquitous departure-scene [sic]', a wide range of images over a singular medium, pottery, has allowed an almost formulaic construct of the departure scene to be formed.[9] A hoplite is seen departing from a woman – most commonly assumed to be his mother – and often an old man who is either sitting on a stool or leaning on his staff.[10] While the woman is depicted as youthful, possibly allowing for a secondary identification of her as the wife of the hoplite, the man is characteristically balding or bedecked with white hair, indicating the advanced years of a father, if not a mentor.[11] The woman is often a central participant in the scene, preparing or assisting the hoplite as he pours his libations, helping him to don his armour, or similarly handing the final piece of the *hopla* to the warrior, such as his helmet or shield, before he departs.[12] The scenes are, at times, scantily decorated with domestic objects, which works alongside the familial scene to highlight the *oikos*-context of the departure.[13] However, some vases are decorated with a column and/or an altar emphasising the pious nature of the hoplite, the *oikos* he is departing from and the religious nature of the rite itself.[14] While there are, of course, small variations of this model throughout the period under review, it is possible to identify the motif of a departure by these key identifying features.

The topic under review here, however, is not the artistic representation of a warrior's departure but rather the real-world form that departure took, the identification of the participants, and the rituals involved. This raises two distinct problems when using these vases to reconstruct a process or ritual for a warrior's departure. Firstly, the vase paintings that form the bulk of analysis on the theme of departure were, most likely, for individual use within a domestic setting.[15] It is therefore unsurprising that the 'departure scenes' envisaged a domestic departure based upon a distinct set of rituals and ideals suited to the *oikos*-sphere. Similarly, 'departure scenes' that appear on funerary materials such as *lekythoi* vases follow this pattern of individualism and domesticity, rather than embodying a sense of comradery with the military group to whom the man belonged as a warrior. The second problem arises from the iconography of the depicted warrior on all available media. He is most frequently illustrated with his *doru* sometimes wearing his *linothorax* and and with either his *aspis* and/or his helmet:[16] he is not an archer, nor a rower, he is specifically characterised as a hoplite. Thus, it is necessary to acknowledge that the experiences and transitions under consideration here may not reflect those undergone by rowers, light armed troops or even cavalry.

All Greek men called up for military service would have needed to depart on some level, so the question remains to what extent do these departure scenes reflect an 'average' departure, both ritualistically and ideologically? A secondary, but no less pertinent, question must arise from the overt domestic bias inherent in these images: are they telling the full story of a warrior's departure? From a purely geographical perspective, these hoplites are shown to be leaving their family so they could arrive at their mustering point – they are not departing for battle *per se*.[17] It stands to reason that a secondary departure would have taken place where the warrior was no longer a member of a domestic unit but was instead member of his military group and departed accordingly within this new context. The images available on these pots have not been identified as depicting any such departure. Was it then a non-ritualised, uneventful occurrence that was secondary to the domestic scene? Was the departure of the army simply one of physical relocation, without any precursory act? While this may not fit with our understanding of Greek religio-military practices on the whole, when ritual sacrifices and libations pre-empt almost any action while on campaign, the lack of a formalised group departure cannot be dismissed as a possibility.[18]

2.2 Departure from the *oikos*

The domestic departure is, ostensibly, the most visible incarnation of a warrior's parting in the late archaic and classical Greek period. According to Lissarrague, most often, the women in relation to the hoplite designate the space of the *oikos*.[19] Clemente Marconi concurs with this sentiment, emphasising the representations of mothers, fathers and wives, which define the 'family network around the warrior, his *oikos*'.[20] For Susan Matheson these scenes emphasise the family, while Nathan Arrington embodies the woman in a departure scene with a symbolism of the 'domestic world that the warrior leaves'.[21]

The focus of the warrior's departure on the *oikos* has a pivotal role on possible emotional interpretations of the image. During an analysis of archaic departure scenes, Lissarrague observed the continuity of ideals that the *oikos*-centrism had with epic and therefore heroic ideology.[22] The epic imagery is certainly overt, with the common motif of a chariot best exemplifying the interpolation of anachronistic iconography.[23] Nevertheless, an important shift occurred at the start of the early classical period and the departure scene was adapted to reflect a change in either artistic fashion or social attitudes to the departure. The archaic departure scene was often filled with bodies: a group of warriors departing; more than two family members, or non-military personnel; one or more horses either carrying a rider, or else pulling a chariot, which formed the central focus of the scene with the departing warrior often pushed to the outer wing. Nevertheless, by the turn of the fifth century BC, chariots had all but disappeared from the motif and had been resolutely replaced with the new form of military ideal: the hoplite.[24] With the hoplite came further change: a new emphasis, a simpler image and a more emotive scene.[25]

During the classical period, we see the number of people depicted within these scenes reduce to a standard of two or three individuals; some exceptional instances present as many as four individuals, but these are not as common.[26] The hoplite took centre stage at all times, with the pouring of a libation forming the most common scene.[27] This new form focused on the core elements of the departure, leaving the heroic motifs of the archaic period behind; these images centred on war and the oikos. The acquired space that came from the removal of people from these stock scenes also allowed a greater emphasis on minor details. Often, these are inconspicuous in their subtlety and come in the form of domestic iconography, such as hanging vessels or other items on the wall, or the chair on which the older man is often depicted sitting..[28] These minor artistic additions create an ambiance and set the contextual scene without overwhelming the image. Nevertheless, their impact has still led one commentator to conclude that when no contextual iconography is available in the scene, a military departure should be assumed to be set within the home.[29]

There are instances where an icon of domesticity and, in essence the *oikos*, does take a more prominent position within the scene. The domestic dog can take a central role in departure scenes, without getting lost in the background as often happened on earlier vases.[30] Within one famous departure scene on a mid-fifth century *stamnos*, attributed to the Achilles painter (see Figure 2.1), a dog shares the central space with the hoplite while he shakes hands with his father. Within this archetypal departure scene, the domestic nature of the event is emphasised, not only by the presence of the animal, but also by the detailed collar that sits around its neck.[31] The dog mirrors the direction and gaze of the hoplite; its alert stance, with pricked ears, similarly echoes that of the departing warrior.[32] The close physical relationship between the two implies a bond between master and dog, creating a second departure unseen and unresolved within the tableau: that of man and beast. The poignancy is magnified by the dog's apparent unawareness of what is occurring;[33] an image that recalls Argos, the loyal hound of Odysseus, who sat pining for his master until his return and the dog's subsequent and immediate death thereafter.[34] Furthermore, the dog is painted in a small set of dimensions, so he does not interfere with the negative

Figure 2.1 Red figure *stamnos*, attributed to the Achilles Painter, with a hoplite departing from his *oikos*. *c.* 450–440 BC London, British Museum: E448. © The Trustees of the British Museum. All rights reserved.

space within the scene. This distance between the three human agents creates the beginnings of the space that will engulf the position of the hoplite once he departs, pre-empting a void that will not be filled until his return.

This focus on empty space adds greater potency to scenes with only two agents, where the imminent departure, allied with the overwhelming emptiness around the figures, invites us to imagine the parental/wifely figure on their own.[35] However, this artistic focus on loss and emotional longing does not preclude the idolisation of the hoplite within this form of imagery, as artists continued the use of heroic-style nudity and the naming of individuals as characters from Homeric epic.[36] That being said, departure scenes of a warrior with only one other agent, most often a woman, are frequently found on *lekythoi*.[37] The funerary-ritual context of, especially white-ground, *lekythoi* adds a gravitas to these scenes that can be pushed too hard on non-funerary iconography.

An indisputable instance of war and *oikos* colliding can be seen in an image attributed to the Athens painter (see Figure 2.2a), which recreates the standard departure scene motif of a man with some form of accoutrement pertaining to the hoplite taking hold of his helmet before he leaves.[38] The scene deviates from our archetypal image: the woman could not have handed him his helmet. By moving the man to the edge of the scene, reflecting the position of the woman, emphasises the items in their hands. The helmet's eyes are turned to the man, just as those of the babe-in-arms are turned toward the woman. The emphasis on the two gender roles for the *polis*, for the man to fight for his *polis* and for the woman to give birth to future fighters, is isolated within the centre; purposefully drawing the viewers' attention to this intertwined duality.[39] However, reminded of the vase's context, this *lekythos* is not an idiomatic commentary of engendered civic roles, but is rather an expression of loss, of mourning and of death. The woman's eyes do not meet that of the man, there is no libation of farewell and there is no recognition between them. The content of the scene in many ways reflects the mythical trope of Amphiaraos who went to battle as one of the Seven of Thebes, knowing, through his gift of prophecy, that he was destined to die, the departure for which was chosen for ceramic art (see Figure 2.2b).[40] The presence of the child reinforces, in both examples, the ideological presence of the *oikos* from which the warrior is departing and that it is the *oikos* who will miss him when he inevitably dies.[41] So this scene in Figure 2.2a is best read in its simplest form: the man has died, most likely in combat – hence the limited, un-heroicised military iconography and the absence of the shield that failed him – and the woman has been left to mourn with a fatherless babe-in-arms.

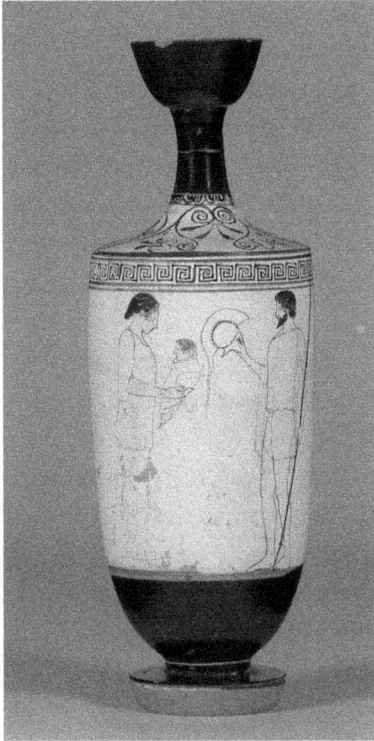

Figure 2.2a White-ground *lekythos*, attributed to the Athens Painter, with a hoplite departing from his wife and baby. Early to mid-fifth century BC. Antikensammlung, Staatliche Museen Zu Berlin – Preussischer Kulturbesitz, photographer: Johannes Laurentius, F 2444.

Figure 2.2b Red-figure *hydria*, attributed to the 'Dwarf' Painter, depicting Amphiaraos [named] departing from his wife and child. Mid-fifth century BC. Boston (MA), Museum of Fine Arts: 03.798. © Rebecca Weston.

2.2.1 The *polis* in the *oikos* departure?

Matheson argues that departure scenes do not merely show the individualist concerns of the members of the *oikos*, but similarly emphasise the civic role of the hoplite as a member of the *polis* and the roles of the hoplite's family.[42] To David Pritchard, the presence of the older man and woman in departure scenes highlights those who must stay behind in the *city*, thus placing the entire scene within a *polis*-specific framework.[43] For Lissarrague, this hoplite-*polis* relationship is epitomised by the handful of examples that exist where Athena is present, often in the position and role of the regular female figure of the scene.[44] But, much like Marconi asked of vase scenes depicting the retrieval of bodies from battle, where is this perceived *polis* in the departure scene?[45]

It is only Lissarrague who presents a recognisable icon that can be seen to be outside of the *oikos* context and it requires further exploration. Lissarrague's Athena is actually a rare icon on vases within the departure scene motif;[46] out of 1,126 suspected depictions, Athena appears in ten alleged departure scenes.[47] To put this into iconographical perspective, the god Hermes has been labelled within fifteen alleged departure scenes, so Athena's numbers are by no means unique within the Olympian pantheon. Of the ten scenes in which Athena appears, seven may be discarded as they are either a mythical scene, depict Athena herself as the departing warrior, or simply they are too fragmentary to conclusively allocate a departure scene label.[48] Within the three remaining images her representation is quite consistent:[49] in all three of these scenes she holds a spear and wears her aegis, and in two of them she also wears a helmet.[50] Athena embodies her role as a warrior goddess and, conceivably, fulfils Lissarrague's icon of a *polis*.[51]

Within the classical period, however, Athena appears in only one known red-figure departure scene. The scene portrays the hero, Ajax, seemingly in the midst of his preparations to depart; one of the female members in the scene is explicitly labelled as Athena.[52] Noticeably, regarding Lissarrague's characterisation of Athena's presence in such scenes, she does not take an active role in the departure as a mother/wife figure. In fact, the lack of any form of ritual practice being represented does raise the issue as to whether this scene should even be categorised as a departure scene. As the evidence stands to date, the goddess' overall presence in departure scenes is miniscule, while the sole image within the classical period does not fit within Lissarrague's interpretation. In fact, until more scenes are identified with Athena as an active participant, it is more accurate to describe her appearances as rare, if not anomalous. A more common depiction of the divine in the warrior departure motif comes in the guise of Nike, who is more likely to replace the role of the female figure of the scene.[53] Nike appears in eighteen departure scenes:[54] she is most commonly depicted holding a *phiale* and/or an *oinochoe*, fulfilling the role of the mother/wife pouring the libations. However, one exception presents Nike on the opposite side of the vase to the female figure and the goddess is in the process of handing the warrior his sword.[55]

While it could be argued that Nike is, in part, a manifestation of Athena and her presence constitutes possible evidence to support Lissarrague's characterisation, this ignores three key elements. Firstly, Nike was a separate deity to Athena and, while the Athenians merged the two in their worship, there is no evidence to suggest this was a Panhellenic synthesis.[56] Secondly, even if it is accepted that Nike was a representation of Athena, it must similarly be accepted that she was not a manifestation of the goddess' role as a *polis* patroness, but as the manifestation of victory, giving her an uneasy syncretism with the ideals of the *polis*. Thirdly, from a purely iconographical point of view, there is no way to be sure that these winged women are indeed Nike. On seven different vases, another winged woman appears in the departure scene; in each one she is participating in the role of the mother/wife, in six of the seven she is holding a *kerykeion* which allows her to be identified as Iris, while on the seventh vase she is not holding her staff but is instead named.[57] Figure 2.3 best exemplifies the difficulty with labelling a winged women Nike without further iconographic clues; as one side ostensibly shows Nike with a woman, and on the other side is Iris in the midst of a departure ritual. If Iris had been without the addition of the *kerykeion* – and there is one instance of this being so – it would be a reasonable assumption to identify the second winged women as Nike.[58] This raises the question is the other winged woman not meant to be considered Nike, but in fact Iris again, or yet another winged deity?[59]

The very presence of Nike in a departure scene demands some explanation, with the most overt attempt being Matheson's suggestion that this should change the reading of the scene to a dedication of, rather than a departure, of a warrior, making Nike the object of the dedication.[60] However, this does not quite fit with what we are seeing in the scene, where 'Nike' is making a dedication on behalf

Figure 2.3 Red-figure amphora, attributed to the painter of the Berlin Hydria. On the left is 'Nike' with a woman holding a staff; on the right is Iris preparing a libation for the warrior. Mid-fifth century BC. London, British Museum: E275. © Rebecca Weston.

of the warrior as the mother/wife figure. Perhaps Iris, in her role as a messenger goddess, is a more natural fit in that she is helping the warrior to communicate his libation to the gods, acting within the human realm and the divine simultaneously.[61] This is a characterisation that can be found reflected within the *Iliad*, where Iris is actually portrayed as helping a warrior's libation and prayer reach the ears of the gods, a characteristic which is so far missing from the mythology of Nike.[62] While the identification of the winged women from these scenes cannot be resolved here, suffice to say that her identification with Nike is not without its problems; similarly, she cannot be considered a reliable manifestation of Athena nor, indeed, as an iconographic manifestation of the *polis*.

Unlike Lissarrague's Athena, the interpretations of Matheson and Pritchard, that a *polis*-centric ideology was being transmitted through the departure scenes, is not based on an additional icon, but on the presence of the hoplite himself. This interpretation assumes that there was a seamless continuity of military ideology between the *oikos* and the *polis*, which must be brought into question. In these classical scenes, the hoplite is most often depicted as a solitary warrior, devoid of any military context other than the hoplite equipment he, or his mother, holds. The hoplite of these scenes is an individual, with full influential agency and involvement in all aspects of his experience. He and his *oikos* prepare him for battle, they organise his armour, they pour the libations and they part at the door.[63] This is particularly clear when an older element of the departure motif is included in the discussion. Whereas the classical scenes focus upon the literal moment of departure, like Figure 2.1, or an 'arming-scene', the imagery of the late archaic period reflected a further ritual practice of the departing warrior and his *oikos*; hieroscopy.[64]

A popular departure scene within the late archaic period, the reading of the liver and entrails, became less frequent as the departure scene became simplified in the classical era.[65] It was replaced by the libation, which became the most popular form of iconographic acknowledgement of the religious rites involved in the departure. The variance between the two forms of ritual in the scene has not attracted much in the way of scholarly interest. The differences are subtle, but interesting, with regard to the ideological projections of war and of individual participation. The reading of the entrails gave the man control and input into his decision making.[66] The hoplite is either depicted as inspecting his own sacrifice, or his father was, giving him and his *oikos* a semblance of influence on the future ahead.[67] By playing this role he is enacting his duty to conduct religious rituals on behalf of his wife and children.[68] This choice of iconography, by the vase painter, creates the illusion that military service was a decision agreed upon in the last instance; if the omens were not good then, theoretically, the man could excuse his absence.[69]

Conversely, the libation offers a shift in emphasis. It is not an act of control over the future by reading it, but of a supplicatory dedication to a deity to look over the warrior.[70] The *oikos* had no control over the fate of the warrior, but instead tried to influence a god or goddess to support the hoplite in being valiant.[71] A point that becomes emphasised by the presence of Iris, whose role as messenger to and for the gods reinforces this narrative. This shift in ritual accentuation may reflect a shift in the socio-military experience of the *oikos* as the classical period brought with it a more structured form of enlistment, exemplified through the *katalogos*.[72] This new system called up men for hoplite service, making it harder to pretend that the hoplite or his *oikos* had any real influence in the decision for the individual to depart for war. The discontinuity of hieroscopic representation into the classical period does not dictate a discontinuity of practice. The shift in religious iconographic preference may reflect an *oikos*-driven imperative for the head, or heir, of the family to survive in the face of the ever-growing casualty lists of war that faced many of the classical Greek *poleis*.

The depiction of the hoplite as an individual, with personal control and influential agency over the military sphere, contrasts starkly with the military ideology of collective unity within the fighting force he must enter.[73] The hoplite ideal, within the civic and military sphere, was one of collective identity within the phalanx. In essence, the ideal hoplite would be set within a de-individuated state of awareness, one that has removed the personal identity of the individual and replaced it with a sense of collective identity. As will be more thoroughly discussed below, the individual had no influence on the religious rites enacted by the army he entered, he had minimal influence in the decision making for battle and, on the battlefield itself, he had no identity beyond that of the collective formation of which he was part. There were only two occasions within the military sphere that reflected something akin to the individualism that is revealed within these departure scenes: prizes awarded for valour and the naming of the war-dead. A prize was awarded for *aristeia* after the conclusion of a battle, which normally constituted an individual receiving a hoplite panoply and a crown of olive leaves.[74] However, the statistical likelihood of an individual receiving such recognition was minimal and it seems even men deserving of the prize were known to be overlooked for reasons beyond the battlefield.[75] Therefore, while the existence of this prize must be accepted as a form of recognisable individualist acknowledgement, its reach was largely symbolic and its impact on a hitherto unprized individual minimal.

Returning to the individual identification of the war-dead on *stelae*; the concept of having a name inscribed permanently for all to see must epitomise a social acceptance of individual agency within battle. These lists were laid out by tribe, while some later examples show that chosen officers were given their military titles and, most importantly, the names of the war-dead were inscribed without any patronyms.[76] With a lack of patronymic identity the individual is isolated for eternity within his military role, with his defining feature being the name of the tribe that had called him for duty. In essence, these lists denied the link between the hoplite and the *oikos*, defining the dead solely by his duty to Athens and his place within the tribe.[77] The reverse also stands: that the *oikos* was refused any public recognition for the war dead.[78] This was the ethos of the *polis*: the hoplite stopped being a member of an *oikos* at the point he met at the mustering point. He lost any recognised individuality unless he achieved greatness in battle or, more commonly, he died, at which point, his individual identity would be acknowledged as a name, but no more. Returning to the original question regarding the ideological representation of the *polis* in departure scenes: *if* we are to believe that the painted departure scenes under review were in any way reflective of this form of civic ideology, it must be expected that this *polis*-centrism be reflected beyond the circumstantial iconography of the hoplite himself. But it is not.

2.2.2 The voice of the *oikos* during a departure

While the artistic representations of the departure offer important evidence in ascertaining some of the rituals involved and in identifying participants, they cannot express in words the emotions involved, this is only available from the few passages of literary evidence available. The most famous example of a warrior departing from his *oikos* is that of Hector in Book 6 of the *Iliad*. Yet, from an historical perspective, the *Iliad*, while undoubtedly influential, cannot be used in isolation as a reliable source for ascertaining thoughts and feelings during the classical period.[79] However, there are two similar scenes that date from the classical period, although much shorter in length, which will benefit from a comparison and contrast with the Homeric masterpiece. The first scene appears in Xenophon's *Cyropaedia*, an early fourth-century BC novel about Cyrus the Great, and shows the departure of Abradatas, king of Susa, from his wife Panthea.[80] The second example comes from the lost Euripidean play *Erectheus* (written and performed *c.* 422 BC), which is partially quoted by the logographer Lycurgus in *Against Leocrates*.[81] Lycurgus chose to quote a passage of speech by Praxithea, who describes her disgust for how some women act during their sons' departure for war

Neither piece of classical evidence is without its methodological difficulties. Abradatas' departure is not actually from the home, as he had already left to join his captured wife with the army of Cyrus.[82] Furthermore, the relationship between Abradatas and Panthea is romantically idealised, verging on a perfect and rare marital paradigm, culminating in Panthea's suicide over the body of her dead husband.[83] More generally, the use of the *Cyropaedia* is never without its difficulties. It is very hard to discern fact from fiction and, in this emotive scene, whether we are reading the ideals of a fictional writer or the accurate projection of societal norms and values.[84] Regarding Lycurgus, there is the question of whether his use of Euripides' fragment is an accurate reflection of what Euripides intended when he wrote it as it lacks any original dramatic context.[85] Yet, the manner in which both scenes approach and deal with the themes of departure are constructive in trying to explore the perspective of the *oikos*; even if what we discover is an idealistic construct of how our authors, or maybe even Athenian society, thought that the *oikos* should feel about it.

The scene of Andromache and Hector is the longest of the three and involves a highly emotive dialogue between wife and husband. For the sake of comparison, it is necessary to set out the main focal points of the Homeric scene. It is set by the Scaean Gates of Troy, just as Hector is about to re-join the battle and sees Andromache appeal to Hector not to go to battle because he will die.[86] She refers to his role as a father and as a husband, exposing the *oikos* to his failure if he was to die and she captured, his son orphaned.[87] To reiterate this, Andromache details how Achilles had destroyed her own family in war; adding greater, *oikos*-focused, pathos by describing Hector as a father to her, a mother, a brother, as well as her virile lover.[88] Finally she begs him to stay on the ramparts and defend the walls, offering observations of the Achaean assaults in a bid to convince him of the dangers.[89] Hector's reply explicitly states that he, too, had experienced these thoughts.[90] But his concern lay with the views of the Trojan people, the shame of not fighting and of cowardice. His personal worry lay not with the fall of Troy, nor the death of his father and his brothers, but with the fate of his wife:

> But may I be dead and the piled earth hide me under I learn of your capture by way of your cries.[91]

The dialogue is broken by an intimate moment between the pair and their baby son, who becomes frightened by his father's helmet.[92] Hector takes off his helm and plays with Astyanax, before kissing him and praying to Zeus that the child would become far greater than himself and that he would delight the heart of his mother.[93] When the child is returned to Andromache, Hector finally gives her a caressing touch as she smiles through her tears.[94] Hector must eventually send Andromache away so that he may depart, but he himself lingers, watching them walk away.[95]

The common links between Homer's scene and that of Xenophon has already received scholarly attention, however no emphasis has yet been placed on what this comparison may reveal about the military departure.[96] Xenophon appears to invert, purposefully, the Homeric scene, attempting to rebalance the role played by Andromache with a more ideal portrayal of a woman.[97] The departure takes place in Cyrus' military camp, following the King's decision to face the Assyrians in battle and Abradatas' own decision to take up a position in the most dangerous area of the battlefield.[98] The parting occurs within the narrative sandwiched between Cyrus making a sacrifice and then receiving his positive omens, adding an emotive dimension to a common military process.[99] Deborah Gera seems correct in her assertion that the scene appears to begin indoors, with complete privacy, although Xenophon does not make this explicit.[100] It begins with a Homeric-style arming scene, in which Panthea gives Abradatas a new golden panoply which she had bought with her own personal jewellery; although she denies this to him when questioned.[101] Like Andromache, Panthea is shown in tears, failing in her attempts to hide them.[102] The scene moves outside, with Abradatas holding the reins of his chariot, while Panthea sends her servants away for more privacy. In this private, intimate moment, Xenophon puts the sentiment of Hector's reply into the mouth of his own 'Andromache'.[103] Panthea professes her love for Abradatas and uses words that echo Hector's quoted above:[104]

> I would far rather go down into the earth with you, if you show yourself a valiant man, than live disgraced with one disgraced.[105]

Panthea's concern is not the survival of her husband, as Andromache's was, nor the impact of his death on their *oikos*, but on the honourable actions of Abradatas in battle and him repaying the honour bestowed upon them by Cyrus.[106] Contrary to Hector's famous rebuke to his wife, that war shall be the concern of men, Abradatas is in awe of his wife's exhortation.[107] He prays to Zeus, as did Hector, that he, rather than Astyanax, would live up to the reputation that precedes him, in this case the honourable actions of Panthea.[108] The dialogue is then broken by him entering the chariot, where the roles revert to the Homeric prototype. Panthea, not knowing how she could kiss him good-bye, kisses the chariot and then follows behind as Abradatas begins to ride off, delaying his departure for as long as possible.[109] When she is noticed by her husband, he turns to her and bids her farewell before ordering her back, where she is hidden from view by her servants.

Xenophon's scene is a careful allusion to Homer, while at the same time a purposeful manipulation of the motif. As Valla argued, Panthea appears, on the surface at least, to be a rebalance for the less than honourable actions – to the eyes of classical Greece – of Andromache.[110] This is reinforced by the fates of both heroines: the death of Hector leads to Andromache being captured and taken as a mistress for Neoptolemus, bearing three new children;[111] whereas Panthea held Abradatas' dead body on the battlefield and then chose to kill herself. Seemingly the ideal Athenian wife, Panthea of Susa extolls the virtues of manhood to her husband: she fully supports his role in war, she feels the necessary emotions and sadness expected of a woman but does not let it affect her duty and she offers herself as a final sacrifice as a way of following the honourable actions of her beloved. However, something Valla did not consider is that Xenophon dramatically shatters this illusion when Panthea and Cyrus the Great have their one and only conversation.[112] Cyrus finds her on the battlefield cradling the dismembered body of Abradatas and, while saddened, he describes Abradatas' bravery and loyalty, the sort of traits that Panthea urged her husband to possess at their departure. Panthea, however, has completely reversed her thoughts on war and finds no comfort in these words.[113] She blames herself for prevailing upon him the need to show himself a virtuous man and a good servant to Cyrus.[114] In turn, she blames Cyrus for her husband's death. She damns the military ideology that she had been holding aloft in awe of her husband, declaring that while he has died a blameless death, she, who urged him towards it, sits there alive and well as, by implication, does Cyrus. Thus, Xenophon presents two distinct elements of a departure from the *oikos*, symbolised here by Panthea as the wife. On the one hand, he shows the ideal wife, the sort of woman that Pericles was calling for in his funerary oration: one who cared for the military reputation of her husband or sons, who considered his honour over her own and one who considered the authority of the state/ruler to be paramount.[115] On the other hand, Panthea is reduced to the emotional hardships faced by Andromache at the point when she is finally faced with the harsh realities of war.[116] Xenophon's inversion of the departure scene amplifies the emotional power of this realisation for Panthea: that all of this military ideology and her part in its dissemination has been the cause of Abradatas' death and ultimately her pain.[117]

The third source under review, Euripides' *Erechtheus*, highlights very similar themes to Homer and Xenophon, but presents the cognitive dissonance between civic duty and familial love within two separate people, rather than as an inner turmoil within one character. In a speech made by the mythic Queen Praxithea, after consenting to the sacrifice of her daughter for the sake of victory in battle, Euripides seemingly defines the patriotic Athenian woman.[118] Praxithea bore children to protect the altars of Athens, which she deems the greatest of all the *poleis*.[119] She emphasises that the sacrifice of one child would mean the saving an entire population of *autochthones* and compares the decision to that of a woman's sons leaving for war.[120] If Praxithea had sons she would send them to war to stand out among other men, unafraid of their fate or impending death.[121] To cement her ideological stance on motherhood she describes the daughter she gave in sacrifice as not being hers, except by birth.[122] Within this rhetoric, Praxithea breaks from her personal, hypothetical, narrative to describe the type of women she hates, the type of woman who does not live by these lofty ideals:

> A mother's tears, whenever they send children off, have made women out of many men heading for battle: I hate women who prefer to have their children live and give them bad advice rather than what is good.[123]

Contrary to the first two scenes discussed above, Praxithea's speech emphasises the role of the mother, rather than that of the wife, in a warrior's departure. What is clear from even this one fragment is that Praxithea is not meant to be considered as expounding a common view held by the women in her world nor, by extension, the views of the women in the world of Euripides' audience. She derides the tears of a mother sending her son to do his duty; tears that she herself would not shed for her own daughter. Within this speech, Praxithea, much like Panthea, and Hector before her, seems to be claiming that the 'state' superseded the concerns of the family. But, unlike Panthea and Hector, within this fragment there is no evidence of any inner turmoil over this ideological stance.[124] The emotions of the departure that have been seen in the tears of Andromache and Panthea, the lingering of Hector and the prolonged goodbye of Panthea, are not found with Praxithea. In fact, these emotions define the sort of woman she hates. Her speech reflects the first set of views given by Panthea and the ideological view of contemporary Athens; that honour, acting well in battle and dying for 'the cause' were the prime markers by which warriors should be judged.[125] However, in her characterisations of the 'other' mothers, we see a continuation of Andromache's pleas to her husband. These mothers see off their sons with tears in their eyes, and with final pleas to stay alive no matter the cost, just as Andromache begged Hector to stay on the walls. In these four lines, Euripides creates a miniature Homeric scene so that his character can attack the type of sentiment expressed by Andromache. This raises the important question, why?

Lycurgus, who gives us the largest fragment of this scene, considered this speech to be a great example worthy of emulation and capable of instilling patriotism.[126] Is this the image that Euripides appears to be creating, the perfect example of civic ideology being expressed by the words and actions of a wife and mother? Was his Praxithea meant to be a homage to the strength of the women of Athens?[127] Ultimately, the answer must be no. What Lycurgus chose to omit from his speech is as revealing as what he chose to quote. The sacrifice of Praxithea's daughter was not enough to save her husband, Erechtheus, nor did it stop Poseidon from almost destroying Athens, but for the intervention of Athena.[128] In fact, Praxithea's proclamation that the sacrifice will save her, Erectheus and their two remaining daughters is steeped in dramatic irony; not only does Erechtheus die in battle, but the two daughters also commit suicide. This certainly implies, in line with Pietro Pucci, that the audience of Euripides may have been shocked by what they were hearing, rather than motivated by its overt manifestation of a civic ideology.[129] It is pertinent to observe that, like Panthea during Abradatas' departure scene, Praxithea is yet to be influenced by the impact of the ideology which she is articulating. Firstly, she is yet to feel the impact of her husband's death and the ultimate fruitlessness of her motherly sacrifice. Secondly, Praxithea is hypothesising about a scenario she will never experience. She does not have sons to send off to war, so cannot understand the emotional pain that is expressed during the departure scenes she criticises so vehemently. In fact, the women that Praxithea hates are portrayed in the same vein as both Andromache throughout the departure and Panthea while indoors and later, when holding Abradatas' body. Therefore, what Praxithea embodies is an antithesis of the normative behaviour of the woman, whether mother or wife, during a warrior departure.

The Military Departure

Once the warrior had departed from his home, leaving his family behind, he would then perform a secondary departure as part of the military group. Elements of this departure have been well studied in the scholarship, in particular the systems of mobilisation and conscription, but the experience of the departure, the experience of this transition from the city out onto campaign, has not garnered much attention. Once again, it is necessary to consider the logistical organisation of the transition to allow a full picture to emerge. This includes the differences in mobilisation between the *katalogos* system and a *pandemei*, the regularity with which Athens was mobilising its forces and the location(s) of the musters after which it becomes pertinent to examine what limited evidence we have for an army's departure.

Once this secondary departure has been established, it will be possible to highlight any continuity or contrasting experiences between it and the domestic departure discussed in Chapter 2. Only after the two forms of departure are established will it be possible to understand the sociological framework from which the Greek warrior departed and into which he would later return because it will incorporate both the domestic and the military ideologies and experiences.

3.1 Joining the muster

Once a hoplite had departed from his home and family, he began the second stage of his departure, one that saw him join his comrades in arms, before departing from the *polis* as part of a united military force. However, the hoplite and his comrades did not initiate the military departure at this reference point, but rather joined an active mechanism that had already begun preparing for departure; the final stage of which was the mustering of the men. To understand this last stage of a hoplite's departure, from his civic setting, it is necessary to set out an overview of the mobilising system he joined. For this topic, there are two key elements: the call to arms and the muster itself. Once a broad image of this process has been established, an examination of the army's departure and the rituals involved in that departure, can occur. Finally, having established how a hoplite was called up for service, how and where he mustered and what rituals took place on behalf of the army before departure, it can be asked to what extent this military departure differed from the domestic one discussed above, both in terms of ideology and personal participation.

3.1.1 The mobilisation

A large, complex socio-political system such as the classical Athenian *polis* required a systematic process by which it could mobilise its forces, which were drawn from all over the large region of Attica. During the classical period, Athens utilised three forms of mobilisation: (1) the *katalogos* – a system of enlistment based on a theoretically fair distribution of commitment from all ten of the Athenian tribes; (2) the mass levy (*pandemei/panstratia*) – a general call to arms for all men obliged to serve; and (3) a late fourth-century replacement of the *katalogos*, which called men to arms by age groups.[1] Within all three systems, selection liability was automatic, ostensibly based upon Solon's property classes.[2] The poorest class of the Athenian citizenry, the *thetes*, were the exception to this rule, for they rowed in the navy or served as light infantry and there is still no concrete evidence to suggest that either form of military service was subject to a mandatory summons.[3] The *zeugitai* were a landholding leisure-class and were expected to serve as hoplites.[4] The *hippeis* were wealthier still and, as their name suggests, were expected to serve as cavalry. The richest of the classes were the *pentacosiomedimnoi*, who would reinvest their wealth into the Athenian military by becoming a *trierarchos*, a commander of a trireme that they would sponsor for a year.[5]

As Hans van Wees has persuasively argued, this rigid system would not have been capable of producing the large numbers of hoplites that Athens possessed, especially at the start of the Peloponnesian War, when it could boast almost 30,000.[6] Van Wees originally calculated that the formal criteria for the status of a *zeugitai* would have necessitated a farm of approximately twenty-two acres, thus an area the size of Attica could only facilitate 10,000 suitably sized farmsteads.[7] Recently, van Wees has re-assessed this estimate and increased the bare minimum for classification as a *zeugitai* to thirty acres, further reducing the number of estimated *zeugitai*.[8] These figures are simply incongruent with the hoplite-strength that was available to Athens during the classical period.[9]

There is, however, an inherent flaw within van Wees' calculations, as he overlooks the issue that one farm may have been supporting more than one warrior. Knowing that Athens used its youngest and eldest hoplites for garrison duty, the age disparity between them being anywhere up to forty years, it is not implausible that father and son(s) were being simultaneously drawn into a legally obligated military service, determined by the ownership of a single property.[10] In Lysias' *For Polystratus*, the speaker defends the actions of his father as a member of the 400 and, in so doing, outlines the military career of Polystratus' sons, himself included.[11] Based on this testimony, the house of Polystratus had three young men serving in Sicily, Attica and the Hellespont concurrently. Two of these sons, we are informed, were part of the Athenian cavalry and, while there is no verification of the third son's manner of service, it is not unreasonable to presume he was also a cavalryman. The speaker goes on to state that the large estate, one capable of maintaining these three military men, was built upon Polystratus' skilful farming.[12] But the Spartan invasions of Attica took that income away, inciting the sons to perform great acts in war. This direct link between the loss of Polystratus' financial fortune and the son's actions in war, allied with the concerns of the speaker for the estate, suggests that some, if not all, of these three sons were living off the income of this one farm. The military costs of three sons were not unmanageable for such a farm –we hear from Demosthenes of another estate that needed to be split between five sons, many of which would have been militarily active at the same time, and all of which would have had to be supported by the single *oikos* until they had established their own.[13] Isaeaus similarly describes two sons of military age serving in Thrace under Iphicrates, one of whom is adopted into the *oikos* of Menecles before being married off.[14] While Isaeaus' speech is late in the period, it reflects the same logistical reality: that a single *oikos* would frequently be responsible for the maintenance of more than one hoplite. Yet, while van Wees' arguments are flawed, it is still hard to explain how an extra 20,000 men could have appeared.

Van Wees' solution to this numerical quandary comes in the form of his concept of the 'working-class' hoplite, by which the hoplite numbers were swelled by the *thetes*.[15] In addition to supplementation from below, hoplite figures would have seen recruitment from the higher property classes as well. The reasons for this were varied, not least because the military service expected of the two richest classes were based on an assumed assessment of real wealth but, of course, each of these men would have had varied forms of outgoings based on unforeseen factors, such as their dependents. Alternatively, there may have been a social allure to being a part of the hoplite phalanx and the desire to serve in the most prestigious element of the Athenian military was motivation enough for some of the richer citizens.[16] Therefore, while the evidence is not yet conclusive, it seems reasonable to observe that the system by which the muster was announced, the rigid system of class identification, did not, in all likelihood, match perfectly the demographics of those who appeared for muster.

3.1.2 The mechanism of the muster

As a system of mobilisation, the *katalogos* was the most prolific in Athens, so it will form the basis of this analysis; however, the two remaining systems will be discussed as forms of contrast at relevant points of divergence.[17] An Athenian army was not permanently mustered, waiting to be called upon when the need arose; its very existence needed to first be agreed upon by the Assembly. Once the Assembly had voted to raise a force of a set size, they appointed a commanding *strategos*, or at times *strategoi*, from the ten who held office that year.[18] The appointed general was then responsible for the recruitment process, beginning a distinct four-stage process of mobilisation.[19]

The army was drawn from the ten Cleisthenic tribes, each of which was to be led by a *taxiarchos*. These *taxiarchoi* aided the *strategos* with the compilation of conscription lists of hoplites required to serve for their respective tribes, possibly further aided by the tribal *strategos* who held office.[20] The original source of these lists has been the subject to in-depth historical enquiry, with a common consensus beginning to appear that the *katalogos* was not a central register, but the synthesis of numerous *katalogoi*.[21] This still raises the question of origin; where was the information held from which these tribal lists could be formulated? The tribe itself was simply too large and too disparate, split as it was by its three *trittyes* – one from the urban centre, one from the countryside, and one from the coast. Neither the tribe nor the *trittyes* were socially cohesive enough to establish such a detailed and updated format of registration for its members.[22] It is for this reason that the tribe's smallest political element, the deme, has been identified as the most likely source with the original source of information being found in the *deme* register: the *lexiarchikon grammateion*.[23] Once the *strategos* recevied these smaller conscription lists, he was now capable of compiling the *katalogoi* for his campaign, with the added assistance of the personal knowledge from his tribal representatives, the *taxiarchoi*, or, possibly by notations from the *demarchos* who supplied the list of demesmen.[24]

The second phase of mobilisation was the notification to those who had been listed for service. The current historical explanation for this notification is not without its difficulties. Each of the ten tribal *katalogoi* were placed under their respective eponymous hero's statue, at the *Eponymoi* monument in the agora.[25] These lists would have been written on erasable whitened boards and must have specified details such as the mustering point, the relevant date and time, as well as the amount of personal rations to bring.[26] However, only one-third of each tribe lived in the city and Christ rightly questioned the likelihood of hoplites, living in the wider proximities of Attica, coming to Athens simply to check a list.[27] Christ tried to resolve this issue; he suggested a logical solution by which notification was taken to the *demes* via heralds.[28] Yet, each of the strands of evidence he uses to support this hypothesis do not actually completely support his argument, but rather highlight that this method of notification produced a speedily mobilised *pandemei*, rather than the slow, methodical process that Christ imagined the *katalogos* to be.[29] Lamachus, in Aristophanes' *Peace*, was ordered by a herald to muster some troops to deal with marauders on the Attic borders. Plutarch's Phocion ordered an unusual muster of men up to the age of 60, by way of a heralds, at a purposefully fast pace to unsettle his crowd, which he succeeded in doing.[30] Andocides was discussing the use of heralds in an emergency muster within Athens. The only exception is the passage Christ cites from Aristophanes' *Clouds*. The meaning of this passage is, unfortunately, uncertain, due to its poetic contrast between the heraldic proclamation that had just been made that peace was going to be released and a non-specified summons to war. For this dramatic contrast to work, the herald's proclamation needed to be conceptually congruent with a real-life form of notification for mobilisation, which has already been shown to be true in states of emergency or, at least, states of rapid mobilisation. It is also noteworthy that, contrary to Christ's solution, not one of these examples is depicting a herald calling the men to read the *katalogoi*, but are, instead, the call to arms.

Another possibility is that the summons to read the *katalogoi* was made by *salpinx*-calls, but this suggestion has similar uncertainties.[31] One piece of evidence comes from the same section in Andocides' speech in reference to the *salpinx*, which has already been discussed as referring to a state of emergency. Furthermore, the relevant passage only states that the *hippeis* were called by the *salpinx* to their mustering point, after dark, not the hoplites or the army as a whole.[32] The second substantial piece of evidence can be found in Bachhylides' *Ode to Theseus*:

> King of sacred Athens, lord of the luxuriously-living Ionians, why has the bronze-belled trumpet just now sounded a war song?
>
> Does some enemy of our land beset our borders, leading an army? Or are evil-plotting robbers, against the will of the shepherds, rustling our flocks of sheep by force? What is it that tears your heart?[33]

In these two instances, it can be seen that the *salpinx* were deployed in states of emergency, or situations requiring a rapid response. Bacchylides' speaker only associates this bugle sound with enemies at the border, or sheep rustling marauders, not anything akin to an Assembly-sanctioned muster and campaign outside of Attica. This interpretation of the *salpinx's* usage is supported by Christ's other sources;[34] Demosthenes describes its use during a state of emergency following the fall of Elatea, while Polyaenus describes its use during a state of emergency due to an anticipated attack by the Thebans.[35] So the image that emerges, from the use of heralds and the salpinx, is not that they were frequently used, nor that they were used to advise men to check the *katalogoi*, but that they were employed for a particular attribute that they gave to the muster – speed. Additionally, these examples of fast messages for mobilisation all have a further facet in common: their sources do not mention the *katalogoi* and fit best with our understanding of the mass levy. This, of course, did not require any discernment of liability for service, therefore, a mass form of notification would suffice.

Unfortunately, there is no evidence yet available which supports any other hypothesis for how notification was announced to the men. Realistically, each *deme* only needed one person to go and collect the list of names, before returning and informing the relevant demesmen.[36] In theory, this could have been anyone, but one would expect that the same person, or a person in that same position, was given the responsibility. The most logical candidate would be the deme's member at the *boule*, who had more reason to be in Athens regularly.[37] This solution would also save the agora from becoming a scene of chaos anytime the *katalogoi* were listed, as it would have prevented 13,000 men from descending upon the *Eponymoi* at a moment's notice. While this suggestion can only remain theoretical, it would support the use of heralds and trumpets, which we do read about in the sources, as a different system that sped up the entire process and fits with our understanding of the *pandemei*. Governed by the power of the Assembly, this secondary system could bypass the usual, slow *katalogos* that was reliant on the movements of these individuals and speed the entire process up.

3.1.3 Locations of the muster

The third stage of mobilisation, the granting of exemptions, is not relevant to the discussion here, as the departure of a hoplite necessitates him being present in the army.[38] The fourth stage of mobilisation was the muster itself. Frustratingly, there is no unique ancient Greek term for the mustering of an army. Thucydides, for instance, uses the various cognates and compounds of ἀθροίζω (to gather together, collect), and σύλλογος (assembly, meeting), to describe the gathering together of an army.[39] However, these terms do not exclusively describe the mustering of an army before departure.[40] Sophocles uses the term ἀφορμή (starting-point), as does Diodorus on one occasion, but again neither instance distinguishes itself as being the mustering point, but rather a single point of departure at some point on a military campaign.[41] Yet, to understand the sequence of a hoplite's departure, it must be established where he departed from and therefore to where he mustered. While the terminology does not aid this particular enquiry, there are a selection of possibilities for mustering grounds that scholars have observed, which warrant a mention. Before this can occur, however, a few factors need to be considered before analysing the suitability of a particular location to be a regular mustering point.

Locating the place of muster is not simply a matter of looking for any location that was big enough to host the Athenian army, because different armies varied in size greatly, depending on their purpose. Having extracted the military figures of Athenian musters and battle figures given by three of the main historians that covered the classical Greek period – Thucydides, Xenophon and Diodorus – it becomes clear that an Athenian muster had a great range of sizes.[42] Table 3.1 shows a collation of Athenian musters in which a numerical strength is declared by the historians. It should be noted that these figures cannot be presumed to be accurate mustering figures but have been collated to form the parameters of analyses regarding the regularity of mustering and the plausible size of mustering space. Table 3.2 shows the size of Athenian armies when in battle, which have been quantified by the relevant listed sources.

For the sake of determining likely mustering points in Athens, a minimum requirement of 1,000 men was deemed necessary. This parameter negated the possibility that smaller forces could have met at impractical locations and therefore could not be considered as an official mustering point for an army of any great strength. Following this data extraction, an accumulation of historically attested fighting strengths for the Athenian army in battle was required, to observe the numerical commitment of Athenian hoplites in combat who may not have been specifically described as a mustering force within the histories. With these two sets of data brought together, a more accurate understanding of the rate and size of Athenian hoplite mobilisation can emerge.

From the subsequent data, there are a few factors worthy of note. The first is that the (modal) average army raised by the Athenians was 1,000 hoplites strong; forming a 41% majority. This means that the most frequently attested summons for service required 100 hoplites from each tribe, or 33/4 from each *trittys*, which was split between the number of *demes* each *trittys* possessed. However, the (mean) average-sized army that Athens put directly into the field of battle during the classical period was 4,679 hoplites strong. This equated to roughly 468 hoplites from each tribe, or 155/56 from each *trittys*. The largest number of hoplites put into battle, after discarding Diodorus' exaggerated number of 20,000

Table 3.1 Athenian mustering figures

Reference	Year of muster	Purpose of muster	Hoplite numbers
Thucydides:			
1.57	433	To Potidaea	1,000
1.60-1	432	To Macedonia	2,000
1.64	432	To Potidaea	1,600
1.107	457	To Megara	13,000
1.113	447	To Boeotia	1,000
2.23	431	Raid Peloponnese	1,000
2.31	431	To Megara	10,000
2.56-8	430	Raid Peloponnese/to Potidaea	4,000
3.17	433/2-431	Besieging Potidaea	3,000
3.18	428	To Mytilene	1,000
3.91	426	To Melos then Tangara	2,000
4.42	425	To Corinth	2,000
4.53	424	To Cythera	2,000
4.68	424	To Megara via Eleusis	4,000
4.129	423	To Mende and Scione	1,000
5.2	422	To Chalcidice	1,200
5.55	419	To aid Epidaurus and Caryae	1,000
5.61	418	To Argos	1,000
5.75	418	To Epidaurus	1,000
5.84	416	To Melos	1,600
6.43	415	To Syracuse	1,500
8.25	412	To Miletus	1,000
Xenophon, *Hellenica*:			
1.1.34	410	For Thrasyllus	1,000
7.1.41	366?	To area around Corinth	2,000

Reference	Year of muster	Purpose of muster	Hoplite numbers
Diodorus:			
11.84.3-6	456	To Laconia	4,000
11.85	455	Raid Peloponnese	1,000
12.34.4	435	To Macedonia	2,000
12.47.3	429	To Thrace	1,000
12.55.4	427	To Mytilene	1,000
12.65.1	424	Raid Peloponnese	1,000
12.65.8	424	To Cythera	2,000
12.69.4	424	Delium	20,000
12.79.1	419	To Arcadia	1,000
12.84.3	415	To Sicily	5,000
13.9.2	413	Reinforcements to Sicily	5,000
13.52.1	410/9	To attack after victory at Cyzicus	1,000
13.65.1	409	To Megara	1,000
15.26.2	378/7	To Thebes	5,000
15.29.7	377/6	Levy, readying for war with Sparta	20,000
15.32.2	377/6	To Thebes	5,000
15.63.2	369/8	To help Sparta against Thebes	12,000
15.71.3	368/7	To Thessaly	1,000
15.84.2	362	To Mantinea	6,000

Athenians at Delium (424) and the mass levy of 377/6, is found at the battle of Tanagra (457) where Athens called a mass levy and mobilised 13,000 Athenian hoplites. This means that the largest mobilisation that we know of required 1,300 hoplites from each tribe, or 434 from each *trittys*.

Table 3.2 Athenian battle figures

Battle[43]	Source	Year	Hoplite Numbers
Marathon	Paus. 10.20.2; Plut. *Mor.* 305b; Nep. *Milt.* 5	490	9,000
Plataea	Hdt. 9.28-29	479	8,000
Tanagra	Thuc. 1.107.5	457	13,000
Potidaea	Thuc. 1.61.4	432-1	3,000
Spartolus	Thuc. 2.79.1	429	2,000
Solygeia	Thuc. 4.42.1	425	2,000
Delium[44]	Thuc. 4.93-94	424	7,000
1st Mantinea	Thuc. 5.61.1	418	1,000
Syracuse	Thuc. 6.43	415	1,500
Miletus	Thuc. 8.25.1	412	1,000
Ta Kerata	Diod. 13.65.1-2	409	1,000
The Nemea	Xen. Hell. 4.2.17	394	6,000
2nd Mantinea	Diod. 15.84.2	362	6,000

The data also suggests that the Athenian military was often mobilising small forces and sending them throughout their empire at the same time. Between the years of 433 and 431, Athens mobilised at least five forces numbering over 1,000 men each, or 15,600 collectively. Although 3,000 of these were stationed at the siege works surrounding Potidaea and would not return to Athens until the city fell in 431 it cannot be assumed that the remaining 12,600 hoplites were all unique individuals, but that these different levies contained many of the same men.[45] This is especially relevant because one of these musters was a *pandemei* of 10,000 hoplites, who took part in one of the biannual raids in Megara in 431.[46] Similarly, in 424, Athens mustered two separate armies to go to Cythera and Megara, with strengths of 2,000 and 4,000 hoplites respectively and this was also the same year that Hippocrates ordered the *pandemei* of 7,000 hoplites which would face defeat at Delium.[47] Therefore, the image that reveals itself from these figures, especially during the Archidamian War, is one where Athens was calling thousands of men to muster throughout the height of the summer campaigning season. While these specific examples were not, by any means, a common occurrence in terms of committed hoplites, they do demand that Athens was capable of hosting the regular mustering of large groups of hoplites within its vicinity, possibly simultaneously. This record of mustering strength, allied with the regularity by which these musters were being called, required an infrastructure capable of managing the movement of anywhere between 33 and 434 fully armed hoplites from every one of the 30 *trittyes* spread throughout Attica, while not interrupting the day-to-day lives of people, businesses, and general trade.[48] From this theoretical foundation, the question can now be asked; where did the Athenian army muster?

Following Hansen and Christ, there are nine potential mustering points in and around the city of Athens: (inside the city) Agora, Theseum, Anacaeum, Odeum and Pnyx, (outside the city) Academy, Lyceum, Piraeus and the Hippodamian Agora.[49] These locations have been identified because they had either been named in one of the sources as a place where an army had set up camp during the classical period, whether Athenian or Peloponnesian, or they have been specifically mentioned in the sources as the location of Athenian musters by *katalogos* or *pandemei*. Of these locations, only the Agora and the gymnasium at the Lyceum offer any secondary evidence to imply an institutional recognition of their role as a mustering point. For the Agora this is loosely implied by the placement of the Eponymoi, from where the *katalogoi* were placed. Nevertheless, there is direct evidence for the Agora as a muster point. Xenophon describes a review under arms of 3,000 hoplites in the Agora during the rule of the Thirty, while the remainder of the hoplites in Athens mustered 'here and there'.[50] Andocides describes the Agora as the location for the mustering of all hoplites inside the main city walls during an emergency.[51] Polyaenus describes a similar instance of emergency which resulted in Iphicrates mustering his men in the Agora.[52] Indirect evidence can also be found which connect any agora as a possible scene of military muster, such as the mustering of men in the Trojan agora depicted by Bacchylides, or Aeneas Tacticus' suggestion to muster men in the agora during a siege.[53] However, the Agora was primarily a market place and centre of government, any role as a mustering point would only be secondary to these more primary roles. In other words, the Agora may have seen some armies muster, but it cannot be considered a permanent mustering point.

It is the grounds of the Lyceum that holds greater potential to be a recognised, permanent, mustering point. Xenophon describes it as a point of muster for the forces of Thrasyllus and as a location to hold a cavalry review.[54] Yet, more interestingly, Aristophanes presents the Lyceum as the standard venue for military duty:

> We have been killing ourselves long enough, tiring ourselves out with going to the Lyceum and returning laden with spear and shield.[55]

The statement, made by the citizen chorus in the play, describes the Lyceum as a place to which the men would often be called, with their arms in tow. This does not necessarily have to equate to a muster, it could be describing a military review. Either way, this not only implicates the Lyceum as a location for military service, but also indicates that the Lyceum was an *obvious* location and, therefore, it was able to be the focal point for the chorus' frustrations. The scholia to this passage affirms that military reviews or parades used to occur in the Lyceum, due to its close proximity to the city. It is also possible that the Lyceum had long-term connotations with the military, due to its position as the seat where the *polemarchos* could make judgements on cases within the realms of his own authority before the reforms of Solon.[56]

The most tantalising piece of evidence for the Lyceum being a permanent fixture in the Athenian muster system, is provided by an epigram, *IG* I³ 138, which describes a tax on active warriors claimed by the temple:[57]

[.........23..........χσυμβάλλεσθαι δὲ τ]-
[ὸ]<ς> h<ι>ππ[έ]ας δ[ύο δρ]αχμ<ὰ κα>ὶ <τ>ὸς [ὁπλίτας δραχμὲν]
καὶ τὸς τοχσότας τός τε ἀστ[ὸς καὶ τὸς χσένος τρ]-
ἐς ὀβο<λ>ὸς τõ ἐνια[υτ]õ ἀπò τõ[ν καθ' ἑκάστος μισθõν].
[5] ἐκπραττόντον δὲ hοι δέμαρ[χοι παρὰ ἀπάντον τõν]

ἐς τὸ λεχσιαρχικὸν γρ<α>μματ[εῖον γραφέντον, οἱ δ]-
[ἐ] <τ>όχσαρχοι παρὰ τὸν τοχσο<τ>[ὸν· ἐὰν δέ τινες μὲ ἀπ]-
οδιδõσι, ἐκπράττ<ε>ν καὶ [τὰς ἀρχὰς αἳ τὸς μισθὸς ἀ]-
ποδιδόασιν παρὰ τούτον ἐκ [τõν μισθõν. hε δὲ βολὲ]
[10] hε ἀεὶ βολεύοσα σφõν αὐτõν [hαιρέσθο ταμία δύο ἄ]-
νδρε τõ ἀρ<γ>υ[ρί]ο τõ Ἀπόλλον[ος ὅταν τὸς τõν τἐς Με]-
τρὸς χρεμάτον αἱρεῖται· το[ύτοιν δὲ ἐς θόλον ἐλθό]-
ντοιν παραδιδόντον ho<ί> τε [δέμαρχοι καὶ οἱ τόχσ]-
αρχοι καὶ <h> οἱ πρυτάνες hὸ ἂν [ἐκπράττοσι ἀργύρι]-
[15] ον. τ<ὸ> δὲ ταμία μετὰ [τõ] <h>ι<ε> [ρέος τõ Ἀπόλλονος τõ τε]-
μένος τõ Ἀπόλλονο [ς ἐπιμελέσθον, ὅπος ἂν κάλλισ]-
τα θεραπεύ <ε> ται καὶ [....] ευ[.......17........]
νει· χρεματίζεν δὲ αὐτοῖ[ς ὅταμπερ πρõτον ἐ βολὲ]
καθἐται πρότοι<ς με> [τὰ τὰ hιερὰ ......14......]
[20] —

[...] the cavalryman
will contribute
two drachma and from the hoplite one drachma,
and from the archer, both those from the city and foreigners,
three obols each year from their pay.
[5] Let the demarchoi collect this from all those recorded
in the lexiarchikon grammateion, and the archery-commander
from the archers; and if ever somebody does not pay,
the paymasters will render what is due from their pay.
[10] Let the Boule appoint two treasurers for the silver of Apollo,
both of whom are always from the boule, as whenever someone
is appointed to the finances of the Mother. Let the demarchoi, the archery-
    commander
and the prytanes hand over whatever silver they collect to both of them [the
    treasurers],
once both have entered into the Tholos.
[15] The treasurers, with the priest of Apollo,
are to take care of Apollo's precinct, caring for it in the most beautiful way and
    [...]
And the boule, after the preliminary sacrifices, will sit to do business [....]

The tax was imposed, by the Athenian assembly, in the latter half of the fifth century, on all men serving as *hippeis*, hoplites or archers.[58] The money was collected from those listed on the *lexiarchikon grammateion* by the *demarchoi*, while the archers had theirs collected by their own captains (*toxarchoi*).[59] This money was given to two treasurers and was intended to aid the maintenance of the *temenos* (precinct) of Apollo.[60] The specific identity of this Apollo is never made clear and scholars have suggested a few possible cults as the recipient.[61] However, Michael Jameson convincingly argues for this Apollo to be none other than Apollo Lykeios.[62] His argument is based on the accumulation of various strands of evidence. First, there is no mention of a temple in the decree, only the surrounding grounds, which suggests that this tax is not necessarily for the cult itself but merely for its location.[63] Second, only land forces are mentioned as paying this tax, there is no mention of the navy.[64] This last point, Jameson argues, implies that the tax was not for a general war cult, or defensive cult of any sort, as the primacy of the Athenian navy would demand their inclusion somewhere. Jameson then combined his assessment with the literary sources regarding the Lyceum mentioned above, to connect the specific tax for Apollo's precinct with the upkeep of the grounds for the Lyceum.[65] Jameson's suggestion is that the land forces were being taxed for the upkeep of the muster grounds they most commonly used; in turn, I would argue, this might suggest an institutional recognition for the Lyceum being a permanent, military muster point.

The question still remains, why is there so much evidence for numerous mustering points around Athens, if there was a permanent site at the Lyceum? The statistical evidence discussed earlier puts these musters and the mustering points into their military context. Athens needed to be able to muster numerous forces simultaneously, a demand epitomised by the Andocides' description during an emergency:

> Then they summoned the Generals and urged them to proclaim that citizens resident in Athens proper were to proceed under arms to the Agora; those between the Long Walls to the Theseum; and those in Peiraeus to the Agora of Hippodamus. The cavalry were to be mustered at the Anaceum by trumpet before nightfall.[66]

These orders reveal two important factors to a muster: (1) the speed that was demanded dictated the location of each mustering point, that which was nearest to the position of each group;[67] (2) the objective of each muster determined its location (see Map 3.1). Xenophon describes this clearly when Iphicrates was placed in charge of an army that was sent to assist the Spartans during the Theban invasion of 370.[68] From the Academy, Iphicrates was able to muster his men on route to the Corinthian Isthmus to Athens' northwest, but the lack of urgency required allowed for his communal meal and night spent in situ.

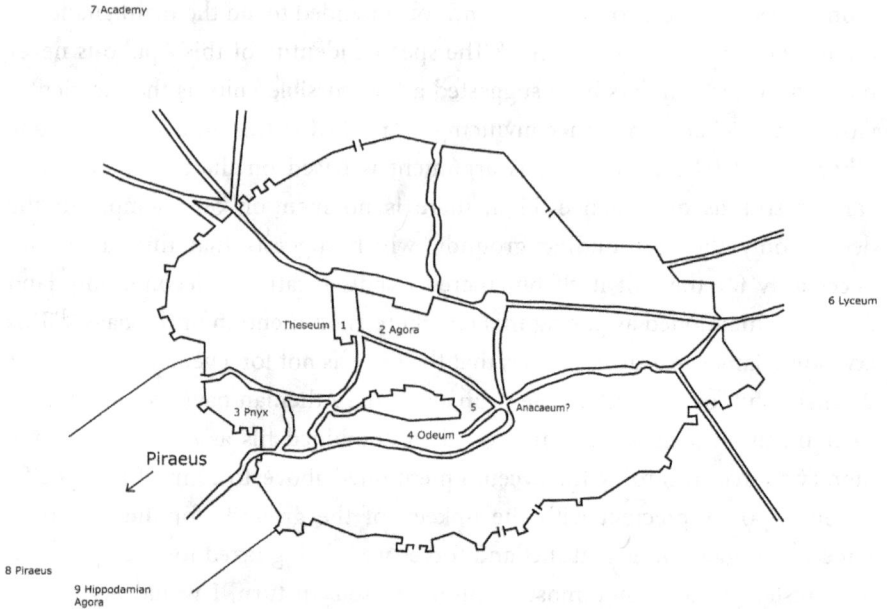

Map 3.1 Map of possible mustering points in and around Athens.

Thucydides' account of the Sicilian expedition, discussed more fully below, where the hoplites mustered in the Piraeus shares a similar logic. Firstly, the men had time to muster wherever they wished, so a location outside of the city was not an obstacle. Secondly, the purpose of the muster was to send a hoplite force overseas, making the harbour an obvious choice. Whereas the Lyceum, as a place of muster, positioned the army outside of the city, yet deep into Attic country, making it a better vantage point from which to attempt to counter invasions from the north, from the sea to the east and south, as well as from the Isthmus region. This is shown by Xenophon, who describes a counter-attack mounted against the army of Agis, coming from the northeast at Decelea, under the command of Thrassylus.[69] This army mustered at the Lyceum and defended the city by engaging with the enemy outside the walls.

Returning to Andocides' speech, the disparate muster that he describes, over numerous locations in Athens, meant that the city had four independent battle groups to defend against a variety of possible attacks. This was achieved by a logical and systematic allocation of muster points, which reduced the time and distance required to make the defence of the city viable. The men in the Peiraeus were not required to enter the main city, through the crowds in the Long Walls.

Those in the Long Walls were to muster away from the crowds by going to the Theseum, one of the nearest points inside the city.[70] The men inside the city were to muster in the Agora, which was a central focal point and more than capable of holding the large numbers at short notice. Finally, the most disruptive element to muster was the cavalry. The introduction of a large number of horses into a city that was crowded, frantic with activity and panicked, needed to be controlled. This was achieved first by mustering the cavalry away from the hoplites, at the Anacaeum to the east of the Acropolis, which reduced the possibility of converging traffic between the two forces and, secondly, officially calling the cavalry to muster at nightfall, presumably after the hoplites had already congregated.

Thus, the image that appears from the Athenian muster is that it could – and did – occur in a multitude of locations, each of which were chosen based on these two factors of required speed and strategic intent. This means, referring to the army's departure under discussion here, that the location of the departure was focused on the strategic requirements for that army, not for the location's ritualistic significance. We can deduce that, once the *katalogoi* had been compiled and the men notified, they would congregate either at the Lyceum or a separate, temporary, mustering point based on the criteria of speed and tactical objectives. There is one final question concerning the experience of the hoplite during the muster that needs resolving: did the individual hoplite simply leave his home and join the army at the central mustering point by himself?

3.1.4 The rolling muster

In his provocative work on the Athenian *trittyes*, Peter Siewert argued that the Cleisthenic tribal reforms were established specifically for military purposes.[71] One of his core arguments rested on the position of roads throughout Attica, asserting that they allowed for a fast and efficient mustering of the tribal-based army in the Agora.[72] The many merits and flaws of his thesis have been addressed by previous scholars and do not concern the matter at hand, however Siewert proposed another factor in the mustering of the Athenian army that has received very little recognition or opposition – a rolling muster.[73]

Siewert's model was based solely on Polybius's account of a covert muster made by the Achaean League at the turn of the second century BC, ordered by the great strategist Philopoemen.[74] Siewert argued that the method Philopoemen utilised – where one city would muster its men, and then march to the next city along a designated road, hand over a dispatch ordering that city to muster and then both forces march to the next city, and so on, until the army was assembled – was an obvious meaning to the *trittys*-road system that Siewert himself had proposed for Attica.[75] Siewert's model would allow for the demesmen to muster and then join with the next *deme* along the road; then they would move on to the next deme until the whole *trittys* had been brought together. This proposal suited another of his arguments, that the *trittys* formed the basis of the *lochos*.[76] This devised system allowed Siewert to identify a military sub-unit independent of the *taxeis*, which then marched to the central muster point to join the main army. Unfortunately, he offers no substantive evidence for this hypothesis. It is not known how the *lochos* was configured, there is no evidence which suggests that the *trittys* was itself a specified constituent of the Athenian army, nor is there any direct evidence of a rolling muster of this magnitude in the classical evidence.[77] Siewert's intention, to link his idea of a rolling muster with his larger hypothesis of an Attic military-logistic infrastructure and his subdivisions of the Athenian army, could perhaps explain the lack of scholarly interest in his suggestion. Yet, his initial concept of the rolling muster, however constructed, does merit some consideration.

If the focus of Siewert's idea is moved away from the military infrastructure of Athens and towards the personal experience of the individual hoplite, it appears an obvious suggestion that the men of the *deme* would meet first before marching to muster.[78] However, the only direct evidence comes from a speech of Lysias, in *For Mantitheus,* which describes a muster of demesmen before a departure:

> Now, when the demesmen had assembled together before their setting out, as I knew that some among them, though true and ardent patriots, lacked means for expenses of service, I said that those with the means ought to provide what was necessary for those in needy circumstances.[79]

It has been rightly observed that this reference does not clearly state the location of the gathering, so it does not necessarily suggest that the men gathered in the *deme* first, before departing for the mustering point.[80] However, if this scene is not set within the deme, then the content of the passage raises a few questions. Firstly, why would the demesmen have cause to meet at the large mustering point if they had not gone as a group, or if their *taxis* had not been officially split into *deme* sub-divisions? It could be understood if the speaker was describing a gathering of a few friends, but he is not. Secondly, the speaker goes on to claim he gave 60 drachmae to two men and asked the other wealthy men to follow suit.

This raises an unanswerable question, how much money do we expect men to have carried on campaign? Based on the speaker's donation, it must be assumed that he would also personally need, as a minimum, 30 drachmae but decided to carry to the muster at least 90 drachmae for himself.[81] Furthermore, he was able to assume that the wealthier men among his *deme* would have carried a similar amount of money. While this is plausible, this scenario makes for a simpler reading if the scene occurs in the deme, where the full wealth of the individuals present can be called upon to aid the poorer elements of the hoplites. In another of Lysias' speeches, a similar sentiment is expressed by Philon, who offered to equip his fellow demesmen but, unlike *For Mantitheus*, he makes no mention of an imminent departure nor of a muster.[82]

Tangentially, there is evidence available that reveals a small-scale, central focus of the individual on his deme.[83] In terms of military service, specifically, these include the calling of demesmen to supply evidence of a hoplite's actions in battle,[84] the description of one speaker that he served on campaign with his tribe and deme,[85] the calling of demesmen in battle to witness one's actions[86] and the making of military vows as a *deme*.[87] This points to both a personal interest in deme-peer assessment and a close proximity between a hoplite and his demesmen, in battle and on campaign. Neither of which were encouraged, nor formulated, by the structure of the Athenian army, as it is understood. However, the personal experience of the campaign was one that was influenced by and shared with a hoplite's fellow demesmen, making it more likely that they would begin their service together from the very start.

Furthermore, the entire mustering system in Athens was underpinned by the role of the *deme*. The registering of an adult into the *deme* made him liable for hoplite service and participation in the *katalogos*, a system which drew its names from the *deme*-register, *lexiarchikon grammateion*. The compilation of these lists required the cooperation of the *demarchoi*, and the announcement of who were to serve may have been made within the *deme* itself.[88] Finally, it was from the use of these registers, and the actions of the *demarchoi*, that military taxes were taken from all of the men serving in the military every year. Every stage of the bureaucratic process required, or at times solely relied on, the *deme* serving the administrative role of the muster. Therefore, with the *deme* serving as both a strong psycho-social motivational factor on the hoplite himself, and as a pivotal administrative centre for the army in its entirety, it seems that Lysias' speech quoted above should be read as pertaining to a micro-muster in the *deme* itself, before the demesmen went to join the official muster.[89]

3.2 The army departs

Once the army had mustered at its designated point, our ancient evidence becomes rather bereft of any specific information about its departure from the city. Commonly, our sources simply declare that the army departed, without any description of the ritualistic element involved. This omission is, on the one hand, very strange and anomalous in Greek military practice but, on the other hand, it is entirely understandable. The incongruity this absence of evidence, compared to the fastidious nature of Greek rituals during military campaign, is quite blatant.[90] However, if we consider the Athenian army as mustering regularly, every year, then the mundanity of this departure for readers, who would have experienced it first- or second-hand on a regular basis, must be acknowledged. This may go some way to explain why the one clear example of a military departure we have during the classical period comes from Thucydides' account of the Sicilian expedition. In turn, this inclusion by the historian raises a major methodological concern: why has Thucydides chosen to break his habitual silence on the departure of armies in this instance, if not for its unique nature?

3.2.1 Departure for the Sicilian expedition

As Thucydides relates, the Athenian assembly voted to muster 5,000 hoplites, under the command of Nicias, to help their Sicilian allies against Syracusan intervention.[91] Of these 5,000 hoplites, only 1,500 would be Athenian citizens from the lists (ἐκ καταλόγου), a further 700 were volunteer *thetes* who served as marines, with the remainder of the force consisting of *metics*, foreigners and mercenaries.[92] These hoplites, escorted by their friends and families, mustered in the Piraeus at daybreak and began boarding their vessels. To transport these men, Athens had provisioned 60 triremes (τριήρεις) and 40 troopships (στρατιώτιδες). Numerically this expedition was not without precedent, a point that Thucydides himself dwells upon and, in fact, the Athenian commitment is entirely in keeping with those figures collated in Table 3.1.[93] For Thucydides, the main difference was that this expedition had received greater funding and the men were better equipped than usual.[94] Another difference was, seemingly, that this was the furthest an armada like this had ever been sent.[95] Finally, the collective feeling behind this venture was, of course, amplified by the fact that Athens had not long begun to recover from the plague, so this was the first major venture by Athens with its newly recovered adult generation.[96] With these comments in mind, the description of the rituals involved can be explored, with the understanding that we may expect to see more wealth on display than would be 'normal'. We may also expect to see a greater outpouring of emotion than is normally depicted, due to the dual factors of the distance and the emotional connection involved in sending this new generation to war for the first time.[97]

> [T]he trumpet commanded silence, and the prayers customary before putting out to sea were offered, not in each ship by itself, but by all together to the voice of a herald; and bowls of wine were mixed through all the fleet, and libations made by the marines (ἐπιβάται) and their officers in gold and silver goblets. They were joined in their prayers by the crowds on shore, by the citizens and all others that wished them well. The paean sung and the libations finished, they put out to sea, and first sailing out in column then raced each other as far as Aegina, and so hastened to reach Corcyra where the rest of the allied forces were also assembling.[98]

First and foremost, it is evident that there are three participating elements to these rituals: the herald and ritual organisers, the marines and commanders on the ships and the citizens and 'all the others' on the shore.[99] All these elements are actively engaged in two of the rituals, namely the prayers and the *paean*, but those on land are not involved in the libations. Interestingly, the hoplites are not named as active participants and Thucydides seems purposefully to declare this through his use of the term ἐπιβάται, when a more generic term such as μαχόμενοι or στρατιῶται would have been more inclusive.[100] Thucydides' work clearly identifies the ἐπιβάται as a distinct naval fighter, ten of which formed part of the fighting crew of a trireme, alongside four archers, so it is valid to assume that the historian has purposefully made this distinction.[101] This observation is reinforced by Thucydides' opening qualifier; that the prayers offered were those customary before putting out to sea. More specifically, the hoplites were not involved because this was a naval departure, so only the naval personnel took part in the physical ritual, excluding the rowers who are also left unmentioned.[102] Another, more pragmatic, reason behind this ritualistic selectivism is one of logistics. Even within the confines of a single trireme, with a crew of anywhere up to 200 men, the inclusion of every person in a physical ritual is difficult, so only the elite members of the naval crew were involved, pouring libations on behalf of the trireme as a whole.[103] They were, in effect, no longer individuals involved in the ritual, but rather a collective singularity who had these rituals done on their behalf. This state of de-individuation would not have prevented from them from performing collective practices, such as joining in the prayers and the paean.

Another important caveat to Thucydides' description is his statement that the prayers were not offered on each ship but were instead made collectively. The only reason he would have for making this observation would be because it is a break from standard practice, so we can assume it was more usual for each ship to hold its own prayers and rituals separate from one another.[104] Thucydides makes no mention of any other rituals, which at first glance is surprising, because we know, from a fragmentary inscription of a decree relating to the Sicilian expedition, that the Assembly had allocated a set sum of money in the pursuit of 'auspicious sacrifice'.[105] Yet, Thucydides makes no mention of these sacrifices in his vivid departure scene. This absence of sacrifice and divination in the narrative is in keeping with Thucydidean historical practice; it is a habit he only ever broke when the presence of omens were needed to explain a counterintuitive action, or used as a rhetorical device, so this may be a simple way to explain this absence.[106]

However, another possibility is that, in this one instance, Thucydides is purposefully portraying a communal affair. The historian is almost at pains to include as many people as possible in these rituals. This accentuates a symbiosis between the crowds and those who are departing, reinforcing the emotional bonds mentioned above, that Thucydides masterfully manipulates through the use of dramatic irony, knowing, as we do, that this voyage will end in disaster for the men, as well as the families left to mourn them. The crowds on the shore are taking part as much as they physically can and the libations are poured by as many as is realistically possible. While these actions are unprecedented, they are not outside the realms of possibility or reality. Thucydides can explain away a breach in naval protocol, whether actual or invented by the historian, so that all of the ships are homogenous in their religious rites. While unusual, this is, again, not beyond what was possible and it can be assumed that his explanation was satisfactory to his readers. Perhaps the sacrifice was the one ritual that stretched reality too far. As will be explored more fully below, the sacrifice may have been purposefully omitted by Thucydides because only the *strategos*, his *mantis* and, at most, a select few others witnessed it. For Thucydides to present this ritual as a communal event at a military departure would not have been possible because the only communalised aspect of any sacrifice was the feast that followed it. This would not fit his overarching aim of presenting a communal group of warriors and citizens, bound by communalised worship, right before their departure. As will be examined shortly, the sacrifice was an important element of the military departure and there is no question that at least one took place, but Thucydides' purposeful silence on the matter reveals more about his own narrative design than it does about military departure rituals.

Therefore, it can be seen that Thucydides' account is clearly representing a distinctly naval departure. The unique nature of this event is highlighted by the expensive gold and silver goblets, by the throngs of people on the shore, and by the collective nature of the rituals involved – not the rituals themselves.[107] While this departure may not be used as direct evidence for military departures on land, it does provide evidence for the likely rites that would have been involved. Thus, with a basic template of prayers, paeans and libations being led by a central figure and Thucydides' absent sacrifice, the rituals involved in military departures for hoplites can now be explored.[108]

3.2.2 Interacting with the gods

There are snippets of evidence that suggest that the wider community may have held a small level of responsibility for garnering divine support on behalf of a departing army. In Aeschylus' *Seven against Thebes*, the chorus of old women in the city describe themselves not only as making prayers to the gods but also awaiting the right time to adorn the statues with robes and garlands as prayer-offerings.[109] This Aeschylean image has a later companion in Aristophanes' *Acharnians*, which describes the busy sights of Athens in the wake of an announced mustering notice.[110] Through the hustle and bustle of Dicaeopolis' descriptions, with men preparing for their departure, we are told that the Pallas Athena statues are being gilded.[111] However, these small examples cannot be used to argue, convincingly, that Thucydides' crowds at the Piraeus were in any way a common occurrence for two distinct reasons. First, these dramatic portrayals have no historical comparisons, beyond the exceptional circumstances surrounding the Sicilian departure, making them less reliable to be portraying classical Athenian experiences. Secondly, in neither example are the women involved in the army's own departure rituals, unlike in Thucydides' crowds, where they joined them in prayer. In addition, Euripides constructs a similar scene of pre-battle preparations within a civic setting, in which he distinguishes between the sacrifices and rites made by the army, to those being made throughout the city.[112] While it is possible that these plays may reflect customs during war, maybe even during a period of military departure, they are portrayed as background noise that does not directly affect the army and its rituals.

The rituals involved in the military departure all have one common goal: to secure the approval of the gods, or, if divine approval could not be guaranteed, then at least the protection from divine hostilities.[113] The importance of securing this support was as much psychological as it was theological:

[F]or I with my own good fortune will take command, a new leader with a new army. One thing alone I need, the favour of the gods who reverence justice; for the presence of these things gives victory. For valour carries nothing for mortal men, unless it has the god on its side.[114]

The way to secure divine support was not simply to ask for it: the gods needed something in return. The most prolific form of evidence for this comes in the guise of military vows, where an army, or its leaders, would make a vow on behalf of the collective and offer the god(s) a prize in return for aid. The most famous example from historical times is the vow made by the Athenians before the battle of Marathon, when they vowed to sacrifice to Artemis the same number of nanny goats as there would be Persian dead.[115] Herodotus describes a similar vow made collectively by the Greeks to Apollo of Delphi, to take a tithe from all of the medising Greek *poleis*, if the god helped them to overcome the Persians.[116] Diodorus reflects this practice when he describes the vows made to Zeus and Apollo by the Athenians, before the battle of Arginusae in 406 BC.[117] One late classical letter, attributed to Demosthenes, suggests that not only were these vows normal practice, but that they also took place before the campaign.[118] This paradigm was taken to its greatest extreme by a very late source, Justin, who describes the vows made by the people of Kroton during a war against Lokroi (*c.* 555 BC), in which the Krotonians vowed a tithe of the spoils to Apollo.[119] The men of Lokroi vowed a ninth of the spoils, thus the god granted them victory, the moral of the story being that vows could win you success. These vows would often be mandated by the assembly of a *polis* such as on an inscription in Selinous, Sicily, celebrating a military victory, in which it describes a single vow made to no less than ten gods, and also 'all the others'.[120]

On its own, Thucydides' template of departure rites – prayers, hymns and libations –forms a rather basic, almost ubiquitous, series of rites that do not distinguish a military departure from any other form of ritual. However, as has been argued above, in a small unit such as a single trireme, the logistics of a formal libation do not permit complete inclusive involvement for the hoplites. It is unrealistic to presume that thousands of individuals would take part in the libations, outside of an informal setting such as a communal meal.[121] The individual hoplite at the muster point, would most likely have watched his commanding officers pour libations on his behalf, before joining a communal prayer and paean. To these departure rituals we can add the more specific military vow which, in this instance, is made on behalf of the army, seemingly within the assembly.[122] There is one further, omnipresent, feature of Greek religion missing from Thucydides' own picture highlighted earlier: there are no sacrifices. While Thucydides may have had his own reasons for such an omission, to a seasoned military commander such as Xenophon, their importance could not be overstated.[123] Opening his treatise on being a cavalry commander, he states that a commander's first duty was to sacrifice to the gods and pray to them.[124] It is advice he would repeat, stating that after drawing together a cavalry force, the commander should sacrifice to the gods on behalf of the men (ὑπὲρ τοῦ ἱππικοῦ).[125] Xenophon depicted his own, pseudo-historical, Cyrus the Great as performing such a sacrifice on behalf of his men, before departing with a small army against the Armenians.[126] Numerous sacrifices are also described in Xenophon's *Anabasis* preceding military marches.[127] Onasander, a much later military-manual author, reinforced this advice by stating that a general should not lead his army on a journey without first making sacrifices.[128] He went one step further than Xenophon and suggested that the general should have his own official sacrificers and diviners to accompany him.[129] Within the classical Greek army, this role was already filled by the *mantis*, who studied omens and advised the generals on creating a relationship with the divine.[130]

3.2.3 Reading the signs

There was an exceedingly close relationship between sacrifice and omen in ancient Greece.[131] From a military perspective, the omen was the more important element, as these were the signs from the gods that determined action or inaction. While there are numerous examples of positive omens being read and deciphered while an army was on campaign, or preparing for imminent battle, there are very few instances of this occurring before an army had departed.[132] Herodotus mentions the Peloponnesians, as a collective, marching out to join the Spartans at Eleusis after the omens of sacrifice had proven to be favourable.[133] The generalised manner in which he describes the remaining Peloponnesians all receiving their omens by sacrifice, does suggest a Panhellenic custom that could be seamlessly attributed by Herodotus to a large collation of *poleis*. There is a passage in Pausanias that shows the mirror image of Herodotus' positivist impetus. During the conflict between Sparta and Aristomenes of Messenia, 300 Arcadians delayed their departure to join the Messenian king due to unfavourable readings of the sacrificial victims, implying that a formal omen reading took place before the departure.[134] However, these instances are rare in the historical record.

More commonly, our sources describe sacrifices at the borders (διαβατήρια) of an army's home territory and subsequent omen readings. Thucydides recounts three separate instances in which the Lacedaemonians marched to their borders before performing the διαβατήρια, subsequently returning home due to the poor omens.[135] Xenophon gives more examples, allowing the notoriously pious Spartans to receive seven positive διαβατήρια rituals, which resulted in direct Spartan action.[136] The prolificacy of these border rites could be seen to imply that the main departure ritual did not occur at the muster but rather at the border, raising the wider question as to whether the διαβατήρια should be considered a departure ritual from the civic sphere, or the first of the rituals of a military campaign. Within context, the latter seems most pertinent because the forces had already been mustered, removed from their domestic roles and had set out from the *polis* – departure had already occurred before any of these rituals. The διαβατήρια, by contrast, was the first real act of military decision making by the commander in charge, aligning it with campaign sacrifices and omen readings, rather than a ritualised movement from the civic to the purely military world.[137]

Our best source for the διαβατήρια is Xenophon's *Constitution of the Spartans*, which presents it as the final part of a complex departure ritual led by the Spartan king.[138] According to Xenophon, the Spartan king first offered sacrifices to Zeus Agetor (Leader) and associated gods. If these were favourable, the fire-bearer (πυρφόρος) would take the flame from the altar, lead the army to the border, and they would be used during the διαβατήρια rites. The unique status of this Spartan departure is emphasised by Xenophon when he described this as proof that every other *polis* were mere improvisers in war compared to the Spartans who he considered skilled in this regard.[139] Indeed, the only comparable instance of this format is found in the later work of Plutarch, drawing on Theopompus, who described the rituals of a departing mercenary force on Zacynthus in similar fashion.[140] The commander, Dion, led his men on a solemn procession to the temple with full armaments before making a sacrifice to Apollo. After this, he led them to the Zacynthian stadium where he held a banquet, something that finds no comparison in Xenophon's description, but was institutionally enforced on the Spartans by their *syssitia*. Returning to Athens, Plutarch/Theopompus' description of a communal meal has a precedent in Xenophon's *Hellenica*, when Iphicrates was appointed commander of a newly raised force and, following his favourable sacrifices, ordered his men to eat together at the Academy before departing the following day.[141]

Perhaps then, the Spartan rituals were not unique for their content, but rather in their execution.[142] In Athens, the departure of an army had no set location, therefore, no set format, whereas the Spartans could methodically replicate the same rites every time. Even the uniquely Spartan διαβατήρια has comparisons in the rites at 'obstacle' crossings, such as rivers, that we see in the actions of other Greeks.[143] Similarly, Jameson persuasively argues that the Athenian venerated their borders, implying that the Spartan ritual appears to be a continuation of a Panhellenic form of worship, aimed specifically at their two principal gods, Zeus and Athena. While Jameson was reluctant to draw direct parallels between the διαβατήρια and these other forms of border and 'obstacle' rituals, Robert Parker perhaps takes it too far when he describes the διαβατήρια as being 'peculiar to Sparta'. Rather it stands as an example of Spartan variance, rather than Spartan uniqueness. The emphasis placed, by Xenophon especially, on the pre-departure sacrifices made by the commander of the Athenian army, either on his own or with his *mantis*, contrasts with his Spartan ritual system that was witnessed by the hierarchy of the army, as well as the leader of the baggage train and commanders of foreign contingents.[144]

For the Athenian hoplite, his role in the rituals of the military departure mirrored his role in all other military rituals: he was a passive witness, presuming that he could see it at all.[145] The two military treatises, mentioned earlier, were very clear about the role of the commander. Xenophon's cavalry commander was to make sacrifices on behalf of his men, while the officers described by Onasander should be able to read the omens so that they could 'tell the men to be of good courage, because the gods have ordered them to fight', implying that the men themselves were not present to watch the reading.[146] Xenophon repeats this format in his Cyropaedia on two separate occasions: the first sees Cyrus sacrificing on behalf of his military expedition;[147] while the second instance repeats this topos while out on campaign, culminating in Cyrus drawing his officers together, after the sacrifice, to explain the good omens.[148] Finally, the fourth-century BC inscription, known as the decree of Themistocles, clearly states that the generals and the *boule* were to offer sacrifices to the gods *before* manning the ships.[149] While our sources differ slightly in their timing of the sacrifice, whether at the muster or before it, the same conclusion can be drawn in regard to the individual hoplite – he is not included.

Once the omens had been read, the commander conferred with his *manteis* before telling his officers of the decision to march. In so doing, he brought an end to the transition between the domestic and military world and completed the hoplite's departure. From this exploration of the various elements to an army's departure, a model for the military departure can be presented from the moment the *strategos* had been assigned by the assembly: the lists of potential hoplites are compiled by the *demarchoi* and given to the *strategos*, via the *taxiarchoi*. The *strategos* is then assisted in compiling the final list that would make his campaign *katalogos*. Final arrangements are confirmed, including the amount of rations required for each man. The location of the muster is judged, based on the operational objective of the newly raised force and the speed required and then set. The *katalogos* is then posted up at the *Eponymoi* monument and is read by a representative from each *deme* (if this is a mass levy, rather than a *katalogos*, this element is overridden by heralds and trumpet calls, speeding up the entire process). Following this, an assigned hoplite departs from his home and meets at a set location within his *deme*. With his fellow demesmen he marches out to the pre-arranged muster point in or around Athens. While Athens itself is abuzz with activity, the hoplites are registered and the fighting strength is confirmed to the *strategos*. When the commander is content, the army prepares to depart. The *strategos*, with his *mantis/eis*, perform the sacrifices and read the omens. These are then relayed to the *taxiarchoi* with final orders. If the muster occurs late in the day, the army may be ordered to take a communal meal the evening before finalising the departure the following morning. If the muster occurs early in the day, libations are poured by the officers, followed by communal prayer and a paean sung by the hoplites. The army is led to the borders of their homeland, assuming they are assigned a foreign duty, where another sacrifice is made before crossing the final threshold.

By examining the process by which an Athenian hoplite departed for his military service it has become apparent that there was a vast experiential difference between his domestic and military transitions. The domestic departure was not solely dictated by a public ideology, emphasising civic duty, but presents the individual as the centre of focus, offering him an active role in his departure and the rituals involved. This contrasts with his place in the military departure, during which he had joined a large-scale system of recruitment that inevitably stripped the individual of his ability to participate in the rituals on a personal level.

Importantly, the hoplite underwent a process of de-individuation during the military transition, yet there is no suggestion that this resulted in any friction between the hoplite, his family and the Athenian army he was joining. What the evidence does show is a clear acknowledgement of the tensions and fears inherent in the domestic departure. While this is to be expected when loved ones depart for war, the reticence in the departure scenes and its articulation in the words of Xenophon's Panthea, suggest that Crowley's proposition of a seamless transition of ideals between the civic and military spheres is, at the very least, questionable.[150] As Panthea's speech holding Abradatas' dead body shows, the experiences of war could quite drastically change the thoughts and beliefs of even the most ardent of advocates for civic duty and military service.

Military Homecoming

One unique feature of classical Greek warfare, which separates it so distinctly from later Hellenistic and Roman traditions, is the absence of military victory processions.[1] At times of great Athenian victory such as the battles of Marathon or Plataea, which we know were later commemorated and celebrated in Athens, there is no mention of a triumphal army marching back to Athens, no celebration of the victorious hoplites.[2] Indeed, even during the Peloponnesian War, when military action was most prevalent for the Athenians, neither Thucydides nor Xenophon actually describe an Athenian army returning to their mother city. This strange gap in our understanding of the Athenian military experience transcends the literary sphere and has also been observed within art.[3]

As Lisa Hau has successfully shown, the greatest difference between the after-battle actions of the classical Greeks and the Republican Romans, as described by Greek historians, is the absence of victory celebrations and processions.[4] Indeed, it is very noticeable that the entire classical Greek world was void of anything akin to the famous Roman triumphs, not just Athens.[5] Hau concludes her research by asserting that the ancient historians must have been averse to writing about these celebrations, due to a form of class prejudice. This conclusion is based upon Hau's own stated assumption that the Greeks did, in fact, celebrate their victories regularly, in the absence of any direct evidence to support this.[6] Hau's focus is precisely on this lack of victory celebration, which she links with Greek concerns for appearing hubristic. However, she does not attempt to reconcile this absence of evidence with the various accounts available that describe Greek athletes receiving their own triumphal marches and celebrations.[7] This disparity surely implies that the celebration of a victory was not necessarily hubristic, for an individual at least, but that a military victory was somehow different and it was the military context that made a celebration unseemly.

Matthew Trundle considered a similar line of thought, suggesting that the lack of triumphal marches and the leading of captives through the streets may reflect the Greek perception of war as 'sorrowful and destructive'.[8] He further observes that there is no record of the return of a Greek army to its own city, which Trundle finds anomalous and in direct contrast with the clear military participation in civic festivals and, indeed, of festivals based around significant battle sites.[9] Similarly to Hau, Trundle's emphasis here is on victory and the celebration of that victory; yet this only accounts for one side of a battle. The defeated needed to go home as well. By focusing on the military homecoming as an exercise in triumph and celebration, something that is absent from the historical record, scholars have allowed the topic to remain unexplored. As a result, the subject does not feature in many of the influential works of Greek socio-military history.[10] However, as I aim to show in this section, when the restrictions of victory and celebration are removed from the enquiry, it becomes possible to piece together elements of the military homecoming and, as a result, create a more complex image of the experience of homecoming for the hoplite.

4.1   Arriving in Athens

Thucydides regularly uses the aorist passive of the verb διαλύω, to describe an army being disbanded, followed by a prepositional phrase such as κατὰ πόλεις (to their cities), κατα ἔθνη (to their 'peoples') and ἐπ᾽ οἴκου ἕκαστοι (to their own home).[11] Remarkably, not one of these descriptions refer to the Athenians themselves, but rather allied armies; creating an image of military contingents parting to go back to their own territories. In addition to cognates of διαλύω, Xenophon also uses the set phrase διαφῆκε το στρατευμα ([the general] dismissed the army), but this, similarly, does not refer to an Athenian army.[12] There are, in fact, no direct references to an Athenian army being disbanded in any of the surviving sources, neither are there any descriptions of an Athenian army being sent home, nor of them entering the city of Athens, which raises the question: what happened to them?[13]

To answer this, it must first be ascertained how Athenian armies most frequently travelled. If our image of the Athenian army is one which most frequently marched out of Attica to raid Megara, or invade the Peloponnese, then there is the distinct possibility that the absence of a military homecoming in our sources reflects a reality. The armies could have crossed into Attica and the men then dispersed to their *demes*, without entering Athens itself. However, the statistics collated in Chapter 3 reflect a different image of Athenian military transportation, as can be seen in a modified version given in Table 4.1.

This table shows the geographical destinations of every Athenian muster that numbered over 1,000 hoplites, as described by Thucydies, Xenophon and Diodorus. It also collates the number of ships that were assigned to the mission and the means of transport used by the army. For our enquiry here, the exact destination is not as important as the geographical scope of the journey. By sending an army to an island, it is obvious that they must have travelled by ship. What is perhaps less obvious is that many of the assaults on the Peloponnese were also carried out by ship. It is only when the Isthmus was raided, or an army was sent into Boeotia, that an Athenian force left Attica by land. A change in pattern appears during the Theban Hegemony, when it became safer for the Athenians to enter the Peloponnese by land, either as an ally of Thebes, or as an ally of Sparta.

Of the 44 Athenian musters we are given by our sources, 29 were transported by ship. This means that 65% of all Athenian musters that we are informed about, of a size that has been previously argued needed specific logistical considerations, were transported by ships. The importance of this comes, once again, from a logistical consideration: the hoplites who went out on campaign, would have needed to be aboard a ship to return home. Demosthenes describes a group of Athenian sailors in service, who chose to remain with their commanders to ensure their safety when travelling home, from where the commander would then discharge them.[14] Demosthenes is purposefully contrasting the loyal behaviour of citizens with the disloyalty of mercenary sailors, who simply moved on to the next paymaster. The significance of this passage comes from who these Athenian sailors were; they were οἵ γε ἐκ καταλόγου (those [sailors] drawn from the *katalogos*). This means that they were of the same social group as conscripted hoplites, if not experienced hoplites themselves. Two elements are relevant here: the association between staying as a group and feeling safe and the fact that they returned home safely *before* they were discharged.[15] A return home, for these ships, would have meant a return to the Piraeus from where they had launched and, if Demosthenes is to be believed, it would have been here that the men were discharged, at the earliest.[16]

There is direct evidence of a homecoming force entering the Piraeus, when Alcibiades returned from his exile in 408/7 BC, having been named one of the Athenian generals for that year. He sailed into the Piraeus with 20 ships and received a hero's welcome, according to Xenophon, who was apparently an eyewitness.[17] A slightly different version, based on the accounts he had read by Xenophon, Theopompus, Ephorus and Daris of Samos, is given by Plutarch who dismisses their overly extravagant portrayal of the event.[18] Plutarch does not give

Table 4.1 Athenian musters and methods of transportation

Reference	Year of muster	Destination	Muster size	Transport	Number of ships
Thucydides:					
1.57	433	Chalcidice	1,000	Ship	30
1.60-1	432	Chalcidice	2,000	Ship	40
1.64	432	Chalcidice	1,600	Ship	Unknown
1.107	457	Corinthian Isthmus	13,000	On foot	N/A
1.113	447	Boeotia	1,000	On foot	N/A
2.23	431	Peloponnese	1,000	Ship	100
2.31	431	Corinthian Isthmus	10,000	On foot	N/A
2.56-8	430	Peloponnese	4,000	Ship	100
3.17	433–431	Chalcidice	3,000	Ship	N/A
3.18	428	Island	1,000	Ship	Unknown
3.91	426	Island	2,000	Ship	60
4.42	425	Peloponnese	2,000	Ship	80
4.53	424	Island	2,000	Ship	60
4.68	424	Corinthian Isthmus	4,000	On foot	N/A
4.129	423	Chalcidice	1,000	Ship	40
5.2	422	Chalcidice	1,200	Ship	30
5.55	419	Argolid	1,000	On foot	N/A
5.61	418	Argolid	1,000	On foot	N/A
5.75	418	Argolid	1,000	On foot	N/A
5.84	416	Island	1,600	Ship	30
6.43	415	Island	1,500	Ship	100
8.25	412	Island	1,000	Ship	48
Xenophon, *Hellenica*					
1.1.34	410	Island	1,000	Ship	50
1.4.21	407	Island	1,500	Ship	100
7.1.41	366?	Peloponnese	2,000	On foot	N/A
Diodorus:					
11.84.3-6	456	Peloponnese	4,000	Ship	50
11.85	455	Peloponnese	1,000	Ship	50
12.34.4	435	Chalcidice	2,000	Ship	Unknown
12.47.3	429	Chalcidice	1,000	Ship	Unknown
12.55.4	427	Island	1,000	Ship	Unknown

12.65.1	424	Peloponnese	1,000	Ship	60
12.65.8	424	Island	2,000	Ship	60
12.69.4	424	Boeotia	20,000	On foot	N/A
12.79.1	419	Peloponnese	1,000	Ship	Unknown
12.84.3	415	Island	5,000	Ship	100
13.9.2	413	Island	5,000	Ship	80
13.52.1	410/9	Unknown	1,000	Ship (?)	30
13.65.1	409	Corinthian Isthmus	1,000	On foot	N/A
15.26.2	378/7	Boeotia	5,000	On foot	N/A
15.29.7	377/6	Peloponnese	20,000	Ship	200
15.32.2	377/6	Boeotia	5,000	On foot	N/A
15.63.2	369/8	Peloponnese	12,000	On foot	N/A
15.71.3	368/7	Thessaly	1,000	On foot	30
15.84.2	362	Peloponnese	6,000	On foot	N/A

the number of ships that Alcibiades had with him, but he does specifically describe them as triremes and being adorned with shields and the spoils of war.[19] He also diverges from Xenophon by describing Alcibiades' own concerns and reticence during the event. To Xenophon, Alcibiades was received by the mob from the city, but Plutarch emphasises the faces in the crowd that Alcibiades was hoping to see:[20]

> [H]e was in fear as he put into the harbour, and having pulled in, he did not disembark from his trireme until ... he saw that his cousin Euryptolemus was there, with many other friends and family members, and heard their calls.[21]

Plutarch then describes the rest of the crowd, Xenophon's mob, ignoring the other generals that they saw and instead ran to Alcibiades. This presents Alcibiades' return as part of a larger military homecoming, in which Alcibiades is not the only *strategos* present.[22] Xenophon does not describe such a large array of ships in this instance; however, he does describe a similar scene with the return of Thrasyllus briefly before that of Alcibiades.[23] Thrasyllus sailed home to Athens with the 'rest of the fleet', that is the remainder of the fleet after subtracting 20 ships for Alcibiades and a further 30 ships for Thrasyboulos who went raiding the Thracian coast. Thrasyllus had been originally given charge of 50 ships when he first set out in 410 BC and, as Xenophon does not mention any loss of ships during Thrasyllus' campaign, it is fair to assume that he returned with a similar number.[24] Therefore, much like with Plutarch's Alcibiades, the return of Thrasyllus should be envisioned as a large fleet, filled with hoplites as well as sailors, pulling up to the Piraeus and disembarking there.

Further, albeit indirect, evidence for an organised, collective homecoming can be found in the handling of war captives. Most famously, following the Athenian victory at Sphacteria and the surrender of the Spartan garrison on the island, Cleon and Demosthenes arranged the transportation of the Spartan captives.[25] Two hundred and ninety-two men were taken and distributed among various ships, to be transported back to Athens in bondage.[26] These captives were by no means unique and keeping prisoners in theatre during an extended campaign would have put a strain on resources and manpower.[27] To alleviate this problem, Athenian commanders often sent their captives back to Athens, possibly alongside the wounded or sick combatants.[28] This was not a small undertaking; if we consider that the Sphacterian prisoners were split over numerous ships, while numbering less than 300 men, then the 700 Toronean prisoners sent back to Athens by Cleon, or the four full crews captured by Thrasyllus and sent away, must have required even more ships.[29] These contingents would have sailed back to Athens and landed at the Piraeus, presenting another opportunity for a formal homecoming to occur.

4.1.1 A military *pompe*

There is a great difference between the physical homecoming of troops and a ritualistic homecoming that embodies some form of reintegration or celebration of the hoplite.[30] In the absence of any obvious examples in the sources, a more refined analysis is needed. If a Greek army were to form a victory procession of any description, we would expect this to be reflected in the language of the sources. The two most obvious candidates are θρίαμβος, which is often associated with a hymn to Dionysus but was used by later writers to refer to triumphal marches and πομπή, in the sense of a solemn or religious procession.

Θρίαμβος is not a term that is used by either Herodotus, Thucydides or Xenophon and does not seem to have any basis in the Greek world of the fifth or fourth century BC. The term is used by Plutarch, but only in his works on Roman figures of history and only to describe Roman triumphs. Diodorus uses the term on two occasions to describe the triumphal homecoming of the god Dionysus from India, an event that he compares with the triumphs of Alexander, but again, he does not use the term to describe any such event in the fifth or fourth century.[31] Without any description assigned to Dionysius' triumph, it must be assumed that Diodorus had in mind a Roman-style march, rather than some early Greek variant. The second term, πομπή, is regularly attested in the classical Greek literature. It can describe an escort as well as a procession, but most often holds the meaning of a religious or festive parade. It is a term that can be used in a military context: Xenophon talks about the role of the cavalry in various *pompai*;[32] the Ten Thousand perform their own processions during a long period of respite;[33] Thucydides describes the spear and the shield as being the usual weapons carried at a procession.[34] But there is only one instance in which the term is used to describe the actions of an Athenian army and, what is more, that army was forming a procession to enter the city of Athens itself.

The army in question was not a formal one established by the Assembly, in fact it was the complete opposite. The logographer Lysias, in his speech *Against Agoratus*, describes the rebel forces of Thrasyboulus who, in 403, had mounted a campaign against the Thirty Tyrants and had won a great military victory in the Piraeus. When the Spartan king Pausanias dismissed his army and left Athens, this allowed the rebels to enter the city and re-establish democracy. This entry is labelled by Lysias as a πομπή from the Piraeus into the city, whose speech outlines the removal of a polluted man called Agoratus from the procession.[35] The destination of this procession was an unspecified temple of Athena atop the Acropolis, a fact which amplifies the religious context of this parade: a polluted man could not partake in the religious procession and most certainly could not join them as they entered the sacred ground of a temple.[36] The religious undertone of the march is confirmed by Xenophon's own account, which describes the procession making its sacrifices to Athena on top of the Acropolis before the generals made an appearance in front of the Assembly. Although Xenophon clearly defines the destination and religious context of the procession he refrains from using the term πομπή and merely describes the men as ἀνελθόντες (they went up).

Ostensibly, this is evidence of an Athenian army marching from the Piraeus into the city following a long campaign season and performing a set series of rites before the hoplites were disbanded.[37] But the context of the event, allied with certain textual problems, mean this is not simple to confirm. Stephen Todd describes this as a victory procession, rather than the symbolic act of reconciliation suggested by Athena Kavoulaki.[38] Andrew Wolpert sums up the confusion that this episode elicits in modern scholarship, by describing this as both a solemn procession and a victory procession.[39] The confusion comes from the presence of weaponry in the parade. As Barry Strauss argues, the presence of weaponry 'reminded [the victors] and their former enemies of their military achievement'.[40] Perhaps most revealing is that the original manuscript available to us of this Lysias speech does not refer to the men in the procession as τῶν ὁπλιτῶν, which many commentator's insert, but merely τῶν πολιτῶν.[41] This raises an important question about Lysias' intention: was he trying to assert that these were military men entering the city, or was he trying to emphasise that these were citizens who were forced to arms?

The fact that the men marched into Athens under arms is beyond doubt. They are described as carrying their military kit[42] and when Agoratus was chastised by the commanding officer leading the procession, he had his shield taken from him and thrown away.[43] This is also corroborated by Xenophon's description of the men going to the Acropolis with their arms.[44] However, while Athens may have been a non-weapon carrying society day to day, the presence of arms could be considered quite normal for a religious procession, as mentioned earlier, so we cannot presume that these were specifically military processions.[45]

Taking into account the exceptional circumstances of this single event, as well as the fact that there are no similar instances in the available evidence, it could be concluded that this was a unique parade. Further evidence for this can be found in how the event was memorialised in Athens, with annual thanksgiving offerings being sacrificed on that day, possibly up until the time of Plutarch.[46] Conversely, the unique nature of the event and the importance placed on it for generations to come, may actually explain why a common, but unstated, military ritual was described by our sources. It could be that the exceptional nature of the context allows for an explanation as to why a regular ritual has been given such coverage. After all, this was the first Athenian force allowed to enter the city since the Thirty first took control.[47] Making the (historically) mundane event of a military homecoming a highly emotional, as well as political, watershed moment in the history of Athens.

While it may appear to have been a unique event in Athenian history, the procession does have great similarities with another, as described by Xenophon and, once more, it could have been a procession he witnessed.[48] In 399 BC, the Spartan commander Derkylidas was causing chaos for the Persians in the Troad region. He received a message from Meidias, an ally of the satrap Pharnabazus, asking to begin negotiations. Derkylidas stated his desire to free all the Greek cities and marched his army toward Skepsis. Meidias, knowing that he could not win a confrontation with the Spartan-led army, allowed the commander to enter the city, who went straight up to the acropolis to sacrifice to Athena.[49] He then marched to Gergis and told Meidias to order the gates open so that he could march his men to their temple of Athena on their acropolis and sacrifice to her.[50] Xenophon describes this second event in more detail and even mentions the procession itself. While undoubtedly an army, Derkylidas' men were marching two abreast, allowing Xenophon to assign the procession the adverb εἰρηνικῶς, they were marching peacefully.[51] In other words, they marched in a non-military, non-threatening manner, almost trying to convert themselves from being victorious military men, into being peaceful, pious men feigning humility.[52]

With regard to the Athenian episode, Xenophon does not explain why Derkylidas goes to the temple of Athena on both occasions, nor does he explain the need to march two by two before entering the city. The concept of an army entering a 'welcoming' city and immediately heading to the acropolis, to make a sacrifice to Athena, did not need an explanation.[53] The only element that Xenophon felt the need to clarify was that Derkylidas had performed the procession correctly, in two lines. It is in this construct that the procession from the Piraeus to the Acropolis should be seen. From the moment the campaign was over and the men were able to march into Athens, they needed to ensure that they could not be perceived to be either militarily active, or celebrating in their victory; they possibly used the two-by-two marching line and walking in silence to achieve this.

The absence of any obvious victory celebrations on the part of the Athenian army has allowed the topic of a military homecoming to be neglected. It has been established that the predominant form of transportation was by ship; this, in turn necessitated a collective homecoming for Athens' hoplites. The location was the Piraeus, which has big enough to host large crowds and may have played host to well-wishers and family members looking for their loved ones – in many ways the direct mirror image of the departure scene for the Sicilian Expedition discussed in section 3.2.1.

It is also pertinent that the sole instance we have from the records, which describes an Athenian military force entering Athens, starts from the Piraeus as well. While the context was unconventional, the procession described by both Lysias and Xenophon is a clear example of an Athenian army re-entering the city after a period of prolonged service and embarking on a set pattern of ritual which neither author felt the need to explain. This procession was void of all victorious symbolism and was instigated by the army itself, led by its commanders. Only once the sacrifice to Athena had been made did the army disband and the commanders then entered the Assembly. This lack of political action, or engagement, on the part of the army is echoed by the Spartan example of Derkylidas, who similarly refrains from his plans to take control of the city of Gergis until the sacrifice is complete.

Whether the procession always ended at the temple of Athena, or whether the procession had to enter the centre of Athens itself, is impossible to ascertain from the historical record as it stands. What is very clear, however, is that the Athenian forces being raised on a regular basis were returning to Attica as a unified force. That unified force would not disband until the orders were given by the *strategos*, most likely following a ritual like that atop the Acropolis. Only then does the army end its transition from being a militarily active unit, through to being a band of citizens ready to engage with the political infrastructure and, by extrapolation, the domestic world into which they must next transition.

4.1.2 An athlete's welcome?

Even when an Athenian army had been disbanded and each man had ceased to be an active participant and representative of that army, the official 'homecoming' had not yet reached its completion. Commonly, Athenian commanders would have to enter the next Assembly that was convened and answer any challenges that may exist about their tenure, if they had not already been called for deposition.[54] Unlike the army of Argos, for instance, who had a clear process of resolving their military matters before re-entering the city, marking an explicit liminal space between military and civic life, the Athenians did not.[55] Even when an Athenian hoplite had returned home, he was still at risk of being called to account for his actions on campaign inside a courtroom.[56] For the individual hoplite, this would be in the form of a private legal case brought against him. Equally, the Assembly would systematically call in a *strategos* at the end of his tenure to scrutinise his behaviour in post.[57] Alternatively, a returning *strategos* could petition the Assembly for public honours, on behalf of his army, continuing the military association after homecoming, but in search of positive recognition.[58] Aeschines gives such an example, when he describes the honours given to the Athenians who fought against the Persians at the river Strymon, after they petitioned the Assembly for them.[59] Aeschines himself had received rewards from the Assembly for his own military service at the battle of Tamynae, something for which he had already been awarded a wreath of honour from his field commanders.[60] The honouring of individuals is not unique here: Athens had a tradition of bestowing prizes and favours onto exceptional commanders. References in Aristophanes appear to suggest that Cleon received *sitesis* (food provided by the state) and *prohedria* (honoured with front seats in the theatre), in recognition of his victory at Pylos.[61] By the fourth century BC many *strategoi* were receiving rewards for their service; these included the dedication of commemorative statues, something that Lycurgus boasted was a unique feature of Athens.[62]

It should be stated that generals were not the only Athenians who were given such rewards on their homecoming and a comparison of the various overlaps may be useful in helping to identify the key features of a military homecoming. Pritchard is certainly correct in identifying the awarding of prizes to victorious *strategoi* as analogous with the awarding of prizes for victorious athletes of one of the four Panhellenic Games.[63] Indeed, Lycurgus' boast was that the Athenians did not make statues of athletes, unlike other Greek cities, but of their generals instead. Victorious athletes were likewise given *sitesis* and *prohedria* in recognition of their performance on behalf of the city. The symmetry of celebration is explicit in the source material:

> [The Scionaeans] welcomed Brasidas happily, publicly crowning him with a crown of gold as the liberator of Hellas; while private individuals approached him and crowned him like an athlete.[64]

This was not a unique event. Lysander is described as taking his many crowns, given to him by various cities, back to Sparta in 404 BC.[65] The Spartan *nauarchos*, Teleutias, was crowned by his men on his final day in command before returning home.[66] Aeschines is accused, by Demosthenes, of joining Philip of Macedon in his victory celebrations at Thebes, wearing a crown and singing songs of praise to Philip.[67] Similarly, Plutarch describes Pericles walking through a crowd of women giving him crowns, after performing the speech for the war dead, following his victory at Samos.[68] Much like Thucydides' description of Brasidas' crowning, Pericles is also described as being like a successful athlete.[69] The use of athletic victory as a metaphor for a military one is, again, not unique. Thucydides' Periclean funeral speech describes the Athenian system of giving a funeral speech and the meeting of costs for raising war-orphans of their citizens as the greatest prizes of virtue.[70] During the trial of the naval commanders who fought at Arginusae, Euryptolemus is alleged to have argued that it would be 'more just to honour the victors with crowns' than punish them with death.[71]

Pritchard's nuanced argument describes an athlete's victory at one of the Panhellenic games as displaying 'the same virtues as the city's hoplites and sailors did in military victories'.[72] As such, he explains much of the shared terminology between success in war and success in athletic contests and the shared honours.[73] However, by arguing for the interconnected nature of the two victories, military and athletic, in the Greek imagination, he omits any recognition for ancient authors that show a very clear differentiation between the two. For instance,

Xenophon claims that victory in war gives greater glory than athletics, because the city also shares in it.[74] A fragment of a lost Euripidean satyr play shows an unknown speaker challenging the worth of the athlete as opposed to a hoplite, or a man who leads his city well.[75] Even sources that seemingly support Pritchard's thesis can offer a different interpretation. Pericles' speech describes military victory and death as the greatest prize, which must place it above anything won by an athlete. Similarly, Lycurgus' boast of the commissioning of statues juxtaposed Athenian practice with that seen in the rest of Greece: the meaning is clear, Athens placed military victory above all others.

This Athenian outlook brings into question another of Pritchard's assertions; that Athens must have held homecoming ceremonies (*eiselasis*) for Panhellenic victors, because our sources take for granted that their audiences knew of ceremonial gift-giving.[76] However, some of the evidence that he gives to support this is better suited in a military rather than an athletic context. Thucydides' passage describing Brasidas' entry of Scione follows the Spartan's campaigns in Chalcidice and, following Scione's decision to revolt against Athens, Brasidas spoke in the assembly to offer his support.[77] His reception was because of his military promise to support the town in its revolt, supported by his decision to allocate a garrison to the town once he left to continue his campaign. In *Knights*, the leader of the Chorus calls to the famous general Demosthenes to succeed in his fight and return showered in crowns (στεφάνοις κατάπαστος) for his victory. The fact that this is said to Demosthenes raises questions as to Aristophanes' intended imagery. The play makes many references to the Athenian victory at Pylos (425 BC) and makes a passing mention to the disjointed relationship between the joint commanders of that victory, Demosthenes and Cleon; a victory that took place only the year before this play won first place at the *Lenaea*.[78] Yet, not only does Demosthenes himself elicit a strong military undertone, but the use of the adjective κατάπαστος, implying, with the plural dative noun, a sprinkling or a showering of crowns, does not exclusively fit with an athletic metaphor. After such a momentous victory at Pylos, it is just as likely that Demosthenes witnessed scenes similar to Brasidas at Scione, to Lysander returning to Sparta and Pericles after his funeral oration in Plutarch, he may have been inundated with crowns. Furthermore, not one of these examples actually describes a ceremony or procession of homecoming, but rather the granting of crowns by adoring crowds, something that can be found in both military and athletic contexts.

The final piece of evidence Pritchard uses comes from Euripides' *Electra*, when the eponymous heroine offers her victorious brother a hair band, like an athlete, after killing their father's murderer. There is no question that athletic imagery is used in this instance and the reference to the Olympic Games makes a compelling argument for Pritchard's Panhellenic victor motif.[79] However, in terms of Athenian attitudes to athletic victory, it is perhaps more interesting that the chorus describes Orestes' victory as greater than that won at Olympia.[80] Something that Electra reiterates in her own description:

> Glorious in victory, born to a father victorious in the battle at Troy, Orestes, take this garland for your curls. You have come home, not after running a useless footrace, but from killing our enemy Aegisthus, who killed your father and mine. And you, too, his companion in arms, son of a most loyal man, Pylades, take this crown from my hand.[81]

The athletic imagery of victory is present, but it has been carefully blended with military imagery as well.[82] While Orestes himself is not described in an identifiably military context here, he is welcomed as the son of Agamemnon who won victory at the battle of Troy.[83] Aegisthus is referred to as his πολέμιον, which elicits the concept of a military enemy as opposed to a personal one (e.g. ἐχθρός).[84] Finally, Orestes' companion, Pylades, is called ὦ παρασπίστ', literally a shield-bearer, but in this context a companion-in-arms.[85] Orestes and Pylades receive their crowns for individual excellence in their duties, not for the seemingly valueless victory of athletics, but for a victory more akin to the greatest of all, victory in war.

What the Athenian evidence shows is that a successful Athenian commander received a homecoming reception in line with that of a victorious athlete. It also makes it clear that, ideologically, the Athenians considered a military victory to be of greater importance than an athletic one. Most importantly for this enquiry, it adds credence to Plutarch's description of Alcibiades' homecoming, described in section 4.1. A famous *strategos* attracted huge crowds in the Piraeus, which included the family members of many of the hoplites with him. However, there is no direct evidence that a less famous general would have attracted such a crowd, so the question of whether the families turned out to welcome the men home must remain open.

4.2 Dedications

The awarding of prizes to generals and, indeed, the awarding of penalties to hoplites in court, formed a continual association between that individual and the military identity of a specific campaign. Even though the army was disbanded on its arrival in Athens, the use of prizes and punishments in the civic sphere meant that a citizen could still be associated with his actions as a hoplite in any given campaign, whether he wished to or not.

An alternative way of cementing the military identity of an army, after it had disbanded, was through collective dedications. An Athenian army would use the collected booty from a campaign to pay the men; but, prior to this division, a portion was first allocated to the gods.[86] Depending on the size of this army, the length of its service and the location of its campaigning, the value of this portioned allotment for the gods could reach a great sum. An Athenian army dedicated a bronze chariot pulled by four horses on the Acropolis, to commemorate a victory over the Boeotians and Chalcidians in 506 BC.[87] The estimated cost of this monument, based on it being the product of a tithe drawn from the sale of over 700 captives, is 14,000 *drachmae*, or 2.3 talents.[88] Perhaps the most famous example of a military dedication was the bronze statue of Athena Promachos, said to have been paid for by the tithe taken from the spoils at Marathon.[89] The statue may have cost somewhere in the region of 83 talents, but there is a debate as to whether this entire amount could really have come from the spoils of Marathon.[90] Xenophon, who recounts the tithe dedicated to Apollo at Delphi by the Spartan king Agesilaus, describes a parallel amount. Agesilaus dedicated 100 talents, following his campaigns in Asia Minor and victory at Coronea. The vast sums available to him were made possible by his prolonged campaign through the rich Persian lands of Pharnabazus and Tissaphernes, something that is hardly comparable to the single military victory at Marathon.

These dedications did not always have to be so ostentatious. Two Corinthian-style helmets have been found at Olympia and the Athenian Acropolis respectively, both seemingly commemorate Militiades' campaign on Lemnos.[91] Each bears the same inscription 'Athenians: from those in Lemnos'.[92] If these have been correctly linked with military service – and the medium on which they are inscribed does suggest this – then this would constitute a 'raw' portion taken from the spoils.[93] A more famous example can be seen in the dedicated Spartan shield taken at Pylos; its inscription is more specific: 'The Athenians [took this] from the Lacedaemonians at Pylos'.[94] These forms of dedications have been deemed 'public dedications' by William Pritchett, in which the identity of the dedicators is given as the wider collective 'The Athenians' or, in the example of the bronze chariot, 'The Children of the Athenians'.[95]

What Pritchett does not consider, by separating public (collective) and private (individual) military dedications, is the possibility of a middle ground. A collective dedication does not always fit neatly into the distinct category of 'public', which must derive its categorisation from the use of public funds while on campaign, or by order of the *boule* or *ekklesia*. There is a clear example that contrasts starkly with the Corinthian helmets mentioned above. There is a third helmet which has often been connected with the two from the Athenians on Lemnos previously mentioned; although, the dating of this third helmet has recently been challenged and it seems to date from anywhere up-to 40 years later. Nevertheless, it offers a different form of collective dedication, which requires some consideration.

IG I3 522*bis* is a small inscription on a fragment of a Corinthian-style helmet, found in the Attic *deme* of Rhamnous, which reads: 'The Rhamnousians on Lemnos dedicated [this] to Nemesis.'[96] The dating of the dedication is uncertain, with estimates ranging from 499/8 BC to a period later than 480 BC and the absence of any military detail has persuaded some scholars to try to remove it from the context of Miltiades' campaign.[97] The helmet was dedicated to Nemesis, an important goddess and cult in Rhamnous and was dedicated by Rhamnousians, presumably still present on Lemnos at the time of the dedication.[98] The use of a helmet for the dedication does strongly suggest a military connection so, if members of Miltiades' army did not send it, then the possibility that it was members of an Athenian garrison offers a second solution. The most interesting part of this dedication is the focalisation on the *deme* of Rhamnous. The joint dedication of a sub-group within the wider army implies that the independent group identities with which an Athenian joined the army, in this case his *deme*, was not replaced during his military service. Furthermore, it reinforces the idea that members of the same *deme* considered their service to be connected to such an extent that they, as a group, needed to make an offering to a distinctly local *deme* cult. Regardless of whether this helmet's dedication should be linked, directly, with a specific military action, it shows an attempt by the men of Rhamnous to continue being identified with one specific period of active service, independently of the faceless title of 'Athenians'.

Whereas the Rhamnousian dedication suggests a collective identification and desire to commemorate service at the *deme* level, there is a more concrete parallel that shows this same desire at the *phyle* level. *IG* II² 1155 consists of two inscriptions: the first is a pair of honorific council decrees concerning a *taxiarchos* from the *phyle* of Kerkropis, called Boularchos, the second is a dedication by Boularchos and the men who served under him, to Athena.[99] It is possible that the second inscription formed the base for the first inscription, but it is not certain. Importantly, the honorific decrees reinforce what was discussed above, that the council would reward noteworthy military service; although, the inscription is too fragmentary to offer any explanation as to why a *taxiarchos* was singled out.[100] It is the second inscription, which reflects that of *IG* I3 522*bis*, it states that '[t]he men of Kekropis who served on campaign in the archonship of Lysimachides, and their *taxiarchos*, Boularchos son of Aristoboulos of Phlya, [dedicated this] to Athena'.[101]

The archonship of Lysimachides dates the military service to 339/8 BC, with early commentators eager to associate it with successful engagements between the Greek allies and Philip II of Macedon, but there is no information on either inscription to confirm this.[102] Similar to the Rhamnousians, this inscription offers the possibility that a group identity existed between members of the same *phyle*. However, this collective dedication was not sent to a central cult in one of the various *demes* within the *phyle*, but it was instead set up on the Acropolis itself. So, on the one hand this shows a collective decision to commemorate service and make an offering to Athena, by men linked to an identity that was distinct from the main body of the army. It also shows a desire to identify the specific period of service being commemorated, through the uncommon naming of the eponymous archon. On the other hand, the commemoration shows how disparate their shared identity was; they did not choose to make the dedication to their shared tribal hero that was unique to their identity as Kekropians; instead they made a very public dedication to the goddess of the entire *polis*. Furthermore, if the supposition of Stephen Lambert is correct and the inscriptions were originally placed in the temple of Kekropis, then this interjects an official edict into this collective commemoration.[103] This, in turn, raises a question as to whether the decision to make the dedication arose organically from the men due to their service, like the Rhamnousians, or as a direct result of the council's decision to make the honorary decrees.[104] If we accept the editorial tradition of linking these two inscriptions, then, without the identity of the person who proposed the decrees, it must be assumed that this collective commemoration was a result of the council's decree. Nevertheless, it offers another form of collective commemoration for military service based around an identifiable sub-group within the wider Athenian army.

The only element regarding the provenance of these various collective dedications, which cannot be ascertained, is the gap in time between the military service and the dedication. So, it cannot be confirmed whether these dedications, or often the decision to make a dedication, was made before, during or after the homecoming of the army. However, the presence of subdivisions within the military identity offers the possibility for dedications to focus more specifically on internal group identities and relevant gods. Furthermore, the presence of these collective dedications shows that there were a few different ways in which a hoplite could partake in commemorating his own service, thus prolonging an association with an isolated military identity which only existed for a set campaign.

A final opportunity for the hoplite to choose to commemorate his military service was through a personal dedication. This could be done, as an individual, in a few different ways. Primarily, he could dedicate a tithe of his own earnings from the campaign to any given god, possibly in fulfilment of a vow he had made before departing.[105] This is a revealing practice because the duty of a Greek hoplite to pay a tithe was fulfilled by the collective dedication to the gods made by the army; there was no direct need for the individual to pay a further tithe on his own portion. Theodora Jim resolves this inconsistency by suggesting that maybe the individual was simply replicating the city's religious practice or was extending a customary practice from other aspects of his life, such as his agricultural work.[106] Another possibility is that the individual felt some remoteness from the collective dedication made on his behalf, so the private dedication may have felt more meaningful and personal.[107]

A second possibility for the hoplite was to dedicate a symbolic gesture from his campaign, such as an enemy weapon or piece of armour taken in battle. There is a lot of evidence of *strategoi* doing this, but it was at times looked down upon, especially in Athens.[108] It is possible that many of the bronze weapon votives found on the Acropolis were offerings made by hoplites but, without inscriptions, it is hard to discern whether they should be considered military votives in the first place.[109] However, a speech made by Demosthenes in the mid-fourth century does suggest that the dedication of armour was normal practice. In a small section of his *Against Eubulides*, the speaker, Euxitheus, accuses his own accusers of stealing *ta hopla*, which he had dedicated to the temple of Athena.[110] The term *ta hopla* is vague, as Euxitheus does not describe whether it was his own *hopla* or one taken in battle.[111] Yet, even without a concrete answer, this is still a clear example of a regular hoplite making a religious dedication of armour to a temple.[112]

A third possibility was for the hoplite to make a dedication to a temple based on his military service more generally. This is in contrast to a tithe based on the earnings from a set campaign, or the dedication of armour taken in a battle.[113] A prime example is the statue and inscription dedicated to Athena, by Hegelochus:

Hegelochus, father and son of Ecphantus, dedicated me here to the Parthenos [Athena], a memorial of the toils of Ares; he [Hegelochus], having a share of both great hospitality and all *arete*, inhabits this city. Critios and Nesiotes made it.[114]

The inscription dates somewhere between 470–60 BC and would have sat under a statue, most likely a portrait of Hegelochus' father striking a combative pose.[115] The statue served as a memorial to Hegelochus' military service (the toils of Ares) and possibly that of his deceased father, most plausibly during the Persian Wars.[116] Interestingly, the wording suggests that Hegelochus was an outsider to Athens, possibly a *metic*, during the period of service he commemorates here.[117] The decision made by Hegelochus to commemorate his service in the military, along with his father, reveals a desire by an individual to do this outside the collective forms of dedication made on his behalf.

The practice of making dedications following service would have prolonged the military homecoming beyond the single day in which the army returned to the city. Collective dedications reinforced military identities even after the disbanding of the army to form one homogenous entity. In turn, this encouraged smaller sub-groups of the army to similarly commemorate their service in tandem. Finally, for some men, these collective identities and dedications, were not sufficient. They took it upon themselves to commemorate further their own actions within a period of service, outside these collective groups, such as Hegelochus who only associated himself with one collective identity, his own *oikos*. Importantly, this shows that the military homecoming may have taken place on a given day but it continued for as long as people chose to identify the hoplites with a set campaign and, indeed, how long an individual hoplite chose to do so.

5

The Warrior's Homecoming

To consider the topic objectively, it would be valid to assume that the easiest transition to identify in the source material and, indeed, attempt to reconstruct, would be the moment the warrior returns to his *oikos*. Greek literature is filled with moments of *nostos* that offer a wide spectrum of experiences, from the reunion of Odysseus with Persephone to the murderous homecoming that awaited Agamemnon. However, evidence for warriors returning is not the same as evidence for the rituals involved in that homecoming. Yet, this transition is vital if we are to understand whether there was an ideological continuity between the civic ideology that was so apparent in the military homecoming and that of the home.

In Chapter 2, we saw that underneath the façade of pride and the prospect of glory, there was an underlying fear within the domestic ceremonies. An emotional expression that ran concurrently with the civic ideology that is so commonly on display in our evidence. What then of the domestic homecoming? Once again, a ritualistic framework must first be established: who was involved, what rituals were performed and what were these rituals performed for? The most pivotal aspect of this transition is how the warrior was perceived by his family. Was he the triumphal hero? Was he a changed man? Was he in some way 'othered' and in need of reintegration? This transition was the final step of his metamorphosis, bringing him full circle from civilian to hoplite, back to civilian once again – and arguably this was the most important of them all.

5.1 Homecoming arrivals on red-figure pottery?

In order to examine the nature of the domestic homecoming, it is first necessary to return to a form of source material dealt with in section 2.2, departure scenes on Attic vases. As previously discussed, the warrior departure scene is a well-established motif of Athenian vase painting; however, there is an accepted dilemma involved in their identification, as 'it is not clear if these scenes are departures or returns.'[1] This identification is further compounded, according to Vasiliki Siurla-Theodoridou, when the warrior in question is on foot, which he most frequently is on red-figure vases.[2] While scholars have acknowledged the possibility that a departure scene could, in fact, be an arrival scene, they have not yet tried to identify one.[3] The aim of this section is to try and identify examples of the 'arrival scene' within red-figure artwork.

Alan Shapiro differentiates between the departures and the arrivals of heroes on vases, by examining the gestures and expressions of the people in the scene.[4] In so doing, he was able to identify a scene as a departure, based on such gestures as the presence of a handshake and a mother's embrace, which reflects other such imagery on pots depicting known mythological departures.[5] Following a similar pattern of enquiry, the iconographic clues for a warrior's departure are well established: the positioning of the feet of the warrior, with at least one foot turned away;[6] peripheral figures in the scene holding their heads in their hands, as a sign of grief;[7] the pulling of one's garments as a sign of distress, most often performed by a women in the scene;[8] the downturned heads of many of the participants involved.[9] Scenes with this body language indicate that the warrior is departing and highlight the sadness inherent in the event. However, what does it mean for a departure scene that does not contain these gestures or iconographic markers? Should this type of scene still be considered a 'departure' by default?

5.1.1 Parallel scenes

Not all 'departure scenes' are isolated paintings on a pot. One amphora in Munich, for instance, has a departure scene on the obverse, with the second scene imitating the first in a few characteristics:[10] a non-military man stands between two women, holding a sprig and walking stick in his left hand; one woman holds a wreath, while the other holds a wreath and *phiale*. The context of the scene is hard to deduce, but a libation ritual has been depicted and the scene reduplicates so many elements of the hoplite scene that the two can be considered to be connected in some way. Other departure scenes share space with various, seemingly unrelated, images, such as Heracles fighting with Apollo over a tripod.[11] One vase supplements the departure scene with a non-military, interior scene, showing domestic life.[12] Another shares space with an image of resting athletes and their trainer.[13] One more departure scene shares a vase with a *komos* scene, with pipe players and nonsense inscriptions.[14] This raises the question of whether these adjacent scenes should always be associated together; whether or not they should be considered complementary or paralleled in some way?[15] This has been the focus of decades' worth of scholarly debate, with no satisfactory conclusion.[16] However, a focused version of this question may be profitable: is it possible to use the other scenes on a vase to help identify whether the warrior scene is one of departure or arrival?

There are two sets of examples that share too much to be unconnected. Both vases, show two separate departure scenes that differ in detail enough to suggest they are not to be considered part of the same ritual.[17] On the obverse of a *pelike* in Rome (see Figure 5.1a), a young man, with short hair, takes part in an arming scene, helped by a woman. She holds his shield for him, while passing him his cap; his head band is already on his head and his helmet rests on the ground. On the wall hangs a set of leg greaves, but as the young man is already wearing his these evidently do not belong to him. On the reverse (see Figure 5.1b), an older man, with a beard and long curly hair, wearing a helmet, leans on his staff with a relaxed posture as he watches a woman pour a libation over his shield, which lies on the ground. On the wall hangs a set of greaves, almost in an identical position to the obverse; once again, they are not the hoplite's, because he is already wearing his.

These are quite clearly not meant to present a temporally continuous series of events; however, this does not mean that they are not meant to represent the

Figure 5.1a Red-figure *pelike*, unattributed, with a young man arming for departure with the help of a young woman. Mid-fifth century BC Rome, Mus. Naz. Etrusco di Villa Giulia: 46942. © Rebecca Weston.

Figure 5.1b Red-figure *pelike*, unattributed, with an older hoplite taking part in a libation ritual with a woman. Mid-fifth century BC Rome, Mus. Naz. Etrusco di Villa Giulia: 46942. © Rebecca Weston

same man. Two visual attributes are striking in these images. The first is the size difference between the two men and the women in their respective scenes. In Figure 5.1a, the young man is slightly smaller than the woman and breaks the boundary of the scene with his left elbow. In Figure 5.1b, the man is considerably taller than the woman, and breaks the uppermost boundary of the scene with his helmet crest. In addition, the two women vary in height, with the woman in Figure 5.1a nearly reaching the top of the scene herself. Secondly, the positioning of the greaves hanging on the wall creates a sense of interior continuity between the two scenes. This not only suggests that the two scenes occur inside a room, it also creates the impression that they take place inside the same room. Taking into account these two important elements of the connected images, I think the two scenes should be read syntagmatically, with the first scene being considered a hoplite's departure, maybe his first ever, from the home with the aid of his mother.[18] The second may simply represent an older member of the same house but, more plausibly, it should be seen as the same man taking part in a libation ritual, with the aid of his younger wife.

Identification of the ritual on the reverse is more problematic. The passive posture and lack of general dynamism on the part of the hoplite does not suggest a departure for war. Usually, the hoplite is depicted holding the *phiale*,[19] either holding his arm out to receive something,[20] or holding his armaments in both hands;[21] whereas here, this man only holds his staff, while his right hand rests on his hip. This positioning of the hand is not unique in departure scenes, but other examples offer iconographic suggestion of motion and dynamism, whereas this hoplite is clearly at rest.[22] The shield positioned on the floor, which is identifiable by its distinctive shape and rimmed edge, takes the place of an altar within this scene.[23] Christopher Faraone has shown that the *aspis* was used as a ritual receptacle on a military campaign. Turned inside up, it was used for collecting the blood and flesh of the sacrificial victim in which hoplites would dip their hands, or the points of their weapons, while taking oaths.[24] However, there is no literary support for this image of a shield being used in a libation ritual, convex side up; it is unique outside this one example.[25]

The libation ritual could, on its own, represent either a departure or a homecoming, but the presence of the shield achieves three things: first, it will reflect a socially accepted ritual practice, but not necessarily a common one; second, it confirms the identification of the man as a hoplite, by placing his most iconographic symbol within the centre of the scene; third, it ensures he has an empty hand to place on his hip. It is the relaxed demeanour of this scene, which is so important to identifying its context. The man is not departing for war, but is in a state of relaxation having arrived home. From this reading of the vase, the two scenes come together to show the transition from a young man departing for war with the help of his mother, to a fully grown adult man returning home to his wife after his military service.

There is a similar vase, a *pelike* in New York attributed to the Altamura Painter, which supports the notion that a vase may contain both a departure and homecoming scene. On the obverse (see Figure 5.2a), a young hoplite with long hair stands on the right side of the scene, wearing a crested helmet and body armour. In his right hand, he holds a *phiale*, and his *doru* leans on his left arm. Opposite him is a woman who is pouring a libation from an *oenochoe* into the *phiale* she holds in her left hand. Between the two bodies rests an *aspis*, standing up at an angle, with details of the internal structure on display. On the reverse (see Figure 5.2b) is a near identical scene. A young hoplite, with long hair, stands on the left side of the scene wearing a crested helmet. In his right hand, he holds a *phiale*, which is receiving a libation. Opposite him is a woman who holds an

Figure 5.2a Red-figure *pelike*, attributed to the Altamura Painter. A young hoplite takes part in a libation ritual with a woman, wearing armour and holding his *doru*. Mid-fifth century BC. New York (NY), Metropolitan Museum: 56.171.44.

Figure 5.2b Red-figure *pelike*, attributed to the Altamura Painter. A young hoplite takes part in a libation ritual with a woman, while only wearing his helmet and cloak. Mid-fifth century BC. New York (NY), Metropolitan Museum: 56.171.44.

oenochoe in her right hand, pouring the libation into the hoplite's *phiale*; in her left hand she holds a second *phiale*. Between them rests an *aspis*, almost identical to the one on the opposite side, standing at an angle, with the internal structure on display.

It is unsurprising that Beazley identified these two scenes with an identical description of the decoration and assigned them both to the genre of 'departure scene'.[26] However, because they are so nearly identical, it is therefore both the continuity and the differences between them that interest us here. There is a clear distinction of dress for the hoplite, in Figure 5.2a he wears the cuirass and holds the spear of a hoplite whereas in Figure 5.2b he only wears his helmet and the *chlamys* of a citizen. The woman in Figure 5.2a pours a libation into her own *phiale*, whereas in Figure 5.2b she pours it into the hoplite's. In addition, the male and female figures swap places between the two scenes, with the hoplite moving from the right-hand to the left-hand side. The identical location of the shield's position between the two scenes makes for a strange aesthetic, but undoubtedly maintains a continuity between the two, even more than the greaves on the *pelike* in Rome. Further continuity can be seen in the helmet design, which maintains its folded cheek flaps, long crest, spiral decoration behind the ear and chequered band running between the crest and the top of the helmet. This design is, therefore, purposeful, and the two scenes are meant to be seen as part of a singular narrative.

The continuity between these two scenes suggests that the hoplite and the woman are meant to be identified as the same people. However, the continuing lack of a beard on the part of the hoplite prevents a reading similar to that of the *pelike* in Rome, in which much time has passed between the two scenes. Both libation scenes are undoubtedly military in nature, but this does not mean that they are both departure scenes. The scene on the reverse is the more likely candidate for a departure scene. The young hoplite departs for military service, maybe for the first time, still wearing his domestic clothing, having not yet fully immersed himself into his military role. His positioning in front of the shield suggests that it has yet to be passed to him; the pouring of the libation into his *phiale*, gives him a passive role in the scene. The reverse interpretation is, of course, possible: the young man is dressed for peace, so he must be back home, whereas on the obverse he is dressed for war and therefore must be departing for war.[27] This is undoubtedly a valid reading of the scene, however greater emphasis should be placed on the position of the shield and the young hoplite's passive role in the reverse scene. In addition, if this scene is meant to be one of peace, and homecoming, then the presence of the helmet is peculiar. With my reading of the scene, it contrasts with the fully dressed hoplite who returns from war. The reverse scene emphasises both the transition to war, as he is in a state of only partial military dress and the naivety of the young man, who is being taken through the ritual by his mother. This starkly contrasts with Figure 5.2a, in which the physically mature hoplite stands tall, holding his *phiale* aloft with a sense of purpose. His shield is positioned to suggest that he brought it in and placed it down. His own ornate costume is matched by the woman's, which is no longer plain, but decorated, as is her head band. This scene has a much greater sense of occasion and, when read in contrast to Figure 5.2b, it suggests that this is not an identical ritual but is, rather, the reverse: it is the hoplite's homecoming.

5.1.2 Libation rituals and variation

The variation that is evident within the departure/arrival scenes raises an important question concerning the reflected rituals. If there was a set practice of ritual shared by Athenian families in the departure of their hoplites, why do these particular libation scenes, show such variation? This question specifically concerns the apparatus onto which the libation is being poured. On Munich J326, it was poured onto a palm leaf, possibly symbolising a libation for Artemis. On the Benaki *hydria* 38151, there is no evidence of an object so presumably it was poured onto the floor, something which can be confirmed from other vases.[28] On Rome 46942 (side B) it was poured onto a shield lying on the floor, and on New York 56.171.44, the object of the poured libation is unclear. To these we can also include examples that show an altar onto which the participants pour a libation and one example of an altar with an incense burner on top.[29]

There are a few possible explanations for these differences. The first is simply artistic preference. There is no reason that these images need to reflect ritual practice and the use of a symbolic item, such a as the palm tree on the Munich amphora, does, in such a case, support this point. However, this does not explain the very carefully selected use of the shield or an altar, which are literal in their presentation; they do not automatically conjure a figurative reading, but rather bring to mind only the item that is depicted. A second possibility is that these differences reflect different rituals or stages within the departure/homecoming, where a libation was not only poured onto the ground, maybe around the hearth, but also on the shield and on one of the domestic altars. This is an enticing reading of the scenes, but there is no supplementary evidence elsewhere to support this.

A third explanation is that the mixture of practice and apparatus, shown in the artistic work, reflects the market for which these vases were made. While it is known that Athenian households shared deities and cults, such as Hestia and the two Zeus' Ctesius and Herceius, there is a suggestion that individual *oikoi* had different traditions when it came to performing their rituals.[30] Concerning the domestic cult of Zeus Ctesius, the speechwriter Antiphon describes a murder that took place during a ritual sacrifice to the god.[31] The speaker states that only three people took part: the host, his murderous mistress and the host's guest friend, none of whom were related by blood or marriage.[32] This contrasts with an account of a ritual, given by the speechwriter Isaeus, who describes an old, pious man who performed all of the sacrificial duties due to Zeus Ctesius by himself and only allowed blood family to watch.[33] Isaeus' speaker goes to great pains to state that neither slaves nor freemen outside his family could attend. A third source for this cult comes from Aeschylus' *Agamemnon*, discussed further below, which implies that slaves were included in the sacrificial rites.[34] What this shows is that different families could adapt seemingly shared, domestic cults and rituals. Similarly, not every house would have contained a large standalone altar, or a permanent hearth, so the use of a shield, or simply the floor, is a realistic variance of a wider Athenian practice, as the red-figure art seems to suggest.[35]

5.1.3 Ambiguity

Another factor to consider, regarding these variations in ritual, is that they insert a level of ambiguity into these scenes. As previously mentioned, scholars have struggled to identify whether all these scenes are departures or arrivals. Part of the reason for this is that the two events could potentially look very similar. Unlike mythical departure scenes, which are often identified through the presence of names inscribed into the scene, the majority of red-figure, hoplite departure/arrival scenes are anonymous.[36] This ambiguity is characteristic of red-figure vase painting and, as noted by both Matheson and Neer, it was likely to be purposeful in design.[37] A parallel example within the motif is the ambiguous identification of the 'woman' in the scene. Scholars tend to identify her as the mother of the warrior, based on inscribed mythological scenes where such an identification is made, or as the wife of the hoplite, an interpretation often reliant on the presence of more than one woman in the scene.[38] Yet, when there is only one woman and one man in the departure/arrival scene, there is nothing to indicate whether she should be interpreted as his mother, his wife, his sister or, indeed, as his girlfriend or mistress. While it has been noted that, in departure scenes, the hero Hector is more frequently depicted leaving his mother Hecuba, than he is his wife, Andromache, the important point is that he could be depicted with either woman and the motif ultimately remains the same.[39] This purposeful ambiguity with the woman in the scene would have enabled the vase to appeal to a wider audience: a mother could see herself in the scene, just as easily as a wife could; an unmarried man could have bought the vase, as well as a married one.[40]

Although these warrior departure/arrival scenes continue the tradition of mythological departure scenes, it cannot be assumed that the person who bought the vase realised this, or indeed cared. The moment that the inscribed names were removed from the motif, it became purposefully ambiguous. A scene could be a departure or an arrival, the location of the ritual could be anyone's home, and the female figure could be a multitude of people. Thus, when an Athenian bought a pot it was in response to their own interpretation of the scenes in front of them, with the ambiguity of the scene allowing the artist to widen his market by eliciting more than one possible interpretation.[41] Therefore, it is only possible to identify a departure or an arrival scene based on obvious gestures of sorrow, or from the context of the other artistic scenes that share the same pot, such as the examples above concerning two 'departure' scenes, it cannot be merely presumed.

There is, however, an underlying assumption to this hypothesis of purposeful ambiguity. For this ambiguity to manifest itself, the two ritual scenes – hoplite departure, hoplite arrival – must have closely shared the same identifiable participants, the same locations and, ultimately, the same iconography. Even if it is assumed that these paintings are idealised forms of the scene, for ambiguity to exist, the imagery and ideals projected into the scene must be congruent with both the departure and arrival of a hoplite. One example in which this is certainly not the case is in the emotion that is presented; grief seems to correctly identify a departure and happiness an arrival. This was subsequently dealt with by artists by the choice of omitting gestures of grieving, in essence removing the emotion from their ambiguous scenes. This allows physical mannerisms and gestures to shed their emotional connotations, so the hug of a woman could be one of greeting or farewell, as could a handshake. Nevertheless, this does not account for the libations being poured. For this hypothesis to be correct and the ambiguity inherent in the majority of these scenes purposeful, then it must also be true that the libation ritual would look identical in both the departure and the arrival of hoplites to the home.

5.2 Homecoming arrivals in the literary evidence

To answer this question regarding the similarities between the departure and arrival scene, it is necessary to supplement the artistic evidence with literary source material. Unfortunately, literary evidence for a domestic homecoming, following military service, is surprisingly scarce during the classical period.[42] The most extant examples that have survived, scenes from Aeschylus' *Agamemnon* and Euripides *Heracles*, are, in themselves, highly problematic. However, contemporary dramas offer a window into Athenian norms and values as they need to have been relevant to their audiences. A hero, performing rituals that have no resonance with the audience, is a hard character to empathise with or in any way relate to. So, before an analysis of the scenes can progress, it is first necessary to address their problematic nature as source material for the topic of military homecoming.

5.2.1 Thematic considerations

Agamemnon follows the trials and tribulations of the eponymous king, after his successful return from Troy. Agamemnon returns to his home with his captive, Cassandra, beside him, to be welcomed by his wife Clytemnestra. Aeschylus utilises the dramatic irony available from such a well-known *nostos* story, purposefully casting Cassandra as a wife who acts dutifully and correctly, in direct contrast to Agamemnon's own murderous and adulterous wife.[43] Clytemnestra's double murder is to take place during the rituals of homecoming, making it a potentially valuable source for these domestic rituals. However, the sacrifices that take place are not those of animal victims but, of course, Agamemnon and Cassandra themselves, thus making it an antithetical model of homecoming. This is not problematic in itself: Aeschylus needed to exploit a motif of homecoming that was familiar to his audience in order to accentuate the tragedy of the events that were unfolding. It is Clytemnestra's subversion of cultural and ritual norms that is most shocking – her disregard for the sanctity of what was supposed to be happening.

This may explain why Aeschylus chose the version of the myth that he did. An older tradition of the myth sees Agamemnon killed by Aegisthus, the lover of Clytemnestra, during a feast of celebration.[44] The shift in responsibility, from the lover to the wife and the location, from the banquet hall to a bath, 'underlines the great flaw in Agamemnon's return'.[45] By placing the blame onto Clytemnestra specifically, the sacrilegious element of the murder is amplified. It is not just that the murder took place in Agamemnon's own palace and during his homecoming; it now takes place during the very moment of his transition home and is perpetrated by the one individual responsible for helping him through those rituals.[46]

Euripides' *Heracles* is a more problematic example of a warrior's homecoming. Unlike Agamemnon, it would be incorrect to describe Heracles as a warrior returning home from military duty. He is a hero returning from his own individual exploits, following his final labour, which took him into the underworld to capture the hellhound, Cerberus. His homecoming is described and, similarly to *Agamemnon*, the tragic murder of his family occurs during the rituals inside the house at the precise moment of his own transition home. Unlike Agamemnon, this homecoming is not antithetical; there are no reverse-rites akin to Clytemnestra. The rituals in the house are seemingly ordinary, but it is the influence of Lyssa that drives Heracles mad and provides the catalyst for the massacre.

Scholars have begun to use *Heracles* as an important piece of evidence to argue that the ancient Greeks knew of combat trauma, with Heracles equated with a homecoming warrior.[47] Nevertheless, to date, nobody has attempted to show that this comparison is valid, it is merely assumed. In this regard, there are two important elements of Euripides' text. The first is the chronology of his story, and the second is the playwright's use of athletic and military imagery. Mythological conventions in the ancient world suggest that Heracles was assigned to his legendary labours after the murders of his wife and children, but Euripides chose to reverse this.[48] The murder of his family occurs after his labours are completed. It has been suggested that Euripides reversed the order to maximise Heracles' heroic stature, thus maximising his tragic fall during the play.[49] Yet the famous debate between Amphitryon and Lycus seemingly undermines the heroic quality of Heracles, due to his identification as an archer rather than as a hoplite, so the grand status of his heroism is quickly criticised.[50] A simpler way of interpreting this decision by Euripides is that he was purposefully turning the story into a *nostos* play.[51] By having Heracles returning home from his labours, Euripides placed the hero in the same genre as the stories of heroes like Agamemnon and Odysseus. This play was intended to be a tragedy based around a homecoming gone wrong, yet the question still remains, the homecoming from what exactly?[52]

It has long been established that Euripides' play contains epinician language, and the presence of this language moulds Heracles into the form of a victorious athlete returning home.[53] Marigo Alexopoulou argues that Heracles is put forward as the quintessential paradigm of the victorious athlete.[54] This image of hero-as-athlete is further compounded by the constant repetition of Heracles' epithet *kallinikos*, fair victory or fair conquering.[55] Ostensibly, then, the one image that Heracles is not meant to convey is that of a warrior returning home: he is a hero, he is an athlete and he is an archer; he is most definitely not a hoplite. However, this interpretation would ignore all the militaristic imagery within the play. As highlighted in section 4.1.2, there are many crossovers between athletic and military imagery in the sources, therefore this places a greater level of importance on the context of the terminology being used in the text.

Taking the example of *kallinikos*, Euripides first uses the adjectival form to describe Heracles' spear following his victory over the Minyans, the first of two occasions in which the adjective is associated with a weapon of his.[56] It is further used to describe the victory song that Heracles sang with the gods, following their victory over the Giants.[57] The military undertones of Heracles' labours are similarly present throughout the play. He battled (μάχης) with the Minyans singlehandedly, he fought (μάχη) with Cerberus, and made war (πόλεμον) against the centaurs.[58]

Lycus is described as making war (πόλεμον … μάχην) against the hero and the Chorus lament that their age prevents them from going into battle against the tyrant.[59] Finally, the description given to the murder of his family is tinted with military imagery. The massacre is described as a 'warless war' (ἀπόλεμον … πόλεμον) waged against his children and, in the immediate aftermath, Heracles questions the term 'war' in his reply, not yet realising what has happened.[60] When Theseus arrives, he describes the scene almost like a battlefield, with corpses strewn across the ground.[61] When he realises who these bodies belong to, Theseus remarks that 'children do not stand in the line of battle', thus realising that what he is looking at is not a battlefield, but something more sinister.[62]

Euripides' choice of language portrays Heracles as both a warrior and an athlete, a comparative parallel that was not uncommon in classical Athens.[63] During the debate with Amphitryon, Lycus uses Heracles' heroic exploits, akin to his athletic victories and portrays them as cowardice, synonymous with his use of the bow.[64] Lycus' point is that these victories were meaningless when compared to the victories won with a spear and shield, as part of an army. Once again, Euripides is repeating the same formula we explored in section 4.1.2, while analysing his *Electra*. Athletic victories, heroic victories, do not equal a victory in war. This comes to the fore when Heracles is most vividly placed in the aftermath of a battle, in the midst of the metaphorical battlefield that surrounds him following the carnage done by his own hand. This moment cements the identity of Heracles as a warrior, his tragedy occurs inside his own war.

5.2.2 Homecoming

Within the vase-painting motif discussed above, the locations of the rituals are left vague by the artists. It is generally assumed to be in the domestic sphere, but the precise location is left to the imagination of the viewer. In Chapter 2, the topic of the location for departure rituals never arose, for the simple reason that there is no evidence to guide us. This is most certainly not the case when it comes to homecomings. Agamemnon makes the location of the rituals abundantly clear when he declares his first intention having arrived home: 'I will pass to my palace halls and to my household hearth, and first of all pay greeting to the gods. They who sent me forth have brought me home again.'[65]

It is important, therefore, that the first interaction he has with his wife immediately follows this sentiment. Clytemnestra acts like the doting wife, but is primarily stopping her husband from performing the first set of rites he has deemed necessary before all else, by obstructing his route to the hearth.[66]

Clytemnestra's use of the hearth to describe Agamemnon's homecoming further accentuates the centrality of the hearth to the *oikos*, the focus of the hearth as the point of homecoming and her own obstruction of it.[67] Ultimately, Agamemnon never reaches his hearth, as he is killed in the bath he takes in order to purify himself before the rituals take place.

The importance of the hearth is emphasised in *Heracles* by its regular invocation in the text. On five separate occasions the hearth is used to re-iterate the domestic focus of the play. It is used by Megara to describe the role of Amphitryon, as grandfather, in a metaphorical marriage between her children and the spirits of death, preceding their anticipated execution at the hands of Lycus.[68] Amphityryon describes to Lycus Megara taking refuge at the altar of Hestia, tricking him to enter the house and subsequently be killed by Heracles.[69] Heracles refers to the hearth on two occasions: the first time is to describe his delight at his own homecoming, at which point he greets his roof, his gates, and his hearth.[70] the second time, Heracles is interrogating his wife about their situation and asks her why she has left his home and hearth.[71] So, throughout the first half of the play, the hearth is firmly placed in its ideological context as a central fixture in domestic life: it is the focal point of marriage, it is a source of sanctuary and security, it is the epitome of homecoming and it is synonymous with the home.

The final instance in which it is mentioned, is in a functionary role of domestic life. Heracles, on his return, learns of the injustice his family has been facing and intends to face Lycus immediately, not having yet entered his own house. He is quickly rebuked by his father, who orders him to go and address the hearth within the house.[72] On realising his error, Heracles not only agrees to his father's order, but also articulates his reason for doing so: 'I will not neglect to address, first of all, the gods beneath my roof.'[73] Thus, *Heracles* and *Agamemnon* identify the hearth as the first location of any homecoming ritual.

Both plays offer supplementary locations where further rituals will take place. In *Agamemnon*, the king enters the palace with his wife, but she returns outside to speak with Cassandra. She orders Cassandra to take her place with the many other slaves, who are standing by the altar of Zeus Ctesius and to share in the lustral water of the house.[74] The cult of Zeus Ctesius was predominantly domestic and it was associated with the protection of the house, the health of the family, as well as the giving and protecting of wealth.[75] The physical embodiment of this cult in the Athenian household seems to have varied: one source described a specific jar that was to embody the god, while another suggests that images of the god were set up in the storage room of the house.[76] Further sources imply that the god was envisioned as a snake.[77] In addition to this flexible imagery, the god is described in

Agamemnon as having a specific altar, at which small animal sacrifices would be made.[78] Cassandra, as a new acquisition for the house, was invited to the altar to take part in the sacrifice and to share in the lustral waters.[79] This should have been a preliminary ritual, followed by her introduction to the household via a ritual at the hearth; instead, it becomes the scene of her own murder.[80]

The hearth and the altar are two focal points of the text, but they are not where the murders take place. Agamemnon is famously killed in his bath, yet when Cassandra claims to smell the odour of blood coming from the house, like it would from a fresh funerary rite, she is told it must be the smell of the victims on the hearth.[81] Cassandra's murder is not given a location, so it is plausible that it happened at the altar, but Aeschylus did not feel the need to confirm this in any way. While the analogy is clear, that Agamemnon and Cassandra are being used like sacrificial victims, the action described in the play does not explicitly reflect this.[82]

Euripides' *Heracles* offers a slightly vague secondary location: the altar of Zeus. The altar was used by Heracles and his family to perform purification rituals for the house, following the murder of Lycus. The question of whether purification rituals were necessary following military service is more fully dealt with below, for our purposes here, it is important to note two things. First is the use of separate sacred spaces within the home. Heracles does not use the hearth for every ritual action he makes during his continuing period of transition back home. Second, the homecoming transition does not not seem to involve a single isolated ritual. Much like in *Agamemnon*, there are several ritualistic concerns that need attending to by the warrior and his family. For Agamemnon there was the need for thanksgiving to the gods at the hearth, followed by the incorporation of his human property into his household via the altar of Zeus Ctesius. For Heracles, there was his need to reacquaint himself with the gods at the hearth, followed by the need to purify himself and his household at the altar of Zeus. Therefore, the ideology of homecoming focuses on the centrality of the hearth, as the symbolic heart of the house and family, for its location. Yet, it should not be considered in isolation, but as a core element within the wider network of religious space throughout the home.

5.2.2.1 *The participants*

Within the warrior departure motif on red-figure vases the hoplite is rarely depicted on his own. He is most often shown with a father figure and one, or more, women. In addition to this, there are examples of the motif which include infants, youths or attendants/slaves, other men on military service, and dogs.[83]

This suggests that there was a wide spectrum of participants who were able to take part in the departure ritual. For the running hypothesis here to be accepted, that arrival rituals shared the same iconography as departure rituals, it is necessary to examine the participants in the homecoming rituals.

Importantly and, perhaps, most obviously, both the arrival scenes under review show that neither warrior took part in the rituals on his own. Agamemnon is led into his house by his wife toward the hearth and Cassandra is sent to the altar of Zeus Ctesius where she was to join the other slaves already waiting for her. This simple picture conforms to wider scholarly understanding of domestic religion in ancient Greece, in which ritual was often male led but still a communal event; members of the *oikos* were usually welcome.[84] In *Heracles*, the hero is sent indoors by his father, but led in by his wife and children. As he enters, and heads toward his hearth, Heracles emphasises the importance of family and a man's love for it.[85] This articulation of family love and family unity not only relates to the terror having been faced by his family at the hands of Lycus, but it also relates to the coming ritual at the hearth. The family home, epitomised by the hearth, will welcome back the *kyrios* and be complete once more.

It may seem very one-dimensional to describe the participants of the homecoming rituals as simply the members of the *oikos*. However, it is important to remember that the *oikos* was not a rigidly defined construct. A clear example of this is found in the evidence for the cult of Zeus Ctesius. Our sources differ in their descriptions of who was invited to take part in rituals around the altar: *Agamemnon* implies that all the household slaves were welcome, Antiphon states that close friends and mistresses took part, whereas Isaeus implies that only close family were able to participate.[86] Nevertheless, all the sources agree that this was a domestic ritual, based on close ties associated with the household.

5.2.2.2 *The rituals*

The most prevalent ritual in the warrior departure motif is the libation, a ritual which took precedence over earlier ritual *topoi* such as the post-sacrificial hieroscopy. The physical imagery offers two main difficulties of interpretation: the first is context – the libation ritual does not usually offer a suggestion of the god or gods to whom the libation is being poured; the second is the continuation of ritual practice – does the disappearance of the sacrifice ritual suggest a change in practice or is it simply a change in artistic design? By way of contrast, the two plays under review do offer some suggestions about the rituals involved during the homecoming. First, it is necessary to set out which rituals are described in each instance and what form they take. Following this, discussion must turn to the question of whether a homecoming warrior needed some form of purification ritual before re-entering the home.

Aeschylus presents three distinct ritual practices within his distorted homecoming. The thanksgiving sacrifice at the hearth, the purifying bath of Agamemnon and the sacrifice during a ritual of incorporation at the altar of Zeus Ctesius.[87] The two sacrifices clearly echo the imagery of early warrior departure scenes but raise an interesting contrast. Within black figure and early red-figure scenes of departure, it is not the actual sacrifice which is commonly depicted, but the reading of the liver. As has been argued in 2.2.1, the depiction of hieroscopy imbues the hoplite with a sense of control by somehow grasping an insight into the future. For a homecoming, this form of ritual is not necessary because the hoplite is not departing into the unknown. Yet there is one example, on the obverse of an amphora in the Michael C. Carlos Museum (see Figure 5.3a), in which a bloody altar serves as the focal point of the scene.[88]

Figure 5.3a Red-figure amphora, attributed to the Niomid Painter (Greek, active ca. 475–450 BC). A warrior returning or departing, before a bloodied altar and with the aid of a woman. Atlanta (GA), Emory University, Michael C. Carlos Museum: 1984.12A.

Figure 5.3b Red-figure amphora, attributed to the Niomid Painter. A young warrior arms for departure while a woman waits ready to pour the libation. Atlanta (GA), Emory University, Michael C. Carlos Museum: 1984.12B.

The pot is fragmentary, so a full analysis is not possible. The man is identifiable as a hoplite, due to his shield apron and *doru*. The woman holds an *oenochoe* in her hand, which compliments the presence of the altar and identifies this as a probable example of the warrior departure/arrival motif. On the reverse of this amphora (see Figure 5.3b) is a separate departure scene that, while fragmentary, offers a greater indication that it depicts a departure. The hoplite is clearly a young man, *sans* beard, and the direction in which his helmet is facing suggests that he has been given it by the woman. His pensive look at the helm in his hand gives the scene the necessary sadness inherent in the departure motif. Finally, the positioning of the shield, with its outer side facing toward him, imitates that scene on the New York *pelike*, creating the impression he has yet to be handed it by the woman. It is unlikely that both scenes depict the same event, since the fragments, as they exist now, do not suggest it is the same man and woman in both scenes. The woman's dress shows a different design on its trim and the man carries one *doru* on the obverse but two on the reverse. The design of the altar also differs on both the base and the top.

Even without a clear identification, the presence of the bloodied altar in Figure 5.3a is important. It is one of the few allusions to the use of sacrifice in the motif, confirming the literary description in the *Agamemnon*. If the woman was not pouring a libation, but instead this was replaced with an image depicting the reading of a liver, there would be no question that the scene should be read as a departure. By replacing the hieroscopy with a libation, the artist allows for an ambiguous reading, enabling the viewer to identify the ritual as a post-sacrifice libation at either the departure or at the arrival. In turn, this corroborates the main ritual activity as described by Aeschylus.

In the *Agamemnon*, there is also a fourth form of ritual practice, alluded to at various points in the play, but never actually performed. The ritual in question is the libation poured to Zeus *sōtēr tritos*, a ritual commonly attested after a meal.[89] Most evocatively, Clytemnestra describes the murder of Agamemnon as a distorted version of these libations:

> Twice I struck him, and with two groans his legs relaxed. Once he had fallen, I dealt him yet a third stroke to grace my prayer to the infernal Zeus, the saviour of the dead. Fallen thus, he gasped away his life: throwing forth a quick burst of blood, he struck me with dark drops of gory dew.[90]

The triadic schema has been maintained by Clytemnestra, but it is not fully revealed until the final strike which kills her husband. Only now does the audience realise that the first two strikes were a perverse form of libation in her mind, followed by the third and final libation to Zeus the Saviour in the form of Agamemnon's own blood.[91] This perversion is further emphasised by her description of Zeus as the saviour of the dead, rather than the living. The libation metaphor is maintained in Clytemnestra's speech by her contemplation of pouring a libation over Agamemnon's head, like one would a sacrificial victim.[92] Finally she describes Agamemnon's accursed wrongdoings like wine, first filling the mixing-bowl to the brim, and then drinking it himself.[93]

The libation was a ubiquitous feature of Greek religion, supplementing almost every prayer and sacrifice.[94] Additionally, in domestic religion, it was commonly associated with hospitality and communal socialising at meals or with drinks. Libations would be poured to recognise new friendships, to begin and end communal meals and during symposiums.[95] A libation would also be poured before a departure on a long journey or, indeed, a departure for war.[96] In other words, libations were often used in domestic rites to cement close relationships and formal bonds. Therefore, Clytemnestra's subversion of the libation ritual simply accentuates the shattering of close bonds between husband and wife.

The motif of hospitality in the *Agamemnon* has been explored by Paul Roth, who has shown that *xenia* and its code of hospitality is plainly evident from the early parts of the play.[97] Clytemnestra was herself a *xenē* both as a stranger to the family brought in by marriage and within the play as a host.[98] She hosts Agamemnon and Cassandra on their arrival, but subverts the code of hospitality.[99] She stops her husband at the entrance, rather than offering a quick invitation inside, she delays his change of clothing, and rather than allowing him to bathe in peace, she murders him.[100] In turn, the *Agamemnon* offers a very different dynamic to the homecoming scenario. The portrayal is one of Clytemnestra purposefully failing in her wifely duty, which was to reintegrate the warrior back into the *oikos* from which he has become estranged.

In his *Heracles*, Euripides only describes two forms of ritual that follow the warrior's homecoming. The first sees Heracles enter his house to address the gods at the hearth, a ritual which the playwright fails to describe in any detail. Following *Agamemnon*, this was likely to be a ritual of thanksgiving on his part and one of reintegration between him and his *oikos*. The theme of reintegration and re-acquaintance is one articulated by Heracles to his children and wife, as they enter the house: 'Come now, children, accompany your father into the house. My entering in is fairer in your eyes, I think, than my going out.'[101]

The second ritual is a purification, following the murder of Lycus and it is this ritual that Euripides subverts into the massacre of Heracles' family.[102] This episode offers a description of the elements involved in the purification ritual:

> Victims to purify the house were stationed before the altar of Zeus, for Heracles had slain and cast from his halls the king of the land. There stood his group of lovely children, with his father and Megara; and already the basket was being passed round the altar, and we were keeping holy silence. But just as Alcmene's son was bringing the torch in his right hand to dip it in the holy water, he stopped without a word.[103]

The messenger describes a sacrifice being made at the altar of Zeus. The underlying purpose of the ritual is described as purification, but, as Parker has observed, the ritual seems to be a normal sacrifice.[104] This may reflect the Athenian attitude to justified homicide, in which the perpetrator could in certain circumstances, be considered unpolluted by his acts.[105] This may explain why there is an absence of specific purification rites, and Heracles' desire to purify himself may simply reflect what Parker describes as 'private scruples.'[106] There is, however, another way of interpreting this ritual, based on Euripides' choice to stage the massacre within it. For he produces a scene which uses similar dramatic constructs to the death of Agamemnon, by choosing to debase the purifying ritual with death and destruction. To understand this decision, and the place of purification within a warrior's homecoming, it is first necessary to establish the polluted status of a homecoming warrior.

In his seminal work on *miasma*, Parker does not deal with military pollution in any great depth, other than to show that purification rituals on campaign were often used to unify the army.[107] The most concrete example for this is found in Xenophon, who describes the Ten Thousand in council, agreeing to restore order and discipline.[108] Following the meeting, Xenophon and the seers proposed that the entire army be purified. Xenophon does not describe the rituals in any detail, and Pritchett is most likely correct in his assertion that this suggests that Xenophon expected his readers to be familiar with the ritual.[109] Otherwise Parker, following Pritchett, does not find any examples of purification rituals at the end of military service. This topic has been left relatively unexplored by scholars.[110] Crowley, in his work on the motivating factors behind an Athenian hoplite's will and capacity to fight, argues that killing in battle was non-polluting, but refrains from exploring other forms of pollution that hoplites were susceptible to during service.[111] Tritle, in his work on the experience of the veteran in ancient Greece, claims briefly that the Greeks had forms of 'rituals involving actual religious sacrifices' which would have facilitated the warrior in his homecoming, but offers no direct evidence to support this.[112]

The most extant attempt to challenge the view set out by Parker is that of Bernard Eck. Eck challenges the assumption that bloodletting in ancient Greek battle did not cause pollution.[113] He combines evidence of pollution as a direct result of action in war, but not killing, with wider ethnographic evidence of purification rituals, none of which come from the classical Greek period. The most compelling piece of evidence to his argument and one that had been observed by Parker before him comes from Aeschylus' *Seven Against Thebes*:[114]

> There are enough Cadmean men to go to battle with the Argives; such blood is cleansed (καθάρσιον). But the death of two men of the same blood killing each other – that pollution can never grow old[115]

The Greek term, καθάρσιος, here in its adjectival form, agrees with αἷμα to form a very condensed clause. It is possible to translate the clause along the lines of the blood already being cleansed, or that it will cleanse itself, which fits into the scholarly consensus that this bloodshed did not cause pollution.[116] However, it is being used as an example with which to contrast the killing of kin. The Chorus is not necessarily saying that killing strangers in battle does not cause pollution, but rather it causes a less severe pollution than the killing of one's own brother. The contrast being made is that the blood-guilt of battle is minimal and can be easily cleansed in ritual, whereas the pollution from fratricide can never be removed.[117] Parker's solution to this passage is the more compelling; that bloodshed in battle could simply be washed away. This does not mean that battle was not polluting, but that it was not a severe form of pollution and caused little to no concern for Athenian men. This may go some way to explaining the contrasting evidence available that suggests that killing in battle was free from blood-guilt; it was not a pollution which lingered for very long.[118]

This does not mean that a hoplite could not become polluted by other acts he performed on a campaign. We have already heard from Xenophon that disobedience and the possible incitement of mutiny in an army was cause for a purification rite. Hoplites were not immune to the many causes of pollution, such as sex or impious actions in temples. Similarly, while the killing of an enemy may not have been very polluting, the touching of the dead still remained a great taboo. The logistics of dealing with the war dead on a battlefield shall be dealt with in section 6.1, but for the topic in question here it is important to note that hoplites seemed to have avoided the collecting of their own dead, leaving it to their slaves.[119]

The importance of this state of pollution, for the topic of homecoming rituals, is that the hoplite was not immune to pollution during his service. Thus, like every other aspect of his religious behaviour, he would have habitually cleansed himself before embarking on a ritual within the home. This cleansing was unlikely to be any more than a standard use of lustral water, as described by both Clytemnestra, and the messenger in *Heracles*, allowing the hoplite to, quite literally, wash his hands of the matter. Therefore, referring to the question of Euripides' decision to place the murders during this point of purification, the playwright has chosen an innocuous, yet omnipresent pre-ritual which focuses the attention of the audience onto the theme that engulfs his entire story – a warrior's homecoming. In turn, by choosing the one aspect of ritual that was least likely to vary between households, the murders resonate both with the theme and with the audience.[120]

5.2.3 Arrivals vs departures

The pivotal question that was asked at the end of section 5.1.3 was whether the rituals involved in the homecoming of a hoplite would look identical to that of a departure. If this was the case, then the previous argument that the warrior departure/arrival motif was often made to be purposefully ambiguous by the vase painters, would hold some validity. By combining the literary evidence with the iconographic evidence dealt with above, it is possible to see a great continuity between the scenes. The two ritual events are closely focused around the domestic environment. The participants involved in both scenes vary between depictions; however, each show a focal emphasis on members of the *oikos*. How different households defined those members seems to have varied, especially in terms of participation in household rituals, but both of the scenes discussed here show the importance of *oikos* members.[121] The actual rituals that took place in a departure or homecoming scene look very similar on paper but are used for different purposes.

One major difference between the two scenes is the overarching emotional context. As discussed in section 2.2.2, a warrior's departure was an emotionally wrought time for the family. This is evident in both the literary evidence and on many of the departure-scene vases; indeed, as argued above, when a red-figure scene notably conveys the emotion of sadness then it should be confidently identified as a departure scene, rather than one of arrival. Conversely, the emotional context of a warrior's homecoming is expected to be one of happiness. While our literary sources purposefully invert this expectation to emphasise their tragic stories, they still express the expectation that their *nostos* should be a happy event.

Only now is it possible to answer the original question. The two scenes reflect one another quite closely. If a vase painting depicts a warrior, surrounded by his family or *oikos* members, participating in a libation ritual with or without an altar, then it is equally plausible that the scene is meant to depict a homecoming, as much as it is a departure. The warrior's homecoming formed a mirror image to his initial departure. It was a domestic affair and included a wide array of *oikos* members. He was greeted by members of his *oikos* before entering the homestead and would have been guided toward the hearth first and foremost. He would first purify himself through a simple wash or maybe a sacrifice, and then perform rituals of thanksgiving to the gods. In turn, this ritual at the hearth would reintegrate the warrior back into his *oikos* by returning him to his rightful role in the household – whether as *kyrios* resuming command of the domestic rites, or as a son having these rites performed on his behalf. Once this was complete, secondary rituals would then be performed, if necessary, such as the integration of slaves or giving thanks to specific gods at their altars.

Military Homecoming of the Dead

The homecoming of the war dead was the final transition available to Athenian hoplites. Scholarship on the Athenian war dead understandably focuses more on their funerals and the famous funeral oration epitomised by that recounted by Thucydides and attributed to Pericles in the first year of the Peloponnesian War.[1] But, for the purposes of understanding the transition of the war dead, it is important to try and reconstruct the entire process of their homecoming, beginning with their processing on the battlefield. Not only will this allow for a broader understanding of the commitment involved in the handling of the dead, but it will also allow any inconsistencies within the evidence to come to the fore.

During the classical period, the Athenian army processed and then transported the remains of their war dead by one of two distinct methods. Either, they buried them on the battlefield, as they did at Marathon and Plataea, or they cremated them and then transported their remains back to Athens for burial in a public *polyandrion*.[2] Thucydides incorrectly states that the Athenians made an exception at Marathon to bury the dead, but otherwise they only used the process of cremation and repatriation, as part of what he describes as an ancestral custom (*patrios nomos*).[3] This assertion has been disproven categorically by the work of Pritchett, who collected every example of battlefield burial and shows that the Athenians followed the wider Greek practice until sometime into the early fifth century BC.[4] Yet, it has proven difficult to date the introduction of battlefield cremations. Pausanias describes the earliest *polyandrion* in the *demosion sema* belonging to the Athenians who fell in battle against the Aeginetans, possibly dated to 490/1 or 487/6 BC.[5] It was not until the time of Cimon that the *demosion sema* was officially designated to accommodate the war dead and bring with such a designation the rituals described by Thucydides.[6] Therefore, it can safely be stated that the Athenians began cremating their war dead from as early as the turn of the fifth century, but the pomp and ceremony associated with their homecoming may not have been introduced until the middle of the fifth century.[7]

6.1 Battlefield cremation

To understand the cremation process, it is necessary to understand one important aspect of how the war dead were interred. Thucydides describes the remains in Athens residing in cypress wood boxes, one for each tribe, so ten in all.[8] If this is correct, it would be valid to assume that the war dead were collected from the battlefield and categorised into a maximum of ten distinct piles. These piles were each then cremated separately, transported back to Athens and placed in their respective boxes. This basic account forms the general scholarly consensus, but it rests on a few assumptions.[9] The first is that the Athenians could identify their war dead accurately.

In her study of the identification of the war dead, Pamela Vaughn follows this consensus, but observes that identifying the bodies would have been made very difficult by the looting of identifiable clothing or armour in the case of a defeat.[10] Nevertheless, she asserts that the presence of the *katalogoi* allowed the Athenians to take accurate stock of their dead.[11] The battle of Solygeia in 425 BC, is a strong example in favour of this; the Athenians won the day, but were forced to retreat before collecting all of their dead, leaving two behind.[12] In the battle, the Athenians lost fewer than 50 men, so it is conceivable that the dead could be found quickly and identified in an organised manner, allowing them to recognise the absence of two bodies.[13] However, the logistics behind the removal, identification and cremation of these men becomes harder to fathom in the aftermath of battles where the Athenians lost greater numbers. To exacerbate the issue further, battles with a higher loss of men commonly followed a defeat, after which the Athenians would have had their dead returned to them naked and possibly in a state of decay, depending on the time delay between the battle and their collection.[14] The battle of Delium resulted in 1,000 Athenians dead, at Amphipolis it was 600 dead and, of the 400 dead at Mantinea, half were Aeginitans who would have first needed to be separated from their Athenian counterparts.[15] While it is true that the *katalogoi* may have informed the officers about who had died, they would not have informed them of which body they were throwing onto which tribal pile.

The second assumption, arising from the standard model, is that the Athenians brought back all the remains of the war dead that were cremated. This assertion brings with it three interlinked questions worthy of further exploration: How then did they burn so many bodies? What constituted the remains they transported home? Is there any evidence that they left any of the remains on campaign?

6.1.1 Pyres and (c)remains

To take the first question, the bodies were burned on outdoor pyres.[16] During the Sicilian Expedition (415–13 BC), Thucydides provides the only account in the classical Greek literature of such a pyre described on a battlefield:

> [The Athenians] having collected their dead and laid them upon a pyre, passed the night upon the field. The next day they gave the enemy back their dead under truce, to the number of about two hundred and sixty, Syracusans and allies, and gathered together the bones of their own, some fifty, Athenians and allies.[17]

This passage is revealing in a few of its details. The first is that the pyre is given in the singular (πυρὰν), there is no suggestion that there were multiple pyres as we would have expected. Secondly, Thucydides suggests that the Athenians were burned with their allies and that the accumulative remains were then collected, in an impossible state of personal identification. These first two observations immediately challenge the assumption that the dead were separated into tribes before cremation and that, somehow, these remains were kept separate up to and including their internment back in Athens. Thirdly, Thucydides gives a timeframe for burning 50 bodies, stating that the army bivouacked overnight before collecting the bones, perhaps suggesting a standard practice.[18] Thucydides does not describe the pyre in any detail, but artistic evidence would suggest that it would have been open, with layers of logs alternating in direction, presuming that there was sufficient time to make such a formal pyre construction.[19] As noted by David Noy, the construction of an adequate pyre was time consuming and, by the Roman period, it was considered to be a job requiring technical competence, so perhaps such a perfect and formal pyre on a Greek battlefield was unlikely.[20]

An ancient pyre was capable of reaching similarly high temperatures to a modern British cremator (which has an operational temperature of 800–1000°C), but was simply inefficient.[21] Unlike modern cremators, a pyre has various factors to contend with: the majority of the energy in the fire is not directed toward the body and much is lost to the atmosphere; a constant temperature is hard to maintain; the weather affects its efficiency, the human body is a poor conductor of heat; and the pyre will collapse the longer it burns, so the body could smother the flames entirely.[22] To counter these issues, the pyre needs constant tending and, towards the end, a greater heat is necessary, as only the least combustible parts of the body remain.[23]

Crucially, to cremate a body successfully takes time and a large amount of fuel. Jacqueline McKinley estimates that an ancient, non-military, cremation would take seven to eight hours, while some experimental pyres have taken up to ten hours;[24] this is in keeping with Thucydides' timeframe in this passage. A comparable instance of mass pyre cremation potentially offers a more nuanced estimate. After the battle of the Alamo in 1836 AD, the defeated Texans were burned on two or three pyres constructed by the Mexicans immediately after the battle. A little under 200 bodies were burned, offering a comparable scale to the losses faced by the Athenian army. The pyres burned for two days and two nights and needed constant replenishing of fuel and grease to keep it going.[25] This offers a minor discrepancy with Thucydides' account; the Mexican pyres burned for twice as long as the Athenians. This may mean that the Mexican pyres were a lot larger than the Athenian pyre, but one source does mention the constant refuelling of the fire, so they were most likely just better managed.[26]

No ancient source describes the necessary amount of fuel for a pyre, but modern comparisons in India would suggest 500–600kg of wood are necessary to completely burn one body.[27] Nevertheless, this information only answers the question of how to burn one body on a pyre, not multiple bodies. As yet, no experimental studies explore open pyre mass cremations, but we know from the mass outdoor cremations of bovine carcasses following the foot and mouth breakout that any estimate of fuel consumption should include a consideration of fuel efficiency – in the case of the bovine carcasses, this reduced the amount of wood per body by one third.[28] This provides the approximation of 330–400kg of (dry)wood per cremated body in the instance of a mass cremation. For the Sicilian example above, the 50 Athenian bodies would have required *c* 20 tonnes of wood to cremate them effectively. Taking into account this only accounts for a single pyre and the disposal of only 50 men, this is a remarkable amount of a finite resource, raising the perplexing issue of where they sourced all of that wood from.[29]

The second question, borne from the standard model for the cremation of the war dead, concerns the cremated remains themselves. In modern British practice, the 'ashes' that are returned to the family of the deceased are not fire ash, but the ground up bones that remain after the raking process.[30] In fact, the human body does not really produce any ash, so it is fitting that Thucydides only uses the term τὰ ὀστᾶ, the bones, to describe the cremated remains in Sicily; it is the same term he uses to describe the remains during the public funeral in Athens.[31] Conversely, Aeschylus paints a very vivid, yet unrealistic, scene in his *Agamemnon*, in which the ashes of the dead are returned in individual urns, without any mention of the bones.[32] This confusion regarding the nature of the remains has caused modern scholars to fluctuate between describing the remains as ash or bone, with Pritchett going so far as to translate ὀστᾶ as ash.[33]

The assumption that ash returned to Athens, rather than bone, influenced Debra Hamel to calculate a plausible amount of ash resulting from the Athenian victory at Arginusae (406 BC).[34] She estimated that the incineration of 2,500 adult male bodies, would produce roughly 5.2 pounds (just over 2kg) of ash each. This would result in 13,000 pounds (roughly 6 tonnes) of ash, which would require a storage vessel measuring 8 cubic yards (roughly 6,100 litres). However, the modern weight estimates of the ashes, used by Hamel, mostly consist of ground bones. For these calculations to be correct, the bones of the war dead would need to have been collected and ground down, but there is no evidence that bones were ground down after a cremation in classical Athens.[35]

If it is assumed, for the moment, that the entire skeletal remains were removed from the pyre, each weighing approximately 1.6kg, then the skeletal remains of 2,500 adult remains would weigh approximately 4,000kg (4 tonnes, or 8,800 pounds).[36] As for volume, Per Holck studied the volume of cremated bones, in a modern crematorium, before they were ground down. Holck found that the average volume of a cremated skeleton was 7.8 litres.[37] By multiplying this estimated volume by the number of dead bodies given by Hamel, we can set a lower estimated volume for the remains at 19,500 litres, or 25.5 cubic yards. So, while the weight estimate is lower than Hamel's original, the space required is a lot higher than her estimate of 8 cubic yards. This, in turn, highlights the great logistical considerations necessary to handle the war dead, not just in terms of weight but also of storage, when it is taken into account that the Athenians were not bringing home ash but actual bone.[38]

A possible solution to this question of whether it was ash, bone, or a mixture of both that was brought back to Athens, could be provided by Plutarch. Admittedly a very late source, Plutarch does not use σποδός or ὀστᾶ to describe the Athenian war dead, but, in his *De Gloria Atheniensium* he uses the phrase τὰ λείψανα τῶν σωμάτων, 'the remains of the bodies'.[39] It is not an isolated example, as he uses the same term, τὰ λείψανα, to describe the cremated remains of various Greek historical figures.[40] We know from the example of the pyres at the Alamo that witnesses described seeing the charred remains of different body parts including heads, arms and legs.[41] Considering that these pyres used an accelerant, and burned for twice the amount of time than is described by Thucydides' narrative in Sicily, the flames still failed to burn every part of the dead bodies. It becomes unrealistic, therefore, to assume that the Athenian pyres were any more successful than those of the Mexicans, so Plutarch's description of 'remains' is an accurate one.

Plutarch's use of abstract terminology to describe whatever is left behind after a cremation, has a modern equivalent: 'cremains'.[42] This has an important advantage in its usage; it does not require the cremation to have been completely successful. The terms 'ash' and 'bones' create an image of complete cremation, in which the bodies are fully broken down by the fire into these two distinct elements. However, these terms brush over the issues discussed above: pyres are not consistently hot, nor is the body a good conductor of heat. Therefore, unless the pyre is tended to continuously, it is unlikely to result in such a clean and pure article, and soft tissue may remain on some of the bones.[43] When the practicalities of the Athenian system are taken into account – building upto ten pyres on a battlefield, watching and tending to them overnight, having sourced enough fuel to complete the job – it is, then, most accurate to describe the war dead as returning home as 'cremains', rather than ash or bone. These would not have been as clean as Holck's test subjects, so his average figure here should be taken as a minimum volume, presuming that all of the cremains were present. This presumption, however, raises the final question on this topic: Did the Athenians really transport all of the cremains home every single time?

6.1.2 Leaving cremains behind

It was an accepted fact of Athenian life, that not all the war dead would return home. This is evident during Thucydides' description of the *patrios nomos*: 'Among these is carried one empty bier decked for the missing, that is, for those whose bodies could not be recovered.'[44] While it was abhorrent for the Athenians to consider their men unburied through negligence, there was a general understanding that there were circumstances in which bodies could be lost, such as at sea.[45] Therefore, the Athenians implemented a symbolic gesture for the missing dead, so that those who were not brought home were still an integral part of the funerary ritual. This, in essence, allowed the war dead to be laid to rest and given due honours, without needing to be wholly present in the grave. Therefore, while the emotions and sanctity surrounding the retrieval of the war dead are apparent, there was still a base understanding and acceptance of the logistical limitations faced by the army.[46] This, perhaps, goes some way to explain a confusing discrepancy in the work of Xenophon.

After the Athenians were defeated in the naval battle of Ephesus in 409 BC, the commander Thrasyllus arranged the customary truce to be able to collect the

400 war dead. Xenophon then describes what the commander did next: 'The Athenians, having collected the corpses under a truce, sailed away to Notium, buried them there, and sailed on[.]'[47] The key phrase is κἀκεῖ θάψαντες αὐτούς, with αὐτούς referring to the corpses. The aorist participle comes from θάπτω, which is conventionally translated 'to bury'. The *LSJ* also observes later usage of the verb that refers to cremation rather than burial, but no examples are given from the classical period.[48] A more inclusive translation would be 'dispose of the dead' or 'honour with funeral rites', but it maintains a default meaning in Athenian literature of bury, or inhume, unless further qualification is provided.[49] It is possible, following Pritchett, that Xenophon meant that the Athenians transported the bodies and cremated them, before sending the ashes on to Athens.[50] This would at least offer credit to Xenophon's writing, as opposed to Felix Jacoby's solution that Xenophon suffered a 'slip of the pen'.[51] However, the use of the adverb κἀκεῖ focuses the rituals within a spatial context, it happened *there*. If the bodies were cremated and transported to Athens, this adverb would not be necessary; however, if this was a burial, the emphasis on location makes more sense. If this was a slip of Xenophon's pen, it was not his only one. The verb θάπτω appears nine times in his *Hellenica*, three of which refer specifically to Athenian burials. The other two instances do not emulate the adverbial description, but instead use the preposition ἐν, which similarly emphasises the spatial parameters, focusing on the placing of the body or remains into the ground via a burial.[52] One of these instances centres on an Athenian *mantis* who, having died at the battle of Mounichia, is described by Xenophon as being buried in the ford of the Cephisus river.[53] Not only does the context of the ford give credence to the translation of 'bury', but the military context of his death offers a tantalising suggestion that not all the Athenian war dead had to be buried communally.[54]

If the Athenians did bury their dead at Notium, as Xenophon suggests, the question still remains why? Thrasyllus had embarked on a large naval campaign that year to try to take control of the Ionian coast, with early success. His defeat at Ephesus was not the end of the campaign. Rather than return to Athens, his fleet moved north to Lampsacus where it was later joined by another Athenian fleet and they continued in their strategic aims. This context may explain the burying of the Athenian dead: they could not be carried around while the fleet was still on active duty. This explains their transportation to Notium, the nearest safe point, and their immediate disposal. What this does not explain is why they buried the cremains, rather than sent them back.[55] Thrasyllus' men collected 400 dead bodies for processing. If, as we would have expected, these bodies had been cremated, then the resulting weight of bone would have been *c.* 640kg (over half a tonne). In turn, the minimum amount of space needed to store this amount of bone would be *c.* 3,120 litres (just over 4 cubic yards). It was certainly possible to send these cremains home, in one or numerous containers, however it would have been a major logistical operation.[56]

There are two further logistical factors which must be considered once the cremains arrived in Athens. The first is the visual impact that such large containers carrying the cremains would have had on the people of Athens when they arrived. Aeschylus dramatises the distress felt by families at the sight of individual urns returning to them, following battle;[57] what, then, would the Athenian citizenry have felt seeing large boxes being brought off the ships at the Piraeus? The second factor is once more of storage. Thucydides is very clear in his description of the public funeral: it occurred in the winter, outside the campaigning season. So where were the cremains kept until it was time for the funeral? The battle of Ephesus was fought in the early summer of 409 BC. If the cremains had been sent back to Athens, they would have been stored for at least four months, if not longer.[58] In addition, they would have been joined by further cremains during the campaigning season. If Donald Bradeen's interpretation of one particular casualty list is correct, then the year 409 BC saw anywhere in the region of 1,400 dead.[59] This means that anywhere up to 1,000 more Athenian dead joined those from Ephesus in storage somewhere in Athens. The issue here is not so much one of space, but rather of Athenian sensibilities. There would have been buildings or warehouses large enough to store the cremains, but the time spent in storage for these fallen men is very hard to reconcile with the great honours and rites that the war dead would receive later in the year.

A possible solution to this issue is that the Athenians did not bring home all of the cremains.[60] Archaeologists researching cremations describe a sub-category of cremation burial in which a significant amount of the skeleton is missing, these are called 'token' cremation burials.[61] A token burial could result from a variety of socio-religious factors, such as the sociological conception of what represents an individual or the social expectation for an individual to be buried in more than one place.[62] Athens would not be historically unique in this regard, not even when it comes to repatriation for the war dead. During the Second World War, Imperial Japan struggled to maintain its custom of the repatriation of cremated remains. White boxes that were sent home were instead filled with sand, wood, paper, a pipe, or sometimes partial cremains. A civil servant by the name of Izumi Tōru had the job of taking receipt of the remains when they arrived in Japan and would later describe the pragmatic, yet harrowing, decision that was made:

Unable to face the greater sadness of families with no remains inside the boxes and believing that the heroic war dead would rest in peace better, we decided to take a few fragments of remains from other boxes. All the while fearing that it was wrong to deceive the bereaved families, we divided the fragments of bones into different boxes, our hands trembling as we did this.[63]

For the Japanese, this was a sacrilegious secret to be kept quiet, whereas it was an open secret in Athens. The presence of a bier for any missing bodies had already averted the potential sacrilege of not burying all the dead in the *demosion sema*. Therefore, on a ruthlessly practical level, there was no need to bring all the dead home.[64] When the sheer size and weight of the cremains are taken into account, alongside their possible long-term storage through the summer months, it may be that a more efficient solution was enacted. Only a few of the bodies were cremated and sent back to Athens as token burials for the rest, who were processed and buried in foreign soil. This solution does not answer every question raised here but it would equally explain Thucydides' lack of tribal pyres in Sicily and Xenophon's description of Thrasyllus' men being buried at Notium.

6.2 *Patrios nomos*

Before the full ceremony of the *patrios nomos* can be analysed, it is first important to highlight two large gaps in our understanding, both of which have been drawn out by the previous sections. First, it is not known where the cremains of the war dead were held before their burial, how they were stored or if any form of ritual had occurred before or during their placement into storage. Second, it is not known how many of the dead men actually had their cremains interred back in Athens.[65] That being said, there is no evidence to suggest that the Athenian public thought, or even suspected, that only a token number of the war dead came home. While this does not, in any way, disprove the notion, it is pertinent for the following section to state that, essentially, the Athenians believed that the majority of their war dead were interred during the public funeral.

6.2.1 The funerary rites

Thucydides describes the public funeral of the war dead on one single occasion, the first such funeral of the Peloponnesian War. The funeral was paid for by public funds during the winter following the first campaigning season. It consisted of extravagant pageantry that lasted for three days, culminating in the burial of the cremains in the Kerameikos. This, Thucydides tells us, was an ancestral custom, a *patrios nomos*. Dating the introduction of the rites has proved difficult for scholars, partly because there is so little evidence for it and partly because of Thucydides' assertion that it was an ancestral custom. The interest here does not concern the implementation of some form of public funeral for the war dead, but rather with the specific rituals described by Thucydides and contemporaneous authors. While not all of these rituals may have been performed throughout the entire period under review, they do reveal the zenith of the ideological construction of both the funeral and, in turn, allow for a more general understanding of the transition undergone by the war dead.

Thucydides' *patrios nomos* – he is the only author to use that term – is intrinsically linked to the tribal system of Athens, which only existed after the reforms of Cleisthenes.[66] If it is accepted that the use of the Kerameikos for *polyandria* coincides with the implementation of the *patrios nomos*, then a start date *c.* 500 BC is appropriate.[67] The original rituals, whatever they had been, were added to over time and made much grander by such innovations as the introduction of the funeral speech (*epitaphios logos*) and also the funeral games (*agon epitaphios*), which is intriguingly absent from Thucydides' description.[68] By describing the funeral, Thucydides' aim was to explain to a non-Attic audience something that was uniquely Athenian.[69] In turn, this gives insight into particular elements of the rituals and the order in which they came.[70]

The first stage of the funeral began two days before the burial;[71] the bones of the war dead were supposedly laid out in a specially constructed tent, possibly in the agora, where people brought gifts for them.[72] This public *prothesis* was a purposeful and stark contrast to the Solonian laws on private *prosthesis*, which only allowed such a display for one day.[73] In his short description, Thucydides does not make clear the state in which the dead were 'laid out' (προτίθενται).[74] More commonly, this verb refers to the laying out of a body before cremation or burial.[75] Yet, this form of public display was simply not possible for the war dead and their burned cremains. Firstly, there was no body, only the fractured cremains of a multitude of bodies, possibly still adorned with charred flesh.[76] Secondly, the cremains must have been categorised into their tribes, so the cremains would have mixed, making such a display of distinct, individual remains impossible.[77] An alternative solution is that the ten *larnakes* were closed but laid in the tent, perhaps with a mark to associate each tribe; it was to these boxes that the family and friends went to place their gifts and pay their respects.[78]

The second stage of the funeral consisted of the ten larnakes being transported by ten carts, carrying out the cremains to the *demosion sema*. This procession, according to Thucydides, could be joined by any male citizen or foreigner in Athens, as well as the female relatives of the dead. Frustratingly, Thucydides is once again unclear in what he is describing. A *larnax* could be a chest or a coffin, but it could specifically refer to a cinerary urn.[79] While the use of cypress wood does suggest a box of some sort, this has not prevented some scholars from perpetuating the idea that ash was returned to and placed into appropriate urns which, in turn, were placed into boxes.[80] From the previous discussion in section 6.1.1, it has been established that the cremains of the dead were not ash, but fragmentary, cremated bone, so the translation of coffin in this context is accurate. As for its size, Thucydides gives no indication. If, for instance, only a select amount of cremains were returned from campaign, then they would only require a standard-size coffin.[81]

Conversely, if this hypothesis is incorrect, and all the dead were returned to Athens, then these *larnakes* must have been very sizeable. The casualty list *IG* I³ 1147 shows that the tribe of Erectheis lost 177 men in just one campaign season. If the traditional model is correct, the cremains of these men would have been placed in a single box; 177 cremated bodies would require approximately 1380 litres of volume, or just under 2 cubic yards.[82] By way of comparison, a fitted coffin, designed for a man who was 5ft 8in, has a volume of 262 litres; this means that the cremains would fill the equivalent space of five fitted coffins.[83]

There is, then, the question of uniformity between the ten *larnakes*. It is highly unlikely that the ten tribes would have suffered equal losses each year, so we must imagine either different-sized boxes for each tribe or a uniform size shared by them all. If it were the former, this would have highlighted the tragedy and sacrifice felt by one tribe over each of the others. If it were the latter, then the campaign year covered by *IG* I³ 1147 would have seen ten identical boxes on parade, each one having the same visual impact on the crowds who saw them. As yet, there are no firm answers or solutions to this line of enquiry, but it does highlight the difficult, logistical practicalities that underpin the traditional model for the burial of the Athenian war dead.

Alongside the ten *larnakes*, Thucydides describes an empty bier (κλίνη) for those whose bodies were not returned to Athens. The term *klinē*, in this context, refers to a funerary couch or bed,[84] not another coffin, as it is sometimes described.[85] The differentiation made by Thucydides, between the *larnax* and the *klinē*, suggests an important contrast in how the two forms of war dead were being treated. The *klinē* was customarily used to transport the dead to their pyre, or their final resting place, during the *ekphora*. The Athenians were symbolically replicating this part of the funerary process; covering the bier with blankets and possibly ribbons.[86] Through the presence of the empty *klinē*, the missing bodies were ritually processed as if they had returned home. While the *larnax* represents the very end of the process, filled with the cremains, ready for internment, the *klinē* offered a symbolic middle, the missing dead were offered their death bed, fully adorned, ready for the next stage of the funeral. So, by the time the *larnakes* were lowered into the *polyandrion*, the missing men were laid to rest alongside them not as a superficial appeasement to the families, but in accordance with the ritual rubric that surrounded the disposal of the dead.

The third stage of the funeral witnessed the burial of the *larnakes*, after which an orator, specially chosen for the job, gave his funeral oration (*epitaphios logos*). Nothing can yet be said on the actual burial of the dead. As Cynthia Patterson astutely observes, it cannot even be discerned whether it was the *larnakes* or just the bones that were placed into the earth.[87] Additionally, it is not known whether the *klinē* was buried.[88] The *polyandrion* itself was a narrow rectangular tomb, lined internally with monumental blocks plastered with lime and possibly subdivided into chambers.[89] The base was paved, and slabs would have been placed on top of the grave after burial. There is also evidence of votive offerings being placed in the graves; although, it is not certain whether these were placed in the *larnakes* or in the grave; all that is certain is that these offerings were not cremated with the bodies.[90] Once the war dead were laid to rest inside these *polyandria*, the chosen orator would begin his speech to the crowd of mourners.

6.2.2 The funeral oration

Each *epitaphios logos* was written for a unique individual occasion, but they maintained certain distinctive elements that defined them as a genre.[91] From antiquity, two speeches have survived relatively intact (written by Demosthenes and Hyperides); one speech survives but is not a verbatim script of the speech delivered (Thucydides' account of the speech of Pericles); two speeches exist that were never intended to be delivered (written by Lysias and Plato); and the final speech exists but only in fragmentary form (written by Gorgias).[92] From these examples a general structure has been identified: a prelude which focuses on the role of the speech; a praising of the dead and the city's past glories; an exhortation giving advice to the living and consolation directed at the parents of the deceased; and an epilogue, followed by a dismissal of the crowds.[93] The speech was laced with political rhetoric, mythical as well as actual history and cultural ideology, but its primary aim was to honour the dead.[94]

The scholarship and debate surrounding the *epitaphioi* is vast and wide-ranging, but the genre's primary relevance to this section is within its role in the homecoming transition of the war dead. There are two particular themes that may be expected in a speech delivered at the graveside of the repatriated dead. The first is the theme of homecoming; the Athenians went through the effort and expense of returning the dead so, if the repatriation was so important to them, then it is to be expected that this would be mentioned in the speeches. The second theme is the transformation of the war dead; the Athenians bestowed upon their war dead a singular, collective, heroic identity, so it can be expected that this transformation, the purpose it served, and any justification for it, would be mentioned in the speeches as well.

The first theme of homecoming is actually conspicuous by its absence. Not one of the surviving speeches offers any attention to the homecoming of the dead. There is no appreciation for their return, no description of the bodies having returned to Attic land, no sense that the return of the bodies has offered any form of completion or closure to their military service. The topic of ἄταφος ('lack of burial') does arise in two of the orations: Lysias and Demosthenes each mention the story of the Seven against Thebes.[95] The mythical reference in the speech is seemingly clear; only the Athenians ensured the correct burial of the war dead back then. Perhaps the implication was clear to the Athenian crowd that they, like their predecessors, were ensuring the correct burial for their war dead, but it is never stated explicitly.[96] This omission is even more startling when considered next to one of the recurring themes in the *epitaphioi*, the reference to the Athenians' status as *autochthones*, and being born from the earth of Attica.[97] As Nicole Loraux has persuasively outlined, the *autochthones* motif commands a central role within the genre.[98] It is, therefore, peculiar that there is no narrative that succinctly ties the returning of the dead to the land from where they were sprung.[99] Even though the limited number of speeches that are available make it difficult to discuss absent concepts in the motif, this lack of examples still suggests that the physical homecoming of the bodies, if present in the motif at all, was certainly not an important ideological feature.[100]

The reason for this absence may be due to the second expected theme – the war dead's transition into heroic status. Pericles comes the closest to describing the physical burial of the dead, but in so doing highlights where the ideological emphasis of the speech lay:[101]

> For this offering of their bodies, made in common by them all, they each
> of them individually claimed that undying praise, and a most glorious tomb,

not so much this resting place, but one in which their glory remains to be eternally remembered upon every occasion on which deed or story shall fall for its commemoration. For renowned men have the whole earth for their tomb ...[102]

Pericles' words undermine the importance of the physical burial place in the Kerameikos, they instead conceptualise an eternal tomb that has no spatial confinement and becomes the whole earth.[103] Pericles builds on this image to state that the memorialisation of these men is not bound to the *stele* at the tomb, but resides in the memories of the people.[104] This imagery is cleverly chosen, it creates the impression of everlasting glory through communal memory, something Pericles uses to entice future generations to take up arms for Athens.[105] It also prioritises a metaphysical tomb of remembrance over the physical one.[106] This shift in emphasis allows for the inclusion of all those men who could not be returned to Attica, thereby alleviating the physical parameters that normally determine and define the burial of a body or its cremains.

Having downgraded the importance of the tomb, the orator looks to a different form of transition for the war dead. The transition from the battlefield to the grave was not physical, but transcendental, taking these men from being individual citizens to a collective embodiment of Athenian ideals. This transformation raises a hotly debated question of whether or not the Athenian war dead became heroes, recipients of heroic cult status.[107] They certainly received all the honours granted to heroes, most notably the commemorative games.[108] Yet, the rhetoric in the *epitaphioi* is slightly reserved in this regard, with no example describing the dead as heroes (ἥρως). Demosthenes describes them as associates (παρέδρους) of the gods below, while Hyperides describes it as plausible (εἰκὸς) that the war dead experience some sort of favour from the gods.[109] This paradox between the war dead being heroes in all but name, honoured in all but official cult, has been best explained by Parker, who rightly observes that the official mandating of heroes would take a long time, suggesting that the Athenians heroised the war dead as 'best as they could'.[110] However, there is a further complication in the characterisation of the war dead. What Parker does not consider is that what was heroised was not the individual who had died, but the institution itself: it was not a man who died in war, but rather the collective 'war dead'. This is emphasised within the *epitaphioi* using two interweaving themes: the removal of individual identity and the reiteration of collective action.

Individual identity does not exist in the rhetoric of the war dead for anyone except, on one anomalous occasion, the *strategos*.[111] The shared ancestry of the dead is emphasised as are the shared motives of the men in battle and their collective death.[112] Pericles even goes as far as to state that the previous errors and misdemeanours of the war dead, in civilian life, were erased by their death in battle.[113] His phrasing is particularly relevant here: κοινῶς μᾶλλον ὠφέλησαν ἢ ἐκ τῶν ἰδίων ἔβλαψαν ('their service together [outweighed] their harm as individuals'). In essence, Pericles is deleting the living memory of the individual warrior and replacing it with the collective identity of the war dead.[114] This erasure of personal identity can also be seen further in Pericles' ideological projection that social status and financial position do not determine valour.[115] This is repeated later in the speech, but this time in direct reference to the dead, when he reminds the crowd that not one of the dead allowed their financial status to affect their actions.[116] It no longer mattered whether they were rich or poor in life, whether they were good or bad as citizens, once they had been consumed into the identity of the war dead. This collective identity extended beyond the names inscribed onto the casualty list for that year, it included all the war dead up to that point.[117] This is implied by the recitation of past wars and sacrifices made by Athenians, thus aligning the war dead with their predecessors. This connection between them is overtly described by Demosthenes, who declares his intention to remind the crowd of the previous war dead, so his praise will include not only that year's war dead, but all the war dead collectively .[118]

Having secured the collective identity of the war dead, the final element of the transition was the need to identify the immortal nature of the dead. The greatest complication in the identification of the war dead as 'heroes' is that they were never named as such. A further complication was that these were mortal men known to the mourning crowd; to transform them into something greater than that was no simple task. As the *epitaphioi* repeat time and again, these men were born in mortal bodies and died mortal deaths.[119] However, their deaths were not the same as a normal death. Within the genre, the descriptions of their deaths laid the groundwork for their transition. According to Demosthenes and Hyperides, the war dead were blessed (εὐδαίμονές) and, for Lysias, they were the most blessed of all people.[120] As mentioned above, their association with the gods was assured by their sacrifice – so, too, was their place in the afterlife in the islands of the blessed.[121] Their death also removed them from the shame of defeat if, indeed, they died in a battle that was eventually lost.[122] Nevertheless, this still resulted in a mortal death, in an elevated and praised form but a death all the same. For their full transformation into a heroic homogeny to occur, they needed to possess some form of immortal asset, something that, like the gods, was ageless.

Within the *epitaphioi*, the war dead are said to exchange their mortal bodies for immortality. That immortality was not metaphysical, but one of memory. The war dead derived their immortality from their valour (ἀρετή), which in turn gave them a right to immortal remembrance.[123] This immortality is generally described in one of two ways: immortal (ἀθάνατος) memory and glory or ageless (ἀγήρατος) memory and glory.[124] Gorgias offers a different interpretation, saying that it was the mourning felt by the living that was immortal, describing it as living on 'immortal in bodies that are not immortal'.[125] This transfers the importance directly onto the survivors, positioning them in an active role of maintaining this immortality, which the abstract notion of memory only offers in a passive sense. This sentiment is echoed in the words of Pericles, who says that it is the praise of the dead that will not grow old;[126] similarly, Demosthenes describes the honours of, and to, the dead as ageless.[127] This clarifies the fragility of the war dead's immortality; it was not the gods who made them immortal, but the people who survived them.[128] For the war dead to be correctly honoured, the crowds could not be passive agents of memory. Instead, they were being urged to actively engage with maintaining that immortality through praising the dead and giving them their due honour.[129]

For an Athenian man to gain this form of immortality, he needed to first give up his life in battle. This exchange of one's life for ageless glory and honour is described, with varying explanations, between the logographers. In Demosthenes, the mortal death and the creation of immortal valour are synchronised events; the mourner then chooses which to emphasise more.[130] In Lysias, the exchange contrasts chance with choice; the dead men happened upon (ἔτυχον) their mortal bodies, but bequeathed (κατέλιπον) an immortal memory arising from their valour.[131] Whereas, in Hyperides, the exchange is described almost like a transaction, he uses the genitive of value to describe the war dead acquiring (ἐκτήσαντο) immortal glory in exchange for their mortal bodies.[132]

In whatever way it was perceived, the war dead had offered up their lives in exchange for this immortality of memory, which identifies the final transition they underwent. From the moment they died on the battlefield, these men were taken on a transitionary journey from physical remains to an immortal memory. During the process they were stripped of their individual identity. In the first instance, this was a product of necessity during the cremations. The bodies were burned together and the cremains collected for storage. From the aftermath of the cremation their individuality had been subsumed into the collective mass of the war dead. In the second instance, the *epitaphioi* articulated the removal of individuality as part of a larger process. The war dead were united as one in their sacrifice, so were offered shared lineage, shared motives and shared action. In death, they joined a new singularity. It was no longer the army which had absorbed them, but now the heroic conception of the war dead. They would be remembered and honoured, not for the man that they were, but for the collective they had joined.

The Domestic Reception of the War Dead

The political usurpation of the war dead significantly distanced the domestic household, both as a location and as a social unit, from the rites and reception for the dead. Although the families of the dead were invited to give offerings to the boxed remains of their family member's tribe and to attend the funeral, they were but one of many families doing the same. By the time of the procession, the single family, in mourning for their loss, had been joined by thousands of other people, both citizens and foreigners. What the state offered in return was to transform the dead family member into a child of Athens for the entire city to mourn in unison. The political rhetoric portrays this as an honour to the dead man and to his family, but it fails to empathise with their loss; not just the loss of a son or husband, but the loss of direct involvement in the funeral. This final chapter examines three interconnected threads of inquiry: the extent to which families were extricated from the sacred rites; the experiences of the bereaved families; and, finally, asks the question, were the war dead ever returned to the family?[1]

7.1 The family and the funeral

It has long been established that the family of the war dead were purposefully pushed to the margins by the advent of the Athenian public funeral.[2] The traditional funerary role of women, in particular, had been taken from them by the centralisation of death in war.[3] Loraux considered this a part of the democratisation of the war dead, elevating the public funeral from being a ritual for the dead to becoming a statement of democratic unity.[4] However, this 'removal' of the *oikos* from the funeral has never been placed into the wider context of military service.[5] As has been apparent in Chapters 2 and 3, the *oikos* and the individual had been superseded by the army from the very beginning of a hoplite's military service. From the moment the hoplite left his house he became de-individuated by the larger collective that he joined during the muster. This individual identity was not restored until he re-entered his *oikos* and reclaimed it through acts such as the making of thank offerings to the gods, in both public and domestic spaces. For the war dead, they never left their military service. In death, these men were never demobilised but instead were transferred into a heroic collective. To understand the experience of the family members who had survived the hoplite, it is more fruitful to examine it as part of this military continuum. The issue was not so much that the family had been overlooked during the rites, but rather their dead relative was not returned to them; he was never re-individuated.

7.1.1 Subversion of funeral norms

When an Athenian citizen died outside military service, it was the family's obligation to collect the body and perform the necessary rites. This obligation was so ingrained in the Athenian psyche that it was raised as proof, or disproof, of a right for an individual to inherit from the deceased.[6] The *prothesis* took place inside the house and began with a ritual washing of the body by the women of the *oikos*.[7] Once the body was cleaned, clothed and adorned with ribbons and flowers, it was placed upon a *klinē* with the feet facing the door.[8] The body would lie in state for one day, in accordance with Solonian law, before it needed to be buried.[9] During this day, family members would mourn and lament over the body.

The primary actors during these rites were the women of the *oikos*. *Prothesis* scenes on vases show the women taking responsibility of the body once it entered the home.[10] They would prepare the body, dress it and decorate the bier appropriately.[11] They would also take a primary role in the lamentations during the *ekphora* and burial.[12] Women were so integral to the funerary process that some scholars consider that the Solonian laws, brought in to control private funerals, were as much a control over women as they were a control of aristocratic spending.[13] That is not to say that the funeral was a predominantly female affair. As the work of Kerri J. Hame has established, control of the body was ultimately the responsibility of the male members of the family.[14] They would also approach the body during the *prothesis* and mourn over the body.[15] Once the *ekphora* began and the body was taken outside men took a more prominent role in the procession, with the women following behind.[16] While it is tempting to overemphasise this gendered division of responsibility, for the topic at hand, the most important aspect is that the *oikos*, as a collective, had a direct role in every stage of the funerary rites.

This contrasts directly with the preparation of the war dead. The family did not collect the body, the army collected it during a formal truce. The body was not washed or prepared, but ceremoniously burned and was, in the eyes of the family at least, returned to Athens. The war dead lay in state for two days, rather than one and the ritual space for mourning and lamentation needed to be shared with all the other relatives of the dead. However, describing this as the removal of the *oikos* from their ritual obligation would suggest that the family did, at some point in the past, have, or were expected to have, close funerary contact with the war dead. Yet all the evidence available suggests that this was not the case. The introduction of full-scale repatriation for the war dead in Athens replaced the otherwise Panhellenic ritual of burying the war dead out on campaign.[17]

If anything, the public reproduction of the domestic funerary rites offered the family access to rituals that had otherwise been kept from them. The family had the opportunity to be with the remains and give semi-private offerings. Similarly, they could follow the *larnakes* through the streets as part of the *ekphora*. Unlike the private *ekphora*, which most commonly saw the body transported on a bier with the body covered up to the neck in cloth, the public *ekphora* witnessed a large-scale procession with the *larnakes* drawn on carts.[18] Much like the *prothesis*, this was a shared experience for the family. Not only did they walk alongside the other families of the dead, but also any citizen or stranger in the city was permitted to join as well.[19] The same is true of the actual burial. Once the war dead had reached the Kerameikos the women were then permitted to begin their ritual laments.[20]

Without the introduction of a public burial, the family would have continued to miss out on all of the hands-on rituals involved in processing the dead. That being said, there is the issue of the family being allowed to be so close and yet kept distant at the same time. The family could take part in the usual forms of ritual, but under unusual circumstances. They could go to the *prothesis*, but not perform it in their own home. They could mourn in the presence of the dead, but only in front of the collective coffin. They could take part in the *ekphora* and lament at the grave, but they were only a small number in the large crowds. This conflict between expectation and reality is reflected quite neatly in Euripides' *Suppliant Women*, when Adrastus encourages the mothers of the dead to approach their sons on their biers following battle:

Adrastus   Draw near, unhappy mothers, to your sons!

Theseus   That is not a good idea, Adrastus.

Adrastus   Why? Should mothers not touch their sons?

Theseus   To see them so changed would be their death.

Adrastus   Yes, the blood and wounds of the dead are a painful sight.

Theseus   Why then do you want to add to these women's grief?[21]

Importantly, the first reaction is for the mothers to want to touch the corpses. Although the act of touching the body was, in itself, polluting, this did not concern the members of the relevant *oikos*. This desire to touch the bodies of dead children, of any age, is similarly reflected in *Medea*. Jason begs Medea to allow him to bury his murdered children, but she refuses and declares that she will bury them with her own hand.[22] He then requests to kiss them, or at least touch them, but to no avail.[23] Finally he calls upon the gods to witness her actions in preventing him touching the bodies of his children.[24] It is pertinent to observe that this desire to touch the corpses transcended the orthodox compartmentalisation of gendered roles.[25] Not only did Jason wish to perform the necessary rites, but his desire to touch his children is also repeated throughout the short exchange. The desire of fathers to touch their children's bodies also occurs elsewhere in Greek tragedy, showing that this urge was not based on a gender or maternal bond but was a desire that permeated the *oikos*.[26] Yet, within historic Athenian practice, touching the war dead was not possible. Much like the distraught Jason, family members of the war dead were denied the ability to conduct a funeral, and then refused the simple consolation of embracing the body one last time.

The funerary status quo that was subverted by the public funeral was not actually the female control of the funerary rites, nor the taking of responsibility away from the *oikos*. The *oikos* did not have control of the war dead's burial to begin with. The subversion was something much worse; the *polis* of Athens returned the bodies of the dead home and invited the families to join in an appropriated set of rituals, that were normally the privilege of the family, but stopped them short of touching distance. Like the torture of Tantalus, the family could see the prospect of having the body returned to them, only for it to move away the closer they tried to get. Simply put, the family was left as part of a wider audience to their relative's burial.

7.1.2 Public memorialisation

Although the *oikos* had never been in control of the funeral for the war dead, before or after the introduction of repatriation, they could still commemorate them. Yet, as has been discussed in Chapter 6, one of the main functions of the *epitaphioi* was to give responsibility for the memorialisation of the war dead to the wider Athenian population. The most obvious manifestation of this public attempt to control the memory of the dead individual is with the casualty lists.

The casualty lists were large marble *stelae* erected in the *demosion sema*, containing the names of all the men who had fallen in battle during that year, organised by their tribal affiliation.[27] As Arrington has identified, these were symbols of defeat as much as they were symbols of memory.[28] The greater the defeats in that year, the more names on the lists and the larger the memorial. These lists have been compared to the large Vietnam War memorials in the United States of America, in that they served as powerful memorials that would have elicited a similar emotive response to the Athenians who read them.[29] There is, however, one important discrepancy between the modern war memorial and that of ancient Athens: how the names were recorded.

Contrary to the modern war memorial, which often records the full names of the deceased, the Athenian casualty lists bear only the given names of the dead, without patronyms. The only way that a name could be identified was by tribal heading or, more commonly, subheadings.[30] There are eleven *stelae* which have one or more of the names partnered with a designated formal position, such as *strategos, trierarchos, phylarchos, taxiarchos* and *mantis*, but these are rare and do not account for the majority of names on the lists.[31] The removal of patronyms, allied with the tribal organisation of the lists, has been interpreted by many scholars as indicative of the democratic overtones of the funeral.[32] To quote Polly Low, the identification of the hoplite was 'not his ancestral lineage, but his tie to the democratic structure of the *polis*'.[33] However, as the work of Low goes on to show, this sweeping identification of democratic intent within this memorialisation does not stand up to scrutiny, especially when compared to other Greek *poleis* who also erected casualty lists. These non-Athenian lists offer a mix of tribal and non-tribal organisations, as well as patronymic and non-patronymic identifiers, from both democratic and oligarchic regimes.[34] The individual elements of the Athenian casualty list were not exclusive to democratic regimes; although, Low is most probably correct in assuming that Athens still considered their memorialisation intrinsically Athenian and intrinsically democratic.[35] If the addition or omission of patronyms crossed political ideologies, then perhaps it is more accurate to consider that the omission, in particular, was not solely to cement democratic ties, but rather to cut familial ties.

It has long been argued that the severing of family ties for the dead was part of a larger movement stemming from the early sixth century BC to restrict aristocratic power.[36] This resulted in the banning of ostentatious funerals under Solon and, in turn, by the classical period, meant that many of the old aristocratic funerary honours were being given to the war dead alone.[37] While there is, of course, validity to this explanation of the Athenian system, it ignores the majority of the men listed on the *stelae* who were not from wealthy families. They would not necessarily have appreciated this purpose nor, indeed, would they have cared. The lack of patronyms is not the only conspicuous omission, there are also no demotics. There may be a very practical reason behind this – there were, after all, 129 more *demes* than tribes, which would require more space and more effort at a greater cost – however, this had adverse effects on the family. Firstly, it made it harder to identify their loved one, as they would have to read the entire list to make sure there were not two people with the same name; only then would they know they had identified them.[38] Second, there are examples where the same name appears more than once under the same tribal heading, so there would be no sense of having found the name of a loved one.[39]

The lack of demotics brings into question the statement by Arrington that this purposeful anonymity absorbed the dead man into a collective identity of military men and that the 'tie that binds is military service for the city'. On the one hand, this is correct: the only way these men are identified is by their military action; on the other hand, the foundation of that military experience was the man's place in the *deme*. As has been established in section 3.1, the *deme* was the building block of military service, and the removal of the war dead from the *deme* is worthy of note. It was not just the *oikos* that lost ownership over the dead hoplite, but also his fellow comrades-in-arms, the very men he died fighting alongside.

The only defining feature afforded to a dead hoplite by the *polis* was his tribal denomination.[40] The tribe was a disparate community split throughout Attica, whose important political role never resulted into a close-knit community.[41] Yet, the one thing that the tribes did have were specific eponymous heroes, so the symbolism here may be more important than the practicalities involved.[42] The war dead were listed by the Attic heroes who they were deemed to have followed. If the ten *Eponymoi* were representative of the citizen army, then it makes sense that the war dead were categorised by their relationship with them.[43] While the *deme* was of fundamental importance to the individual hoplite, it held little to no official position in the Athenian army. Therefore, it is not necessary to see the memorialisation only in terms of political structure and ideology, it is equally apparent that the war dead were kept within their official military framework.[44] Because of this, the casualty lists echo many of the sentiments from the *epitaphioi*. *IG* i³ 1162 contains an epigram dedicated to the Athenians who died in the

Chersonnese in the mid-fifth century BC, describing the casualty list as an 'immortal memorial of their excellence (ἀρετές)'.[45] This reinforces two sources of the immortal nature of the war dead, as identified in section 6.2.2: their valour (ἀρετή) and their memory. The wording of the casualty lists also emphasises the military rhetoric of manhood, emphasising the deaths in combat, sometimes depicting the dead as fighting against larger forces.[46] Similarly, the casualty lists continue the silences in the *epitaphioi*, the men are kept in their de-individuated state. By only recording the first name and tribe of a dead hoplite, the individual was effectively deleted from public memory; he was stripped of his family, his community and his own personal military identity within the *deme*.

7.1.3 Private memorialisation

Before the instigation of the public funeral, the memorialisation for the war dead was the sole responsibility of the relevant *oikoi*. This could have manifested itself in ostentatious monuments of remembrance, such as those Solon's laws intended to curb, or within private actions that rarely receive any mention in the source material.[47] However, when the *polis* took control of the war dead and, in turn, their memorialisation, the *oikos* finally had something taken from them. They lost the sole right to remember their relative.

After the instigation of the public cemetery in the mid-fifth century BC, there was a sharp decline in the number of private monuments.[48] Evidence from vase paintings seems to suggest that families would go to the public grave and tie ribbons to the *stelae*, thus privately engaging with the public memorial. One fine example from a white ground *lekythos* in New York (see Figure 7.1) shows a woman and a mature youth making their offerings to two *stelae*, both of which are already covered in fillets and votive offerings.[49] The *stelae* are, unfortunately, shown side on, so there is no way to be certain these are meant to be casualty lists. However, these have been identified on vase paintings, showing that the medium was not averse to such a depiction.[50] So, while the identification of these graves as being those for the war dead is not certain, nevertheless the large number of offerings and ribbons is quite unusual, which would suggest that these are meant to be public graves, tended to by an entire community.[51] The *lekythos* serves as a double reminder of this process, not only does it depict personal offerings, the vase itself would also have been used as one. Therefore, it is important to set down, before moving on to more personal memorialisation, that families would have engaged with the public memorials and this *lekythos* is a prime example of that.

Figure 7.1 White ground *lekythos*, attributed to the Vouni Painter, with a woman and youth standing before two *stelae* and grave. New York (NY), Metropolitan Museum, 35.11.5.

That being said, most of our evidence for private memorialisation for the war dead shows a degree of separation from public monuments. The majority of these are visually striking, often grand pieces of art, whether sculptural or ceramic. However, private memorials did not need to be visually ostentatious or, indeed, very grand. The Chorus in Euripides' *Suppliant Women* paint an emotive and private picture of the home in mourning for a dead son:

> Tears are all I have left; in my house, sad memories of my son are stored; mournful tresses shorn from his head, garlands that he wore, libations for the dead departed, and songs, but not such as golden-haired Apollo welcomes; and when I wake to weep, my tears will ever drench the folds of my robe upon my bosom.[52]

The focus of the pain felt by the Chorus is centred on small items of remembrance that are still in the house – specifically locks of hair and former garlands that he wore. To take them in order, cutting a lock of hair was a standard trope, which features in the story of the *Seven Against Thebes*.[53] This is replicated on a few departure scenes, which lack the necessary iconography to align them with this specific story. On a red-figured *lekythos* in Cleveland, a lone hoplite stands armed, but for his helmet and shield which rest on a stool in front of him.[54] In his hand, he holds his sword and he is in the act of cutting a lock of hair from his head. The isolated figure offers no indication that he is meant to be a hero of some sort, nor that he is a member of a larger group of men preparing for imminent battle. Similarly, a fragment of a kalyx krater shows the arm of a hoplite extending toward the hand of a child, passing over a lock of his hair.[55] The presence of the child holds no parallel, neither iconographically nor literarily, so should be similarly considered as separate from the story of the Seven. This would suggest that the motif transcended its mythical boundaries and may have been part of a pre-battle or pre-departure ritual.

When the shearing of the hair is combined with the garlands, Euripides' Chorus is describing personal, intimate items of remembrance. The scene that is being portrayed is one of sorrow and constant remembrance. As the family walk around the house, they see these items and mourn their lost relative. The lock of hair is symbolic of mourning, being placed on the porch to indicate that there was a death in the house.[56] The garland was so often associated with festivities, joy and success that it would bring sorrow to think of those joyous times coming to an end.[57] The Chorus also mentions songs of mourning, implying that a personal rite of singing could also take place in the home. Of course, being a scene from tragedy, it cannot be assumed that this reflects actual Athenian practices. However, it does offer an insight into the emotionally charged nature of the mourning *oikos*. Similarly, it shows an appreciation for how even the smallest items from the deceased can serve as a memorial within the home.

Unlike the use of pottery, ribbons and personal trinkets, families could also choose to commemorate their dead relative with a *permanent* structure, a cenotaph. The use of private cenotaphs to commemorate the war dead is evident in both historic and archaeological records. Lysias describes a cenotaph erected for Diodotus following his death in battle in 410/9 BC, worth just under 25 minae (2,500 drachmae).[58] Xenophon also suggests that those who died at Phyle, during the civil war of 403 BC, were collected by their families and buried privately.[59] In addition to these sources, there is overwhelming archaeological evidence. Although it is often noted that the establishment of the *demosion sema* brought with it a steep decline in private cenotaphs, Arrington correctly observes that there is still evidence that the practice persisted before the conventional watershed of 394/3 BC, with the erection of the Dexileos monument.[60] One such cenotaph, dating from the third quarter of the fifth century BC, suggests that this form of private memorial was not just for the wealthy. In the Kerameikos, archaeologists uncovered a small pyre with a flat stone at its centre. With it, they found accoutrements pertaining to ritual activity, such as animal bones, olive stones and broken pottery. Rather uniquely, they also found two spearheads and one butt spike, but no human remains. This certainly validates the assessment that this was meant to be a memorial for a member of the war dead.[61] Ursula Knigge's beguiling explanation for the flat stone is that it was a substitute for the missing body, which was interred in the public cemetery.[62] Combining the overt military objects with the missing body and the presence of ritual activity, it would appear that this pyre was an attempt not only to commemorate a dead relative, but to actually reclaim and reproduce the funerary process.

This example is, thus far, unique. The most common forms of cenotaph are the large marble monuments erected by wealthy Athenian families. The earliest known monument, that can be successfully dated, is the famous cenotaph of Dexileos (see Figure 7.2).[63] The inscription beneath the monument informs the reader that he was a young cavalryman who died at Corinth during the archonship of Euboulides, allowing a preliminary dating of 394/3 BC. The relief depicts a valiant Dexileos astride his horse, raising his javelin high above his head. Beneath him, between the legs of his horse, cowers an enemy hoplite, accentuating the power and dominance of Dexileos. The image is accompanied by this inscription: 'Dexileos son of Lysanias of Thorikos. He was born in the archonship of Teisandros; he died in that of Euboulides, at Corinth, one of the five cavalrymen.'[64]

The monument's value for this topic is not its overt projection of aristocratic ideals nor, indeed, the design of the sculpture itself. It is more important to try to understand the purpose behind the family's commission. Why did they feel the need to commission it and why did they choose certain characteristics in their portrayal of Dexileos? In the first instance, the need to commemorate Dexileos may seem misguided. He would have appeared on potentially two casualty lists for that campaign season, both the standard tribal-based lists and a list for the cavalry.[65] Yet, importantly, there is a discrepancy between the cavalry list and Dexileos' own inscription. According to the private cenotaph, Dexileos was one of five cavalrymen to have died outside Corinth, yet the official casualty list names 11 men.[66] There is no logical reason for this to have been a purposeful mistake; it offers no ideological or political merit to downplay the number of dead.[67] This discrepancy would suggest that the original commission was made before the official casualty list was erected. In the year of Dexileos' death, the

Figure 7.2 Relief for the cenotaph of Dexileos. 394/3 BC. Height: 1.75 m. Athens, Kermaeikos Museum: P1130.

Athenian cavalry were present at two major battles, the Nemea and Coronea.[68] The Nemea was fought outside Corinth and this was where Dexileos died. It stands to reason that when the Athenian army returned home from Corinth it brought with it a list of five dead cavalrymen, but potentially more badly wounded casualties. It was at this point, almost immediately after the news of his death was received by the family, that the monument was commissioned. By the end of the year, following the death of more wounded warriors and a second battle in Boeotia the list of names had grown, thus the casualty list reveals more names.

The unique element of this inscription is the inclusion of his year of birth: 414/3 BC, during the archonship of Teisandros. It has been noted that the political significance of this information would suggest that its inclusion was to remove the young Dexileos from any association with the oligarchic revolutions of the final decade of the fifth century BC. As a cavalryman, he would have been associated with a pervading stigma, as an obvious member of the aristocracy and part of an institution that was inherently linked with the oligarchy of the Thirty (404/3 BC).[69] However, this over emphasis on the political landscape has led Josiah Ober to identify the crushed hoplite in the relief as representing Harmodius, one of the famous tyrant slayers.[70] To Ober, it is tempting to read the monument as a 'metaphoric overthrow by the aristocratic cavalryman ... of democracy itself'.[71] This interpretation pushes the imagery too far. He assumes, through the presence of an *oinochoe* in the grave that depicts the Tyrannicides, that the family intentionally imitated the iconography to portray the hoplite as Harmodius, presuming, in turn, that the family designed every single element of the relief. However, when the inscription is considered alongside the relief and the presence of the one vase, among at least five, then a different interpretation is possible.[72]

If we consider the emphasis that the inscription places on dating the life and military activity of the young Dexileos, it is clear that the intention was to separate him from the memory of the oligarchies. The presence of the vase showing an historic overthrow of aristocratic tyranny would support this intention; not only was he not associated with the oligarchies, but he was also to be associated with the heroic Tyrannicides no less.[73] Yet, it would seem that the relief forms a picture of elite, aristocratic power over the hoplite. How can this dichotomy be reconciled? In effect, by unshackling our interpretations from a political rhetoric, for it is the contrasting political messages which cause the cognitive dissonance. If the monument is seen simply for what it is, a family's memorial to a fallen son, then the individual elements begin to make sense.

The Dexileos monument had one important purpose for the family, it allowed them to reinstate his identity. By setting up such a monument they had the opportunity to retake control of his memory. Firstly, they reinstated his patronym, in essence returning him to his family and secondly, they offer him back his personal and social identity by listing his *deme*. Furthermore, rather than allowing Dexileos to be consumed by the collective war dead and condemned to a list that categorises him as purely a cavalryman during a period of history where this reflected well in Athenian society, the family took quick action. They took pride in his military role, epitomising the aristocratic ideology the family held, so the action in the relief embodies that pride. The concern would not have been that he was aristocratic, nor that he fought on horseback – if it was, then the relief fails to address these concerns. The problem was the connotation of his service, so the family chose to limit how his memory could be appropriated. It categorically proves that he was not involved in the oligarchic rule and the *oinochoe* reiterates this statement. There is, therefore, no contrasting political message to the monument, only the multiple messages projected by a family in mourning. He was a brave warrior, who died in battle, from a good and wealthy family, upholding aristocratic ideals of military service, all in the name of democracy.

A family's decision to commemorate their lost loved one in a state of glory or heroic posture is understandable. Its purpose is obvious: to portray their relative in a courageous light and to reclaim their personal glory from the anonymity of the casualty lists and the numerous examples of varying postures and designs support this.[74] Thus, when an example arises which does not conform to this method of commemoration, its motives become even more interesting to understand. One such monument is the grave relief of Demokleides (see Figure 7.3).

The relief portrays the dead Athenian sitting on the deck at the front of a trireme.[75] Behind him lies his *aspis* and Corinthian helmet, identifying him as a hoplite, or possibly *epibate*, rather than a rower. The ship's prow is prominent

Figure 7.3 Grave relief for Demokleides. First quarter of the fourth century B C. Height: 0.7m. Athens, National Archaeological Museum: 752.

and the original colours of the *stele* would have offered a clear definition to the man, the ship and the sea beneath.[76] Unfortunately, the relief has not survived intact, so it cannot be known how big the original commission was. The relief is topped by a small epigram, kept to the right-hand side of the sculpture: 'Demokleides, son of Demetrios'.[77] The relief is unique in a few of its elements: the portrayal of a trireme, the commemoration of naval service and the allusion to the manner of the man's death.[78] However, its most defining feature must surely be its use of space. Demokleides is squashed into the top of the relief, surrounding by space, the most striking element being the original deep blue beneath the ship to depict the sea.[79] His own name similarly sits in a confined space above his head: primarily it identifies the man, but it also accentuates the great void that surrounds him.[80]

The choice of imagery would suggest that Demokleides lost his life at sea, while the presence of the *hopla* behind him would suggest that he died during military service. The emphasis on space, the diminutive depiction of the dead and the melancholic posture he holds, with his head in his hands, all point to a sense of longing and of absence. This has led to speculation by scholars that he may have been missing in action, but this assumes that his family had been informed of this.[81] Furthermore, this evaluation is based on the absence of the usual grandeur and heroism in the portrayal of the deceased. We do not see the confusing dichotomy of aristocratic and democratic idealism like that of Dexileos; this is a poignant monument which highlights how one man had become consumed by something larger than himself. The decision to portray the man sitting on a trireme, rather than dressed in his *hopla*, emphasises the larger collective, the navy. The size of the ship and the bright colours of the sea attract the eye away from the small figure in the corner and the small inscription above; he is meant to be a surprise, someone who is found after the image is first scanned.

The relief does seem to be emphasising loss and absence, but not necessarily a physical loss of the body. As a casualty of naval warfare, Demokleides' role was downplayed in Athenian discourse.[82] Although the majority of its citizens would have experienced naval duty, or perhaps because of it, this vital sacrifice of lives went unnoticed. Unlike Dexileos, Demokleides' epitaph offers no demotic identifier but, as mentioned previously, there is space for it. Rather, the family felt no need to reassert his own military identity because the *deme* did not serve this purpose. Instead, as one of the *epibatai*, his military identity is clearly defined by the presence of the trireme and the *hopla*. Importantly, the family has chosen to show his service, but not define him by it. He sits aboard a ship, at melancholic rest. He is not dressed for war he is not engaged in combat and he is in domestic clothing. This non-military dress, added to the patronymic identifier, suggests that the family were reclaiming their son or husband from his military identity. They did not want his death in service forgotten, nor did they want their son consumed by the vast collective identity of the war dead.

The evidence for private commemoration, in the face of such a grand and public funeral, clearly demonstrates that the families of the deceased were not satisfied with the grand rhetoric. In direct contravention to the calls in the *epitaphioi*, the families did not accept that the memorialisation of their relative was now a public duty. The emphasis on re-individuation – patronyms, demotics, one instance of unorthodox iconography of service – seems to be a direct action against the de-individuation being pronounced on a political level. However, this is to look at mourning and remembrance through a purely political lens. While these private monuments were, in many ways, subversive, they were paramount to a family directive to re-establish that which they had lost.[83] They restored the memory of the person and, in so doing, reclaimed a small part of that which the public funeral had most subverted from the *oikos*, the sole right to remember.

7.2 Experience of the *oikos*

Scholarly interest in the Athenian war dead has traditionally rested on the political ideology that underpins it. However, since the 1970s, a secondary focal point of study has emerged, which has explored the role of women within the funeral process.[84] As has been discussed in section 7.1.1, women held a primary function within the funerary practices of Athens and the state's control of the war dead removed them from these traditional roles. However, this emphasis on women has forced researchers to examine the gender dynamic to the detriment of understanding the experience of the family as a unit. Whether the *kyrios* or the female relatives had official 'control' over the funeral is not wholly relevant to this enquiry, what is more important is that both genders held important roles within the process:[85] funerals brought the household together in a mutually reinforcing ritualistic format.

The task of examining the domestic reception of the war dead is undoubtedly complicated by the fact that the household did not receive the body of their deceased family member. The model of the war dead being cremated, returned to Athens, given the honours of the *patrios nomos* and duly commemorated on the casualty lists, only offers a politically relevant narrative and completely bypasses the families who have lost an integral member of their *oikos*. One reason for the pervasiveness of this model is because of the minimal evidence available to elucidate the family's experience. There are, however, two elements of their experience that can be brought to light. The first is an important addition to the entire process of homecoming discussed: the family had to receive notification that their male relative had been killed in battle. The second offers a different slant on the *epitaphioi* discussed in Chapter 6. The family was present, listening to the speech and was referred to directly during the consolation. This allows an examination of how the higher rhetoric of the war dead envisioned the role of the family and can offer insight into the wider experience of family members who had lost a loved one.

7.2.1 Notification of death

The first direct point of contact that the *oikos* had with the war dead was when they were notified that their family member had died. The process by which the Athenian *oikos* was informed of their loss is not made clear within the sources. Xenophon's account of the aftermath of Leuctra (470 BC) gives a clear indication of the Spartan method of notification.[86] He describes a herald returning with the news and passing it on to the *ephors*, who then sent messages to the households of the deceased to disclose the 400 names.[87] This model offers a clear pattern of communication that would reliably disclose the information to the families.[88] The Athenian equivalent to the Leuctra disaster would be the Sicilian campaign, but Thucydides' account does not offer such a clear-cut system of communication. According to Thucydides, the news of the disaster was brought back to Athens by the survivors.[89] For a long time, the men were not believed, which presumably made it harder for the families to know whether their relatives had died. Although Thucydides is the only direct evidence available to guide this enquiry, his account cannot be transferred for the purpose of reconstructing a standard account for the notification of the family. The disaster in Sicily was a unique situation, the Athenian army and navy had lost control of the Great Harbour where they had beached their ships. Without access to the sea from the harbour, it would not have been an easy task to send a herald ahead of the survivors to inform the Athenians. Furthermore, the available indirect evidence would suggest that the families could receive notification before the army had returned from campaign.

There are passing mentions to the *oikos* receiving notification of death, particularly in the court speeches, but they rarely offer any direct information.[90]

The clearest example comes from a fragment of a court speech of Isaeus, which describes a *trierarchos* during the archonship of Cephisodotus (*c*. 358 BC) who returned home from service to find that his *oikos* had been informed that he had died in a naval battle:[91] 'When I was trierarch in the archonship of Cephisodotus, word was brought to my relatives that I had died in the sea battle.'[92] This return from the dead would have categorised the *trierarchos* as a *deuteropotmos*, 'second fated'.[93] This polluted state had consequences, including the prohibition of entry into sacred spaces, not least the precinct of the Semnai Theai under whose protection those presumed dead would have already been placed.[94] If Hesychius is correct in linking a *deuteropotmos* with a *hysteropotmos* described by Plutarch, then the *trierarchos* needed to have undergone an elaborate set of rituals re-enacting a new birth before he could properly reintegrate himself into society.[95] In terms of the mechanism of communication, this fragment offers no suggestion as to the means by which the family were informed, but the fact that this miscommunication was possible is, in itself, revealing. The fact that false news of a death could precede the man's own return suggests that it did not return with the naval forces.

This specific example was a case of accidental misinformation; a more sinister example can be seen in a suit for impropriety in the role of a guardian, written by the logographer Lysias in the early fourth century BC. A man by the name of Diodotus wrote a will before departing on military service, which named his brother Diogeiton (who was his wife's own father) as guardian of his children should he die in battle.[96] Diodotus did not return from his military service, he died at Ephesus in 409 BC, but this news did not reach his wife or children.[97] Diogeiton is accused of having concealed the death from his daughter and is alleged to have taken control of all of the financial documents that Diodotus had left with his will. Then, after much time had passed (ἐπειδὴ δὲ χρόνῳ), he finally revealed to the family that Diodotus had died and they carried out the customary rites.[98] The remainder of the suit explores how this ruse was exploited by Diogeiton to take control of his brother's wealth and abuse his role of guardian to his own niece and nephews. Whilst this speech is a hostile litigation against the accused, and we must be careful not to take it at face value, it is still an important source of information. For the accusation to have effect in the courtroom it must be built around a plausible reconstruction of events. If those events did not conform to normal Athenian processes, then the accusation becomes an obvious fiction.

Lysias does not reveal how Diogeiton came to hear of his brother's death, but there are still important elements from this case in need of consideration. The wife was not informed of the death first hand; if there was a messenger of any sort sent to the houses, similar to the Spartan example mentioned above, then the messenger spoke to the acting *kyrios*. It seems unlikely that Diogeiton would have acted so precisely and blatantly without knowing for certain that his brother had died. This discounts the possibility that it was a rumour, or second-hand news.[99] It seems equally unlikely that, considering the timeframe involved in the deception, the news of the death emerged with the returning fleet. It is hard to fathom how a family could be kept in the dark for so long if there was a list of war dead; other members from the same *deme* who served with Diodotus would also have been aware of his death.[100] The actions of Diogeiton relied on the local population similarly being unaware of his brother's death, suggesting that the other demesmen who survived the battle at Ephesus had yet to return. The speaker states that once Diogeiton finally revealed Diodotus' fate, his family were able to perform the customary rites. Presuming that these are the same rites described in the *patrios nomos*, then it is possible that Diogeiton held onto the information until the last possible moment, to maximise the time he had to secure his brother's assets. This would suggest that he waited until the forces of Thrasyllus returned and with them people who also knew of Diodotus' death. On balance, it would appear that, in a similar vein to the Spartans, Diogeiton was told via a messenger.

A second, yet no less important element to this narrative is the male control of information. While the news of Diodotus' death appears to have arrived at his *oikos* without any problem, the news was then filtered down to the rest of the family in accordance to the intentions of the *kyrios*. In essence, this means that it would be inaccurate to describe the family or the *oikos* as receiving the news; rather it was the *kyrios* who received it. Even within this extreme example, it is clear how separated the various members of the *oikos* were from the war dead, even those who held him most dear.[101] The speaker's mention of the delay to the customary rites, whatever they may have been, emphasises the interruption in the *oikos*' reception of their dead. It is notable that, later in the same speech, mention is made to a memorial erected for Diodotus separate from the public tomb in the Kerameikos.[102] The reason that the speaker mentions it is because it was a part of Diogeiton's financial manipulation; he took from the estate twice the amount it actually cost and erected a smaller memorial as a result. If this was one of the rites mentioned, then Diogeiton's subterfuge not only delayed the necessary memorialisation of a lost family member, it actually allowed him to take control of it.

There is one final piece of evidence that needs to be briefly considered for this topic. It comes from Diodorus' description of the trial of generals after the victory of Arginusae (406 B C). His account varies greatly from the contemporary source Xenophon; most notably Diodorus claims that the generals were tried, in part, for their failure to collect some of the war dead, whereas Xenophon claims that it was a failure to collect the survivors.[103] In Diodorus' narrative, the surviving families of the uncollected dead entered the Assembly in a clear state of mourning and demanded the generals be punished. Conversely, Xenophon reports that the mourning 'families' in the assembly were no more than paid stooges. The conflating information between the two sources is difficult to resolve, but is fortunately not an impediment to our line of enquiry. What is most pertinent is that both sources describe an expected presence of mourning families, during a scenario in which we are categorically told that not all of the dead/survivors had been identified. This, in itself, raises an interesting question: were Athenian families informed if their relative had not been identified?

There is minimal evidence of personal or domestic ritual practice focussed on those missing in action. In Euripides' *Helen* there is the possibility that the characters describe a relevant ritual.[104] It begins with a sacrifice, which is followed by the procession of an empty bier adorned with offerings; finally, the bier is put on a ship and taken out to sea. However, within the play, this ritual forms part of the plan to allow Helen and Menelaus to escape, so it is impossible to say how much, if any, of this is in any way reflective of Athenian practice. There is evidence of memorials to men lost at sea, but they are in a non-military capacity.[105] There is no direct evidence for the pronouncement of the names of those of the war dead who were unidentified or uncollected. However, the example of Isaeus' unnamed *trierarchos* would suggest that the list of the war dead that first came home did not concern itself with who was securely identified. This would suggest that the lists did not state who was missing in action and who was confirmed to be dead. Furthermore, it would serve no purpose to tell a family that their relative had not been identified because it would not prove to them that their relative was dead. All of the evidence we have for familial action following the notification of death, correct or otherwise, must have been based on the surety of the information provided. If they were informed that their relative was missing, presumed dead, it is unlikely that the families would have taken such quick and extreme measures, such as as dividing the estate, before the army returned home.

As the evidence suggests, the system of notification was not refined. It could lead to false information returning home, as well as the control of that information once it had been delivered. Seemingly, the only time a family could be sure of their relative's death was when the original army or naval force, with which he had departed, had returned to Athens. That being said, a form of notification of death appears to have preceded the return of the army. The case of Diogeiton suggests this notification of death was received by the *kyrios*, or acting *kyrios*, which offers one of two possibilities. The first is that this notification was made in a public space where only the *kyrios* was present. This is unlikely because it would entail a public pronouncement of death, which would have made Diogeiton's subsequent machinations very difficult. The second, and more probable, is that some form of messenger was sent to inform the families and that this messenger was met by the (acting) *kyrios* of the house.[106]

7.2.2 Funeral oration

Following from the notification of death, the next direct form of contact that the family had with the war dead was during the *patrios nomos*. Five of the six extant *epitaphioi* include extended sections of exhortation and consolation directly aimed at and addressed to the families of the dead. Within these sections it is possible to read the public rhetoric that the families would have been surrounded by, during their state of mourning. From these five speeches it possible to highlight certain themes that emerge, which suggests that these were the forms of advice and expectations given to the families.

Perhaps the most striking idea declared in the *epitaphioi* was the notion that the family of the war dead were to be envied. Thucydides' Pericles states this bluntly, with no acknowledgement of the grief felt by the family.[107] Similarly, Hyperides lists all of the reasons he considers the family to be fortunate that their relative has died so that, by the time of the consolation, his recognition of grief seems rather hollow.[108] Both Lysias and Demosthenes offer a more sympathetic understanding of what was being stated, while simultaneously maintaining the standard trope.[109] Plato's speech does not allow for such a direct observation to be made by the speaker because, for much of the section, he claims to be relaying the words of the war dead. However, he does have his speaker question the assumption that the loss of a child in war was actually a misfortune to bear.[110]

The emphasis in the *epitaphioi* is not on the family as a unit, but rather its constituent parts. While the speakers often state their envy or sympathy for the family, they direct different reasons to the different elements. Hence, according to this rhetoric, the family can be split into three distinct parts: the parents of the deceased, the children of the deceased and the widows of the deceased.[111] According to Plato's breakdown of the genre, the consolation was particularly aimed at the parents of the deceased. Remember that, up until this point in the funeral, the parents had been unable to see or touch the body of their son, had been made to participate in public funerary rites alongside hundreds of other parents and had stood through a speech which had attempted to remove both the individuality of their child and their familial duty to be responsible for remembrance. There is a general understanding that the parents would feel the loss of a son acutely. In Plato, the parents are in need of healing, for Lysias they are, in particular, worthy of pity; whereas Pericles is aware that that it will be hard to persuade the parents that they are, in fact, fortunate to have lost their child.[112] That being said, most of the speeches call upon the parents to move beyond their grief in some way. Thucydides and Plato are the most hardline here. Pericles calls upon the parents, who can, to go and produce more children so that they too may fight and die for Athens, whereas Plato's use of the hypothetical words of the dead allows him to emphasise the emotional strain put on the parents during the funeral. The parents are called upon by their dead sons to curb the excess of their grief.[113] The fathers, in particular, are called to show courage in their grief, just as their sons showed courage in their own death. Yet, this call for courage is accompanied by the threat that any failure to show courage would ultimately call into question the father's legitimacy in calling the dead man his son.[114] Hyperides accepts the limits of his influence on the grieving, but still calls for courage and for them to control their grief.[115]

Of course, the source of their grief was not simply that their son had died, but had further implications.[116] Both Lysias and Plato highlight the impact that losing a son could have on the parents. To have reared a son old enough to die in war, they themselves must have been elderly; a stage in life which brought with it physical weakness, isolation and friendlessness and an inability to procure a new income.[117] Their protection and guardianship in old age had been their son's responsibility, but the parents are assured that the city will step in and look after them.[118] Lysias' description of this assistance is vague and suggests a form of help that is more symbolic than material. However, Plato mentions a law which states that the parents of the dead were to be looked after (ἐπιμελεῖται), and responsibility for this was held by the highest city official.[119] Again, he is not clear in his details, and this support is not mentioned in any other classical source; however, it is possible that it was an extension of the state sponsorship offered to the war orphans.[120]

These war orphans were the focus of a lot of attention within the *epitaphioi*. Unlike the parents of the deceased, the children were not assumed to be in any great state of mourning. Instead, according to Lysias, they were worthy of envy, as they did not know their fathers well enough to mourn them.[121] Not only had their fathers died, proving that the children were of courageous stock but, as orphans, they would also be well provided for by the state.[122] The precise mechanism is, once again, unclear. Plato describes this as the responsibility of the 'highest authority in the city', which could be considered one of the archons. However, Xenophon makes a tangential reference in his writings to a board of guardians for orphans (ὀρφανοφύλακας) and it may be that this board was specifically responsible for the war orphans.[123] While this is not certain, what is clear is that the war orphans would not have undergone any scrutiny to ascertain the legitimacy of their Athenian citizenship, as evidenced by the fact that adopted and illegitimate children could receive the subsidy.[124] That being said, Ronald Stroud is surely correct in his presumption that orphans would have had prove that their father had, indeed, died in war.[125]

The endowment did not amount to very much financially, most likely equalling one obol a day, the same amount given for an incapacity pension.[126] It is not known how this was delivered, but Loraux's suggestion that it was paid in kind by way of food in the *prytaneion* seems plausible in the absence of any evidence.[127] Once the male orphans reached their majority they were awarded a full *hopla* and then called on to exercise authority over their parental home.[128] By contrast, female orphans do not receive very much attention. It is not clear whether the subsidies were paid for both male and female orphans; females would certainly not have received a *hopla* from the state. There is a highly fragmentary decree of Theozotides, combined with the fragmentary legal case against him, authored by Lysias, which may suggest that both genders would normally have received a subsidy.[129] However, Lysias' attack of this proposed decree was on behalf of bastards and adopted children, suggesting that it was not the gender that was important in the decree, but that legitimacy was a prerequisite.[130] Thucydides does not address female war orphans at all, but does refer to the children (παισὶ). In the important section the 'children' and the brothers of the deceased are both addressed with the same advice, suggesting that his words were aimed solely at male members of the family.[131] Similarly, Hyperides makes no mention of female orphans when he claims that a sister of the deceased will benefit through law to make marriages worthy of them.[132]

To become a (male) war orphan, according to the rhetoric of the *epitaphioi*, was to win a prize (στέφανον, ἆθλον). The death of the father was not simply a manifestation of his own excellence as a citizen, but ultimately as a father. As Plato declares, the death of the father was a noble treasure, as the honours bestowed upon him reflect well upon his descendants.[133] For Demosthenes, the only orator to acknowledge any sadness for the children, the sorrow was assuaged by the inheritance of their father's glory.[134] Thus, within the framework of the *epitaphioi*, the best father was a dead father, and the best child was a war orphan. Yet, the *epitaphioi* placed the most amount of pressure on the youngest generations. Pericles is characteristically blunt on the matter, proclaiming that he foresees a great struggle for the children and brothers of the deceased. For the dead would always be praised and, until the young men in the audience join the fathers or brothers as one of the war dead, they will always be inferior.[135] The orphans, in particular, are said to be honoured, but they hold no right to claim that honour as it was not theirs to begin with.[136] In order to warrant the honour given to them, they must first emulate the deeds of their war dead.[137]

The final category of family which is explicitly mentioned and addressed in the *epitaphioi* is that of the wives, who had become war widows. The war widows receive a mention in three of the surviving speeches, one of which addresses them directly for part of the consolation.[138] This address comes from one of the most notorious sections of Pericles' speech, in which he finishes addressing the issues faced by the sons and brothers of the dead, and moves onto the subject of 'female excellence'. He qualifies this statement, making it clear that the notion of female excellence was not being directed at all of the women in the crowd, but rather the new widows (νῦν ἐν χηρείᾳ) in particular. This excellence stemmed from one trait, being spoken about least among the men; unlike the parents whose emotions were mostly addressed, or the male relative whose need for future valour was defined, the comment for the widows was about their present behaviour.[139] It is difficult to ascertain exactly what this advice is suggesting: should the widows be silent and invisible, should they be quiet in all but their laments, are men speaking about their availability or their poor behaviour?[140] All that is important here is that Thucydides only mentions them to discuss their behaviour, there is no acknowledgement of grief or of a sense of pride for being married to such a valorous man. The reason may be, if we take this sentiment in a similar vein to Thucydides' statement to the mothers, that they had yet to sacrifice a son of their own. Their only duty was to marry another Athenian.

Lysias offers a more emotive response to the war widows. He acknowledges their loss alongside that of the orphans, parents and siblings of the deceased.[141] He also makes reference to the people of Athens offering support to the widows.[142] What is interesting about this statement is that there is no evidence that war widows received any official support from the state. While there is external evidence for the support of both the parents and the orphans, there is no mention, or even the hint of a mention, of an infrastructural basis with which war widows were given any help. It seems likely here that Lysias' words are meant to invoke comfort and an offer of social support. Yet the wording in the subordinate clause is inconclusive; the people of Athens were urged to help the widows 'as [the war dead] did when they were alive'.[143] Notably, the only other *epitaphios* to make a similar claim is Plato's and the suggestion is that the parents of the dead should look after the widows, not the city.[144] Interestingly, the idea of looking after the widows comes from the words of the dead, but when the orator speaks with his own voice, they receive no further mention. This is most starkly apparent because the orator almost purposefully responds to the dead's final points. The city will look after the parents, the city will look after the children; but there is no mention of the widows and their absence is conspicuous. This pervades the two final *epitaphioi*, that of Demosthenes and Hyperides, which fail to mention the widows in any capacity. The widows are again overlooked throughout Plato's own explanation of the exhortation and consolation.[145] Indeed, taking Plato's *epitaphios* as a parody of the genre in many respects, perhaps it is most revealing that the orator ignores them, but the war dead do not. The concerns of the dead do not entirely match the concerns of the city.

For the family of the war dead, the funeral was a grand occasion which brought with it mixed emotions of grief, closure and comfort. Yet the underlying message from the *epitaphioi* was not so much one of solace but of pragmatism. The family was told to restrict their grief, to control their emotions and to behave in a particular manner. The aim of the exhortation was to influence the next generation of war dead. The sons and brothers were told in no uncertain terms that they would be inferior unless they emulated the dead. In consolation, the parents were urged to bring an end to their natural state of grief, to produce new children if possible, or instead to take comfort in the support that the city would now offer them. As for the widows, when they are briefly addressed it is to call on them to act in an appropriate manner befitting their gender. Ultimately, the aim of the *epitaphioi* was to assert control over the families: control over the behaviour of women, control over the aspirations of the next generation, control over the emotions and grief of the parents and control over the fate of the war orphans.

7.3 Return of the war dead

The familial reception of the war dead ran parallel to their military homecoming. It is not, however, possible to describe a domestic homecoming for the dead. For the families, the first stage of their reception occurred at the notification of death. The process is elusive, yet there seems to have been a system of notification prior to the army returning home. Once this news was received, the families would decide on how to begin a process of memorialisation. For the wealthier families this may have consisted of a formal commission for a cenotaph, for the poorer or less ostentatious families this would have consisted of choosing smaller items like *lekythoi*. However, this attempt to claim the memory of the deceased was not in keeping with the rhetoric of the city. The physical and ritual treatment of the Athenian war dead was primarily a continuation of action based on their association with military service. As has been argued above, the family would not receive their dead relative back from the city in either physical or metaphysical form. In both the *patrios nomos* and the culture of public commemoration, the war dead were stripped of all personal identifiers and turned into a collective group for the city to mourn as a whole. Private memorials went a long way to reclaim the right to memory. The presence of patronyms and demotics on *stelae* show a purposeful illumination of the identities of the dead warriors. Similarly, the choice of iconography allowed the families of Dexileos and Demokleides to choose how their sons would be remembered. Both images are a clear indication of control by the family, control of both public and private memory and association.

Following the notification of death, the family would not have direct contact with the dead until the start of the funeral. Following a semi-private visit to the coffin containing the remains of their tribe's dead, they would re-join the collective and commemorate the war dead two days later. As members of the crowd, they heard how the deceased had ceased to be theirs, how his personality and life history had been deleted by his sacrifice. Only then did the city's chosen representative finally address the family. In their state of sorrow and mourning they were offered pity, but also envy. They were urged to act and perform in the city's interest, whether that be to have more children to sacrifice, to emulate the great men who had died, or simply, in the case of the widows, to keep quiet. The entire rhetoric heard by the family was one of control: of their emotions; of their actions; indeed, of their memories. And yet, as has been mentioned previously, there is no direct evidence to suggest that the families did not conform to this way of thinking. Indirect evidence can be found in the commemoration habit that comes to the fore toward the end of the Peloponnesian War, but seems to have begun decades before this. The private grave monuments were not a site of subversive thought, or even behaviour, but rather an attempt by the family to keep a hold of their dead relative. As Arrington neatly describes, these private memorials created 'alternative sites and iconographies of commemoration that encoded and consolidated memories of the individual dead for the family'.[146] They were a supplement to the public rhetoric, but they were also the families' way of making sure their relatives came home. As the city did not intend to return the war dead, their families chose to take them instead.

8

Conclusion

As the introduction to this study set out, the primary aim of this book was to establish the ritualistic and logistical framework that enabled an Athenian hoplite to transition from his domestic environment to his military service and back again. This was achieved through an analysis of three distinct periods of transition: the departure of the hoplite, the homecoming of a living hoplite and the homecoming of the war dead. To further understand these three transitionary periods, they were each bisected into domestic and military designations. Not only did this allow for a wider understanding of the transitions undergone by the hoplite, but it also allowed for the role of the individual to be tracked through each transition.

Chapters 2 and 3 established the process by which an Athenian hoplite would depart for war. Having established the presence of a distinct domestic departure it is apparent that this was not entirely dictated by a public ideology of civic duty and service. The emphasis within the evidence is of families and individuals actively participating in the rituals, consisting of libations, sacrifices and possible omen readings. Once he left the home, the hoplite joined a wide-scale system of recruitment via the implementation of the *katalogoi* or a *pandemei*. It has been argued that the hoplite initially joined with his demesmen in a micro-muster, together they made collective vows to specific gods before heading toward their allocated mustering point. Once there, the *strategos* and the mantis would lead the relevant departure rituals in front of the army. These rituals were ostensibly identical to those in the domestic ritual, included offerings of libations, sacrifices and the reading of omens, but in this instance the *strategos* and mantis would perform them on everyone's behalf. The hoplite would partake in a communal prayer and song and then the army would begin its departure from the city.

Chapters 4 and 5 reversed the transitional process, examining the homecoming of a living hoplite. Identifying a military homecoming was not easy, but hopefully it has been shown that such a formal transition did occur. Once an army arrived at the Piraeus, it has been demonstrated that they would march in a non-military fashion, without any air of pomp or victory, and enter a given temple for the *strategos* to perform a sacrifice. Only then was the army disbanded, and a hoplite was free to return home. Following this disbanding, the military identity of the army was often cemented in perpetuity by an act of collective dedication. Contrary to the military homecoming, the evidence for a domestic homecoming of the hoplite was problematic, but this chapter has proposed a new way to identify homecoming motifs on red-figure vases, through the analysis of parallel familial scenes that depict warrior departures/homecomings. The evidence shows distinct variations between households so the proposed template of homecoming here should be considered as part of range of rituals used during a hoplite's homecoming, not a precise list of rituals that occurred every time.

Having analysed the homecoming of the living, it was deemed important to establish the homecoming of the dead in Chapters 6 and 7. Focus was initially placed on the logistical considerations inherent in the Athenian commitment to repatriate their war dead. Through an analysis of the logistics involved, many questions have been raised which are, as yet, unanswerable. The evaluation of the commitment involved, combined with some conflicting evidence in the ancient accounts, has led to the supposition that the war dead may not have been returned home on every single occasion and not always in their entirety. Once the cremains had been tracked back to Athens, it was deemed pertinent to place them into the context of the public funeral. As part of the public funeral, the war dead were kept within the rubric of their military service and were transitioned into a new homogenous state as a heroic collective. At the end of the funeral, the homecoming of the war dead seemingly comes to an end, but such an analysis would ignore the families of the dead and their experience of this homecoming. Although his physical and metaphysical transition had come to an end at the hands and words of the *polis*, following the funeral, there was still an issue surrounding the memory of the dead. It has been shown that the polis removed all personal identity from the war dead and subsequently denied the family the right to remember them for the people that they were. Nevertheless, evidence for familial remembrance and commemorations demonstrates that the political rhetoric did not always run parallel with domestic actions. Thus, the final transition of the war dead was one of memory, with some families reinstating the identity of the war dead in their private commemorations. In essence, they reclaimed their husband or son from the *polis* and, in so doing, enabled his final transition from military service.

During the analysis of these three transitions, an important, overarching theme has been the role of individuation and de-individuation during military service. Throughout all three transitions it has been possible to highlight the direct presence of an individual identity for the hoplite and for that individual identity being removed from him as a part of his military service. This suggests that there was no seamless, experiential continuity between the military and domestic environments. This is further supported by a secondary theme that has been evidence through all three transitions: the contrasting views on military service between the domestic and military spheres.

Having now established a framework for domestic and military transitions undergone by the Athenian hoplite, it is possible for scholars to explore the process of military homecoming and, indeed, re-address the ancient PTSD debate from a firmer methodological foundation. This work has demonstrated that there was a distinct transition, both physically and ritually, between the *oikos* and military service. It has also been shown that the ideologies surrounding military service could permeate into, yet also be at odds with, domestic ideology. By themselves, these two observations, do not prove that the Athenians would have struggled to transition back to civilian life. What they do show is that these transitions into and out of service cannot be considered seamless. It is clear just how complex and nuanced the military to domestic transitions could be and, in turn, this has raised the important issue of variation. Yet, what has been clear throughout is the potential tension between domestic and military ideology and rhetoric. The PTSD debate has attracted some greatly scholarly minds from all sides. Hopefully the debate can now move forward on a stable, culturally and diachronically sensitive basis.

Notes

Chapter 1

1 I have previously published parts of this section on the PTSD debate; see Rees, 'We Need to Talk About Epizelus: "PTSD" and the Ancient World', *Medical Humanities* 46, (2020): 46–47.

2 Jonathan Shay, *Achilles in Vietnam: Combat Trauma and the Undoing of Character* (New York: Atheneum, 1994); Jonathan Shay, *Odysseus in America: Combat Trauma and the Trials of Homecoming* (New York: Scribner, 2002); Lawrence Tritle, *Melos to My Lai: War and Survival* (London: Routledge, 2000); *A New History of the Peloponnesian War* (Oxford: Wiley-Blackwell, 2010); Richard Gabriel, *The Madness of Alexander the Great: And the Myth of Military Genius* (Barnsley: Pen & Sword, 2015), 79–82.

3 Aislinn Melchior, 'Caesar in Vietnam: Did Roman Soldiers Suffer from Post-Traumatic Stress Disorder?' *Greece & Rome* 58, 2 (2011), 209–23; Jason Crowley, 'Beyond the Universal Soldier: Combat Trauma in Classical Antiquity' in *Combat Trauma and the Ancient Greeks*, ed. Peter Meineck and David Konstan (New York: Palgrave Macmillan, 2014), 105–30.

4 Shay, *Achilles in Vietnam*; *Odysseus in America*.

5 Shay, *Odysseus in America*, 141.

6 Shay, *Odysseus in America*, 142.

7 John Keegan, *The Face of Battle: A Study of Agincourt, Waterloo and the Somme* (Guildford, Book Club Associates, 1978).

8 Victor Davis Hanson (ed.) *Hoplites: The Classical Greek Battle Experience* (London: Routledge. 1991), v, dedicates an important edited volume on the experience of being a hoplite to Keegan. The influence of Keegan is clear in Hanson's work, due in no small part to his role as a long standing mentor: Victor Davis Hanson, *The Western Way of War: Infantry Battle in Classical Greece*. Berkeley: University of California Press, 1994/2009), ix–xiv.

9 Tritle, *Melos to My Lai*.

10 Tritle also identifies fictional cases from Greek drama such as Ajax: *Melos to My Lai*, 185–88.

11 Tritle, *Melos to My Lai*, 63–5; 'Men at War', in *The Oxford Handbook of Warfare in the Classical World*, ed. Brian Campbell and Lawrence Tritle (Oxford: Oxford University Press, 2013), 279.

12 Hdt. 6.117.2-3

13 Tritle, *Melos to My Lai*, 8 n 16.

14 Lawrence Tritle, 'Gorgias, the Encomium of Helen, and the Trauma of War' *Clio's Psyche* 16, 2 (2009), 195–9; (2010: 158–59)

15 Gorg. *Hel.* 16–17

16 Tritle, *Melos to My Lai*, 60–1.

17 Melchior, 'Caesar in Vietnam', 223.

18 Medea: Brian Lush, 'Combat Trauma and Psychological Injury in Euripides' Medea', *Helios* 41, 1 (2014): 25–57. Heracles: David Konstan, 'Introduction. Combat Trauma: The Missing Diagnosis in Ancient Greece?' in *Combat Trauma and the Ancient Greeks*, ed. Peter Meineck and David Konstan (New York: Palgrave Macmillan, 2014), 1–14. Ajax: Tritle, *Melos to My Lai*, 74; see also the *Theatre of War Project* which uses Sophocles' *Ajax*, among other plays, in its readings for modern veteran communities. Philoctetes: Nancy Sherman, '"He Gave me His Hand but Took My Bow": Trust and Trustworthiness in the *Philoctetes* and Our Wars' in *Combat Trauma and the Ancient Greeks*, ed. Peter Meineck and David Konstan (New York: Palgrave Macmillan, 2014), 207–24. For an overview of combat trauma in Greek drama see Peter Meineck, 'Combat Trauma and the Tragic Stage: Ancient Culture and Modern Catharsis?' in *Our Ancient Wars: Rethinking War Through the Classics*, ed. Victor Caston and Silke-Maria Weineck (Ann Arbour: University of Michigan Press, 2016), 184–207.

19 Meineck, 'Combat Trauma', although he makes no reference to Jonathan Shay's short article 'The Birth of Tragedy – Out of the Needs of Democracy', *Didaskalia* 2, 2 (1995). Available at: www.didaskalia.net/issues/vol2no2/shay.html (last accessed 4 February 2018) which explores a similar theme.

20 John Hyland, 'The Desertion of Nicarchus the Arcadian in Xenophon's "Anabasis"', *Phoenix* 64, 3/4 (2010): 248.

21 Sara Monoson, 'Socrates in Combat: Trauma and Resilience in Plato's Political Theory', in *Combat Trauma and the Ancient Greeks*, ed. Peter Meineck and David Konstan (New York: Palgrave Macmillan, 2014), 131–62; 'Socrates' Military Service', in *Our Ancient Wars: Rethinking War Through the Classics*, ed. Victor Caston and Silke-Maria Weineck (Ann Arbour: University of Michigan Press, 2016), 115.

22 François Retief and Louise Cilliers, 'The Army of Alexander the Great and Combat Stress Syndrome (326 BC)', *Acta Theologica* 26, 2 (2005): 29–43; Gabriel, *Madness of Alexander the Great*, 79–82.

23 Assyrians: Walid Khalid Abdul-Hamid and Jamie Hacker Hughes 'Nothing New under the Sun: Post-Traumatic Stress Disorders in the Ancient World', *Early Science and Medicine* 19, (2014): 1–9. Romans: Valentine Belfiglio, 'Post Traumatic Stress Disorder and Acute Stress Disorder in the Army', *Balkan Military Medical Review* 18, 3 (2015): 65–71.

24 Dean Worcester, 'Shell-Shock in the Battle of Marathon', *Science* 50, 1288 (1919): 230.

25 The earliest textbook Epizelus appears in is Norman Fenton, *Shell Shock and its Aftermath* (St Louis: C.V. Mosby Company, 1926), 18. For a full overview of the

legacy of Epizelus' story in the medical and psychological disciplines, see Owen
Rees, 'We Need to Talk About Epizelus: "PTSD" and the Ancient World', *Medical
Humanities* 46, (2020): 46–54.

26 Helen King, 'Recovering Hysteria from History: Herodotus and "The First Case of
Shell Shock"', in *Contemporary Approaches to the Science of Hysteria: Clinical and
Theoretical Perspectives*, ed. Peter Halligan, Christopher Bass and John Marshall
(Oxford: Oxford University Press, 2001), 39.

27 James Boehnlein and John Kinzie, 'Commentary. DSM Diagnosis of Posttraumatic
Stress Disorder and Cultural Sensitivity: A Response', *Journal of Nervous and Mental
Disease* 180, 9 (1992): 598; Donna Trembinski, 'Comparing Premodern Melancholy/
Mania and Modern Trauma: An Argument in Favor of Historical Experiences of
Trauma', *History of Psychology* 14, 1 (2011): 80–99; Fernando Forcen and Arlenne
Shapov, 'PTSD: A Recent Name for an Ancient Syndrome', *The American Journal of
Psychiatry Residents' Journal* 7, 2 (2012): 4–6.

28 Abdul-Hamid and Hughes, 'Nothing New under the Sun', 9; Boehnlein and Kenzie,
'Commentary', 598.

29 Hitesh Sheth, Zindadil Gandhi, and GK Vankar, 'Anxiety Disorders in Ancient Indian
Literature', *Indian Journal of Psychiatry* 52, 3 (2010): 289–91.

30 Aiton Birnbaum, 'Collective Trauma and Post-traumatic Symptoms in the Biblical
Narrative of Ancient Israel', *Mental Health, Religion and Culture* 11, 5 (2008):
543–45; Philippe Birmes et al, 'Psychotraumatology in Antiquity', *Stress & Health* 26,
1 (2009): 21–31; Yulia Ustinova and Etzel Cardeña, 'Combat Stress Disorders and
Their Treatment in Ancient Greece', *Psychological Trauma: Theory, Research, Practice,
and Policy* 6, 6 (2014): 746; Karen O'Donnell, 'Help for Heroes: PTSD, Warrior
Recovery, and the Liturgy', *Journal of Religion and Health* 54, (2015): 2389–397;
Miriam Reisman, 'PTSD Treatment for Veterans: What's Working, What's New, and
What's Next', *Pharmacy and Therapeutics* 41, 10 (2016): 632–34.

31 Charles Figley, *Encyclopedia of Trauma* (Los Angeles: Sage Publications, 2012), 445.

32 For instance, Trembinski, 'Comparing Premodern Melancholy', 93, notes that past
melancholic mania cannot be linked to modern trauma in any real way, but then
concludes that a lack of modern terminology does not preclude pre-modern people
from suffering from it. The clearest instance of criticism from a paper designed for
the psychological and/or scientific community comes from Gregory Day et al, 'A
Case Study in the History of Neurology', *The Neurohospitalist* 6, 4 (2016): 182, the
authors question the usefulness of attempted retrospective diagnoses which, they
note, has become popular. Included in their list of examples is the diagnosis of
trauma in the ancient world.

33 Peter Toohey, '(Review) Achilles in Vietnam. Combat Trauma and the Undoing of
Character by Jonathan Shay', *Phoenix* 50, 2 (1996): 162–3; Alan Farrell, 'A Purple
Heart and a Dime . . .' *Arion* 12, 1 (2004): 129–38. For non-analytical criticism, see
also Jean-Christophe Couvenhes, 'De Disciplina Graecorum: Les Relations de

Violence entre les Chefs Militaire Grecs et leur Soldats', in *La Violence dans les Mondes Grec et Romain*, ed. Jean-Marie Bertrand (Paris: Publications de la Sorbonne, 2005), 431, with a response from Lawrence Tritle, '"Ravished Minds" in the Ancient World', in *Combat Trauma and the Ancient Greeks*, ed. Peter Meineck and David Konstan (New York: Palgrave Macmillan, 2014), 93.

34 Allan Young, *The Harmony of Illusions: Inventing Post-Traumatic Stress Disorder* (Princeton: Princeton University Press, 1995), 4–9, with criticism from Tritle '"Ravished Minds" in the Ancient World', 88.

35 Melchior, 'Caesar in Vietnam', 211.

36 Melchior, 'Caesar in Vietnam', 222–3.

37 Korneel van Lommel, 'The Recognition of Roman Soldiers' Mental Impairment', *Acta Classica* LVI, (2013): 157.

38 Crowley, 'Beyond the Universal Soldier'.

39 Crowley, 'Beyond the Universal Soldier', 106.

40 Crowley, 'Beyond the Universal Soldier', 117.

41 Crowley, 'Beyond the Universal Soldier', 108–9, 112–13, 115.

42 Crowley, 'Beyond the Universal Soldier', 116.

43 See, e.g., Lys. 10.9, 21, 23, 28

44 Jason Crowley, *Psychology of a Hoplite: The Culture of Combat in Classical Athens* (Cambridge: Cambridge University Press, 2012).

45 Thuc. 1.105.5–6

46 There is a modern parallel here with veterans of the Vietnam War returning home to abuse from veterans of the Second World War. This abuse was so detrimental to the well-being of Vietnam veterans, it became the basis for Tracy Karner's newly coined term 'toxic masculinity': 'Fathers, Sons, and Vietnam: Masculinity and Betrayal in the Life Narratives of Vietnam Veterans with Post Traumatic Stress Disorder', *American Studies* 37, 1 (1996): 63–94.

47 David Johnson et al, 'The Impact of the Homecoming Reception on the Development of Posttraumatic Stress Disorder: The West Haven Homecoming Stress Scale (WHHSS)', *Journal of Traumatic Stress* 10, 2 (1997): 274. See also Zahava Solomon et al, 'The Implications of Life Events and Social Integration in the Course of Combat-related Post-traumatic Stress Disorder', *Social Psychiatry and Psychiatry Epidemiology* 24, (1989): 46; Alan Fontana and Robert Rosenheck, 'Posttraumatic Stress Disorder among Vietnam Theater Veterans: A Causal Model of Etiology in a Community Sample', *The Journal of Nervous and Mental Disease* 182, 12 (1994): 682; Emily Ozer et al., 'Predictors of Posttraumatic Stress Disorder and Symptoms in Adults: A Meta-Analysis', *Psychological Bulletin Copyright* 129, 1 (2003): 61–3.

48 Maria Steenkamp et al., 'Predictors of PTSD 40 years After Combat: Findings from the National Vietnam Veterans Longitudinal Study', *Depression and Anxiety* 34, (2017): 711–22.

49 Steenkamp, "Predictors of PTSD", 718.
50 Israeli: Solomon, 'The Implications of Life Events', 46. Portuguese: Paulo Correia Ferrajão and Rui Aragão Oliveira, 'Portuguese War Veterans: Moral Injury and Factors Related to Recovery from PTSD', *Qualitative Health Research* 26, 2 (2016): 5, 6. British Reservists: Samuel Harvey et al, 'Coming Home: Social Functioning and the Mental Health of UK Reservists on Return from Deployment to Iraq or Afghanistan', *Annals of Epidemiology* 21, (2011): 670. British forces (including reservists): Elizabeth Banwell et al, 'What Happens to the Mental Health of UK Service Personnel after They Return Home from Afghanistan?', *Journal of the Royal Army Medical Corps* 162, (2015): 4.
51 For a specific overview see Harvey, 'Coming Home', 668–70.
52 Terence Keane et al, 'Social Support in Vietnam Veterans with Posttraumatic Stress Disorder: A Comparative Analysis', *Journal of Consulting and Clinical Psychology* 53, 1 (1985): 100.
53 Łukasz Kamieński, 'Helping the Postmodern Ajax: Is Managing Combat Trauma through Pharmacology a Faustian Bargain?', *Armed Forces & Society* 39, 3 (2012): 395–414. See also O'Donnell, 'Help for Heroes'.
54 He specifically references Victor Davis Hanson, *The Wars of the Ancient Greeks: And Their Invention of Western Military Culture* (London: Cassell, 1999) while stating this, revealing the influence that ancient scholarship has had on his thesis.
55 Kamieński, 'Helping the Postmodern Ajax', 408.
56 O'Donnell, 'Help for Heroes'.
57 O'Donnell, 'Help for Heroes', 2392.
58 O'Donnell, 'Help for Heroes', 2392.
59 Crowley, *Psychology of a Hoplite*, 100–4.
60 Crowley, *Psychology of a Hoplite,* 104.
61 On the importance of reintegration see Shannon Currie et al., 'Bringing the Troops Back Home: Modelling the Postdeployment Reintegration Experience', *Journal of Occupational Health Psychology* 16, 1 (2011): 38–47.
62 Jean-Pierre Vernant, 'Hestia – Hermes: The Religious Expression of Space and Movement Among the Greeks', *Social Science Information* 8, 4 (1969): 133; Robin Osborne, 'The Erection and Mutilation of the Hermai', *Proceedings of the Cambridge Philological Society* 25, (1985): 53; Josephine Quinn 'Herms, Kouroi and the Political Anatomy of Athens', *Greece & Rome* 54, 1 (2007): 91.
63 Thuc. 6.27.1
64 Michael Jameson, 'Domestic Space and the Greek City', in *The Greek City: From Homer to Alexander*, ed. Oswyn Murray and Simon Price (Oxford: Oxford University Press, 1990b), 194; Quinn, 'Herms', 91. *Contra* John Winkler, 'Phallos Politikos: Representing the Body Politic in Athens', *Differences* 2, 1 (1990): 36 and n 9. For the possibility that many herms were made from wood, which would be a

more affordable option, see Jameson, 'Domestic Space and the Greek City', 194 n 40
who cites a red-figure cup attributed to Epiktetos which shows a young boy holding
and carving a herm statue. There is evidence that other deities were chosen as the
boundary marker, eg Apollo Agyieus (Ar. *Thesm.* 489) and Hekate (Ar. *Lys.* 64).
Christopher Faraone, *Talismans and Trojan Horses: Guardian Statues in Ancient
Greek Myth and Ritual* (Oxford: Oxford University Press, 1992), 8-9; Quinn, 'Herms',
91 n 25.

65 Michael Jameson, 'Domestic Space in the Greek City-State', in *Domestic Architecture
and the Use of Space: An Interdisciplinary Cross-Cultural Study*, ed. Susan Kent
(Cambridge: Cambridge University Press, 1990a), 106. For the lack of hearths in
excavated houses see also Vanna Svoronos-Hadjimichalis, 'L'Evacuation de la fumée
dans les maisons grecques des Ve et IVe siècles', *Bulletin de Correspondance
Hellénique* 80, 1 (1956): 483–506; Lin Foxhall, 'House Clearance: Unpacking the
'Kitchen' in Classical Greece', *British School at Athens Studies*, 15, *Building
Communities: House, Settlement and Society in the Aegean and Beyond*, (2007):
233–4. cf. Wolfram Hoepfner and Ernst-Ludwig Schwandner, *Haus und Stadt im
klassischen Griechenland. Wohnen in der klassischen Polis I.* (Munich: Deutscher
Kunstverlag, 1994), 146–50.

66 Xen. *Const Lac.* 9.5

67 Plut. *Ages.* 30.2–4

68 The literary device is apparent because the punishment obviously contradicts the
lifestyle that Xenophon himself depicts of the Spartan adult male: living communally
with his messmates (Xen. *Lac.* 5.2), not marrying until the Spartiate was in his
physical prime (different sources range this from 28–35: Pl. *Rep.*460e; Arist. *Rh.* II
1390b 9–11) and having to sneak home in the night if he wanted to be with his wife
(Xen. *Lac.* 1.5–7). In this context, Xenophon may be merely reflecting a personal or
more general Athenian concern and fear for such a punishment: Nigel Kennell,
Spartans: A New History (Chichester: Wiley-Blackwell, 2010), 158.

69 Soph. *Aj.*493–5. The fact that Tecmessa is not actually Ajax's wife is not relevant
because it is still their relationship within the *oikos* that she is calling upon to
influence his decision. For the calling upon Zeus of the hearth see also Hom.
*Od.*14.158–59; Hdt.1.44. The calling of Zeus, as opposed to Hestia herself, is a
reminder that the hearth meant more to the Greeks than simply the deified version
of the hearth.

70 Aesch. *Ag.*836–9, 966–70; 1055–60. See also Eur. *Hel.*234-5 when Helen describes
Paris coming to her hearth (τὰν ἐμὰν ἐφ᾽ ἑστίαν) to take her as his bride.

71 Soph. *Elek.*881

72 Eur. *Alc.*738

73 Pl. *Leg.* 11.919e. Plato also uses the paternal hearth for emotive emphasis in
*Menex.*249a-b.

74 Libations and prayers: e.g. Soph. *Elec.*270; *Her.* 559–609; Xen. *Cyr.* 1.6; Pl.
   *Leg.*11.913a. Newborn babies: The *amphidromia*, *Suda* s.v. Ἀμφιδρόμια; Ar. *Lys.*757;
   Richard Hamilton, 'Sources for the Athenian Amphidromia', *Greek, Roman and*
   Byzantine Studies 25, (1984): 243–51. New wives: The *katachysmata* is epitomised by
   the description given in Pl, *Leg.*773a, the joining of two hearths (ταῖς τε συνιούσαις
   ἑστίαις); Arist. [*Oec.*] 1344a; *Suda* s.v. Καταχύσματα; Harpokration s.v.
   Καταχύσματα; John Oakley and Rebecca Sinos, *The Wedding in Ancient Athens*
   (Madison: University of Wisconsin Press, 1993), 34–5. Slaves: Ar. *Plut.*795;
   Dem.45.74.
75 See also Themistocles' supplication to the Molossian king, where he is directed to the
   hearth to wait. Thuc. 1.136.
76 Eur. *Alc.* 158–69
77 Aesch. *Ag.* 1035–40. See also Eur. *Alc.* 98–100.
78 Aesch. *Ag.* 1056. See also Ar. *Av.* 850–65; *Pax*, 956–75; *Eccl.* 1033.
79 Eur. *IT.* 380–5; Thuc. 1.134.3; Xen. *Hell.* 5.3.19; Plu. *Dem.* 29.6; Ar. *Lys.* 742f. On
   birth and death as pollutants see also Eur. *Cret.* fr. 79.17–18 and Theophr. *Char.*
   16. Robert Parker, *Miasma: Pollution and Purification in Early Greek Religion*
   (Oxford: Clarendon Press, 1983/1996), 32–4; Robin Osborne, *The History Written*
   on the Classical Greek Body (Cambridge: Cambridge University Press, 2011),
   166–7.
80 Hipponax fr. 104.20; Hes. *Op.* 733, with comment from Parker, *Miasma*, 76–77.
81 E.g. Thuc. 1.136.2. For an attempt to distance a murder from the accusation of
   having been set at the hearth see Lys. 1.27.
82 For restrictions on entering temples and sanctuaries while under a state of pollution
   see Eur. *IT.* 380–4 and *IG* XII 5.593, with Parker, *Miasma*, 36–38.
83 Eur. *Alc.* 100; Ar. *Eccl.* 1033. On the possibility that the water of the house was
   also considered polluted, requiring water to be taken from a neighbour, see
   Pollux 8.65.
84 Similar to the *peirrhanterion*, which is described at the entrance of temples and
   sanctuaries. According to the Hippocratic corpus, their purpose was to prevent the
   boundaries of the divine becoming tainted by human pollution through ritual
   sprinkling. [Hippoc.] *Morb Sacr.* 1.110–12; Susan Cole, *Landscapes, Gender, and*
   Ritual Space: The Ancient Greek Experience (Berkeley: University of California Press,
   2004), 43–46.
85 Antiph. *Chor.*37; Dem. 47.70
86 Janett Morgan, *The Greek Classical House* (Exeter: Bristol Phoenix Press, 2010), 27.
87 Christiane Sourvinou-Inwood, 'Further Aspects of Polis Religion', in *Oxford Readings*
   in Greek Religion, ed. Richard Buston (Oxford: Oxford University Press, 2000), 54.
88 Julia Kindt, 'Polis Religion – A Critical Appreciation', *Kernos: Revue Internationale et*
   Pluridisciplinaire de Religion Grecque Antique 22, (2009): 30.

89 Walter G Runciman, 'Doomed to Extinction: The Polis as an Evolutionary Dead-End', in *The Greek City: From Homer to Alexander*, ed. Oswyn Murray and Simon Price (Oxford: Oxford University Press, 1990): 348.

90 Mogens Hansen, 'Introduction: The Polis as a Citizen-State', in *The Ancient Greek City-State: Symposium on the Occasion of the 250th Anniversary of The Royal Danish Academy of Sciences and Letters 1–4 July 1992*, ed. Mogens Hansen (Copenhagen: Munksgaard, 1993), 7–9.

91 See section 3.1.

92 Not to be confused with a commemoration of general service in the military. Therefore, this is focused on commemorations which state the leading *strategos* and/or the year of service and/or the theatre of war.

Chapter 2

1 For the most in-depth scholarship on departure scenes, see: Walther Wrede, 'Kriegers Ausfahrt in der archaisch-griechischen Kunst', *Athenische Mitteilungen* 41, (1916): 221–374; Athanasia Yalouri, 'A Hero's Departure', *American Journal of Archaeology* 75, 3 (1971): 269–75; Elizabeth Pemberton, 'The Name Vase of the Peleus Painter', *The Journal of the Walters Art Gallery* 36, (1977): 62–72; François Lissarrague, 'The World of the Warrior', in *A City of Images: Iconography and Society in Ancient Greece*, ed. Claude Bérard (Princeton: Princeton University Press, 1989), 39–51; François Lissarrague, *L'autre Guerrier: Archers, peltastes, cavaliers dans l'imagerie attique* (Paris: La Decouverte- École française de Rome, 1990); H Alan Shapiro, 'Comings and Goings: The Iconography of Departure and Arrival on Attic Vases', *Mètis* 5, (1990): 113–26; Robin Osborne, 'Images of a Warrior. On a Group of Athenian Vases and their Public', in *Greek Vases: Images, Contexts and Controversies*, ed. Clemente Marconi (Leiden: Brill, 2004), 41–54; Thomas Mannack, *The Late Mannerists in Athenian Vase-painting* (Oxford: Oxford University Press, 2001), 104–6; Clemente Marconi, 'Images for a Warrior. On a Group of Athenian Vases and their Public', in *Greek Vases: Images, contexts and controversies*, 27–40; Susan Matheson, 'A Farewell With Arms: Departing Warriors on Athenian Vases', in *Periklean Athens and Its Legacy: Problems and Perspectives*, ed. Judith Barringer and Jeffrey Hurwit (Austin: University of Texas Press, 2005), 23–35; Susan Matheson, 'Farewells by the Achilles Painter', in *On the Fascination of Objects: Greek and Etruscan Art in the Shefton Collection*, ed. John Boardman et al (Oxford: Oxbow Books, 2016), 63–75; Amalia Avramidou, *The Codrus Painter: Iconography and Reception of Athenian Vases in the Age of Pericles* (London: The University of Wisconsin Press, 2011), 57–60.

2 Statistics are based upon a search of the CVA/Beazley Pottery database using keywords WARRIOR AND DEPARTING within the category of Decoration

Description AND Same Decorated Area – accurate on 5 September 2020. While it is possible that vases within this list may not depict any form of the departing scene, due to an inaccurate label being awarded for an ambiguous or fragmentary vase; it is also possible that some vases were missed from this search due to the potential allocation of varying keywords within the database. On the balance of which we have a rough figure which show a prolificacy and can, in turn, work as a baseline from which to explore themes.

3 On iconography and iconology see Erwin Panofsky, *Meaning in the Visual Arts* (London: University of Michigan Press, 1955). For the iconography vs iconology debate within classics, see Mary Beard, 'Adopting an Approach II' in *Looking at Greek Vases*, ed. Tom Rasmussen and Nigel Spivey (Cambridge: Cambridge University Press, 1991) 12–35; Brian Sparkes, *The Red and the Black: Studies in Greek Pottery* (London: Routledge, 1996), 114–39; Patricia Hannah, 'The Warrior *Loutrophoroi* of Fifth-Century Athens', in *War, Democracy and Culture in Classical Athens*, ed. David Pritchard (Cambridge: Cambridge University Press, 2010), 267–8; and for a review of the historiography, Cornelia Isler-Kerényi, 'Iconographical and Iconological Approaches', in *The Oxford Handbook of Greek and Roman Art and Architecture*, ed. Clemente Marconi (Oxford: Oxford University Press, 2015), 557–78.

4 Beard, 'Adopting an Approach', 14.

5 Hannah, 'Warrior *Loutrophoroi*', 267.

6 Lissarrague, *L'autre Guerrier*, 3. See also Jean-Pierre Vernant, 'Preface', in *A City of Images: Iconography and Society in Ancient Greece*, ed. Claude Bérard et al (Princeton: Princeton University Press, 1989), 8.

7 Hannah, 'Warrior *Loutrophoroi*', 267, referencing Tonio Hölscher, 'Image and Political Identity: The Case of Athens', in *Democracy, Empire, and the Arts in Fifth-Century Athens*, ed. Deborah Boedeker and Kurt Raaflaub (Cambridge, MA: Harvard University Press, 1998), 178, 180.

8 Tonio Hölscher, 'Images of War in Greece and Rome: Between Military Practice, Public Memory, and Cultural Symbolism', *The Journal of Roman Studies* 93, (2003): 2.

9 Herbert Hoffman, *Sotades: Symbols of Immortality on Greek Vases* (Oxford: Oxford University Press, 1997), 74.

10 Matheson, 'Farewell with Arms', 26.

11 Young woman: Mannack, *Late Mannerists*, 401; Eva Keuls, *Painter and Poet in Ancient Greece: Iconography and the Literary Arts,* Beitrage zur Altertumskunde, 87 (Stuttgart-Leipzig: BG Teubner, 1997), 238; Ronald Ridley, 'The Hoplite as Citizen: Athenian Military Institutions in their Social Context', *L'antiquité classique* 48, 2 (1979): 516. Old man: Matheson, 'Farewell with Arms', 26.

12 Libations: New York, Metropolitan Museum: 56.171.44, *BA* 206877; St Petersburg, State Hermitage Museum: ST1592, *BA* 207221; Paris, Cabinet des Medailles: 394, *BA* 207309. Armour: Wurzburg, Universitat, Martin von Wagner Mus: 504, *BA* 205438;

Cambridge, Trinity College, *BA* 202996. This specific topos is often categorised as an arming scene, related, but not identical to, the departure scene (e.g., Lissarrague, *World of the Warrior*, 44–50). However, the interrelated nature of these themes – arming, offering of libations, divination (discussed below), and the departure – result in them mirroring each other in terms of the iconography and the portrayed participants. So, while artistically they are technically separate forms, historically they form an almost unbroken sequence of ritualistic events and present a continuity of ideological representation that allows for their interconnected exploration. Helmet or shield: Sotheby's sale catalogue: 12-13.12.1983, 84, NO.315, *BA* 8580; Milan, Civico Museo Archeologico: 3643.2, *BA* 214625.

13 Lissarrague, *L'autre Guerrier*, 238; Matheson, 'Farewell with Arms', 26; Osborne, 'Images of a Warrior', 46.

14 Matheson seems correct when she identified the inherent religious nature of these scenes as a depiction of domestic religion, as opposed to the rites taking place outside of the *oikos*: 'Farewell with Arms', 26.

15 Matheson, 'Farewell with Arms', 30.

16 Munich, Antikensammlungen: J381, *BA* 212266; New York, Metropolitan Museum: 17.230.13, *BA* 213926.

17 On the mustering point within Athens, see Aristoph. *Ach.* 197, *Peace*, 311–12, *Wasps*, 243, Diod. Sic. 11.81.4, with Matthew Christ, 'Conscription of Hoplites in Classical Athens', *Classical Quarterly* 51, (2001): 403 and Crowley, *Psychology of a Hoplite,* 30. For more on Athenian mustering points see section 3.1.3.

18 William Prichett, *The Greek State at War, Vol 1* (Berkeley: University of California Press, 1979), 59–61.

19 Lissarrague, *L'autre Guerrier*, 67.

20 Marconi, 'Images for Warriors', 37.

21 Matheson, 'Farewell with Arms', 33; Nathan Arrington, *Ashes, Images and Memories: The Presence of the War-dead in Fifth-century Athens* (Oxford: Oxford University Press, 2015), 268. See also Robert Sutton, 'Family Portraits: Recognizing the "Oikos" on Attic Red-Figure Pottery', *ΧΑΡΙΣ: Essays in Honor of Sara A. Immerwahr. Hesperia Supplements* 33, (2004): 331 who argues that the only safe indicator of the *oikos* on vase paintings is the presence of children.

22 Lissarrague, *L'autre Guerrier*, 239; Osborne, 'Images of a Warrior', 46; Mannack, *Late Mannerists*, 104.

23 Osborne, 'Images of a Warrior', 46-7; Matheson, 'Farewell with Arms', 24; Mannack, *Late Mannerists*, 104. Eg. Frankfurt, Liebieghaus: 550, *BA* 4964; Tours, Musée des Beaux-Arts: 863.2.64, *BA* 5600; Madrid, Museo Arqueologico Nacional, coll. Varez Fisa: 1999.99.61, *BA* 7462; Sotheby's sale catalogue: 5-7-1982, 122, NO.342, *BA* 7130; Paris, Musée Auguste Rodin: 959, *BA* 10845.

24 Lissarrague, 'World of the Warrior', 44.

25 Osborne, 'Images of a Warrior', 50–1; Arrington, *Ashes, Images and Memories*, 268; Susan Matheson, *Polygnotos and Vase Painting in Classical Athens* (Madison: University of Wisconsin Press, 1995), 270–1. The reasons for the change in iconography within the motif are not relevant for this discussion, the importance being that they did change. For a possible explanation for the change, based around its temporal links with the Persian Wars see Osborne, 'Images of a Warrior', 51, and Pemberton, 'The Name Vase', 65 n 16, who raised this issue without conclusively rectifying it.

26 E.g. Vienna, Kunsthistorisches Museum: 984, *BA* 2196.

27 E.g. New York (NY), Metropolitan Museum: 17.230.13, *BA* 213926.

28 Items on the wall: BM. 1891,0806.85. Chair: Berlin, Antikensammlung: 1970.9, *BA* 318. Matheson, 'Farewell with Arms', 26; Mannack, *Late Mannerists*, 104.

29 Matheson, 'Farewell with Arms', 26.

30 Kurashiki, Ninagawa: 23, *BA* 7307; Paris, Musée du Louvre: F207, *BA* 10711. Another icon of domestic husbandry is the bird, which often serves in a similar purpose to the dog; Arrington, *Ashes, Images and Memories*, 268. However, the agency given to the dog within these scenes allow for a greater sense of emotion than the birds. A notion best exemplified by an earlier vase painting attributed to Exekias (Vatican City, Museo Gregoriano Etrusco Vaticano: 344, *BA* 310395), which sees Pollux and Kastor returning home and a dog jumping up on Pollux.

31 Dog collar: Xen. *Cyn*, 6.1. The slight detailing on the collar depicted may imply that this dog is a symbol of a favourite for the hoplite, as opposed to a standard hunting hound of which he may have many.

32 As Peter Connor and Heather Jackson commented in *A Catalogue of Greek Vases in the Collection of the University of Melbourne at the Ian Potter Museum of Art* (Victoria: Macmillan Art Publishing, 2000), 98, in a similar scene attributed to the circle of the Antimenes painter: the dog seems to think it is departing too.

33 The representation of canine naivety is not unusual for the departure scene and seems purposefully to imitate the common behaviours of the dog: see the dog's cocked head looking up at the mother in Wurzburg, Universitat, Martin von Wagner Mus.: HA120, *BA* 201654, or the excited dog trying to lie close to the ground staring at the father in London, British Museum: E254.

34 Hom. *Od.* 17. 291–327.

35 Paris, Cabinet des Medailles: 394, *BA* 207309

36 *Contra* Osborne, 'Images of a Warrior', 50–1. See also Matheson, 'Farewell with Arms', 29.

37 Arrington, *Ashes, Images and Memories*, 267–72.

38 Note the Corinthian style helmet and the large *doru* in his left hand, both symbolic of the hoplite.

39 Matheson, 'Farewell with Arms', 33; Lissarrague, 'World of the Warrior', 45; Nicole Loraux, *The Experiences of Tiresias: The Feminine and the Greek Man*. Trans. Paula Wissing. (Princeton: Princeton University Press, 1995), 28.

40 The scene given in Figure 2b, while fragmentary, does have precedence that allows it to be identified as a departure scene. See Chiusi, Museo Archeologico Nazionale: 1794, *BA* 301779 which similarly shows the hero's wife holding her child. For other examples of departure scenes with children see Toledo (OH), Museum of Art: 23.3123, *BA* 6154; Bochum, Ruhr Universitat, Kunstsammlungen: S1085, *BA* 46410; Paris, Cabinet des Medailles: 215, *BA* 301745; Paris, Musée du Louvre: CP10656, *BA* 12168. Furthermore, the absence of the necklace, for which Amphiaraos' wife betrays him, implies that this image was not necessarily specific to the myth but rather a known hero departing to his pre-ordained death.

41 This echoes Paolo Arias' assessment of the Kleophon *stamnos* in Munich (Munich, Antikensammlungen: J382, *BA* 215142): 'The warrior and his young wife radiate a humanity which is conscious of its fate': *History of Greek Vase-painting* (London: Harry N Abrams, 1962), 368. That is not to say that death was inevitable, but that in Figure 2a at least, the medium of the *lekythos* tells us that the man within the scene is meant to be considered dead. For the child as a symbol of the *oikos* within attic vase painting see Sutton, 'Family Portraits', 337–45.

42 Matheson, 'Farewell with Arms', 33.

43 David M Pritchard, 'Thetes, Hoplites and the Athenian Imaginary', in *Ancient History in a Modern University, Vol. 1: The Ancient Near East, Greece and Rome*, ed. Tom Hillard (Cambridge: Eerdmans Publishing, 1998), 125, possibly echoing the sentiment of Lissarrague, 'World of the Warrior', 45.

44 Lissarrague, 'World of the Warrior', 46.

45 Marconi, 'Images for a Warrior', 38.

46 The hoplite could arguably be another symbol of the *polis* but, as a symbol, it fits equally within either sphere; as an adult male citizen enacting his duty for the *polis*, or as a member of the *oikos* about to depart it.

47 Based on a search on the CVA/Beazley Pottery database using keywords WARRIOR AND DEPARTING AND ATHENA/HERMES – plus the addition of one image published in Lissarrague, 'World of the Warrior'.

48 Mythical: Paris, Musée du Louvre: F25, *BA* 310431. Athena as Warrior: Brussels, Musées Royaux: A1329, *BA* 12147; Basel, market, Jean-David Cahn AG, *BA* 9032315. Too fragmentary: Brussels, Musées Royaux: R322TER, *BA* 12135; Athens, National Museum, Acropolis Coll: 2112, *BA* 300497; Florence, Museo Archeologico Etrusco, *BA* 9031204; Athens, National Museum, Acropolis Coll: D68, *BA* 46636.

49 Sotheby's sale catalogue: 10–11.7.1989, 60–62, No 171, *BA* 41543; Bologna, Museo Civico Archeologico: PU273, *BA* 217210; Lissarrague, 'World of the Warrior', Figure 64. These three constitute the total of available images where Athena takes on

a role within the scene that is equivalent to the 'female' figure of the topos, as described by Lissarrague.

50 Lissarrague, 'World of the Warrior', Figure 64.

51 See also Matheson, 'Farewell with Arms', 32. Although this does rest on the assumption that these pots were solely for Athenian usage, outside of the Athenian context her symbolic currency as a *polis* can be brought into question.

52 Bologna, Museo Civico Archeologico: PU273, *BA* 217210 which dates to the latter half of the fifth century BC

53 *Contra* Crowley, *Psychology of a Hoplite,* 99–100, who assigns Athena this role.

54 Based on a search on the CVA/Beazley Pottery database using keywords WARRIOR AND DEPARTING AND NIKE/NIKAI.

55 Athens, Benaki Museum: 38151, *BA* 9029956.

56 Hes. *Th.* 384 gives Nike a lineage not derived from Athena but from Pallas and Styx, *Hom. Hymn Ares,* 4 gives Ares as her father. Paus. 1.1.3, 5.11.1 tells us of different statues which placed Nike in the hands of Zeus rather than Athena; see EE Sikes, 'Nike and Athena Nike', *The Classical Review* 9, 5 (1895): 280–3, who went as far as to argue that Nike should be automatically associated with Zeus rather than Athena.

57 Holding *kerykeion*: Bari, Museo Archeologico Provinciale: TOMB11, *BA* 8482; Paris, Musée du Louvre: G165, *BA* 206952; London, British Museum: E275, *BA* 207126; Cambridge (MA), Harvard University, Arthur M Sackler Mus: 1925.30.130, *BA* 211593; Syracuse, Museo Archeologico Regionale Paolo Orsi: 24644, BA 214056; Cambridge, Fitzwilliam Museum: GR11.1917, BA 214410. Named: Berlin, Antikensammlung: F2264, BA 200457.

58 Berlin, Antikensammlung: F2264, *BA* 200457

59 There are many candidates: Ananke, Eos, Eris, Psyche, Nemesis, Nyx. But perhaps another logical choice of symbol for these departure scenes, especially for beardless warriors, would be the deification of youth, Hebe: Jenifer Neils, 'Hera, Paestum, and the Cleveland Painter.' In Marconi, C (ed) *Greek Vases: Images, Contexts and Controversies* (Leiden: Brill, 2004): 77.

60 Matheson, *Polygnotos,* 207.

61 Hom. *Il.* 2.786–806, 3.121, 8.397–8, 11.185, 15.53–7, 15.144, 18.166–8, 23.198–9, 24.77, 24.143–4; Hes. *Th.* 780–1; Ar. *Av.* 1196–1259; Plato, *Crat.*, 408a–b.

62 Hom. *Il.* 23.198–210

63 Athens, Benaki Museum: 38151, *BA* 9029956.

64 E.g. Brussels, Musées Royaux: R291, *BA* 320062; Cambridge, Fitzwilliam Museum: GR5.1917, *BA* 12716; Paris, Musée du Louvre: CA3277, *BA* 5730; Tarquinia, Museo Nazionale Tarquiniese: 640, *BA* 5728; London, British Museum: B171, *BA* 5725. While most *hieroscopy* scenes depict the reading of the liver (*hepatoscopy*), there were more signs to be found within the internal organs, as described by Aesch. *PV.* 493–5. For the Greek practice of hepatoscopy see Derek Collins, 'Mapping the

Entrails: The Practice of Greek Hepatoscopy', *The American Journal of Philology* 129, 3 (2008): 319–45.

65　See section 2.1.

66　Lissarrague, 'World of the Warrior', 48–50.

67　See, especially, Wurzburg, Universitat, Martin von Wagner Mus: HA120, *BA* 201654 for an archetypal image; Copenhagen, National Museum: 3241, *BA* 8570; Jean-Louis Durand, 'Greek Animals: Toward a Typology of Edible Bodies', in *The Cuisine of Sacrifice Among the Greeks*, ed. Marcel Detienne and Jean-Pierre Vernant. Trans. Paula Wissing. Chicago: University of Chicago Press, 1979/1990), 98–9.

68　Aristot. *Pol.* 7.1336b

69　There is no instance of this explicitly occurring, but the ritualistic situation most likely resulted in a positivist mentality for both the hoplite and his family, as they felt they had power and control over the uncontrollable: that is, both fate and socially enforced military service.

70　Xenophon (*Ages.* 11.2) articulates succinctly a difference in ritual motive between the sacrifice, with omen reading and libations, with prayers: '[Agesilaus] offered more sacrifices when confident than prayers when in doubt.'

71　This view of prayer, articulated by Plato (*Menex.*247d), does not seem to assuage the mourning and loss felt by the women who lose their sons and husbands.

72　The date for the implementation of the *katalogos* is contentious but seems, in all probability, to occur around the time of Cleisthenes, or after – as the reforms were vital to the undertaking of the *katalogos* system. See Christ, 'Conscription of Hoplites', 398–9; Crowley, *Psychology of a Hoplite,* 27; and n 59.

73　Crowley, *Psychology of a Hoplite,* 65; Hans van Wees, *Greek Warfare: Myths and Realities* (London: Duckworth, 2004), 180–1. The trait of individual daring was admired by the Greeks, but it could not supersede the duty of the military group; see for instance Hdt. 9.71.3.

74　Plat. *Resp.* 468b-c; *Menex.* 240e-1a; Aeschin. 2.169. David Pritchard, 'The Symbiosis between Democracy and War: The Case of Ancient Athens', in *War, Democracy and Culture in Classical Athens*, ed. David Pritchard (Cambridge: Cambridge University Press, 2010), 18; Crowley, *Psychology of a Hoplite,* 119–20; Matthew Christ, *The Bad Citizen in Classical Athens* (Cambridge: Cambridge University Press, 2006), 110–11; Debra Hamel, *Athenian Generals: Military Authority in the Classical Period* (Leiden: Brill, 1998), 64–70.

75　Plat. *Symp.* 220d-e.

76　Polly Low, 'Commemorating the War Dead in Classical Athens: Remembering Defeat and Victory', in *War, Democracy and Culture in Classical Athens*, ed. David Pritchard (Cambridge: Cambridge University Press, 2010), 343; Robin Osborne, 'Democratic Ideology, the Events of War and the Iconography of Attic Funerary Sculpture', in *War, Democracy and Culture in Classical Athens*, ed. David Pritchard

(Cambridge: Cambridge University Press, 2010), 248; Nicole Loraux, *The Invention of Athens: The Funeral Oration in the Classical City*. Trans. Alan Sheridan (Cambridge, MA.: Harvard University Press, 1986/2006), 52; Ridley, 'The Hoplite as Citizen', 513.

77 Agreeing with Loraux, *The Invention of Athens*, 52.

78 Discussed in more detail in section 7.1.2.

79 Not least because of its final formulation dating somewhere in the eighth–seventh century BC.

80 Xen. *Cyr.* 6.4.2–12

81 Lyc. 1.100 = Eur. *Erechth.* fr. 50, Austin.

82 Xen. *Cyr.* 6.1.45–7.

83 Stewart Oost, 'Xenophon's Attitude toward Women', *The Classical World* 71, 4 (1977): 231, 234, 235.

84 Philip Stadter, 'Fictional Narrative in the *Cyropaideia*.' *The American Journal of Philology* 112, 4 (1991): 461–4.

85 Christos Tsagalis '*CEG* 594 and Euripides' *Erechtheus*', *Zeitschrift für Papyrologie und Epigraphik* 162, (2007), 11.

86 Hom. *Il.* 6.406–10.

87 Hom. *Il.* 6.408, 432.

88 Hom. *Il.* 6.429–30.

89 Hom. *Il.* 6.421–39.

90 Hom. *Il.* 6.441. Trans. Lattimore (1951 [Adapted]): ἦ καὶ ἐμοὶ τάδε πάντα μέλει γύναι. 'My wife, I have also been concerned by all of this.'

91 Hom. *Il.* 6.464–65. Trans. Lattimore (1951 [Adapted]): ἀλλά με τεθνηῶτα χυτὴ κατὰ γαῖα καλύπτοι πρίν γέ τι σῆς τε βοῆς σοῦ θ' ἑλκηθμοῖο πυθέσθαι.

92 Hom. *Il.* 6.466–70

93 Hom. *Il.* 6.471–81

94 Tears: Hom. *Il.* 6.405, 484, 496

95 Hom. *Il.* 6.515. The lingering of Andromache is implied by the verb used to describe her as she walks back to the house: ἐντροπαλίζομαι (turn around repeatedly): Hom. *Il.* 6.490.

96 D Valla, 'Il Mito di Pantea', *Atene e Roma* 3, (1922): 120–1; Deborah Gera, *Xenophon's* Cyropaedia: *Style, Genre, and Literary Technique* (Oxford: Oxford University Press, 1993), 235–7; Sophie Trenkner, *The Greek Novella in the Classical Period* (Cambridge: Cambridge University Press, 1958), 26; John Hilton, 'War and Peace in the Ancient Greek Novel', *Acta Classica* 48, (2005): 61; James Tatum, *Xenophon's Imperial Fiction: On the Education of Cyrus* (Princeton: Princeton University Press, 1989), 179–80; Anna Santoni, 'Figure femminili nell'opera di Senofonte: il caso di Pantea', in *Donne Che Contano Nella Storia Greca*, ed. Umberto Bultrighini and Elisabetta Dimauro (Lanciano: Carabba, 2014), 365.

97 Valla, 'Il Mito di Pantea', 121.

98 Xen. *Cyr.* 6.3.35–37. Abradatas volunteers to face the Egyptian phalanx, and even though Cyrus decides to cast lots, he still wins the right to take the position.

99 M Beck, 'Xenophon', *In Time in Ancient Greek Literature: Studies in Ancient Greek Narrative, vol. 2.*, ed. Irene De Jong and René Nünlist (Leiden: Brill, 2007), 393, similarly suggests that this simultaneous presentation of the two scenes presents a holy element to the couple's final parting.

100 Gera, *Xenophon's* Cyropaedia, 238.

101 Xen. *Cyr.* 6.4.3.

102 Xen. *Cyr.* 6.4.3 with Santoni, 'Figure femminili', 364.

103 As Gera, *Xenophon's* Cyropaedia, 236, interestingly notes this use of privacy to *not* exchange final words of intimacy contrasts with Andromache's regrets for not having such an opportunity (Hom. *Il.* 24. 744–5).

104 A similarity also noted by Santoni, 'Figure femminili', 365. However, contrary to Santoni, it is incorrect to presume that this speech is intended to echo the reputations of Spartan women, who were famously said to have urged their fighting men to return either with their shield or on it. There are two reasons why this is the case: (1) the Spartans were buried on the battlefield, so Plutarch's famous maxim (Plut. *Apophth. Lac.* 241F 4.) is not relevant to the classical period; (2) Xenophon never makes any mention of Spartan women urging their men on in this way, in fact he expresses disappointment in their behaviour when they are faced by war: Xen. *Hell.* 6.5.28. The closest parallel is between Panthea and Andromache/Hector and it is the distortion of the Homeric scene by which this episode should be aligned.

105 Xen. *Cyr.* 6.4.6. Trans. Miller (1914 [Adapted]): ἦ μὴν ἐγὼ βούλεσθαι ἂν μετὰ σοῦ ἀνδρὸς ἀγαθοῦ γενομένου κοινῇ γῆν ἐπιέσασθαι μᾶλλον ἢ ζῆν μετ' αἰσχυνομένου αἰσχυνομένη.

106 Gera, *Xenophon's* Cyropaedia, 236–7. On Panthea's almost obsessive compulsion to talk about Cyrus with Abradatas see Gera, *Xenophon's* Cyropaedia, 233.

107 Hom. *Il* 6.493: πόλεμος δ' ἄνδρεσσι μελήσει. Xen *Cyr* 6.4.8: ἀγασθεὶς τοῖς λόγοις.

108 Xen. *Cyr.* 6.4.9. For a different comparison between the two prayer scenes see Tatum, *Xenophon's Imperial Fiction*, 180, and Gera, *Xenophon's* Cyropaedia, 237.

109 As opposed to Hector who delays his own departure. Xen. *Cyr.* 6.4.10 with Gera, *Xenophon's* Cyropaedia, 238.

110 Valla, 'Il Mito di Pantea', 120–1.

111 Son of the Achilles, the man responsible for the demise of her own paternal household: Pausanias 1.11.1.

112 Xen. *Cyr.* 7.3.8–14. Gera, *Xenophon's* Cyropaedia, 240.

113 Gera, *Xenophon's* Cyropaedia, 241. See also Christopher Nadon, *Xenophon's Prince: Republic and Empire in the Cyropaedia* (Berkeley: University of California Press, 2001), 156–57; Santoni, 'Figure femminili', 368.

114 An act that she describes as her folly, Xen. *Cyr.* 7.3.10: ἡ μώρα πολλά.

115 Thuc. 2.44. For analysis on this passage see section 6.2.2.

116 I remain unconvinced by Nadon's attempt to portray Panthea as manipulatively constructing this scene, knowing long in advance of its inevitability: *Xenophon's Prince*, 156. Nadon does not consider the contrast between the experiences of Panthea and Andromache and is perhaps overly cynical regarding the bond between Panthea and Abradatas. See also Santoni, 'Figure femminili', 368, who describes Panthea as returning to the conventional female role within these scenes when the realities of war finally affect her.

117 For a very different reading of this novella and of Panthea, see Stadter, 'Fictional Narrative', 484, who considers Panthea to be contrasted with Croesus' personal description of becoming a wife, following his defeat by Cyrus. Stadter's Panthea defines a different kind of wife, one whose true happiness is founded in encouraging virtue in herself and others. Stadter does not approach the apparent turn in her views, which appear after Abradatas' death.

118 Nicole Loraux, *Mothers in Mourning: With the Essay, Of Amnesty and Its Opposite.* Trans. Corinne Pache (Ithaca: Cornell University Press, 1998): 13–14, describes Praxithea as more of an 'Athenian' than a mother. For similar views see Thalia Papadopolou, *Euripides: Phoenician Women* (London: Bloomsbury Academic, 2008), 64; Christ, *Bad Citizen*, 83.

119 Eur *Erechth.* fr. 50, Austin, 15.

120 Eur *Erechth.* fr. 50, Austin, 1–21; esp 16–21. Sons: Eur *Erechth.* fr. 50, Austin, 22–27.

121 Eur *Erechth.* fr. 50, Austin, 25–6.

122 Eur *Erechth.* fr. 50, Austin, 38–9.

123 Eur. *Erechth.* fr. 50 Austin, 28–31. Trans. Worthington et al (2001 [Adapted]):
τὰ μητέρων δὲ δάκρυ' ὅταν πέμπῃ τέκνα, πολλοὺς ἐθήλυν' εἰς μάχην ὁρμωμένους. μισῶ γυναῖκας αἵτινες πρὸ τοῦ καλοῦ ζῆν παῖδας εἵλοντ' ἢ παρήνεσαν κακά.

124 We do not have the play in full, so no major conclusion can be made about Praxithea as a character in this regard.

125 Pietro Pucci, *Euripides' Revolution under Cover: An Essay* (Ithaca: Cornell University Press, 2016), 100–1.

126 Lyc 1.100: τὸ τὴν πατρίδα φιλεῖν.

127 Guilia Sissa and Marcel Detienne, *La Vie Quotidienne des Dieux Grecs* (Paris: Hachette, 1989), 245: 'la force des femmes d'Athènes', cf Loraux, *Mothers in Mourning*, 14.

128 Apoll *Bibl* 3.15.4. Mary Lefkowitz, *Euripides and the Gods* (Oxford: Oxford University Press, 2016), 86; Pucci, *Euripides' Revolution*, 101.

129 Pucci, *Euripides' Revolution*, 102.

Chapter 3

1 It is often stated that there were only two forms of mobilisation and the mass levy is omitted as a formal mobilisation. See Hamel, *Athenian Generals*, 23–8; Christ, 'Conscription of Hoplites' 408–9 and Crowley, *Psychology of a Hoplite*, 27. However, as shall be explored in section 3.1.2, the Athenians were capable of overriding their slow *katalogos* through a specific procedure of notification, making it an institutional form of mobilisation; see, however, Pritchard, 'The Symbiosis, 10–11. For analysis of the fighting capabilities of the forces brought together by these three forms of mobilisation see Crowley, *Psychology of a Hoplite*, 27, 34–5.

2 Arist. [*Ath. Pol.*] 7.3-4, *Pol.* 3.1274a; Thuc. 6.43.1; Lys. 21.5-10; Plut. *Sol.* 18.1-2. However, scholars have recently shown that these neat categorisations do not always appear in our sources. See David Pritchard, 'The Symbiosis', 23–7, and his extensive bibliography therein.

3 See also, Miriam Valdés Guía and Julián Gallego, 'Athenian "Zeugitai" and the Solonian Census Classes: New Reflections and Perspectives', *Historia: Zeitschrift für Alte Geschichte* 59, 3 (2010): 259–60, who acknowledge that the *thetes* were not subject to the *katalogos*, but argue that they were still obliged to serve, following Vincent Gabrielson, 'The Impact of Armed Forces on Government and Politics in Archaic and Classical Greek Poleis: A Response to Hans van Wees', in *Army and Power in the Ancient World*, ed. Angelos Chaniotis and Pierre Ducrey (Stuttgart: Franz Steiner Verlag, 2002), 83–98. The issue of conscription lists being used for naval participation, discussed by both papers, is an interesting hypothesis, but is formulated by assumptions based on historical precedent using later sources.

4 Van Wees, 55–6; Crowley, *Psychology of a Hoplite*, 23. See also Vincent Rosivach, 'Zeugitai and Hoplites', *Ancient History Bulletin* 16, 1 (2002): 33–43, with criticisms from Crowley, *Psychology of a Hoplite*, 143 n 6. See also Valdés Guía and Gallego, 'Athenian "Zeugitai"', 257–81, who question the leisure status of all *zeugitai*.

5 Van Wees, *Greek Warfare*, 56; Crowley, *Psychology of a Hoplite*, 23. On the qualifications of the *pentacosiomedimnoi* as a class, without reference to the military obligations, see Vincent Rosivach, 'Notes on the Pentakosiomedimnos' Five Hundred Medimnoi', *The Classical Quarterly* 55, 2 (2005): 597–601.

6 Van Wees, *Greek Warfare*, 55–56; Thuc. 2.13.6-7. Thucydides describes 13,000 heavy infantry (ὁπλίτας) who could enter the field, a further 16,000 drawn from the oldest and youngest conscripts and qualifying metics, who were used for garrisoning outposts and also for guard duty in Athens itself. The number given by Thucydides has been subject to much scholarly attention, due to the disparity in number between the first- and second-tier troops, see Sterling Dow, 'Thucydides and the Number of Acharnian Hoplitai', *Transactions and Proceedings of the American Philological Association* 92, (1961): 67 n 2, and Mogens Hansen, 'The Number of

Athenian Hoplites in 431 B.C.', *Symbolae Osloenses* 56, (1981) 19–32 for an historiographical overview and assessment. The importance here is that all these hoplites needed to be able to sustain the necessary income to both afford and qualify for hoplitic service.

7 Van Wees, *Greek Warfare*, 55–6. Of course, this assessment purposefully ignores the land required to maintain the wealth of the two richer property classes.

8 Hans van Wees, 'Farmers and Hoplites: Models of Historical Development', in *Men of Bronze: Hoplite Warfare in Ancient Greece*, ed. Donald Kagan and Gregory Viggiano (Princeton: Princeton University Press, 2013), 230–1.

9 For further discussion see below. For Athenian hoplite figures during this period see Tables 3.1 and 3.2.

10 Obligation for hoplite service was between the ages of 18 and 59, with the age categories of 18–19 and 40–59 usually excused from field duty. Arist. [*Ath. Pol.*] 53.4. Christ, 'Conscription of Hoplites', 404; Mogens Hansen, *Three Studies in Athenian Demography* (Copenhagen: Det Kongelige Danske Videnskabernes Selskab, 1988), 23; Pritchard, 'The Symbiosis', 22.

11 Lys. 20.26-29.

12 Lys. 20.33.

13 Dem. 43.19.

14 Isae. 2.6-11.

15 Van Wees, *Greek Warfare*, 55. See also Pritchard, 'The Symbiosis', 24–5, on the use of the word *thetes* to describe volunteer warriors.

16 Crowley, *Psychology of a Hoplite,* 23, 100–4. For a different interpretation of Athenian 'motivations' to serve in the military see Christ, *The Bad Citizen*, 45–86 and 'Conscription of Hoplite', 399, who emphasises the presence of draft evasion and cowardly behaviour present in the sources.

17 My great debt to Matthew Christ's model of the *katalogos* will be self-evident, with only small divergences of source analysis being dwelled on herein.

18 For the prescription of army size Hamel, *Athenian Generals*, 25, 201–3, with Xen. *Hel* 1.1.34 and Thuc. 6.26.1.

19 Hamel, *Athenian Generals*, 23–31; Christ, 'Conscription of Hoplites', 399.

20 Lys. 16.16. Christ, 'Conscription of Hoplites', 400; Crowley, *Psychology of a Hoplite,* 27–29; Douglas MacDowell, 'The Case of the Rude Soldier (Lysias 9)', in *Symposion 1993. Vorträge zur griechischen und hellenistischen Rechtsgeschichte*, ed. Gerhard Thür (Cologne: Böhlau, 1994), 155. This form of collaboration was mirrored by the cavalry lists, which were drawn up by the *hipparchoi*, with the aid of *phylarchoi*. Lys. 16.6-7, with Glenn Bugh, 'Introduction of the Katalogeis of the Athenian Cavalry', *Transactions of the American Philological Association* 112, (1982): 23–32; *The Horsemen of Athens* (Princeton: Princeton University Press, 1988), 53–5, 169–73; and Christ, 'Conscription of Hoplites', 400 n 8. For the question of whether the

notion of the tribal *strategos* continued throughout the classical period see Hamel, *Athenian Generals*, 84–7.

21 Hansen, 'The number of Athenian hoplites', 24–6; Christ, 'Conscription of Hoplites', 400–3; Crowley, *Psychology of a Hoplite*, 28.

22 Nicholas Jones, 'The Athenian Phylai as Associations: Disposition, Function and Purpose', *Hesperia* 64, (1995): 504; *The Associations of Classical Athens: The Response to Democracy* (Oxford: Oxford University Press, 1999), 169–72); Crowley, *Psychology of a Hoplite*, 29.

23 Christ, 'Conscription of Hoplites', 401; Nicholas Sekunda, 'Athenian Demography and Military Strength 338–322 BC', *The Annual of the British School at Athens* 87, (1992): 324; Crowley, *Psychology of a Hoplite*, 29; Geoffrey Bakewell, 'Written Lists of Military Personnel in Classical Athens', in *Politics of Orality*, ed. Craig Cooper (Leiden: Brill, 2007a), 90–3.

24 Christ, 'Conscription of Hoplites', 401, Crowley, *Psychology of a Hoplite*, 30.

25 Ar. *Av.* 450; *Peace*, 1179-1184. T. Leslie Shear Jr, 'The Monument of the Eponymous Heroes in the Athenian Agora', *Hesperia* 39, 3 (1970): 145, 204 n 88; Christ, 'Conscription of Hoplites', 403; Crowley, *Psychology of a Hoplite*, 30; Bakewell, 'Written Lists', 92–3.

26 Crowley, *Psychology of a Hoplite*, 30.

27 Christ, 'Conscription of Hoplites', 403–4, followed by Crowley, *Psychology of a Hoplite*, 30. This observation is supported by a comic scene in Ar. *Peace*, 1181–4, which depicts a hoplite from the countryside in tears after finding out, by chance, that he was due for service the following day.

28 Christ, 'Conscription of Hoplites', 404, citing Ar. *Peace* 311–12, *Ach.* 1083; Plu. *Phoc.* 24.4, Andoc. 1.45.

29 Christ, 'Conscription of Hoplites', 408.

30 Obligatory military service in Athens ended at age 60, however men over the age of 50 were usually exempt from active field duty. See n 10.

31 Christ, 'Conscription of Hoplites', 404, using Peter Krentz, 'The Salpinx in Greek Battle', in *Hoplites: The Classical Greek Battle Experience*, ed. Victor Davis Hanson (London: Routledge, 1991), 114–16.

32 Andoc. 1.45. For more on this passage see section 3.1.3.

33 Bacchyl. 18.1-11. Trans. DA Svarlien (1991): βασιλεῦ τᾶν ἱερᾶν Ἀθανᾶν,τῶν ἁβροβίων ἄναξ Ἰώνων, τί νέον ἔκλαγε χαλκοκώδων σάλπιγξ πολεμηΐαν ἀοιδάν; ἦ τις ἁμετέρας χθονὸς δυσμενὴς ὅρι' ἀμφιβάλλει στραταγέτας ἀνήρ; ἦ τί τοι κραδίαν ἀμύσσει; ἦ λῃσταὶ κακομάχανοι ποιμένων ἀέκατι μήλων σεύοντ' ἀγέλας βίᾳ; ἦ τί τοι κραδίαν ἀμύσσει;

34 Christ, 'Conscription of Hoplites', 404.

35 Dem. 18.169; Polyaen. 3.9.20

36 For the importance of the *deme* in Athenian mobilisation see section 3.1.

37 Following the suggestion by Peter Liddel, related in Crowley, *Psychology of a Hoplite,* 149 n 102.

38 For a methodical and illuminating analysis of this stage see Christ, 'Conscription of Hoplites', 404–7, with Crowley, *Psychology of a Hoplite,* 31–32.

39 ἀθροίζω: Thuc. 1.50.3, 3.97.1, 5.6.5, 7.33.6; Xen, *Cyr.* 2.4.17–18, 3.1.2–5, 5.5.16, 6.1.42, 7.1.30; 8.8.6; *Hel.* 1.4.3, 1.63, 2.2.8–9, 5.2.24-25, 7.3.9; Eur. *Hel.* 50; *Phoen.* 78; Plut. *Alc.* 19.4; *Them.* 11.2; *Agis* 13.4. σύλλογος: Thuc. 7.31; Xen. *Cyr.* 6.2.11, 14; *Oec.* 4.6. For a thorough analysis of the term σύλλογος, including its use for assembly points, see Johnny Christensen and Mogens Hansen, 'What is *Syllogos* at Thukydides 2.22.1?', in *The Athenian Ecclesia II: A Collection of Articles, 1983–1989,* ed. Mogens Hansen (Copenhagen: Museum Tusculanum Press, 1989), 195–212.

40 For other, non-muster related, military uses for ἀθροίζω see: Thuc. 6.44.3, 6.70.4; Xen. *Hell.* 3.4.22. For non-military usage see, eg, Plato, *Rep.* 6.487b, 8.565a; Xen. *Cyr.* 8.4.36; *Hel.* 1.4.12.

41 Soph. *Aj.* 289–90; Diod. 11.81.5. The same term can be used for a base of operations (Thuc. 1.90.2) and also as a metaphorical starting point for your personal enemies (Plut. *Them.* 23.1).

42 Herodotus was also reviewed, but he fails to give a numerical strength for any Athenian muster and so cannot be included in the data.

43 This is not an exhaustive list of battles that the Athenians participated in, but rather the collection of battles for which we are specifically told their fighting strength. A secondary mitigating factor was that the fighting strength described is in keeping with the realistic figures that Thucydides gives for the number of hoplites available for battlefield commitments (ie, 13,000, see above).

44 Diodorus' figure is 20,000 Athenians, which is simply too high to be exclusively hoplites. It is plausible that this may include the cavalry and the light infantry, who were said to have left before the battle, but there is no direct evidence to support this.

45 Lys. 9.4.

46 Thuc. 2.31. These raids into Megara became a biannual event during the Peloponnesian War, although they were not always enacted by a mass levy. See Thuc. 2.31.3, which states that these raids would sometimes be a purely cavalry-based excursion.

47 Thuc. 4.90.1.

48 Aristotle (*Pol.* 7.1327a) describes these two importance factors for an ideal city to consider: (1) the ability to communicate effectively with its wider territory, to send military assistance; and (2) the accessibility for the movement of agricultural produce, timber and other trade goods.

49 Mogens Hansen, *The Athenian Ecclesia II: A Collection of Articles, 1983–1989* (Copenhagen: Museum Tusculanum Press, 1989), 207 n 44; Christ, 'Conscription of Hoplites', 407 n 39.

50 Xen. *Hell.* 2.3.20: ἄλλων ἀλλαχοῦ.

51 Andoc. 1.45.

52 Polyaen. 3.9.20.

53 Bacchyl. 15.40–5; Aen. Tac. 2.5.

54 Xen. *Hell.* 1.1.33; Xen. *Eq. mag.* 3.

55 Ar. *Peace*, 355–60. Oates and O'Neill Jr (1938 [Adapted]): καὶ γὰρ ἱκανὸν χρόνον ἀπολλύμεθα καὶ κατατετρίμμεθα πλανώμενοι ἐς Λύκειον κἀκ Λυκείου ξὺν δορὶ ξὺν ἀσπίδι.

56 *Suda* s.v. Ἄρχων

57 The Greek text follows that of *PH* 141. I am indebted to Dr Peter Liddel and Dr Alexandra Wilding for their useful comments and assistance regarding my translation.

58 *IG* I³ 138, 1–4.

59 *IG* I³ 138, 5–7.

60 *IG* I³ 138, 15–16.

61 Homer Thompson, 'Excavations in the Athenian Agora: Buildings on the West Side of the Agora', *Hesperia* 6, (1937): 113, n 7; Douglas Feaver, 'The Historical Development in the Priesthoods of Athens', *Yale Classical Studies* 15, (1957): 142.

62 Michael Jameson, *Cults and Rites in Ancient Greece Essays on Religion and Society*, ed. Allaire Stallsmith (Cambridge: Cambridge University Press, 2014), 41–61, followed by Matthew Trundle, 'Light Troops in Classical Athens', in *War, Democracy and Culture in Classical Athens*, ed. David Pritchard (Cambridge: Cambridge University Press, 2010), 150–1.

63 Lines 15–16.

64 Lines 1–4.

65 Jameson, *Cults and Rites*, 51–2.

66 Andoc. 1.45. Trans. KJ Maidment (1968 [adapted]): ἀνακαλέσαντες δὲ τοὺς στρατηγοὺς ἀνειπεῖν ἐκέλευσαν Ἀθηναίων τοὺς μὲν ἐν ἄστει οἰκοῦντας ἰέναι εἰς τὴν ἀγορὰν τὰ ὅπλα λαβόντας, τοὺς δ' ἐν μακρῷ τείχει εἰς τὸ Θησεῖον, τοὺς δ' ἐν Πειραιεῖ εἰς τὴν Ἱπποδαμείαν ἀγοράν, τοὺς δ' ἱππέας ἔτι πρὸ1 νυκτὸς σημῆναι τῇ σάλπιγγι ἥκειν εἰς τὸ Ἀνάκειον.

67 For a similar disposition of forces see Aen. *Tact.* 3.5.

68 Xen. *Hell.* 6.5.49.

69 Xen. *Hell.* 1.1.33–4.

70 The nearest point would have been the Pnyx, which either was not used during the period, contrary to later evidence or, more plausibly, the Pnyx was not a viable point during such an emergency muster due to the need for the Assembly to meet there.

71 Peter Siewert, *Die Trittyen Attikas und die Heeresreform des Kleisthenes* (Munich: Beck, 1982).

72 Siewert, *Die Trittyen Attikas*, 138–53.

73 Merits and flaws: DM Lewis, 'Review: Die Trittyen Attikas und die Heeresreform des
   Kleisthenes', *Gnomon* 55, 5 (1983): 431–6; GR Stanton, 'The Tribal Reforms of
   Kleisthenes the Alkmeonid.' *Chiron* 14, (1984): 1–41. Rolling muster: see,
   specifically, Siewert, Siewert, *Die Trittyen Attikas*, 138–41.

74 Polybius, 16.36.

75 Siewert, *Die Trittyen Attikas*, 140.

76 Siewert, *Die Trittyen Attikas*, 141–5.

77 *Lochos*: It has recently been suggested that the *lochos* may have fluctuated in size,
   maybe even in number, depending on the size of the army under question. Crowley,
   Psychology of a Hoplite, 39; see, also, Van Wees, *Greek Warfare*, 100. *Trittys*: Lewis,
   'Review', 435. However, Siewert is not the only scholar to make such an assertion,
   see, eg, Peter Bicknell, *Studies in Athenian Politics and Genealogy* (Wiesbaden: Franz
   Steiner Verlag, 1972) 21 and n 67.

78 For the importance of the *deme* in the motivation of the Athenian hoplite see
   Crowley, *Psychology of a Hoplite,* 40–69.

79 Lys. 16.14. Trans. WRM Lamb (1930 [Adapted]): συλλεγέντων τοίνυν τῶν δημοτῶν
   πρὸ τῆς ἐξόδου, εἰδὼς αὐτῶν ἐνίους πολίτας μὲν χρηστοὺς ὄντας καὶ προθύμους,
   ἐφοδίων δὲ ἀποροῦντας, εἶπον ὅτι χρὴ τοὺς ἔχοντας παρέχειν τὰ ἐπιτήδεια τοῖς
   ἀπόρως διακειμένοις.

80 Crowley, *Psychology of a Hoplite,* 152–3 n 142. See, also, William Wyse, *The Speeches
   of Isaeus* (Cambridge: Cambridge University Press, 1904), 268.

81 Over a month's wage for a hoplite. The wage of a hoplite fluctuated during the classical
   period, with a height of two drachmae (Thuc. 3.17.4). During the period in which
   Lysias is writing, a hoplite was likely to earn three obols a day: William Pritchett, *The
   Greek State at War, vol. I* (Berkeley: University of California Press, 1979–91) 14–24.

82 Lys. 31. 15–16.

83 Crowley, *Psychology of a Hoplite,* 43–8. Crowley explores both indirect evidence,
   such as the socio-economic and religious cohesion of the *deme*, as well as specifically
   military related pieces of evidence, to build up his argument that the *deme* formed
   the hoplite's 'primary-group'. See also David Whitehead, *The Demes of Attica –
   508/7-ca. 250 B.C.: A Political and Social Study* (Princeton: Princeton University
   Press, 1986), 224–6.

84 Lys. 20.23.

85 Isae. 2.42.

86 Theophr. *Char.* 25.3, 6.

87 The best evidence for this is found in temple dedications, such as the helmet
   dedicated to Nemesis by the demesmen of Rhamnous. See ch 3 for further analysis.

88 See section 3.1.1.

89 Similar interpretations, through different threads of logic, have been made by Crowley,
   Psychology of a Hoplite, 33, 46–7 and much earlier by Wyse, *Speeches of Isaeus*, 268.

90 For the plethora of examples available in the historical records showing military rituals see Pritchett, *Greek State, vol.* III, 47–90; Michael Jameson, 'Sacrifice before Battle', in Hanson, VD (ed.) *Hoplites: The Classical Greek Battle Experience*, ed. Victor David Hanson (London: Routledge, 1991), 197–227; Robert Parker, 'Sacrifice and Battle', in *War and Violence in Ancient Greece*, ed. Hans van Wees (Oxford: Classical Press of Wales, 2009), 299–309.

91 Thuc. 6.8-25.2.

92 On Thucydides' usage of this prepositional phrase see Christ, 'Conscription of Hoplites', 402–3. Thucydides (6.43.1) describes 5,100 hoplites when the armada reached Corcyra, but it is not clear if these extra 100 men were mustered in Athens or were brought by allies.

93 Thuc. 6.31.2 repeats his information about the forces that Athens had sent to Epidaurus and to Potidaea (2.56.3, 58.3), which took 4,000 Athenian hoplites and 100 Athenian triremes.

94 Thuc. 6.31.3-5. Lisa Kallet, *Money and the Corrosion of Power in Thucydides: The Sicilian Expedition and its Aftermath* (Berkeley: University of California Press, 2001), 48ff.

95 Thuc. 6.31.3, 6. There is an internal inconsistency within Thucydides, for he described a fleet of 200 Athenian and allied ships sailing to Egypt *c.* 460, to aid an uprising against the Persians. Either Thucydides has forgotten this and, therefore, mistakenly described the Sicilian expedition thus, or he has purposefully excluded the Egyptian venture within this assessment. The latter could be rationalised because the Egyptian journey did not depart from Athens; the fleet was redirected from its campaigns in Cyprus.

96 Thuc. 6.26.2. John Morrison et al, *The Athenian Trireme: The History and Reconstruction of an Ancient Greek Warship.* 2nd edn (Cambridge: Cambridge University Press, 2000), 110.

97 However, see Crowley, *Psychology of a Hoplite*, 50. Crowley's main evidence to claim these troops were experienced veterans comes from a Syracusan speech relayed by Thucydides (6.91.2–5), but he does not explain where this experience came from. However, in this speech, Hermocrates purposefully overemphasises the experience of these Athenian troops to the Syracusan assembly to explain their recent defeat in battle and as part of an attempt to introduce a new structure for the Syracusan army.

98 Thuc. 6.32.1-2. Strassler (2008 [Adapted]): τῇ μὲν σάλπιγγι σιωπὴ ὑπεσημάνθη, εὐχὰς δὲ τὰς νομιζομένας πρὸ τῆς ἀναγωγῆς οὐ κατὰ ναῦν ἑκάστην, ξύμπαντες δὲ ὑπὸ κήρυκος ἐποιοῦντο, κρατῆράς τε κεράσαντες παρ᾽ ἅπαν τὸ στράτευμα καὶ ἐκπώμασι χρυσοῖς τε καὶ ἀργυροῖς οἵ τε ἐπιβάται καὶ οἱ ἄρχοντες σπένδοντες. [2] ξυνεπηύχοντο δὲ καὶ ὁ ἄλλος ὅμιλος ὁ ἐκ τῆς γῆς τῶν τε πολιτῶν καὶ εἴ τις ἄλλος εὔνους παρῆν σφίσιν. παιανίσαντες δὲ καὶ τελεώσαντες τὰς σπονδὰς ἀνήγοντο.

99 τῶν τε πολιτῶν καὶ τις ἄλλος.

100 Matteo Zaccarini, 'Thucydides' Narrative on Naval Warfare: Epibatai, Military
 Theory, Ideology', in *Ancient Warfare: Introducing Current Research Vol. 1*, ed.
 Geoff Lee et al (Newcastle-upon-Tyne: Cambridge Scholars Press, 2015), 211.
 Thucydides, at one point, refers to the men in the expedition as στρατιῶται
 (6.31.5), when he is referring to the preliminary preparations for the voyage,
 reinforcing his exclusion of the hoplites in this instance.

101 Epibatai as a distinct naval fighter: Best demonstrated by Thuc. 8.24.2, which
 describes hoplites from the *katalogos* being compelled to serve as *epibatai*;
 Zaccarini, 'Thucydides' Narrative', 212. Archers: *SEG* 18.153, 23–6; Michael H
 Jameson, 'The Provisions for Mobilization in the Decree of Themistokles', *Historia:
 Zeitschrift für Alte Geschichte* 12, 4 (1963): 386–8. Morrison et al, *Athenian Trireme*,
 109–10.

102 Simon Hornblower, *A Commentary on Thucydides, vol III* (Oxford: Oxford
 University Press, 1991–2008), 394, seems correct in his observation that this
 in-depth narration from Thucydides serves a paradigmatic function, in place of the
 many rituals that would have taken place due to the quantities of naval departures
 described in books VI and VII. For Thucydides' emphasis on the naval forces of the
 expedition, to the detriment of the land forces see Kallet, *Money and the Corrosion
 of Power*, 54.

103 Size of crew: Morrison et al, *Athenian Trireme*, 107. Elite members of the crew: *Viz.*
 the *epibatai* and their officers. Arnold Gomme, *A Historical Commentary on
 Thucydides, vol. IV* (Oxford: Clarendon Press, 1945-81), 296. On the *epibatai* as
 part of the *hyperesia* see Morrison et al, *Athenian Trireme*, 109–11.

104 Pindar, *Pyth.* 4 193–200 depicts these libations being acted out by the leader of the
 ship, in that instance Jason on the Argo, but in a historical context this would be
 the *trierarchos*. For a strong comparison between Thucydides' account of the
 Sicilian departure and the naval departure of Jason and the Argonauts, given by
 Pindar, see Simon Hornblower, *Thucydides and Pindar: Historical Narrative and the
 World of Epinikian Poetry* (Oxford: Oxford University Press, 2004), 330–2.

105 *IG* I³ 93.23: καλλιέρεσιν.

106 Thucydides only refers to the omens read at the Spartan διαβατήρια rituals on
 three occasions (see section 3.2.3), all of which resulted in the Spartans returning
 home from their own borders. Thucydides (4.92.7) also uses omens as part of the
 pre-battle speech of Pagondas, before the Theban victory at Delium 424 BC; Parker,
 'Sacrifice and Battle', 304.

107 Hornblower, *Commentary, vol. III*, 393–4. The crowd itself is unprecedented with
 regard to Greek military expeditions, with the only close parallel being found in
 Alcibiades triumphal return to Athens in 407 BC, but that was the return of a
 popular individual, not an army.

108　It is interesting that no sacrifice or omen reading is mentioned by Thucydides. For
　　　more on this see section 3.2.2.

109　Aesch. *Sept.* 101–2

110　Ar. *Ach.* 545–56

111　παλλαδίων χρυσουμένων.

112　Eurip. *Heraclid.* 398-401

113　Jameson, 'Sacrifice Before Battle', 197.

114　Eur. *Supp.* 593–5. Trans. Kovacs (1998 [Adapted]): ἐγὼ γὰρ δαίμονος τοὐμοῦ μέτα
　　　στρατηλατήσω καινὸς ἐν καινῷ δορί. ἐν δεῖ μόνον μοι: τοὺς θεοὺς ἔχειν, ὅσοι
　　　δίκην σέβονται: ταῦτα γὰρ ξυνόνθ᾿ ὁμοῦ νίκην δίδωσιν. ἀρετὴ δ᾿ οὐδὲν λέγει
　　　βροτοῖσιν, ἢ μὴ τὸν θεὸν χρῄζοντ᾿ ἔχῃ.

115　Something that was swiftly adapted into an annual sacrifice of smaller numbers,
　　　due to a shortage of goats available following the heavy Persian losses. Xen. *Anab.*
　　　3.2.12; Ael. *VH.* 2.25. Pritchett, *Greek State, vol. III*, 232.

116　Hdt. 7.132.2. *GHI²* 19 shows that the Athenians at least did pay some tithe to Apollo.

117　Diod. 13.102.2.

118　[Dem.] *L.* 1.16. Trans. DeWitt (1949 [Adapted]): καὶ κατὰ τῶν νικητηρίων ἅπασιν
　　　αὐτοῖς εὐξάμενοι, μετὰ τῆς ἀγαθῆς τύχης ἐλευθεροῦτε τοὺς Ἕλληνας. 'and having
　　　vowed to all [the gods] for victory, with good fortune, set free the Greeks'.

119　Justin 20.3.1.

120　*IG* XIV.268. Giacomo Manganaro, 'L'Elaphos Di Oro Dedicato Dai Selinuntini Nell'
　　　Apollonion (*IG* XIV, NR. 268)', *Zeitschrift für Papyrologie und Epigraphik* 106,
　　　(1995): 162–64. Gods named (Lines 2–6): Zeus, Phobos, Hercules, Apollo,
　　　Poseidon, the Dioscuri (named as the Tyndarids), Athena, Demeter Malophoros
　　　and Artemis Pasicrateia.

121　This meal setting is the most frequently attested scenario for hoplites pouring
　　　libations, as was customary before and after any Greek meal. See, eg, Xen. *Anab.*
　　　6.1.5; Xen. *Hell.* 4.7.4, 7.2.23. It is also a custom that Xenophon transplants onto his
　　　fictional Persians: Xen. *Cyr.* 2.3.1, 6.4.1.

122　For private vows and their subsequent dedications see ch 3.

123　Parker, 'Sacrifice and Battle', 304 is rightly cautious of assuming that the two
　　　historians contrast two sets of ideals: Xenophon's piety, to Thucydides' non-belief.

124　Xen. *Eq. mag.* 1.1. Parker, 'Sacrifice and Battle', 300, suggests that this may be
　　　Xenophon's due diligence for when cavalry detachments are sent away from the
　　　army. Something Parker does not consider is that, in addition to his pertinent
　　　observation, the cavalry was mustered separately from the hoplites (Lys. 16.13;
　　　Xen. *Eq. mag.* 1.8–12; plus, the new system described by Artist. [*Ath. Pol.*] 49.2), so
　　　it is also likely that the *hipparchos* would conduct his own version of the army
　　　departure, including the sacrifice and omen reading. Bugh, '*Katalogeis* of the
　　　Athenian Cavalry', 23–5.

125 Xen. *Eq. mag.* 3.1.

126 Xen. *Cyr.* 2.4.18.

127 Xen. *Hell.* 4.6.23, 6.4.9, 20, 6.5.8, 7.6.44. Xenophon also lauds the attitude of the Spartans, who take many sacrificial victims with them on campaign and offer numerous sacrifices before decisions are made. He claims that this makes them the most skilled in war, making all others look like amateurs in contrast: Xen. *Lac.* 13.2-5.

128 Onasand. 10.10.25.

129 Xenophon believed it was important for the general himself to be able to read the signs and omens of the gods: Xen. *Eq. mag.* 6.6.

130 For the evidence of *manteis* being present with the military see: Pritchett, *Greek State, vol III*, 47–90.

131 The original view, masterfully compiled by Pritchett, *Greek State, vol I*, 109–15, that the two terms for sacrifice, *hiera* and *sphagia*, denote sacrifice with and without divination, has been neatly disproven by Jameson, 'Sacrifice Before Battle', 200–2, 204–5, who argues that both terms denote divination as well as sacrifice. See also Parker, 'Sacrifice and Battle', 308.

132 These include not only sacrificial readings but also a variety of different portents. An extensive list has already been compiled: Pritchett, *Greek State, vol III*: 91–153. See also Jameson, 'Sacrifice Before Battle', 204–21; Parker, 'Sacrifice and Battle', 307–9; Pritchett, *Greek State, vol III*, 83–90.

133 Hdt. 9.19.2.

134 Paus. 4.22.5.

135 Thuc. 5.54.2 and 5.55.3 occurred in the same summer, when the Spartans tried to march against Argos. The third instance (5.116.1) was another failed march against the Argives. See also Hdt. 6.76, for Cleomenes doing the exact same thing when trying to cross into Argive territory in 494 BC; Pritchett, *Greek State, vol III*, 79.

136 Xen. *Hell.* 3.5.7, 4.1.22, 4.7.2, 5.1.33, 5.3.14, 6.5.12, 3.4.3.

137 On the complex balance between religious piety and military prudence see Parker, 'Sacrifice and Battle', 304–7.

138 Xen. *Lac.* 13.2–5.

139 Xen. *Lac.* 13.5.

140 Plut. *Dio.* 23.3–4.

141 Xen. *Hell.* 6.5.49.

142 *Contra* Pritchett, *Greek State, vol I*, 113.

143 See, eg, Xen. *Anab.* 4.3.17; Aesch. *Sept.* 377–9; Hdt. 6.76.2. Jameson, 'Sacrifice Before Battle', 202.

144 Xen. Lac. 13.4: πολέμαρχοι, λοχαγοί, πεντηκοντῆρες, ξένων στρατίαρχοι, στρατοῦ σκευοφορικοῦ ἄρχοντες.

145 It is plausible that the reason Thucydides was silent about sacrifices at the Piraeus was because they had already occurred before the muster. Xenophon describes

something similar when Iphikrates ordered his men to meet in the Academy, after a fortuitous sacrifice (Xen. *Hell.* 6.5.49); but it is not clear whether his men were already mustered when the sacrifice took place.

146 Xen. *Eq. mag.* 3.1 ὑπὲρ τοῦ ἱππικοῦ; Onasand. 10.25. Trans. Tichener and Pease (1928 [Adapted]): θεασάμενοι τοῖς ὑποταττομένοις θαρρεῖν λέγοιεν ἀπαγγέλλοντες, ὡς οἱ θεοὶ κελεύουσι μάχεσθαι.

147 Xen. *Cyr.* 2.4.18: ἐθύετο ἐπὶ τῇ πορείᾳ.

148 Xen. *Cyr.* 3.2.3-4. See also the indignation vocalised by Philesius and Lycon of Acheaea against Xenophon, in his *Anabasis*, for daring to sacrifice on behalf of the army for a decision he had not yet discussed with the men. In his response, Xenophon works hard to distinguish between his personal sacrifices and omen readings and those in the function as *strategos*: Xen. *Anab.* 5.6.28.

149 *SEG* 18.153, 37–8. The aorist participle θύ]σαντας denotes that the sacrifice took place before the ships were manned, further implying that the men may not have been present to witness the ritual. Whether the decree is an authentic third/fourth-century replica of a fifth-century original is the source of much scholarly debate. Its use here is permitted because the inscription reflects common or expected practice within whichever of the two time periods it was written, both of which fall within the remit of the classical period. For a thorough analysis of the vast scholarship on the debate see Mikael Johansson, 'The Inscription from Troizen: A Decree of Themistocles?', *Zeitschrift für Papyrologie und Epigraphik* 137, (2001): 69–78.

150 See section 1.1.2.

Chapter 4

1 The terms military victory and military homecoming here are used to identify that of an army, as opposed to that of an individual.

2 The battle of Marathon was followed by an emergency march back to Athens, to defend it against a Persian fleet sailing around Attica, which may explain the lack of parade home. After Plataea, the Athenians were part of the joint Hellenic force that pushed the Persians out of Europe. Herodotus (9.121) tells us that, after their victories in the Chersonese, the Athenians simply sailed back to Hellas with their spoils and that 'nothing more happened in this year' [κατὰ τὸ ἔτος τοῦτο οὐδὲν ἐπὶ πλέον τούτων ἐγένετο]. On the lack of triumphal march see Bernd Steinbock, *Social Memory in Athenian Public Discourse: Uses and Meanings of the Past* (Ann Arbor: University of Michigan Press, 2013), 110–11.

3 Hölscher, 'Images of War', 14; Sonya Nevin, 'Animating Ancient Warfare: The Spectacle of War in the Panoply Project Vase Animations', in *War as Spectacle:*

Ancient and Modern Perspectives on the Display of Armed Conflict, ed. Anastasia Bakogianni and Valerie Hope (London: Bloomsbury Academic, 2015), 346. See Shapiro, 'Comings and Goings', for an overview of the problems which surrounding the identification of a painted scene depicting either a departure or an arrival.

4 Lisa Hau, 'Nothing to Celebrate? The Lack or Disparagement of Victory Celebrations in the Greek Historians', in *Rituals in Triumph in the Mediterranean World*, ed. Anthony Spalinger and Jeremy Armstrong (Leiden: Brill, 2013), 58–9, 63–4, 65.

5 For a clear example that reveals the sheer scale of the Roman triumph see Tac. *Hist.* 2.89.

6 Hau, 'Nothing to Celebrate?', 72, 74.

7 E.g. Pind. *Nem.* 5.50–4; 8.13–16; *Ol.* 9.10–12. For the athletic-style homecoming of generals in Greece see section 4.1.2, with Michael Blech, *Studien zum Kranz bei den Griechen* (Berlin: de Gruyter, 1982), 112–13 n 17; Peter Liddel, *Civic Obligation and Individual Liberty in Ancient Athens* (Oxford: Oxford University Press, 2007), 178; Steinbock, *Social Memory*, 89–90; David Pritchard, *Sport, Democracy and War in Classical Athens* (Cambridge: Cambridge University Press, 2013), 86.

8 Matthew Trundle, 'Commemorating Victory in Classical Greece: Why Greek Tropaia?', in *Rituals in Triumph in the Mediterranean World*, ed. Anthony Spalinger and Jeremy Armstrong (Leiden: Brill, 2013), 124.

9 Referencing the collation of military festivals found in Pritchett, *Greek State, vol. III*, 154–229.

10 The theme is absent from Pritchett's great compendium, *The Greek State at War, vols I–V* including vol. III which is specifically focused on religion, where we may have expected to find homecoming rituals discussed. It is similarly absent from Hanson, *Hoplites*; *The Western Way of War*; John Rich and Graham Shipley, ed., *War and Society in the Greek World* (London Routledge, 1993); Michael Sage, *Warfare in Ancient Greece: A Sourcebook*. London: Routledge (1996); Van Wees, *Greek Warfare*; Louis Rawlings, *The Ancient Greeks at War* (Manchester: Manchester University Press, 2007); Pritchard, 'The Symbiosis'; Garrett Fagan and Matthew Trundle, ed., *New Perspectives on Ancient Warfare* (Leiden: Brill, 2010); Crowley, *Psychology of a Hoplite*; Krzysztof Ulanowski, *The Religious Aspects of War in the Ancient Near East, Greece, and Rome* (Leiden: Brill, 2016); Matthew Dillon et al, ed., *Religion & Classical Warfare: Archaic and Classical Greece* (Barnsley: Pen & Sword, 2020). Christ, *Bad Citizen*, 113 has a section discussing the returning home of a hoplite but does not explore the form in which that homecoming took and his research focused on the aftermath of that homecoming. Scholarly works that specifically focus on the homecoming of a hoplite frequently emphasise the experiential transition home, from military into domestic life and possible evidence of friction but do not consider the moment in which the army actually returns home: Shay, *Odysseus in America*; Tritle, *Melos to My Lai*; *A New History of the Peloponnesian War*; Peter Meineck and

David Konstan (ed.), *Combat Trauma and the Ancient Greeks* (New York: Palgrave Macmillan, 2014), esp. 87–130.

11 κατὰ πόλεις: Thuc. 2.23.3, 2.79.7, 3.26.4, 4.74.1. κατα ἔθνη: Thuc. 2.68.9, 5.83.2. ἐπ᾿ οἴκου ἔκαστοι: Thuc. 5.60.4.

12 Cognates of διαλύω: Xen. *Hell.* 2.3.3, 3.5.24, 4.7.7, 5.1.35, 6.3.18, 6.4.2–3, 6.5.22. διαφῆκε το στρατευμα: Xen. *Hell.* 4.4.13, 3.2.24.

13 The nearest instance we have comes from Thuc. 3.7.3, who describes the fleet of Asopius being split and the majority of the ships being 'sent back to their homes' [ἀποπέμπει τῶν νεῶν πάλιν ἐπ᾿ οἴκου]. But this is purely a naval force and there is no suggestion that it contained any land troops.

14 Dem. 50.16

15 A similar sentiment is described by Hdt.9.117 when the Athenian were besieging Sestus. The Athenian men were discontent (ἤσχαλλον) from being away from home (ἀποδημέοντες) and urged their commanders to lead them home (ἀπάγοιεν). Notably, the Athenians did not consider the option of just disbanding there and heading home, they needed to be led home as a group.

16 See, for instance, the preparations for the Sicilian Expedition (section 3.2.1), where all the ships in the fleet are described as launching from the Piraeus.

17 Xen. *Hell.* 1.4.12–13. Edmund Bloedow, *Alcibiades Reexamined* (Wiesbaden: Franz Steiner Verlag, 1973), 69 n 404; Marc Gygax, 'Plutarch on Alcibiades' Return to Athens', *Mnemosyne* 59, 4 (2006), 484.

18 Plut. *Alc.* 32.2–3

19 Christ, *Bad Citizen*, 113, identifies this as the closest Athenian armies came to triumphal processions, drawing attention to their victory through these displays.

20 Xen. *Hell.* 1.4.13: ὁ ἐκ τοῦ ἄστεως ὄχλος.

21 Plut. *Alc.* 32.3. Trans. B. Perring (1916 [Adapted]): ἀλλ᾿ ἐκεῖνος καὶ δεδιὼς κατήγετο, καὶ καταχθεὶς οὐ πρότερον ἀπέβη τῆς τριήρους, πρὶν στὰς . . . ἰδεῖν Εὐρυπτόλεμόν τε τὸν ἀνεψιὸν παρόντα καὶ τῶν ἄλλων φίλων καὶ οἰκείων συχνοὺς ἐκδεχομένους καὶ παρακαλοῦντας.

22 Diod. 13.69.1–2 presents a similar scene which reflects Plutarch's quite closely.

23 Xen. *Hell.* 1.4.10

24 See Table 3.

25 Thuc. 4.38.4–5.

26 Thuc. 4.38.5, 41.1, 57.4; Plut. *Nic.* 9.4; Diod. 12.63.4.

27 For a catalogue of instances when the Athenians enslaved their enemies after victory see Pritchett, *Greek State, vol V*, 226–29. For the Greek practice of taking prisoners after battle, see Pierre Ducrey, *Le Traitement des Prisonniers de Guerre dans la Grèce Antique, des Origines à la Conquête Romaine* (Paris: E. De Boccard, 1986) and Jason Crowley, 'Surviving Defeat: Battlefield Surrender in Classical Greece', *Journal of Ancient History* 8, 1 (2020): 1–25.

28 Dem. 50.19, 24; Peter Krentz, 'War', in *The Cambridge History of Greek and Roman Warfare, vol 1: Greece, the Hellenistic World and the Rise of Rome*, ed. Philip Sabin et al (Cambridge: Cambridge University Press, 2007), 193.

29 Sphacterian prisoners: Thuc. 5.3.4; Diod. 12.73.3. Thrasyllus' captives: Xen. *Hell.* 1.2.13. See also the unrecorded number of captives from Corcyra and Aegina, as described by Thuc. 4.46.3 and Diod.12.65.9 respectively. The exact location of the prison where these captives were held has not been identified. Eugene Vanderpool, 'The State Prison of Athens', in *From Athens to Gordion: The Papers of a Memorial Symposium for Rodney S. Young*, ed. Keith DeVries (Philadelphia: The University Museum, 1980), 19 and Virginia Hunter, 'The Prison of Athens: A Comparative Perspective', *Phoenix* 51, 3/4 (1997): 322 n 64, seem correct in their assertion that war captives would have been held separately from the civic prison, due to their sheer numbers if nothing else, but no location has yet been suggested.

30 Raoul Lonis, *Guerre et religion en Grèce à l'époque classique. Recherches sur les rites, les dieux, l'idéologie de la victoire.* (Besançon: Université de Franche-Comté, 1979), 303–4, argues that the return of Alcibiades discussed above is evidence of a Greek version of a triumphal march but he relies too heavily on the supposed account of Douris of Samos, an account of which Plutarch himself is sceptical.

31 Diod. 17.72.1–6. Diodorus does not actually use the term θρίαμβος to describe Alexander's victory parade, but rather τὸν ἐπινίκιον κῶμον.

32 Xen. *Eq. mag.* 2.1, 3.1–2.

33 Xen. *Anab.* 5.5.5.

34 Thuc. 6.58.2.

35 Lys. 13.80–2.

36 Lys. 13.81. Trans. Todd (2000 [Adapted]): οὐ γὰρ ἔφη δεῖν ἀνδροφόνον αὐτὸν ὄντα συμπέμπειν τὴν πομπὴν τῇ Ἀθηνᾷ. 'He said that he [Agoratus], as a murderer, must have no part in the procession to Athena.' See more generally Parker, *Miasma*, 64–66.

37 Commentators on this passage have not yet produced an analysis which highlights the military homecoming inherent in this episode. It is more commonly discussed in relation to the inner social dynamics of a fractured Athenian populace: whether or not this was a parade to promote unity, or to further emphasise a division between the victors and the defeated. See, especially, Barry Strauss, 'Ritual, Social Drama, and Politics in Classical Athens', *American Journal of Ancient History* 10, 1 (1985): 70 and Julia Shear, *Polis and Revolution: Responding to Oligarchy in Classical Athens* (Cambridge: Cambridge University Press, 2011), 288. Strauss, 'Ritual, Social Drama', 89, also observed that Lysias' account of Agoratus does, in itself, symbolise the themes of disunity that would consume the next generation of Athenian citizens; Agoratus having been a previous supporter of the Thirty before trying to change sides.

184 *Notes to pp. 69–72*

38 Stephen Todd, *Lysias* (Austin: University of Texas Press, 2000), 156 n 52; Athena Kavoulaki, 'Processional Performance and the Democratic Polis', in *Performance Culture and Athenian Democracy*, ed. Simon Goldhill and Robin Osbourne (Cambridge: Cambridge University Press, 1999), 304; Strauss, 'Ritual, Social Drama', 70.

39 Andrew Wolpert, *Remembering Defeat: Civil War and Civic Memory in Ancient Athens* (Baltimore: Johns Hopkins University Press, 21, 62, 84.

40 Strauss, 'Ritual, Social Drama', 70.

41 See Christopher Carey's apparatus: *Lysiae Orationes cum Fragmentis* (Oxford: Oxford University Press, 2007), 144–5.

42 Lys. 13.81: τὰ ὅπλα.

43 Lys. 13.81: τήν τε ἀσπίδα αὐτοῦ λαβὼν ἔρριψε.

44 Xen. *Hell.* 2.4.39: σὺν τοῖς ὅπλοις.

45 Thuc. 1.6.1-3; Arist. *Pol.* 1268b40ff. Hans van Wees, 'Greeks Bearing Arms: The State, the Leisure Class, and the Display of Weapons in Archaic Greece', in *Archaic Greece: New Approaches and New Evidence*, ed. Nick Fisher and Hans van Wees (London: Duckworth, 1998a), 333–4.

46 Plut. *De Glor. Athen.* 7

47 Kavoulaki, 'Processional Performance', 304–5.

48 At the end of his *Anabasis*, Xenophon hands over the Cyrean Greek mercenaries to the Spartan commander Thibron. Thibron turned them into a unit of his army (*Hell.* 3.1.6), which Derkylidas took over when he succeeded command in 399 BC (*Hell.* 3.1.8). It is generally considered that Xenophon remained with the Ten Thousand during this time, as one of their commanders, making him an important eye witness to the events he describes with Derkylidas. John Dillery, *Xenophon and the History of his Times* (London: Routledge, 1995), 271 n 29, 274 n 63); Torrey Luce, *The Greek Historians* (London: Routledge, 1997), 73; Michael Flower, *Xenophon's Anabasis, or The Expedition of Cyrus* (Oxford: Oxford University Press, 2012), 54.

49 Xen. *Hell.* 3.1.21.

50 Xen. *Hell.* 3.1.22.

51 Xen. *Hell.* 3.2.22. Xenophon states that they remained armed throughout the procession and the sacrifice to Athena: Xen. *Hell.* 3.1.23.

52 This was, after all, a ruse designed to allow the Spartan commander to take control of the city without any bloodshed.

53 Skepsis is specifically described as welcoming Derkylidas: Xen. *Hell.* 3.1.21.

54 Hamel, *Athenian Generals*, 140–57, for a list of all possible trials of Athenian strategos between the years 501/0–322/1 BC.

55 Thuc. 5.60.6.

56 Lys. 15.5; Plat. *Leg.* 12.943 a–b.

57 See n 61.

58 Christ, *The Bad Citizen*, 113.

59 Aesch. 3.183–6 describes the erection of three inscribed herms, honouring the victorious men.

60 Aesch. 2.169.

61 *Prohedria*: Ar. *Eq.* 702–4. *Sitesis*: Ar. *Eq.* 280, 709, 766, 1404; *IG* I³131. The chorus of *Knights* is also made to lament a change in incentive for the men of Athens, compared to earlier generations: 'our present men refuse to fight, unless they get the honours of the Prytaneum (*sitesis*) and precedence in their seats (*prohedria*)'.

62 Dem. 13.21-2, 20.84, 23.130, 196-8; Aesch. 2.80, 3.243. Generals who are so described include Conon, Iphicrates, Chabrias and Timotheus. Liddel, *Civic Obligation*, 178; Steinbock, *Social Memory*, 89–90; Pritchard, *Sport, Democracy and War*, 86. Lycurgus: Lyc. 1.51.

63 David Pritchard, 'Public Honours for Panhellenic Sporting Victors in Democratic Athens', *Nikephoros* 25, (2012): 209. For wider considerations of the *sitesis* in classical Athens, see Michael Osborne, 'Entertainment in the Prytaneion at Athens', *Zeitschrift für Papyrologie und Epigraphik* 41, (1981): 153–70; Alan Henry, *Honours and Privileges in Athenian Decrees* (Hildesheim: George Olms, 1983), 275–8; Douglas MacDowell, 'Hereditary "Sitesis" in Fourth-Century Athens', *Zeitschrift für Papyrologie und Epigraphik* 162, (2007): 111–13.

64 Thuc. 4.121.1. Strassler (2008 [Adapted]): ... τὸν Βρασίδαν τά τ᾽ ἄλλα καλῶς ἐδέξαντο καὶ δημοσίᾳ μὲν χρυσῷ στεφάνῳ ἀνέδησαν ὡς ἐλευθεροῦντα τὴν Ἑλλάδα, ἰδίᾳ δὲ ἐταινίουν τε καὶ προσήρχοντο ὥσπερ ἀθλητῇ.

65 Xen. *Hell.* 2.3.8.

66 Xen. *Hell.* 5.1.3.

67 Dem. 19.128.

68 Plut. *Per.* 28.3-4.

69 Plut. *Per.* 28.4: ὥσπερ ἀθλητὴν νικηφόρον.

70 Thuc. 2.46.1.

71 Xen. *Hell.* 1.7.33: πολὺ δικαιότερον στεφάνοις γεραίρειν τοὺς νικῶντας.

72 Pritchard, 'Public Honours', 218.

73 Interest here lies solely with victory and the homecoming of warriors and athletes and the prizes they are awarded, rather than analysing the relationship between athletics and war in the ancient Greek world, for which there is a long-standing debate. For the various arguments see Michael Poliakoff, *Combat Sports in the Ancient World: Competition, Violence, and Culture* (New Haven: Yale University Press, 1987), 89–103; Tim Cornell, 'On War and Games in the Ancient World', in *The Global Nexus Engaged: Past, Present, Future Interdisciplinary Olympic Studies. Sixth International Symposium for Olympic Research*, ed. Kevin Wamsley et al (London, Ontario: International Centre for Olympic Studies, 2002), 32–3; Nigel Spivey, *The Ancient Olympics: A History* (Oxford: Oxford University Press, 2004), 1–29; David Pritchard, 'Sport, War and Democracy in Classical Athens', *The International Journal of the History of Sport* 26, 2

(2009): 223–6, Hans van Wees, 'Rivalry in History: An Introduction', in *Competition in the Ancient World*, ed. Nick Fisher and Hans van Wees (Swansea: Classical Press of Wales, 2011), 27; Paul Christesen, 'Athletics and Social Order in Sparta in the Classical Period', *Classical Antiquity* 31, 2 (2012): 235–9.

74 Xen. *Eq. mag.* 8.7.

75 Eur. *TrGF* F 284.

76 Pritchard, 'Public Honours', 211.

77 Thuc. 4.120.

78 Ar. *Knights.* 55, 76, 355, 702, 742, 846, 1005, 1058-59, 1167, 1201. Carl Anderson, 'Themistocles and Cleon in Aristophanes' Knights, 763ff', *The American Journal of Philology* 110, 1 (1989): 14. Demosthenes and Cleon were not originally named in the play but modern critics and editors now generally accept their identities, who are called Slave 1 and Paphlagonian respectively: Kenneth Dover, 'Aristophanes, Knights 11–20', *The Classical Review*, 9, 3 (1959): 198; Walter Connor, *Thucydides* (Princeton: Princeton University Press, 1984), 117 n 18; Keith Sidwell, *Aristophanes the Democrat: The Politics of Satirical Comedy During the Peloponnesian War* (Cambridge: Cambridge University Press, 2009), 155–6. For an analysis of the scholia tradition, which name these characters, see Sidwell, *Aristophanes the Democrat*, 155–6, n 2.

79 On the athletic imagery see Laura Swift, *The Hidden Chorus: Echoes of Genre in Tragic Lyric* (Oxford: Oxford University Press, 2010), 162–70.

80 Eur. *Elec.* 863.

81 Eur. *Elec.* 883–5. Trans. Luschnig & Woodruff (2011): ὦ καλλίνικε, πατρὸς ἐκ νικηφόρου γεγώς, Ὀρέστα, τῆς ὑπ' Ἰλίῳ μάχης, δέξαι κόμης σῆς βοστρύχων ἀνδήματα. ἥκεις γὰρ οὐκ ἀχρεῖον ἐκπλεθρον δραμὼν ἀγῶν' ἐς οἴκους, ἀλλὰ πολέμιον κτανὼν Αἴγισθον, ὃς σὸν πατέρα κἀμὸν ὤλεσε. σύ τ', ὦ παρασπίστ', ἀνδρὸς εὐσεβεστάτου παίδευμα Πυλάδη, στέφανον ἐξ ἐμῆς χερὸς δέχου.

82 W. Geoffrey Arnott, 'Double the Vision: A Reading of Euripides' "Electra"', *Greece & Rome* 28, 2 (1981): 188.

83 Eur. *Elec.* 880–1

84 For the difference between these two terms and their infrequent interchangeability see Mary Blundell, *Helping Friends and Harming Enemies: A Study in Sophocles and Greek Ethics* (Cambridge: Cambridge University Press, 1991), 39, 92–3.

85 Euripides uses the term on two other occasions within his corpus: once in *Cyc.* 6, when Selinus describes himself taking his position in battle against the Giants and a second time in *Phoen.* 1165, when a messenger describes Tydeus and his shield-bearers throwing their javelins in the siege.

86 Descriptions of the process for this division are surprisingly scarce in the literary record but famous instances are found during the Persian Wars: Hdt. 8.121-2, 9.80-1. cf. Hdt. 8.27.4-5. For the issues of reconstructing the process of this division and possible solutions, see Pritchett, *Greek State, vol I*, 82–4; *Greek State, vol* V: 363–438;

Angelos Chaniotis, *War in the Hellenistic World: A Social and Cultural History* (Oxford: Blackwell Publishing, 2005), 132–42; Theodora Jim, *Sharing with the Gods: Aparchai and Dekatai in Ancient Greece* (Oxford: Oxford University Press, 2014), 177–81.

87 *IG* I³ 501. Hdt. 5.77.3-4; Paus. 1.28.2.

88 Jim, *Sharing with the Gods*, 181–2, n 21.

89 Paus. 1.28.2, 9.4.1.

90 William Dinsmoor, 'Attic Building Accounts. IV. The Statue of Athena Promachos', *American Journal of Archaeology* 25, 2 (1921): 126; Jim, *Sharing with the Gods*, 182. Part of the controversy comes from the dating of the monument's construction, which seems to be the latter half of the fifth century. For the question of dating see Ronald Stroud, *Athenian Empire on Stone* (Athens: Hellēnikē epigraphikē hetaireia, 2006), 34. For the question of whether the battle of Marathon could provide the necessary spoils see Evelyn Harrison, *Athenian Agora XI: Archaic and Archaistic Sculpture* (Princeton: The American School of Classical Studies at Athens, 1965), 11 n 68; Werner Gauer, 'Das Athenerschatzhaus und die marathonischen Akrothinia in Delphi', in *Forschungen und Funde. Festschrift für Bernhard Neutsch*, ed. Bernhard Neutsch et al (Innsbruck: Verlag des Instituts für Sprachwissenschaft der Universität Innsbruck, 1980), 127–37.

91 Hdt. 6.137–40.

92 *IG* I³ 1466 and 518.

93 Reinhard Stupperich, *Staatsbegräbnis und Privatgrabmal im klassischen Athen* (PhD diss. Münster: Universität Münster, 1977), 207; Christoph Clairmont, *Patrios Nomos: Public Burial in Athens during the Fifth and Fourth Centuries BC: The Archaeological, Epigraphic-Literary, and Historical Evidence* (Oxford: BAR International Series 161, 1983), 89–90, 92–3; Mario Rausch, 'Miltiades, Athen und, die Rhamnusier auf Lemnos' (*IG* I3 522bis)', *Klio* 81, 1 (1999): 7–8. For the various forms in which the tithes could take in military dedications, including 'raw', see Jim, *Sharing with the Gods*, 180–1.

94 Athens, Agora Museum: B 262.

95 For the distinction between public and private military dedications see Pritchett, *Greek State, vol. III*, 241–2.

96 Ῥαμνόσιοι ὁι ἐν Λεμνο[ι ἀ]νέ[θεσαν Νεμ]έσει. Following Michael Hornum, *Nemesis, the Roman State and the Games* (Leiden: Brill, 1993), 202.

97 Vasileios Petrakos, Ὁ δῆμος τοῦ Ῥαμνοῦντος, *vol. 2* (Athens: Ἡ ἐν Ἀθήναις Ἀρχαιολογικὴ Ἑταιρεία, 1999), no. 86; Sekunda, 'Athenian Demography', 325–6; Argyro Tataki, 'Nemesis, Nemeseis, and the Gladiatorial Games at Smyrna.' *Mnemosyne* 62, 4 (2009): 642; Stupperich, *Staatsbegräbnis und Privatgrabmal*, 207; Clairmont, *Patrios Nomos*, 89–90, 92–3. Rausch, 'Miltiades', 13–16, gives a well-rounded argument, concluding that there are two likely dates, either 498 BC after the action of Miltiades, or a later action by Lenmian-born descendants fighting in the 470s. For a similar conclusion see Emma Stafford, *Greek Cults of Deified Abstractions* (PhD diss. London: University College London, 1998), 81.

98 The importance of the cult of Nemesis was elevated in the early fifth century, possibly as a result of the Athenian victory at Marathon for which Nemesis was given some responsibility for the Persian defeat (Paus. 1.33.2-3). Margaret Miles, 'A Reconstruction of the Temple of Nemesis at Rhamnous', *Hesperia* 58, (1989): 138–9; Vasileios Petrakos, *Rhamnous* (Athens: Ministry of Culture, 1991), 7; Stafford, *Greek Cults*, 104–5.

99 Following the recent edition of Stephen Lambert, 'Dedications and Decrees Commemorating Military Action in 339–8 BC', in *Axon: Studies in Honor of Ronald S. Stroud*, ed. Angelos Matthaiou and Nikolaos Papazarkadas (Athens: Greek Epigraphical Society, 2015), 237–41.

100 For the anomalous appearance of a *taxiarchos* being honoured for his military duties, see Lambert, 'Dedications and decrees', 242–4.

101 Trans. Lambert (2015: [Adapted]): Κεκροπίδος οἱ στρατευ[σ]άμενοι ἐπὶ Λυσιμαχίδου ἄρχοντος [κ]αὶ ὁ ταξίαρχος Βούλαρ[χος] Ἀριστοβούλου Φλυεὺς Ἀθηνᾶι.

102 Lambert, 'Dedications and Decrees', 241–2.

103 Lambert, 'Dedications and Decrees', 236.

104 There is a tantalising fragment within *IG* II² 1155, which suggests that a dedication was authorised by the council, possibly referring to the one to Athens: ἐπὶ τὸ ἀνάθημα ἐπιγρ[άψ]αι καθάπ[ερ]. 'inscribe it on the dedication as well as …'.

105 See section 3.2.2.

106 See Jim, *Sharing with the Gods*, 194.

107 Note the dedication made by Xenophon on behalf of his dead friend Proxenus, following their service in the army of Cyrus the younger. Xen. *Anab.* 5.3.5, with Catherine Keesling, 'The Callimachus Monument on the Athenian Acropolis (*CEG* 256) and Athenian Commemoration of the Persian Wars', in *Archaic and Classical Greek Epigram*, ed. Manuel Baumbach et al (Cambridge: Cambridge University Press, 2010): 113.

108 See the compiled evidence in William Rouse, *Greek Votive Offerings* (Cambridge: Cambridge University Press, 1902), 105–48, with additional comments by Pritchett, *Greek State, vol III*, 269–76. Famously, Themistocles attempted to make a private dedication at Delphi, from the spoils of the Persian Wars, but was refused: Paus. 10.14.5-6. See also Dem. 23.196-8.

109 See Rouse, *Votive Offerings*, 109.

110 Dem. 57.64. For further evidence, see Lys. 10.28.

111 It is more likely to be the latter. The evidence for Greek warriors dedicating their own weaponry or armour is sparse and, if this is what Euxitheus has done, this would be the first identifiable case that relates to a classical Athenian. For an overview of the available evidence for this practice see Rouse, *Votive Offerings*, 111–14 and Pritchett, *Greek State, vol III*, 249–52.

112 Euxitheus was not a rich man, while still seemingly able to fulfil the criteria of hoplite service. He describes the financial constraints on his family in the speech (Dem. 57.25, 31) and makes no assertion about his military service, something that would be expected had he served in any form of leadership capacity. William Lacey, 'The Family of Euxitheus (Demosthenes LVII)', *The Classical Quarterly* 30, 1 (1980): 60.

113 It should be noted that the dedication of armour does not automatically mean the commemoration of the battle/campaign from which that armour was taken. Without a thorough dedicatory inscription it is impossible to ascertain this. However, the contrast made here is that the armour taken in battle is still a memento from one battle or campaign, as opposed to a unique dedication created outside of the military experience to commemorate a man's time in service.

114 *IG* I³ 850. Trans. Keesling (2017: 124 [Adapted]): [Πα]ρθένοι Ἐκφάντο με πατὲρ ἀνέθεκε καὶ hυιὸς / ἐνθάδ᾽ Ἀθεναίει μνεμα πόνον Ἄρεος / Ἐγέλοχος μεγάλε<ς> τε φιλοχσενίες ἀρετε̃ς τε / πάσες μοῖραν ἔχον τένδε πόλιν νέμεται. Κριτίος : καὶ Νεσιότες : ἐποιεσάτεν.

115 Catherine Keesling, *The Votive Statues of the Athenian Acropolis* (Cambridge: Cambridge University Press, 2003), 187–90); *Early Greek Portraiture: Monuments and Histories* (Cambridge: Cambridge University Press, 2017), 124–5; Arrington, *Ashes, Images and Memories*, 189.

116 Josine Blok, *Citizenship in Classical Athens* (Cambridge: Cambridge University Press, 2017), 255; Keesling, *Greek Portraiture*, 124.

117 On the metic status of Hegelochus and the question of his award of citizenship following military service, see Blok, *Citizenship*, 254–7.

Chapter 5

1 Pemberton, 'The Name Vase', 64.

2 Vasiliki Siurla-Theodoridou, *Die Familie in der griechischen Kunst und Literatur Des 8. Bis 6. Jahrhunderts V. Chr.* (Munich: V. Florentz, 1989), 274; Martina Seifert, 'Oikos and Hetairoi: Black Figure Departure Scenes Reconsidered', in *Athenian Potters and Painters, vol III*, ed. John Oakley (Oxford: Oxbow Books, 2014): 219 n 4.

3 See, in addition, Tim McNiven, *Gestures in Attic Vase Painting: Their Use and Meaning, 550–450 BC* (PhD diss. Ann Arbor: University of Michigan, 1982), 37–8, and Lissarrague, 'World of the Warrior', 44–5.

4 Shapiro, 'Comings and Goings', 113–26.

5 Shapiro, 'Comings and Goings', 118–21.

6 Pemberton, 'The Name Vase', 65.

7 Matheson, 'Farewell with Arms', 26.

8 Connor and Jackson, *Catalogue of Greek Vases*, 98; Matheson, 'Farewell with Arms', 26.

9 Elisabeth Tetlow, *Women, Crime and Punishment in Ancient Law and Society: Volume 2: Ancient Greece* (New York: Continuum International Publishing Group, 2005), 64. The avoidance of eye contact is especially prevalent in departure scenes painted onto white *lekythoi*, emphasising the funerary context of the vase: Arrington, *Ashes, Images and Memories*, 269–70.

10 Munich, Antikensammlungen: J326, *BA* 206994.

11 Malibu, The J. Paul Getty Museum: 79.AE.139, *BA* 14731

12 ARV² 339, *BA* 204336

13 Munich, Antikensammlungen: J411, *BA* 201657

14 Wurzburg, Universitat, Martin von Wagner Mus.: HA120, *BA* 201654

15 Thematic unity and its identification has become the orthodox enterprise in the study of Greek vase painting: Jeffrey Hurwit, 'Reading the Chigi Vase', *Hesperia* 71, 1 (2002): 2.

16 On the methods of combining the scenes on a vase see, in particular, Herbert Hoffman, 'Why Did the Greeks Need Imagery? An Anthropological Approach to the Study of Greek Vase-Painting', *Hephaistos* 9, (1988): 143–62); Andrew Stewart, *History, Myth, and Allegory in the Program of the Temple of Athena Nike, Athens*, (Washington DC: National Gallery of Art, 1985), 53–73; Mark Stansbury-O'Donnell, *Pictorial Narrative in Ancient Greek Art* (Cambridge: Cambridge University Press, 1999), 118–57; Hurwit, 'Chigi Vase', 1–22), with further bibliographic information (2 n 7). This view is not universal, however. Even structuralists such as Christiane Bron and François Lissarrague, 'Looking at the Vase', in *A City of Images: Iconography and Society in Ancient Greece*, ed. Claude Bérard et al (Princeton: Princeton University Press, 1989), 21, admit that there is very often no link between the images on vases, other than proximity. Whereas scholars such as Jocelyn Small, 'Time in Space: Narrative in Classical Art', *The Art Bulletin* 81, 4 (1999): 573 n 24, firmly reject the notion that vases can be read in such a unified way, stating that the problem of iconographic unity is 'solely a modern one'.

17 Figure 4: Rome, Mus. Naz. Etrusco di Villa Giulia: 46942, *BA* 17982. Figure 5: New York (NY), Metropolitan Museum: 56.171.44, *BA* 206877.

18 The distinction of syntagmatic and paradigmatic relationships between narratives is based on a literary model and its approach to art was first implemented by Stewart, 'Stesichoros and the François Vase', in *Ancient Greek Art and Iconography*, ed. Warren Moon (Madison: University of Wisconsin Press, 1983), 57–60). For the literary model see Jonathan Culler, *Structuralist Poetics. Structuralism, Linguistics, and the Study of Literature* (Routledge: London, 1975), 12–14. My reading of the vase here aligns itself with Stansbury-O'Donnell, *Pictorial Narrative*, 118, who shows that a syntagmatic relationship can include a set of connected stories that are different, as

long as they follow a linear development of time, such as activities by different members of the same family.

19 See, e.g, Ferrara, Museo Nazionale di Spina: T740, *BA* 206934; Quebec, Laval University: D19, *BA* 207330; Athens, Benaki Museum: 38151, *BA* 9029956; Syracuse, Museo Arch. Regionale Paolo Orsi: 24644, *BA* 214056; Berlin, Antikensammlung: 1970.9, *BA* 318.

20 See, e.g, London, British Museum: E385, *BA* 213871; Bologna, Museo Civico Archeologico: 467, *BA* 216977; Sotheby's, sale catalogue: 5.7.1982, 153, NO.391, *BA* 8580; London, British Museum: E329, *BA* 213854. This includes the shaking of hands, see, e.g., Paris, Musée du Louvre: G429, *BA* 21439; London, British Museum: E448.

21 See, e.g., Berlin, Antikensammlung: F2521, *BA* 205786; London, British Museum: E576, *BA* 207693; Cambridge (MA), Harvard Univ., Arthur M. Sackler Mus: 1925.30.130, *BA* 211593.

22 See, for instance, London, British Museum: E275, *BA* 207126; Newcastle-upon-Tyne, Great North Museum, Shefton Collection: 55, *BA* 213855; Christie's, Manson and Woods, sale catalogue: 28.4.1993, 57-59, No.24, *BA* 214837; Ferrara, Museo Nazionale di Spina: T350, *BA* 207182; London, British Museum: E412. All of these offer a sense of motion or departure through the direction of the feet, either pointing forward towards the viewer, or with an open stance. None of these reflect the foot position of Figure 4b, where the hoplite's feet point toward the woman. For a possible interpretation that this gesture indicates the man is listening to words being spoken by the woman, see McNiven, *Gestures*, 172, 193–4.

23 Gunnel Ekroth, 'Theseus and the Stone. The Iconographic and Ritual Contexts of a Greek Votive Relief in the Louvre' in *Divine Images and Human Imaginations in Ancient Greece and Rome*, ed. Ioannis Mylonopoulos (Leiden: Brill, 2010), 165–66. There is another variation found in the 'departure scene' motif, in which the shield leans against an altar while a libation is poured: London, British Museum: E412, *BA* 215324; Ekroth, 'Theseus and the Stone', 166.

24 Aesch. *Sept.* 42–53; Xen. *Anab.* 2.2.9. Christopher Faraone, 'Molten Wax, Spilt Wine and Mutilated Animals: Sympathetic Magic in near Eastern and Early Greek Oath Ceremonies', *The Journal of Hellenic Studies* 113, (1993): 68; Ekroth, 'Theseus and the Stone', 166-7.

25 There is reference in the literature to the act of pouring something onto a shield, and it comes from Ar. *Ach.* 1128-8, which describes the pouring of oil on the shield while Lamachus prepares to depart. The pouring of oil seems to be used to polish the bronze, through which he can see the reflection of Dicaeopolis and on which he comments. There is no suggestion that this is a religious ritual of any sort.

26 ARV² 594.53. Dietrich Von Bothmer, 'Greek Vases from the Hearst Collection', *The Metropolitan Museum of Art Bulletin* 13, (1957): 166, 175.

27 My gratitude to Prof. Tim McNiven for this observation.

28 The clearest example of this common practice can be seen in a humorous amphora, attributed to the Berlin Painter (Angers, Musee Pince: 12, *BA* 202133), in which the libation is being poured toward the ground, only to be drunk by a waiting dog that stands beneath.

29 Altar: E.g. Paris, Musée du Louvre: G431, *BA* 206987; Oxford, Ashmolean Museum: 1927.3, *BA* 207777; London, British Museum: E412, *BA* 215324; Syracuse, Museo Arch. Regionale Paolo Orsi: 30747, *BA* 215270; Paris, Musée du Louvre: G538, *BA* 216030. Incense burner: London, British Museum: E269, *BA* 201835. For the common use of incense in Greek ritual see Aesch. *Ag.* 1312; Ar. *Ran.* 871; Soph. *OT.* 4; Dem. 21.52; Diod. 16.11.1.

30 Deborah Boedeker, 'Family Matters: Domestic Religion in Classical Greece', in *Household and Family Religion in Antiquity*, ed. John Bodel and Saul Olyan (Oxford: Blackwell Publishing, 2008), 230–4.

31 Antiph. 1.16-7.

32 Boedeker, 'Family Matters', 230.

33 Isae. 8.16.

34 Aesch. *Ag.* 1037-8.

35 Jameson, 'Domestic Space and the Greek City', 192; Morgan, *The Greek Classical House*, 149–53; Kimberly Bowes, 'At Home', in *A Companion to the Archaeology of Religion in the Ancient World*, ed. Rubina Raja and Jörg Rüpke (Oxford: Wiley Blackwell, 2015), 215.

36 See, e.g., The inscription on Theseus' departure in Bologna, Museo Civico Archeologico: PU273, *BA* 217210; Angela Spieß, *Der Kriegerabschied auf attischen Vasen der archaischen Zeit* (Frankfurt: Peter Lang, 1992), 2–25, 85–9.

37 Richard Neer, *Style and Politics in Athenian Vase-Painting: The Craft of Democracy, ca. 530-460 BCE* (Cambridge: Cambridge University Press, 2002), 2, 6, 183–4; Matheson, 'Farewell with Arms', 24.

38 Sian Lewis, *The Athenian Woman: An Iconographic Handbook* (London: Routledge, 2002), 40; Matheson, 'Farewell with Arms', 26.

39 Lissarrague, *L'autre Guerrier*, 43–4, 89–91; Lewis, *Athenian Woman*, 41–42.

40 On the female market for red-figure vases see, especially, Sue Blundell and Nancy Rabinowitz, 'Women's Bonds, Women's Pots: Adornment Scenes in Attic Vase-Painting', *Phoenix* 62, 1/2 (2008): 116; with Oakley and Sinos, *The Wedding*, 47; H Alan Shapiro, 'Correlating Shape and Subject: The Case of the Archaic Pelike', in *Athenian Potters and Painters: The Conference Proceedings*, Oxbow Monographs 67, ed. John Oakley (Oxford: Oxbow Books, 1997), 65, 69 n 29.

41 As Avramidou, *Codrus Painter*, 57, points out, this use of ambiguity would have widened the market to audiences outside Attica and even to people outside Greece.

42 The most obvious example should be Homer's *Odyssey* but, while it was undoubtedly influential, it was ultimately written centuries before the period under review.

43 Helene Foley, *Female Acts in Greek Tragedy* (Princeton: Princeton University Press, 2001), 92; Andrea Doyle, 'Cassandra – Feminine Corrective in Aeschylus's "Agamemnon"', *Acta Classica* 51, (2008): 65–73. For the marital imagery present in the play see Lynda McNeill, 'Bridal Cloths, Cover-ups, and Kharis: The 'Carpet Scene' in Aeschylus' "Agamemnon"', *Greece & Rome* 52, 1 (2005): 1–17.

44 Hom. *Od.* 4.519-37

45 Marigo Alexopoulou, *The Theme of Returning Home in Ancient Greek Literature: The Nostos of the Epic Heroes* (Lewiston: Edwin Mellen Press, 2009), 59.

46 Barbara Goff, *Citizen Bacchae: Women's Ritual Practice in Ancient Greece* (Berkeley: University of California Press, 2004), 301.

47 See section 1.1.1.

48 Diod. 4.11.1-2; Apoll. 2.4.12. There is evidence that both the stories of Heracles' *mania* and the murder of his children were in circulation before Euripides' play: Paus. 9.11.2; Pherec. fr. 14F. However, the evidence is too fragmentary to be able to place the episodes within the story's chronology. For discussion on these fragments see Godfrey Bond, *Euripides' Heracles. With Introduction and Commentary* (Oxford: Clarendon Press, 1981), xxviii–xxx); Stafford, *Heracles* (London: Routledge, 2012), 89.

49 Bond, *Heracles*, xxix; Kathleen Riley, *The Reception and Performance of Euripides' Herakles: Reasoning Madness* (Oxford: Oxford University Press, 2008), 5; Stafford, *Heracles*, 89.

50 Eur. *Her.* 140–235. with Bond, *Heracles*, 108–9. The contrast between the bravery of using a spear and shield, like a hoplite, with the cowardice of the bow was a commonly held truism in classical Athens. The fact that this assertion of Heracles' cowardice comes from the mouth of Lycus is, therefore, very relevant. Amphitryon's rebuttal is unsatisfactory and – following Richard Hamilton, 'Slings and Arrows: The Debate with Lycus in the Heracles', *Transactions of the American Philological Association*, 115 (1985): 21–3 – it is undermined by the words of both Megara (Eur. *Her.* 275–311) and Heracles later in the play (Eur. *Her.* 1348–57).

51 Rush Rehm, *The Play of Space: Spatial Transformation in Greek Tragedy* (Princeton: Princeton University Press, 2002), 100; Riley, *Reception and Performance*, 14–15; Marigo Alexopoulou, *The Homecoming Pattern in Greek Tragedy* (PhD diss. Glasgow: University of Glasgow, 2003), 129–35; *Theme of Returning*, 61.

52 Alexopoulou, *Homecoming Pattern*, 134.

53 Hugh Parry, 'The Second Stasimon of Euripides' Heracles (637–700)', *The American Journal of Philology* 86, 4 (1965): 363–74; Alexopoulou, *Homecoming Pattern*, 131–2; Swift, *Hidden Chorus*, 121–2.

54 Alexopoulou, *Homecoming Pattern*, 131.

55 The word appears eight times in the play referring to Heracles or an item in his possession: Eur. *Her.* 49, 180, 570, 582, 681, 789, 961, 1046. On the athletic undertones to this word, see Swift, *Hidden Chorus*, 133–4.

56 Eur. *Her*. 49: καλλινίκου δορὸς. The second being his club, Eur. *Her*. 582.

57 Eur. *Her*. 179–80. On the association with Heracles, this epithet and the Gigantomachy, see Lillian Lawler, 'Orchêsis Kallinikos', *Transactions and Proceedings of the American Philological Association* 79, (1948): 254–5, 266.

58 Minyans: Eur. *Her*. 220. Cerberus: Eur. *Her*. 612–13. Centaurs: Eur. *Her*. 1273.

59 Lycus: Eur. *Her*. 1168. Chorus: Eur. *Her*. 436–41.

60 Eur. *Her*. 1133–4.

61 Eur. *Her*. 1172. For an historical comparison, see Xenophon's description of the battlefield following the battle inside the Long Walls of Corinth: Xen. *Hell*. 4.4.12.

62 Eur. *Her*. 1176: οὐ γὰρ δορός γε παῖδες ἵστανται πέλας.

63 Epinician language is present in *Agamemnon*, also: Deborah Steiner, 'The Immeasures of Praise: The Epinician Celebration of Agamemnon's Return', *Hermes* 138, 1 (2010): 22–37. But no scholar would challenge the identification of Agamemnon as a warrior coming home, rather than an athlete.

64 Eur. *Her*. 157–64.

65 Aesch. *Ag*. 851-3. Trans. Smyth (1926 [adapted]): νῦν δ' ἐς μέλαθρα καὶ δόμους ἐφεστίους ἐλθὼν θεοῖσι πρῶτα δεξιώσομαι, οἵπερ πρόσω ἔμψαντες ἤγαγον πάλιν.

66 See n 183.

67 Aesch. *Ag*. 968-69. Trans. Smyth (1926 [adapted]): '[N]ow that you have come to the domestic hearth, you show that warmth has come in wintertime.' καὶ σοῦ μολόντος δωματῖτιν ἑστίαν, θάλπος μὲν ἐν χειμῶνι σημαίνεις μολόν.

68 Eur. *Her*. 481-83.

69 Eur. *Her*. 715.

70 Eur. *Her*. 523

71 Eur. *Her*. 554.

72 Eur. *Her*. 599–600.

73 Eur. *Her*. 608-9. Oates & O'Neill (1938 [Adapted]): οὐκ ἀτιμάσω θεοὺς προσειπεῖν πρῶτα τοὺς κατὰ στέγας.

74 Eur. *Her*. 1035-38.

75 Isaeus 8.15–16. Boedeker, 'Family Matters', 230; Martin Nilsson, *Greek Folk Religion* (New York: Harper Torchbooks, 1940), 71; Christopher Faraone, 'Household Religion in Ancient Greece', in *Household and Family Religion in Antiquity*, ed. John Bodel and Saul Olyan (Oxford: Blackwell Publishing, 2008), 216–17, 222.

76 Jar: Athen. 473b–c; with Arthur Cook, *Zeus: A Study in Ancient Religion, vol. 2, part 2* (Cambridge: Cambridge University Press, 1925/2010), 1054-7. Images: Men. *Ps. Her*. fr. 519 K. For discussion of these variations see Faraone, 'Household Religion', 216-17; Boedeker, 'Family Matters', 231.

77 Nilsson, *Greek Folk Religion*, 71-2; Jennifer Larson, *Ancient Greek Cults: A Guide* (New York: Routledge, 2007), 21; Faraone, 'Household Religion', 217.

78 Aesch. *Ag.* 1038. Clytemnestra describes the κτησίου βωμοῦ, the altar of the god of possessions, Zeus. The animal sacrifices are those described in Isae. 8.15–16.

79 The invitation made by Clytemnaestra was in response to an original request made by Agamemnon, that she receive Cassandra into the house (Aesch. *Ag.* 950–5). This request alludes to the rites of incorporation that were offered to both slaves and wives: McNeil, 'Bridal Cloths', 3.

80 For the incorporation rituals of the house see section 1.2.

81 Aesch. *Ag.* 1310.

82 See section 5.2.1 for an earlier discussion on these themes.

83 Infants: Berlin, Antikensammlung: F2444, *BA* 209215; Bochum, Ruhr Universitat, Kunstsammlungen: S1085, *BA* 46410. Youths, attendants or slaves: Wurzburg, Universitat, Martin von Wagner Mus.: HA120, *BA* 201654; Paris, Musée du Louvre: G538, *BA* 216030; Paris, Musée du Louvre: S1431, *BA* 11286; Paris, Musée du Louvre: G46, BA 202097. Other military men: Wurzburg, Universitat, Martin von Wagner Mus.: HA120, *BA* 201654; Bologna, Museo Civico Archeologico: 189, *BA* 202882; Paris, Musée du Louvre: G46, *BA* 202097. Dogs: Athens, Benaki Museum: 38151, *BA* 9029956; Paris, Musée du Louvre: G46, *BA* 202097.

84 Importantly, *oikos* does not mean blood family but rather the household, which clearly, in this instance, includes the slaves.

85 Eur. *Her.* 631–6

86 Aesch. *Ag.* 1037–38; Antiph. 1.16–17; Isae. 8.16.

87 For the thematic motif of sacrifice and its corruption in *Agamemnon*, see Froma Zeitlin, 'The Motif of the Corrupted Sacrifice in Aeschylus' Oresteia', *Transactions and Proceedings of the American Philological Association* 96, (1965): 463–83; 'Postscript to Sacrificial Imagery in the Oresteia (Ag. 1235–37)', *Transactions and Proceedings of the American Philological Association* 97, (1966): 645–53.

88 Atlanta (GA), Emory University, Michael C Carlos Museum: 1984.12, BA 16673.

89 Peter Burian, 'Zeus Swthr Tritos and Some Triads in Aeschylus' Oresteia', *The American Journal of Philology* 107, (1986): 332. Most commonly, three libations were poured: one to Olympian Zeus and the other Olympians, one to the heroes, and a final one to Zeus the Saviour.

90 Aesch. *Ag.* 1384–90. Trans. Smyth (1926 [Adapted]): παίω δέ νιν δίς· κἀν δυοῖν οἰμωγμάτοιν μεθῆκεν αὐτοῦ κῶλα· καὶ πεπτωκότι τρίτην ἐπενδίδωμι, τοῦ κατὰ χθονὸς Διὸς νεκρῶν σωτῆρος εὐκταίαν χάριν. οὕτω τὸν αὑτοῦ θυμὸν ὁρμαίνει πεσών· κἀκφυσιῶν ὀξεῖαν αἵματος σφαγὴν βάλλει μ᾽ ἐρεμνῇ ψακάδι φοινίας δρόσου.

91 For the blasphemy inherent in this revelation see Zeitlin, 'Corrupted Sacrifice', 473; AF Garvie, *Aeschylus' Choephori* (Oxford: Oxford University Press, 1986): xxxviii; Alexopoulou, *Homecoming Pattern*, 78.

92 Traditionally, scholars have interpreted this as the libation one would pour
over a victim; see, e.g., DW Lucas, 'Epispendein nekroi: Agamemnon 1393-8',
Proceedings of the Cambridge Philological Society 15, (1969): 60–68; Burian, 'Zeus Swthr
Tritos', 335 n 10. This view has been challenged by Kerri J. Hame, 'All in the Family:
Funeral Rites and the Health of the Oikos in Aischylos' Oresteia', *The American Journal
of Philology* 125, 4 (2004): 523, who argues that it should be contextualised with
funerary rites and that this would be a grossly inappropriate way to treat a body.
Hame's argument is valid, in that the mistreatment of the body was a gross taboo in
Greek culture, but this does not undermine the position of traditional scholarship. The
reason Clytemnestra is debating the act is surely because she is treating her husband as
a sacrificial victim but is well aware that he is not one. Ultimately, she decides not to do
it even though she feels justified, as it is one step too far.

93 Aesch. *Ag.* 1398–9.

94 Kimberley Patton, *Religion of the Gods: Ritual, Paradox, and Reflexivity* (Oxford:
Oxford University Press, 2009), 33–4.

95 Friendships: Hom. *Od.* 7.163-64. Communal meals: Athen. 15.692; Diod. 4.3.
Symposiums: Pind. *Isth.* 6.1–9; Xen. *Cyr.* 2.3.1.

96 Pind. *Isth.* 4.193–200; Antiph. 1.18.

97 Paul Roth, 'The Theme of Corrupted Xenia in Aeschylus' "Oresteia"', *Mnemosyne* 46,
1 (1993): 2–8.

98 Xenos can refer to a friend, a stranger, a foreigner, a friend, a guest, as well as a host.
For the close association between marriage and xenia see Roth, 'Corrupted Xenia',
3–4. For their use to forge alliances see Moses Finley, *The World of Odysseus*, 2nd
edn (London: Penguin, 1978), 99; Gabriel Herman, *Ritualised Friendship and the
Greek City* (Cambridge: Cambridge University Press, 1987), 36.

99 Roth, 'Corrupted Xenia', 5–6.

100 Quick invitation: Hom. *Il.* 11.776-79; *Od.* 1.113-25, 4.20-43. Bathe: Hom. *Od.*
3.464-68, 4.48-50, 8.426- 55, 10.358-65, 17.87-90 19.320-2.

101 Eur. Her. 622-4. Oates & O'Neill (1938 [Adapted]): ἀλλ᾽ εἶ᾽, ὁμαρτεῖτ᾽, ὦ τέκν᾽, ἐς
δόμους πατρί: καλλίονές τἄρ᾽ εἴσοδοι τῶν ἐξόδων πάρεισιν ὑμῖν.

102 On the purposeful subversion of this ritual see Richard Seaford, 'Homeric and
Tragic Sacrifice', *Transactions of the American Philological Association* 119,
(1989): 94.

103 Eur. *Her.* 922-30. Oates & O'Neill (1938): ἱερὰ μὲν ἦν πάροιθεν ἐσχάρας Διὸς
καθάρσι᾽ οἴκων, γῆς ἄνακτ᾽ ἐπεὶ κτανὼν ἐξέβαλε τῶνδε δωμάτων Ἡρακλῆς:
χορὸς δὲ καλλίμορφος εἱστήκει τέκνων πατήρ τε Μεγάρα τ᾽: ἐν κύκλῳ δ᾽ ἤδη
κανοῦν εἵλικτο βωμοῦ, φθέγμα δ᾽ ὅσιον εἴχομεν. μέλλων δὲ δαλὸν χειρὶ δεξιᾷ
φέρειν, ἐς χέρνιβ᾽ ὡς βάψειεν, Ἀλκμήνης τόκος ἔστη σιωπῇ.

104 Eur. *Her.* 940, 1145. Parker, *Miasma*, 114, n.39. See also Louis Moulinier, *Le Pur et
l'impur dans la pensée des Grecs d'Homère à Aristote* (Paris: Librairie C. Klineksieck,

1952), 88, and Jean Rudhardt, *Notions fondamentales de la pensée religieuse et actes constitutifs du culte dans la Grèce classique* (Geneva: Librairie Droz, 1958), 270.

105 On the topic of justifiable homicide see also Joseph Hewitt, 'The Necessity of Ritual Purification after Justifiable Homicide.' *Transactions and Proceedings of the American Philological Association* 41, (1910): 99–113.

106 Parker, *Miasma*, 114.

107 Parker, *Miasma*, 22–23, 32, 113 n 37, 226.

108 Xen. *Anab.* 5.7.13–35.

109 Pritchett, *Greek State, vol III*, 202.

110 Parker, *Miasma*, 113 n 37. Pritchett, *Greek State, vol III*, 196–202, collected seven disparate pieces of evidence to explore pollution and purification in Greek military history, the majority of which came from outside the classical period.

111 Crowley, *Psychology of a Hoplite*, 94–5.

112 Tritle, *Melos to My Lai*, 191.

113 Bernard Eck, *La mort rouge. Homicide, guerre et souillure en Grèce ancienne* (Paris: Les belles lettres, 2012), 49–87.

114 Parker, *Miasma*, 113, n 37.

115 Aesch. *Sept.* 679-82. Trans. Sommerstein (2008 [Adapted]): ἀλλ᾽ ἄνδρας Ἀργείοισι Καδμείους ἅλις ἐς χεῖρας ἐλθεῖν· αἷμα γὰρ καθάρσιον. ἀνδροῖν δ᾽ μαίμοιν θάνατος ὧδ᾽ αὐτοκτόνος, οὐκ ἔστι γῆρας τοῦδε τοῦ μιάσματος.

116 See Sommerstein's unedited translation.

117 The reading of this small section has been debated for over a century. Much of the debate stems not from the Greek in particular, but from the form of the cleansing being described. Arthur Verrall, *The 'Seven Against Thebes' of Aeschylus* (London: Macmillan and Co., 1887), 81, argued that all bloodshed was polluting, thus killing in war brought with it a need for purgation via sacrifices. Thomas Tucker, *The Seven Against Thebes of Aeschylus* (Cambridge: Cambridge University Press, 1908), 139–40, directly opposed Verrall's argument, arguing that the language suggests that no purgation was needed but that the blood could simply be washed from the hands and that was the end of it.

118 Eur. *Ion.* 1334; Pl. *Leg.* 869d; Dem. 13.55; Xen. *Cyr.* 4.6.4-6; Andoc. 1.97.

119 Eur. *Supp.* 763–68, 939. See also the unusual behaviour of the Thessalians who wanted to handle Pelopidas' body as a mark of respect after his death: Plut. *Pel.* 33.

120 That is to say the presence of some form of purification ritual would be a social continuum, not necessarily the form that ritual took.

121 One other participant who makes an appearance in both forms of ritual scene is the goddess Iris. This observation should not be pushed too far, yet it is at least worthy of note that Iris is the harbinger of Lyssa in *Heracles*. Her presence as a

messenger goddess is at least fitting for both rituals, due to her role as a messenger
goddess, passing prayers from men to the gods in the departure and offering
prayers of protection, and in the homecoming, prayers of thanksgiving.

Chapter 6

1 Thuc. 2.34.8.
2 Burial on the battlefield: Thuc. 2.34.5; Hdt. 9.85; Paus. 1.29.4, 1.32.3. Cremation as
   the normal process of disposing of Athenian war dead: Schol. Thuc. 2.34.1;
   Pritchett, *Greek State, vol IV*, 251.
3 Thuc. 2.34.5. For a defence to Thucydides' famous 'blunder', see Mark Toher, 'On
   "Thucydides' Blunder": 2.34.5', *Hermes* 127, 4 (1999): 501, who argues that it was a
   purposeful generalisation for his non-Attic readers.
4 In opposition, see Noel Robertson, 'The Collective Burial of Fallen Soldiers at
   Athens, Sparta and Elsewhere: "Ancestral Custom" and Modern Misunderstandings',
   Echoes du Monde Classique/Classical Views 27, (1983): 78–92, who argues that the
   Greek norm was to bring their dead home rather than bury them on the field. His
   view fails to convince because of the mass of evidence accumulated by Pritchett, if
   nothing else. For a similar dismissal of his argument see Stephen Hodkinson,
   Property and Wealth in Classical Sparta (Swansea: The Classical Press of Wales,
   2000/2009), 268 n 54.
5 Paus. 1.29.7. This contradicts his earlier assertion that the first to be buried in the
   demosion sema were those who fought at Drabescus. This may come down to a
   simple manuscript error, where the polyandrion of Brabescus is not the first
   chronologically (πρῶτοι) but the first geographically (πρῶτον). For further
   discussion on this error see Felix Jacoby, 'Patrios Nomos: State Burial in Athens and
   the Public Cemetery in the Kerameikos', *The Journal of Hellenic Studies* 64, (1944):
   40–1; Pritchett, *Greek State, vol IV*, 112–13; Nathan Arrington, 'Topographic
   Semantics: The Location of the Athenian Public Cemetery and its Significance for
   the Nascent Democracy', *Hesperia* 79, 4 (2010b): 503 n 19. Pausanias simply says
   that they were killed before the Persian invasion but does not describe whether that
   was during the kingship of Darius or Xerxes.
6 Clairmont, *Patrios Nomos*, 11–13; Pritchett, *Greek State, vol IV*, 113 n 61; Geoffrey
   Bakewell, 'Agamemnon 437: Chrysamoibos Ares, Athens and Empire', *The Journal of
   Hellenic Studies* 127, (2007b): 127.
7 This follows the sensible argument made by Arrington, *Ashes, Images and Memories*,
   33-49), who proposes that the *patrios nomos* developed over time, beginning with
   the fundamental cremation and public burial sometime *c.* 500 BC For a similar
   assessment see Stupperich, *Staatsbegräbnis und Privatgrabmal*, 206–24; 'The

Iconography of Athenian State Burials in the Classical Period', in *The Archaeology of Athens and Attica under the Democracy*, William Coulson et al (Oxford: Oxbow Books, 1994): 93. For a later date see Jacoby, 'Patrios Nomos', 46–50; Clairmont, *Patrios Nomos*, 3; Hornblower, *Commentary, vol I*, 292; Raphaela Czech-Schneider, 'Das Demosion Sema und die Mentalität der Athener: Einige Überlegungen zur Einrichtung des athenischen Staatsfriedhofes', *Laverna* 5, (1994): 22–37; Angelos Matthaiou, Ἀθηναίοισι δὲ τεταγμένοισι ἐν τεμένεϊ Ἡρακλέος (Hdt. 6.108.1)', in *Herodotus and His World: Essays from a Conference in Memory of George Forrest*, ed. Peter Derow and Robert Parker (Oxford: Oxford University Press, 2003), 199–200.

8 Thuc. 2.34.3.

9 Jacoby, 'Patrios Nomos', 37 n 1; Sally Humphreys, 'From a Grin to a Death: The Body in the Greek Discovery of Politics', in *Constructions of the Classical Body*, ed. James Porter (Ann Arbor: The University of Michigan Press, 1999), 140 n 21; Walter Connor, 'Early Greek Land Warfare as Symbolic Expression', in *Studies in Ancient Greek and Roman Society*, ed. Robin Osborne (Cambridge: Cambridge University Press, 2004), 25; Bonnie Honig, *Antigone, Interrupted* (Cambridge: Cambridge University Press, 2013), 102; Debra Hamel, *The Battle of Arginusae: Victory at Sea and Its Tragic Aftermath in the Final Years of the Peloponnesian War* (Baltimore: Johns Hopkins University Press, 2015), 73; Arrington, *Ashes, Images and Memories*, 34; Sara Phang et al, *Conflict in Ancient Greece and Rome: The Definitive Political, Social, and Military Encyclopedia, vol 1* (Santa Barbara: ABC-CLIO, 2016), 208. See also Pritchett, *Greek State, vol IV*, 256–7 who lays out this same view but with concerns over the logistical realities involved, describing them as 'impracticable'. Pritchard, 'The Symbiosis', 33–4, and Low, 'Commemorating the War Dead', 347–8, base their reconstructions of the *patrios nomos* on this model, while not explicitly describing it. See Robert Garland, *The Greek Way of Death*, 2nd edn (Ithaca, NY: Cornell University Press, 1985/2001), 92; Eleni Georgoulaki, 'Religious and Socio-Political Implications of Mortuary Evidence: Case Studies in Ancient Greece', *Kernos* 9, (1996): 109, who argue that the war dead were cremated individually.

10 Pamela Vaughn, 'The Identification and Retrieval of the Hoplite Battle-Dead', in *Hoplites: The Classical Greek Battle Experience*, ed. Victor Davis Hanson (London: Routledge, 1991), 47; Arrington, *Ashes, Images and Memories*, 33–4.

11 Vaughn, 'Identification and Retrieval', 44, 49–50.

12 Thuc. 4.44.

13 See also Crowley, *Psychology of a Hoplite*, 165, n 111, who offers a different interpretation, arguing that it is more likely that the two missing men were noticed in their absence by their fellow demesmen.

14 As an extreme example, the Athenians did not receive their war dead for seventeen days following the defeat at Delium (Thuc. 4.101.1).

15 Delium: Thuc. 4.101.2. Amphipolis: Thuc. 5.11.2. Mantinea: Thuc. 5.74.3. On Athenian losses in battle see Pierre Brulé, 'La mortalité de guerre en Grèce classique. L'exemple d'Athènes de 490 à 322', in *Armées et sociétés de la Grèce classique. Aspects sociaux et politiques de la guerre aux Ve et IVes. av. J.-C.*, ed. Francis Prost (Paris: Errances, 1999), 51–68; for an examination of the proportional losses of armies during the classical Greek period see Peter Krentz, 'Casualties in Hoplite Battle', *Greek, Roman and Byzantine Studies* 26, 1 (1985): 13–20.

16 I have previously published parts of this section on the logistical considerations of the repatriation process; for a deeper discussion regarding the points raised here see: Owen Rees, 'Picking over the Bones: The Practicalities of Processing the Athenian War Dead', *Journal of Ancient History* 6, 2 (2018): 167–84.

17 Thuc. 6.71. Strassler (2008 [Adapted]): ξυγκομίσαντες δὲ τοὺς ἑαυτῶν νεκροὺς καὶ ἐπὶ πυρὰν ἐπιθέντες ηὐλίσαντο αὐτοῦ. τῇ δ᾽ ὑστεραίᾳ τοῖς μὲν Συρακοσίοις ἀπέδοσαν ὑποσπόνδους τοὺς νεκρούς (ἀπέθανον δὲ αὐτῶν καὶ τῶν ξυμμάχων περὶ ἑξήκοντα καὶ διακοσίους) τῶν δὲ σφετέρων τὰ ὀστᾶ ξυνέλεξαν (ἀπέθανον δὲ αὐτῶν καὶ τῶν ξυμμάχων ὡς πεντήκοντα).

18 Arrington, *Ashes, Images and Memories*, 34.

19 See the assorted imagery collated by Jonathan Musgrave, 'Dust and Damn'd Oblivion: A Study of Cremation in Ancient Greece', *The Annual of the British School at Athens* 85, (1990): 275 n 22. The later writer Vitruvius (2.19.15) describes the process of placing the layers at right angles to the ones beneath them.

20 David Noy, "Half-Burnt on an Emergency Pyre': Roman Cremations Which Went Wrong', *Greece & Rome* 47, 2 (2000): 30–1. For examples of informal pyres in Greek artwork see Musgrave, 'Dust and Damn'd', 275 n 22.

21 Jacqueline McKinley, 'In the Heat of the Pyre', in *The Analysis of Burned Human Remains*, ed. Christopher Schmidt and Steven Symes (London: Academic Press, 2008), 183; Musgrave, 'Dust and Damn'd', 272.

22 McKinley, 'In the Heat', 183–5; 3. Rees, 'Picking over the Bones', 170–1.

23 Noy, 'Half-Burnt', 187.

24 Jacqueline McKinley, 'Cremations: Expectations, Methodologies and realities', in *Burial Archaeology: Current Research, Methods and Developments*, ed. Charlotte Roberts et al (Oxford: British Archaeological Report S211, 1989), 67. Experimental pyres: Janusz Piontek, 'Proces kremacji i jego wpływ na morfologię kości w świetle wyników badań eksperymentalnych', *Archeologia Polski* 21, 2 (1976): 247–80.

25 Juan Antonio Chavez, in *San Antonio Express*, 19 April 1914, as transcribed in Timothy Matovina, *The Alamo Remembered: Tejano Accounts and Perspectives* (Austin: Texas University Press, 1995), 116.

26 Juan Antonio Chavez, in *San Antonio Express*, 19 April 1914.

27 Shilpa Badge et al 'Design and Analysis of Energy Efficient Crematorium for Eco Body Burning', *International Journal on Emerging Trends in Technology* 3, 2 (2016): 4129.

28 AUVEST Plan version 3.1, (2015), Appendix 7.

29 On the finite nature of timber as a resource, especially to the Athenians, see Russell Meiggs, *Trees and Timber in the Ancient Mediterranean World* (Oxford: Clarendon Press, 1982), 118–19, 204–6; Eugene Borza, 'Timber and Politics in the Ancient World: Macedon and the Greeks', *Proceedings of the American Philosophical Society* 131, 1 (1987): 32–6.

30 Jacqueline McKinley, 'Bone Fragment Size in British Cremation Burials and its Implications for Pyre Technology and Ritual', *Journal of Archaeological Science* 21, 3 (1994): 339. The largest bone fragment noted by McKinley in her research of modern crematoria was 2.5cm long.

31 Thuc. 2.34.3.

32 Aesch. *Ag.* 435–6, 443–4. The lack of realism stems from the need to cremate each of the bodies individually and it implies that each urn was somehow identifiable to the families. Nevertheless, it has been influential: see, for instance, Garland, *Greek Way of Death*, 92; Georgoulaki, 'Religious and Socio-Political Implications', 109. Arrington, *Ashes, Images and Memories*, 34–5, tries to resolve the issue by envisaging the bodies burned by tribe, then the remains being collected into vases for transportation, although he does not make clear if these are collective vases or individual urns.

33 Pritchett, *Greek State, vol IV*, 195. Pritchett, *Greek State, vol IV*, 103 n 25 explains that his choice of translation stems from the verb ὀστολογίαν, which he says was used to describe the collection of ashes after a cremation, referencing Diodorus (4.38.5). However, Diodorus' use of the term only fits with the word's standard definition, the collection of the bones. The reference in question describes Iolaüs approaching the pyre of Heracles to collect his bones; it focuses on Iolaüs' revelation that the bones of Heracles are missing from his pyre, not that he collected the ashes.

34 Hamel, *Battle of Arginusae*, 73.

35 See Theresa Huntsman and Marshall Becker, 'An Analysis of the Cremated Human Remains in a Terracotta Cinerary Urn of the Third-Second Century BCE from Chiusi, now in the Metropolitan Museum of Art in New York', *Etruscan Studies* 16, 2 (2013): 158–9, for the suggestion that the Etruscans did sometimes perform a form of crushing process after a cremation. Nevertheless, as McKinley, 'Bone Fragment Size', 339, has argued, it was not a common process in ancient Europe as a whole.

36 For the mean weight of cremated remains see Jacqueline McKinley, 'Bone Fragment Size and Weights of Bone from Modern British Cremations and its Implications for the Interpretation of Archaeological Cremations', *International Journal of Osteoarchaeology* 3, (1993), 285; Charlier et al, '"In This Way They Held Funeral for Horse-Taming Hector": A Greek Cremation Reflects Homeric Ritual', in *New Directions in the Skeletal Biology of Greece, Hesperia Supplements 43*, ed. Lynne

Schepartz, Sherry Fox and Chrissy Bourbou (Princeton: American School of Classical Studies at Athens, 2009), 50.

37 Per Holck, *Cremated Bones: A Medical-Anthropological Study of an Archaeological Material on Cremation Burials* (Oslo: Universitetet i Oslo, Antropologiske skrifter 1, 1987), 72; with Rees, 'Picking over the Bones', 175–6.

38 Interestingly, this figure is three times the estimated volume of Hamel, which is in keeping with Holck, *Cremated Bones*, 72, who observes that the volume of full cremains is three times that of crushed cremains.

39 Plut. *De Glor. Ath.* 8

40 Plut. *Phil.* 21.2 (Philopoemen); *Alex.* 56 (Demaratus of Corinth), 77.1 (Iolas); *Phoc.* 37.3 (Phocion); *Cim.* 4.2 (Thucydides), 8.6 (Theseus), 19.4 (Cimon).

41 Pablo Díaz, in *San Antonio Express*, 26 March 1911; Journal of Dr. J. H. Bernard, 25 May, as transcribed in Thom Hatch, *Encyclopedia of the Alamo and the Texas Revolution* (Jefferson: MacFarland & Co., 1999), 87–8; Todd Hansen, *The Alamo Reader: A Study in History* (Mechanicsburg: Stackpole Books, 2003), 615; Phillip Tucker, *Exodus from the Alamo: The Anatomy of the Last Stand Myth* (Havertown: Casemates Publishers, 2009), 331–2.

42 Colin Quinn et al, 'Perspectives – Complexities of Terminologies and Intellectual Frameworks in Cremation Studies', in *Transformation by Fire: The Archaeology of Cremation in Cultural Context*, ed. Ian Kuijt et al (Tuscan: University of Arizona Press, 2014), 28. The term is used already by archaeologists looking at the ancient Greek period, but it is not within the common parlance of historians of the period.

43 McKinley, 'In the Heat', 197–9. Experiments with the burning of small pigs show, on a much smaller scale, the unreliability of pyre cremations: Jonas Jæger and Veronica Johansen, 'The Cremation of Infants/Small Children: An Archaeological Experiment Concerning the Effects of Fire on Bone Weight', *Cadernos do GEEvH* 2, 2 (2013): 18.

44 Thuc. 2.34.3. Strassler (2008 [Adapted]): μία δὲ κλίνη κενὴ φέρεται ἐστρωμένη τῶν ἀφανῶν, οἳ ἂν μὴ εὑρεθῶσιν ἐς ἀναίρεσιν.

45 The importance of collecting the war dead is evident at the battle of Solygeia, as discussed above. Examples of bodies being left on the battlefield are rare, but certainly present: Thuc. 7.72.2, with Pritchett, *Greek State, vol IV*, 235–39. Diodorus (13.101.1) claims that the trial of the generals, following the Athenian victory at Arginusae, was because they failed to collect the Athenian dead; although Xenophon's account (*Hel.* 1.7.1-5) states it was a failure to collect the survivors, while Plato (*Menex.* 243c) describes the unburied dead without reference to the trial of the generals. See also Vaughn, 'Identification and Retrieval', 44. Losing men at sea: Eur. *Hel.* 1241–3.

46 Arrington, *Ashes, Images and Memories*, 48–9, makes a similar observation, but only applies this to a singular 'exception' in Athenian history, the battle of Ephesus (409 BC), discussed below.

47 Xen. *Hell.* 1.2.11. Trans. Brownson (1918 [Adapted]): οἱ δ' Ἀθηναῖοι τοὺς νεκροὺς ὑποσπόνδους ἀπολαβόντες ἀπέπλευσαν εἰς Νότιον, κἀκεῖ θάψαντες αὐτοὺς ἔπλεον.

48 E.g. Diod. 3.55. Christopher Collard, *Euripides, 'Supplices'* (Groningen: Bouma's Boekhuis, 1975), 17, argues that Eur. *Supp.* 935 uses the verb in this way, but his example seems uncertain. The discussion in the play falls on the fate of the corpse of Capaneus, who was struck by Zeus' lightning bolt. Adrastus asks Theseus whether Capaneus will be buried (θάπτω) apart from the rest of the dead; Theseus confirms this, stating that the rest will be burned on one pyre. Collard's interpretation that θάπτω should here be translated as cremated would keep it consistent with Theseus' description of the pyre but is not strictly necessary. The conversation then moves on to where Capaneus will have his tomb, emphasising that the burial is the primary concern, not the means of internment. See also Ian Storey, *Euripides: Suppliant Women* (London: Bloomsbury Academic, 2008), 71. For further discussion on the use of the term in this context see Pritchett, *Greek State, vol IV*, 203.

49 Collard, *Supplices*, 17, followed by Pritchett, *Greek State, vol IV*, 203. See also Christopher Carey, *Lysias: Selected Speeches* (Cambridge: Cambridge University Press, 1989), 214 and Michael Edwards, 'Lysias', in *Time in Ancient Greek Literature: Studies in Ancient Greek Narrative, vol 2*, ed. Irene de Jong and René Nünlist (Leiden: Brill, 2007a), 333, who both discuss the passage based on this same interpretation, without any explanation offered for the supposed anomaly.

50 Pritchett, *Greek State, vol IV*, 203.

51 Jacoby, 'Patrios Nomos', 37 n 1.

52 Xen. *Hell.* 1.7.22, 2.4.19. For a non-Athenian example, using the same preposition, see Xen. *Hel.* 7.3.12.

53 Xen. *Hell.* 2.4.19.

54 The battle was fought against the army of the Thirty in Athens, but Xenophon (2.4.19) does show that the usual practice of retrieving the war dead remained intact. It is plausible that an exception to communal burial could have been made for the seer, due to his unique position, but the casualty list *IG I³* 1147 would suggest that a seer who died in battle or on campaign was buried and commemorated with his army.

55 This assumes, with Pritchett, *Greek State, vol IV*, 203, that the bodies were still burned before burial. There is no evidence to argue either way, but the removal of dead bodies from unsafe regions, before their processing, is evident in our sources.

56 For a similar conclusion, based on Xenophon's description alone, see Arrington, *Ashes, Images and Memories*, 49. This size of container is roughly half of the size of that estimated by Hamel, *Battle of Arginusae*, 73, for the war dead at Arginusae and her discussion regarding the logistics involved in transporting the dead is still very valuable.

57 See n 32.

58 The exact month of the *patrios nomos* is subject to debate. Jacoby, 'Patrios Nomos', 56–66, suggested it took place in late September, whereas Gomme, *Commentary, vol II*, 100–2, argues that it was later in the winter. Hornblower, *Commentary, vol III*, 292, following Loraux, *Invention of Athens*, 70–1, observes that we cannot assume that it was always held in the winter, because Hyperides' funeral oration suggests it was delivered in early spring.

59 Donald Bradeen, 'Athenian Casualty Lists', *Hesperia: The Journal of the American School of Classical Studies at Athens* 33, 1 (1964): 50–5; 'The Athenian Casualty Lists', *The Classical Quarterly* 19, 1 (1969): 146, dates the inscription *SEG* 21.131 (later republished as *IG* I³ 1191) to 409 BC, based, in part, on the naval activities of Thrasyllus in that year. For an opposite view, see Pritchett, *Greek State, vol IV*, 203. See also Hansen, *Three Studies*, 18.

60 Another interpretation, less radically following a suggestion in Donna Kurtz and John Boardman, *Greek Burial Customs* (London: Thames and Hudson, 1971), 108, is that the custom of bringing home all of the war dead was not always followed.

61 Quinn et al, 'Perspectives', 28. See also Jacqueline McKinley's remarks concerning a potential correlation between the status of the dead and the amount of time spent collecting the cremains from a pyre: 'Bronze Age "Barrows" and Funerary Rites and Rituals of Cremation', *Proceedings of the Prehistoric Society* 63, (1997): 142.

62 Quinn et al, 'Perspectives', 28.

63 Izumi Tōru, 'What I have Kept in My Heart until Now', in *Senso: The Japanese Remember the Pacific War: Letters to the Editor of Asahi Shimbun*, ed. Frank Gibney (London: ME Sharpe, 2007), 34–5.

64 This is what ultimately separates the Athenians from their Greek counterparts. For a non-Athenian instance of efficient disposing of the war dead while on the march see Plut. *Eum.* 9.2.

65 Even the discovery of four, possibly five, connected late-fifth century polyandria in the *demosion sema* has failed to show a truly mass grave, with the numbers we may expect for the Athenian war dead during the early years of the Peloponnesian War: Charis Stoupa, 'Γ' Εφορεία Προϊστορικών και Κλασικών Αρχαιοτήτων, ανασκαφικές εργασίες: Οδός Σαλαμίνος 35', *ArchDelt* 52, *Chronika*, Β'1 (1997): 52–56; David Blackman et al, 'Archaeology in Greece 1997–98', *Archaeological Reports* 44, (1997–1998): 8–11; Gilles Touchais 'Chronique des fouilles et découvertes archéolo- giques en Grèce en 1996 et 1997', *Bulletin de Correspondance Hellénique* 122 (1998): 722.

66 This is similarly true of the casualty lists, which were also categorised by tribe. For consideration of earlier evidence of communal burial see Cezary Kucewicz, *The Treatment of the War Dead in Archaic Athens: An Ancestral Custom* (London: Bloomsbury, 2021), 120–2.

67 Nathan Arrington, *Between Victory and Defeat: Framing the Fallen Warrior in Fifth-Century Athenian Art* (PhD. diss., University of California, Berkeley, 2010a), 37.

68 Lys. 2.80; Plat. *Menex.* 249b; Dem. 60.36; something Kucewicz astutely refers to as 'a piecemeal process': *Treatment of the War Dead,* 128.

69 Toher, 'Thucydides' Blunder', 499–500, 501.

70 Although I would not go as far as Loraux, *Invention of Athens,* 46 and describe his account as equal to modern anthropological investigations.

71 Gomme, *Commentary, vol II,* 102; Loraux, *Invention of Athens,* 49; Steinbock, *Social Memory,* 51.

72 Loraux, *Invention of Athens,* 50; Arrington, *Ashes, Images and Memories,* 36. Another strong candidate is in front of the Diplyon Gate, which has been suggested by Stupperich, *Staatsbegräbnis und Privatgrabmal,* 32. However, this location relies on the belief that the presence of the war dead would be polluting to the city, a notion that has since been discredited by Parker, *Miasma,* 42–3.

73 Dem. 43.62. Olivier Reverdin, *La Religion de la Cité Platonicienne* (Paris: E. de Boccard, 1945), 116, argues that the discrepancy in the duration between private and public *prothesis* could be explained by the need for less severe prophylactic measures, because the bodies had already been cremated. However, I am more convinced by Loraux, *Invention of Athens,* 49, 432–3 n 15, who suggests that the extra day of *prothesis* was a purposeful attempt to further honour the dead. Furthermore, I would suggest it allowed the relevant families time to pay their respects to the coffins before the burial – although this suggestion may be too rationalistic for Loraux.

74 The difficulty in visualising what happened at this stage has influenced much of the scholarship on the topic. Either the issue is left silent, or the bodies are described as being 'exposed' for two days (e.g. Loraux, *Invention of Athens,* 49, 50), without clarification of what this actually means. Steinbock, *Social Memory,* 51, describes the bones of the dead being laid out in the tent, before being collected on the day of the funeral and placed in their tribal coffins, whereas Ian Morris, *Death-Ritual and Social Structure in Classical Antiquity* (Cambridge: Cambridge University Press, 1992), 106, speculates on an earlier stage of exposure and decomposition of the flesh, before the day of the funeral. However, he fails to make clear the need for this exposure when we consider the original cremation on the battlefield.

75 E.g. Hdt. 5.8; Eur. *Alc.* 644; Eur. *Supp.* 50–53; Ar. *Lys.* 611; Lys. 12.18.

76 This would make it both impossible to identify which cremains belong to which body, and to ensure that each body had all its relevant skeletal parts. Also, the sensory experience of the families visiting the cremains must be considered. Not only the smell of the partially burned, partially rotting remains, but also the visual impact of fractured bones. This offered a rather undignified presentation for the

war dead, while the impact of seeing the bodies so changed would have been unbearable to the families: Eur. *Supp.* 941–6. For more on this Euripidean passage see section 7.1.1.

77 See Steinbock, *Social Memory*, 51.

78 A modern comparison can be made with the modern British war dead, where the family are invited to sit next to their relevant coffin, which is covered in a Union Flag. The difference here is that the Athenian coffin was communal, so there was no distinction of individuality among the dead.

79 Cinerary urn: Hom. *Il.* 24.776.

80 Johannes Engels, *Funerum sepulcrorumque magnficentia: Begräbnis- und Grabluxusgesetze in der griechisch-römischen Welt mit einigen Ausblicken auf Einschränkungen des funeralen und sepulkralen Luxus im Mittelalter und in der Neuzeit* (Stuttgart: Franz Steiner Verlag, 1998), 110; Colleen Chaston, *Tragic Props and Cognitive Function: Aspects of the Function of Images in Thinking* (Leiden: Brill, 2010), 134.

81 The volume of an interred body (*c.* 66 litres) is that much larger than the volume of a cremated one, so numerous individual cremains could fit inside the coffin. Visual examples of Greek coffins can be seen on late black-figure vases Athens, National Museum, CC688, *BA* 480; Brunswick (ME), Bowdoin College: 1984.23, *BA* 361401.

82 Based on the allocation of 7.8 litres per person. See section 6.1.1.

83 See www.midlandfuneralsupplies.co.uk/coffin_sizes_02.html (last accessed 5 September 2018).

84 For two clear, artistic examples dating from the fifth century BC see H. Alan Shapiro, 'The Iconography of Mourning in Athenian Art', *American Journal of Archaeology* 95, 4 (1991): 647–49, figs. 18 and 19, with discussion.

85 See Gertrude Smith, 'Athenian Casualty Lists.' *Classical Philology* 14, 4 (1919), 363; Morris, *Death-Ritual*, 131; Christoph Clairmont, 'New Evidence for a Polyandrion in the Demosion Sema of Athens?', *The Journal of Hellenic Studies* 101, (1981): 132; Hanson, *The Western Way of War*, 207; Tritle, *Melos to My Lai*, 150–1; Barry Strauss, *Salamis: The Greatest Naval Battle of the Ancient World* (London: Arrow Books, 2005), 178; Karen Bassi, 'Spatial Contingencies in Thucydides' History', *Classical Antiquity* 26, 2 (2007): 191–2; Everett Wheeler and Barry Strauss, 'Battle', in *The Cambridge History of Greek and Roman Warfare, vol 1: Greece, the Hellenistic World and the Rise of Rome*, ed. Philip Sabin et al (Cambridge: Cambridge University Press, 2007), 236; Edith Hall, *Greek Tragedy: Suffering under the Sun* (Oxford: Oxford University Press, 2010), 74.

86 Garland, *Greek Way of Death*, 24.

87 Cynthia Patterson, '"Citizen Cemeteries" in Classical Athens?' *The Classical Quarter* 56, 1 (2006): 54 n 35.

88 Presumably it was, or else its ritual role loses its purpose during the most pivotal point of the funerary rites. Its symbolic representation of the missing dead, aligned

with its physical role as a carrier of dead bodies, not cremains and ash, would lead to the expectation that it was buried, maybe even cremated beforehand. This would bring an end to the symbolic ritual and take the missing dead into the final stage of their journey, in the same state as their comrades inside the *larnakes*.

89 Blackman et al, 'Archaeology', 8; Arrington, 'Topographic Semantics', 517-9.

90 Blackman et al, 'Archaeology', 9–10.

91 The various *topoi* of the genre was compiled by Theodore Burgess, *Epideictic Literature* (Chicago: University of Chicago Press, 1902), 148–57. For common patterns within the genre see John Ziolkowski, *Thucydides and the Tradition of Funeral Speeches at Athens* (New York: Arno Press, 1981), 31–57, 100–37; Loraux, *Invention of Athens*, 279–81; Christopher Carey, 'Epideictic Oratory', in *A Companion to Greek Rhetoric*, ed. Ian Worthington (Chichester: Blackwell Publishing, 2010), 243–4. For discussion around variation and originality in the genre see Vassiliki Frangeskou, 'Tradition and Originality in Some Attic Funeral Orations', *The Classical World* 92, 4 (1999): 315–36.

92 Lys. 2; Dem. 60; Hyp. 6; Thuc. 2. 35–46; Plat. *Menex.* 236d–249c; Gorg. fr.6. Of these, only the speeches made by Demosthenes and Hyperides were actually made during the *patrios nomos*. There is some debate surrounding the authenticity of the speeches of Lysias and Demosthenes in particular. Doubts were raised, mainly in the nineteenth century, but the scepticism continued into twentieth-century scholarship: Max Pohlenz, 'Zu den attischen Reden auf die Gefallenen', *Symbolae Osloenses* 26, (1948): 69–74; SG Korres, 'Οἱ ἐπιτάφιοι λόγοι', *Platon* 5, (1953): 120–5; P. Treves, 'Apocrifi demostenici: Lʼ Epitafio', *Athenaeum* 14, (1936): 153–74. Arguments have generally rested on the style of rhetoric and whether these speeches match the high standards of the two logographers. For a more recent attempt to argue for the authenticity of these speeches see Frangeskou, 'Tradition,' 315–36. With no consensus in sight, I am swayed by the conclusion of Ian Worthington, 'The Authorship of the Demosthenic "Epitaphios"', *Museum Helveticum* 60, 3 (2003): 156–7), who says of Demosthenes' speech 'we should not immediately reject what we have today just because it is so different from Demosthenes' other types of speeches. Its very nature meant that it should be different.'

93 Plat. *Menex.* 236e4-7; Frangeskou, 'Tradition', 319; Franco Trivigno, 'The Rhetoric of Parody in Plato's Menexenus', *Philosophy and Rhetoric* 42, 1 (2009): 34.

94 Thuc. 2.42.1-4

95 Lys. 2.7-10; Dem. 60.8. Plat. *Menex.* 239b also alludes to it briefly.

96 This theme is not unique to oratory, but is also present in tragedies such as Euripides' Suppliants, see Rush Rehm, *Marriage to Death: The Conflation of Wedding and Funeral Rituals in Greek Tragedy* (Princeton: Princeton University Press, 1994), 116.

97 Thuc. 2.36.1; Lys. 2.17; Plat. *Menex.* 237c; Hyp. 6.7. For the use of autochthonism in the *epitaphios logos* see Vincent Rosivach, 'Autochthony and the Athenians', *The Classical Quarterly* 37, 2 (1987b): 301–5; Loraux (1993: 65–9); Frangeskou, 'Tradition', 319–21. For autochthonism as a fundamental aspect of Athenian identity: Rosivach, 'Autochthony', 302–4; Chrisopher Pelling, 'Bringing Autochthony Up-to-Date: Herodotus and Thucydides', *The Classical World* 102, 4 (2009): 471–6.

98 Nicole Loraux, *The Children of Athena: Athenian Ideas about Citizenship and the Division between the Sexes.* Trans. Caroline Levine (Princeton: Princeton University Press, 1993), 50.

99 Especially if Garland, *Greek Way of Death*, 93, is correct and the driving force behind the repatriation of the dead is underpinned by the ideological need for the *autochthones* to be buried in their own soil. The only speech which makes the link is Plat. *Menex.* 237c, but it is part of a larger metaphor of Attica as mother to the Athenians and describes the dead being laid to rest (κεῖσθαι) in their abodes (ἐν οἰκείοις). It is hard to determine if Plato is here parodying the reality that the mothers of the dead were not allowed to receive the bodies and lay them to rest. If so, the reliability of this one small quote must be brought into question. If anything, its unique presence within the genre highlights the potential of it being a purposeful parody.

100 Note Sophie Mills, *Theseus, Tragedy, and the Athenian Empire* (Oxford: Clarendon Press, 1997): 48–9 n 14, and her justified criticism of Loraux's analysis of such absences.

101 The tomb in which the men are buried is sometimes mentioned, but most frequently as a location rather than as part of a ritual process: Lys. 2.1, 60; Dem. 60.1, 13, 30; Hyp. 6.1.

102 Thuc. 2.43.2. Strassler (2008 [Adapted]): κοινῇ γὰρ τὰ σώματα διδόντες ἰδίᾳ τὸν ἀγήρων ἔπαινον ἐλάμβανον καὶ τὸν τάφον ἐπισημότατον, οὐκ ἐν ᾧ κεῖνται μᾶλλον, ἀλλ᾽ ἐν ᾧ ἡ δόξα αὐτῶν παρὰ τῷ ἐντυχόντι αἰεὶ καὶ λόγου καὶ ἔργου καιρῷ αἰείμνηστος καταλείπεται. ἀνδρῶν γὰρ ἐπιφανῶν πᾶσα γῆ τάφος.

103 For a similar observation see Loraux, *Invention of Athens*, 121, following Henry Immerwahr, 'Ergon: History as a Monument in Herodotus and Thucydides', *The American Journal of Philology* 81, 3 (1960): 285–90.

104 Thuc. 2.42.3; Lys. 2.79.

105 For the importance of this over physical memorialisation by way of casualty lists see Nathan Arrington, 'Inscribing Defeat: The Commemorative Dynamics of the Athenian Casualty Lists', *Classical Antiquity* 30, 2 (2011): 181–2.

106 See also Lys. 2.2; Dem 60.33.

107 Loraux, *Invention of Athens*, 71–5; Christiane Sourvinou-Inwood, *'Reading' Greek Death: To the End of the Classical Period* (Oxford: Clarendon Press, 1995), 192–3; Arrington, *Ashes, Images and Memories*, 114–20.

108 First fruits and honours: Hdt. 9.85.1 and Thuc. 3.58.4, with Isoc. 14.61.
    Commemorative games: Lys. 2.80; Plat. *Menex.* 249b-c; Dem. 60.36.6. cf.
    Arrington, *Ashes, Images and Memories*, 119, who emphasises the lack of concrete
    evidence for sacrifices made to the war dead. If the Athenians did not worship and
    give sacrifice to their own war dead, it would make them anomalous with other
    Greek *poleis* such as Sparta (Simonides fr. 531; Xen. *Lac.* 15.9; Diod. 11.11.6),
    Megara (*IG* VII 53, with Paloma Ruano's cautious assessment, '*IG* VII 53, An
    Epigraphicrara Avis in the Corpus of Greek Metrical Inscriptions', *Mare Nostrum* 7,
    (2016): 38; Paus. 1.43.3) and Thasos (Jean Pouilloux, *Recherches sur l'Histoire et les
    cultes de Thasos. Études thasiennes 3* (Paris: E De Boccard, 1954), 371–80).
109 Dem. 60.34; Hyp. 6.43. Robert Parker, *Athenian Religion: A History* (Oxford:
    Clarendon Press, 1996), 135–36.
110 Parker, *Athenian Religion*, 137.
111 Hyperides mentions the dead *strategos* Leosthenes throughout his oration, which
    was a drastic break from the literary tradition: Frangeskou, 'Tradition', 316; Ian
    Worthington et al, *Dinarchus, Hyperides, and Lycurgus* (Austin: University of Texas
    Press, 2001), 129.
112 Shared ancestry: Lys. 2.20; Dem. 60.4; Hyp. 6.7. Shared motives: Gorg. fr. 6; Lys.
    2.23-24; Dem. 60.27; Hyp. 6 16. Collective death: Thuc. 2.43.2.
113 Thuc. 2.42.3; Trivigno, 'Rhetoric of Parody', 43.
114 Katharine Derderlan, *Leaving Words to Remember: Greek Mourning and the Advent
    of Literacy* (Leiden: Brill, 2001), 177–78.
115 Thuc. 2.37.1.
116 Thuc. 2.42.4. For a similar sentiment see Plat. *Menex.* 246e; Dem. 60.2.
117 Elena Franchi and Giorgia Proietti, 'Commemorating War Dead and Inventing
    Battle Heroes: Heroic Paradigms and Discursive Strategies in Ancient Athens and
    Phocis', in *Ancient Warfare: Introducing Current Research Vol 1*, ed. Geoff Lee, et al
    (Newcastle-upon-Tyne: Cambridge Scholars Press, 2015), 235, who argue that the
    honours for the war dead were only for those who died in any given year, but they
    do not discuss the evidence offered here.
118 Dem. 60.12.
119 Gorg. Fr.6; Lys. 2.81; Plat. *Menex.* 247d; Dem. 60.19, 37; Hyp. 6.24. Although, the
    orators used euphemisms and broader concepts such as mortality and immortality,
    in place of using the verb 'to die': Loraux, *Invention of Athens*, 27.
120 Dem. 60.33; Hyp. 6.42; Lys. 2.79.
121 Dem. 60.33. Plat. *Menex.* 235c may be parodying the concept, with Socrates
    describing an overwhelming ability of the orators to influence the listeners of the
    oration. He jokes that he almost believes that he is in the islands of the blessed,
    before coming to his senses once the orator's bewitchment had worn off:
    Trivigno, 'Rhetoric of Parody', 33. For the islands of the blessed (also called the

Elysian Fields) in Greek thought see Hom. *Od.* 4.563–69; Hes. *W&D.* 168-73; Pind. *Ol.* 2.70ff.

122 Lys. 2.31; Plat. *Menex.* 243d; Dem 60.19. Seemingly this was because they had chosen to die nobly rather than live a shameful life: Dem. 60.26; Thuc 2.42.4.

123 Lys. 2.80; Gorg. Fr.6.

124 Immortal: Lys. 2.23, 81; Dem. 60.27; Hyp. 6.24. Ageless: Thuc. 2.43.2; Lys. 2.79; Dem. 60.32; Hyp. 6.42. For the importance of memory and memory formation within the *epitaphioi* see Shear, "'Their Memories Will Never Grow Old": The Politics of Remembrance in the Athenian Funeral Orations', *The Classical Quarterly* 63, 2 (2013): 511–36.

125 Gorg. Fr.6. Trans. Herrman (2004: 25): ἀλλ' ἀθάνατος οὐκ ἐν ἀθανάτοις σώμασι ζῆι οὐ ζώντων.

126 Thuc. 2.43.2; see also Hyp. 6.42.

127 Dem. 60.36

128 On the distinction of civic immortality, as opposed to celestial immortality, see Loraux, *Invention of Athens*, 166–70.

129 The only fragment which seems to describe the war dead themselves explicitly as immortal comes from Stesimbrotus via Plutarch (Plut. *Per.* 8.6 = Stesimbrotus, *FGrH*, 107 F9). He is relating the funeral oration delivered by Pericles in 439, following the Athenian war with Samos. Pericles is alleged to have said that the war dead become immortal, like the gods. Revealingly, Pericles is quoted as describing the gods as unseen, known only from the honours they receive and the blessings they bestow, thus the Athenians conclude that they are immortal; so it was with the war dead. If this account is accurate, it does conform to the analysis here; the two defining features highlighted for immortality are continual honours and the bestowing of favour from the dead.

130 Dem. 60.27.

131 Lys. 2.81.

132 Hyp. 6.24.

Chapter 7

1 This question will be examined below, but it is important to clarify here that this does not refer to the physical body, but rather a symbolic return that allows the family to claim some form of ownership over the memory of the dead.

2 Loraux, *Invention of Athens*, 52–8; Shapiro, 'Iconography of Mourning', 646; Gail Holst-Warhaft, *Dangerous Voices: Women's Laments and Greek Literature* (London: Routledge, 1992), 99; William Tyrrell and Larry Bennett, *Recapturing Sophocles' Antigone* (London: Rowman & Littlefield Publishers., 1998), 9; 'Pericles' Muting of

Women's Voices in Thuc. 2.45.2', *The Classical Journal* 95, 1 (1999): 50; Pritchard, 'The Symbiosis', 45.

3 Margaret Alexiou, *The Ritual Lament in Greek Tradition*, 2nd edn (Lanham, MD: Rowman & Littlefield Publishers, 1974/2002), 21; Shapiro, 'Iconography of Mourning', 646; Helene Foley, 'The Politics of Tragic Lamentation', in *Tragedy, Comedy and the Polis*, ed. Alan Sommerstein et al (Bari: Levante Editori, 1993), 122–3.

4 Nicole Loraux, *The Divided City: On Memory and Forgetting in Ancient Athens*. Trans. Corinne Pache & Jeff Fort (New York: Zone Books, 2001), 27.

5 Mark Toher, 'Euripides' "Supplices" and the Social Function of Funeral Ritual', *Hermes* 129, 3 (2001): 334 n 11.

6 Isae. 4.19–20, 9.4

7 Interestingly there is evidence that families would disagree about which house the *prothesis* should take place. A speech of Isaeus describes the death of a grandfather that resulted in a debate as to whether the body should be kept in his home, as per the wishes of the grandmother, or be moved to the home of the grandson. The implication is that the grandson's request to move the body was the norm, but he concedes and follows his grandmother's wishes: Isae. 8.21–2; Kerri J. Hame, 'Female Control of Funeral Rites in Greek Tragedy: Klytaimestra, Medea, and Antigone', *Classical Philology* 103, 1 (2008): 4 n 18.

8 The best overview of the evidence for the *prothesis* is still to be found in Garland, *Greek Way of Death*, 23–31.

9 Dem. 43.62; Plut. *Sol.* 21.4–5; Robert Garland, 'The Well-Ordered Corpse: An Investigation into the Motives behind Greek Funerary Legislation', *Bulletin of the Institute of Classical Studies* 36, (1989): 3–7; Shapiro, 'Iconography of Mourning', 630–31.

10 Shapiro, 'Iconography of Mourning', 647–8.

11 Plat. *Phd.* 115a; Eur. *Phoen.* 1319, 1667. Douglas MacDowell, *The Law in Classical Athens* (Ithaca, NY: Cornell University Press, 1978), 109; Parker, *Miasma*, 3–5; Matthew Dillon, *Girls and Women in Classical Greek Religion* (London: Routledge, 2002), 289.

12 Shapiro, 'Iconography of Mourning', 646.

13 Shapiro, 'Iconography of Mourning', 630; Hans van Wees, 'A Brief History of Tears: Gender Differentiation in Archaic Greece', in *When Men Were Men: Masculinity, Power and Identity in Classical Antiquity*, ed. Lin Foxhall and John Salmon (London: Routledge, 1998b), 36–40, 43; Alexiou, *Ritual Lament*, 22–3. See, also, Parker, *Athenian Religion*, 50; Josine Blok, 'Solon's Funeral Laws: Questions of Authenticity and Function', in *Solon of Athens: New Historical and Philological Approaches*, ed. Josine Block and André Lardinois (Leiden: Brill, 2006), 198–9.

14 Hame, 'Female Control', 1–4.

15 van Wees, 'Brief History of Tears', 33; Dillon, *Girls and Women*, 279.

16 Dem. 43.62.

17 Pritchett, *Greek State, vol IV*, 249–51. Polly Low, 'Remembering War in Fifth-Century Greece: Ideologies, Societies, and Commemoration beyond Democratic Athens', *World Archaeology* 35, 1 (2003): 104–8, convincingly shows that Athens was not the only *polis* that repatriated its dead during the Peloponnesian War; however, there is no suggestion anywhere that Athens was not the first to introduce this new system in place of burying the dead on campaign.

18 The preparation of the body, with the head uncovered, is clearly seen on a red figure depiction of the *prothesis*: Munich, Antikensammlungen: 2369, *BA* 9028081; Athens, National Museum: CC1168, *BA* 202188.

19 Thuc. 2.34.4.

20 Thuc. 2.34.4.

21 Eur. *Supp.* 941-6. Trans. Kovacs (1998).

22 Eur. *Med.* 1378.

23 Eur. *Med.* 1399–403.

24 Eur. *Med.* 1405–12.

25 Hame, 'Female Control', 6–7. Hame forces the question of who had control of the funeral too far in this instance. Jason's desire to simply touch the corpses shows that he had abandoned any hope of burying the bodies and suggest an emotive plea, rather than a move to retain control of the ritual afforded to him via his gender.

26 Living children: Soph. *OT.* 1466–70. Dead children: Eur. *Phoen.* 1700. This can also be seen in Antigone's description of lifting her brother's corpse by hand (χερί): Sop. *Ant.* 43.

27 The most influential analysis on these monuments can be found in Bradeen, 'Athenian Casualty Lists'; Stupperich, *Staatsbegräbnis und Privatgrabmal*, 4–22; Clairmont, *Patrios Nomos*, 46–54; Pritchett, *Greek State, vol IV*, 139–40; Low, 'Commemorating the War Dead'; Arrington, 'Inscribing Defeat'.

28 Arrington, 'Inscribing Defeat', 189–94; *contra* Tritle, *Melos to My Lai*, 176–7.

29 Tritle, *Melos to My Lai*, 165–72, 181–3; Arrington, *Ashes, Images and Memories*, 94–5.

30 Example of a casualty list for one tribe alone: *IG* I³ 1147. Examples of casualty lists broken down by tribal subheadings: *IG* I³ 1162, *IG* I³ 1186, *IG* I³ 1191, *IG* II² 5221.

31 *Strategos: IG* I³ 1147, *IG* I³ 1162, *IG* II² 5221. *Trierarchos: IG* I³ 1166, *IG* I³ 1186, *IG* I³ 1191. *Phylarchos: IG* I³ 1190, *IG* II² 5222. *Mantis: IG* I³ 1147. *Taxiarchos: IG* I³ 1186, *IG* I³ 1191. With notes from Arrington, 'Inscribing Defeat', 184 n.32.

32 Simon Goldhill, 'The Great Dionysia and Civic Ideology', in *Nothing to Do with Dionysos?: Athenian Drama in Its Social Context*, ed. John Winkler and Froma Zeitlin (Princeton: Princeton University Press, 1990), 111; Hans Rupprecht Goette, 'Images in the Athenian 'Demosion Sema', in *Art in Athens During the Peloponnesian*

War, ed. Olga Palaiga (Cambridge: Cambridge University Press, 2009), 198; Pritchard, 'The Symbiosis', 34–5; Arrington, 'Inscribing Defeat', 187; Nikolaos Papazarkadas and Dimitris Sourlas, 'The Funerary Monument for the Argives who fell at Tanagra (*IG* I³ 1149): A New Fragment', *Hesperia* 81, 4 (2012): 602.

33 Low, 'Remembering War', 99.

34 Low, 'Remembering War', 102. See, in particular, *LSCG* Suppl. 64=Arnaoutoglou 1998.78.

35 Low, 'Remembering War', 109.

36 Louis Gernet & André Boulanger, *Le génie grec dans la religion* (Paris: La Renaissance du Livre, 1932), 132–7; Alexiou, *Ritual* Lament, 18–19; Flavia Frisone, 'Construction of Consensus: Norms and Change in Greek Funerary Rituals', in *Ritual Dynamics in the Ancient Mediterranean: Agency, Emotion, Gender, Reception*, ed. Angelos Chaniotis (Stuttgart: Steiner Verlag, 2011), 182–3.

37 Tyrrell and Bennett, *Recapturing Sophocles*, 7; Carey, 'Epideictic Oratory', 241.

38 *IG* I³ 1147 contains the most, with six pairs and one set of homonymous triplets. See also *IG* i³ 1162 and *IG* i³ 1184.

39 Arrington, 'Inscribing Defeat', 189–90.

40 Lorna Hardwick, 'Philomel and Pericles: Silence in the Funeral Speech', *Greece & Rome* 40, 2 (1993): 157.

41 Jones, 'The Athenian Phylai', 504; *Associations of Classical Athens*, 169–72; Crowley, *Psychology of a Hoplite,* 29.

42 For the practicalities see Arrington, 'Inscribing Defeat', 186.

43 Kurt Raaflaub, 'Father of All, Destroyer of All: War in Late Fifth-Century Athenian Discourse and Ideology', in *War and Democracy: A Comparative Study of the Korean War and the Peloponnesian War*, ed. David McCann and Barry Strauss (Armonk, NY: ME Sharpe, Inc, 2001), 323. Demosthenes goes as far as to claim that the men of each tribe were influenced by the legacies of their tribal heroes in their honourable duty of dying for the *polis.*

44 See also Loraux, *The Invention of Athens*, 52, who argues that the listing by tribe was intended to 'remind the citizen that he owed everything to the *polis*'.

45 *IG* i³ 1162. Trans. Lambert & Osborne (*AIO*, 2017): ἀθάνατον μνε͂μ' ἀρετε͂ς.

46 *IG* I3 1181, with Arrington, 'Inscribing Defeat', 187–8.

47 The prime example of an ostentatious commemoration would be the Kroisos *kouros* (*c.* 540 BC), which commemorates the young man Kroisos who died in battle by way of a statue and epigram: *SEG* 10.461.

48 Arrington, *Ashes, Images and Memories*, 205.

49 New York (NY), Metropolitan Museum: 35.11.5, *BA* 209194.

50 Amsterdam, Allard Pierson Museum: 2455, *BA* 42150.

51 Arrington, *Ashes, Images and Memories*, 80. See also the references to the public ceremony that can be found on warrior loutrophoroi, e.g. Athens, National

Archaeological Museum: 1700, with Stupperich, 'Iconography', 95; Arrington, *Ashes, Images and Memories*, 210. Warrior loutrophoroi: Stupperich, *Staatsbegräbnis und Privatgrabmal*, 155–62); 'Iconography', 95–97; Clairmont, *Patrios Nomos*, 76–81; Stefan Schmidt, *Rhetorische Bilder auf attischen Vasen: Visuelle Kommunikation im 5. Jahrhundert v. Chr.* (Berlin: Dietrich Reimer, 2005), 79–85; Hannah, 'Warrior Loutrophoroi', 266–303.

52 Eur. *Supp.* 971–9. Oates & O'Neill (1938 [adapted]): ὑπολελειμμένα μοι δάκρυα: μέλεα παιδὸς ἐν οἴκοις κεῖται μνήματα, πένθιμοι κουραὶ καὶ στέφανοι κόμας, λοιβαί τε νεκύων φθιμένων, ἀοιδαί θ᾽ ἃς χρυσοκόμας Ἀπόλλων οὐκ ἐνδέχεται: γόοισι δ᾽ ὀρθρευομένα δάκρυσι νοτερὸν ἀεὶ πέπλων πρὸς στέρνῳ πτύχα τέγξω.

53 E.g. Private Collection, Toronto, *BA* 452.

54 Cleveland (OH), Museum of Art: 28.660, *BA* 207549.

55 Samothrace, Archaeological Museum: 65.1055, *BA* 1726.

56 Eur. *Alc.* 98-103, 215-17.

57 Xen. *Hell.* 5.1; Xen. *Ages.* 2.15; Lyc. 1.110; Plut. *Per.* 28.3-4; Soph. *Trach.* 179

58 Lys. 32.21. For more on the story of Diodotus see below section 7.2.1.

59 Xen. *Hell.* 2.4.7. Although, Xenophon does not make it clear whether these burials included the erection of cenotaphs.

60 Arrington, *Ashes, Images and Memories*, 205–7. Decline in private cenotaphs: Kurtz and Boardman, *Greek Burial Customs*, 89–90; Morris, *Death-Ritual*, 146. Watershed: Osborne, 'Democratic Ideology', 263.

61 Ursula Knigge, 'Die Ausgrabungen im Kerameikos 1970–2', *Archäologischer Anzeiger*, (1974): 191 Figure 20, n 17, 193); 'Aison, der Meidiasmaler? Zu einer rotfigurigen Oionchoe aus dem Kerameikos', *Mitteilungen Des Deutschen Archäologischen Instituts (Athenische Abteilung)* 90, (1975): 123; Arrington, *Ashes, Images and Memories*, 207.

62 Ursula Knigge 'Aison, der Meidiasmaler? Zu einer rotfigurigen Oionchoe aus dem Kerameikos', *Mitteilungen Des Deutschen Archäologischen Instituts (Athenische Abteilung)* 90, (1975): 123.

63 Athens, Kermaeikos Museum: P1130.

64 *IG* II² 6217: Δεξίλεως Λυσανίο Θορίκιος. ἐγένετο ἐπὶ Τεισάνδρο ἄρχοντος, ἀπέθανε ἐπ᾽ Εὐβολίδο ἐγ Κορίνθωι τῶν πέντε ἱππέων.

65 Tribal-based list: *IG* II² 5221. Cavalry list: *IG* II² 5222. His name appears on the cavalry list but he is absent from the fragmentary tribal based list: Arrington, *Ashes, Images and Memories*, 206.

66 One *phylarch* and ten cavalrymen.

67 A different historical interpretation that has been made since the late 1800s is that 'the five cavalrymen' was some form of specific, or elite, group, but there no corroborating evidence to support such a notion: Emily Vermeule, 'Five Vases from the Grave Precinct of Dexileos', *Jahrbuch des Deutschen Archäeologischen Instituts* 85,

(1970): 110; Peter Rhodes and Robin Osborne, *Greek Historical Inscriptions: 404–323 BC.* (Oxford: Oxford University Press, 2003), 42.

68 For the question of dating the battles, and reconciling these lists see Rhodes and Osborne, *Historical Inscriptions*, 42.

69 Lys. 16. 3, 6, 8 Arist. [*Ath. Pol.*] 38.2. Bugh, *Horsemen*, 139–40 referencing an unpublished paper by Colin Edmonson; Rhodes and Osborne, *Historical Inscriptions*, 43; Josiah Ober, *Athenian Legacies: Essays on the Politics of Going on Together* (Princeton: Princeton University Press, 2005), 241; Arrington, *Ashes, Images and Memories*, 233.

70 Josiah Ober, 'Tyrant Killing as Therapeutic *Stasis*: A Political Debate in Images and Texts', in *Popular Tyranny: Sovereignty and Its Discontents in Ancient Greece*, ed. Kathryn Morgan (Austin: University of Texas Press, 2003), 242 and again *Athenian Legacies*, 244–5.

71 Ober, *Athenian Legacies*, 244.

72 Vases in the grave precinct: Vermeule, 'Five Vases', 94–111.

73 Vermeule, 'Five Vases', 105–6.

74 For an overview of the different designs of private reliefs, see Stupperich, 'Iconography', 95–9; Arrington, *Ashes, Images and Memories*, 217–37.

75 This seems the more logical reading for the image. For a different interpretation which argues that the man is sitting on land rather than the ship itself, see Nikolaos Kaltsas, *Sculpture in the National Archaeological Museum, Athens* (Athens: Kapon Editions, 2002), 163.

76 Christoph Clairmont, *Classical Attic Tombstones* (Kilchberg: Akanthus, 1993): 316–17; Barry Strauss, 'Perspectives on the Death of the Fifth Century Athenian Seaman', in *War and Violence in Ancient Greece*, ed. Hans van Wees (Oxford: Classical Press of Wales, 2009), 262–3; Arrington, *Ashes, Images and Memories*, 223–4.

77 *IG* II2 11114: Δημοκλείδης ⋮ Δημητρίο.

78 Trireme and naval service: Strauss, 'Perspectives', 262–5; Arrington, *Ashes, Images and Memories*, 223. Manner of the death: Kurtz and Boardman, *Greek Burial Customs*, 139; Garland, *Greek Way of Death*, 16.

79 Felix Wassermann, 'Serenity and Repose: Life and Death on Attic Tombstones', *The Classical Journal* 64, 5 (1969): 198.

80 The short epitaph is not unique, but it is more commonly seen stretching from one side of a *stele* to the other: e.g. Grave *stele* of Stratokles, Boston, Museum of Fine Arts, John H, and Ernestine, A Payne Fund: 1971.129.

81 Erwin Panofsky, *Tomb Sculpture: Four Lectures on its Changing Aspects from Ancient Egypt to Bernini* (New York: Harry N Abrams, 1964), 23; Clairmont, *Attic Tombstones*, 317; Strauss, 'Perspectives', 263; Arrington, *Ashes, Images and Memories*, 224. On the topic of the family receiving notification of death see below section 7.2.1.

82 Strauss, 'Perspectives', 262.

83 Arrington, *Ashes, Images and Memories*, 235.

84 See, e.g., Alexiou, *Ritual Lament*, 21; Shapiro, 'Iconography of Mourning', 646; Foley, 'Politics of Tragic Lamentation', 122–3; Tyrrell and Bennett, 'Pericles' Muting'; Loraux, *The Divided City*, 27.

85 For an illuminating analysis of the gender dynamics inherent in the handling of the dead, see Hame, 'Female Control', 1–15.

86 Xen. *Hell.* 6.4.16.

87 One thousand Lacedaemonians died, of which four hundred were Spartiates: Xen. *Hell.* 6.4.15.

88 As part of the message included an order to the women of the households not to perform their usual lamentations, it can be assumed that this was the first notification that the Spartan *oikoi* received following the battle.

89 Thuc. 8.1.1.

90 See Isae. 9.3.

91 On the dating see the commentary of Michael Edwards, *Isaeus* (Austin, TX: Texas University Press, 2007b), 204.

92 Isae. Fr.15=Dion. Hal. *Isae.* 5: τριηραρχοῦντος γάρ μου ἐπὶ Κηφισοδότου ἄρχοντος καὶ λόγου ἀπαγγελθέντος πρὸς τοὺς οἰκείους, ὡς ἄρα τετελευτηκὼς εἴην ἐν τῇ ναυμαχίᾳ

93 Hesych. s.v. *deuteropotmos*; Garland, *Greek Way of Death*, 100–1; Yulia Ustinova, *Caves and the Ancient Greek Mind: Descending Underground in the Search for Ultimate Truth* (Oxford: Oxford University Press, 2009), 218–19.

94 For the importance of the Semnai Theai for the dead see Sarah Johnstone, *Restless Dead: Encounters between the Living and the Dead in Ancient Greece* (Berkeley: University of California Press, 1999), 280.

95 Plut. *Quaes. Rom.* 5

96 Lys. 32.4–6.

97 He is described in the suit as serving with Thrasyllus (Lys. 32.7), allowing an accurate date of his death to be assigned; Peter O'Connell, *The Rhetoric of Seeing in Attic Forensic Oratory* (Austin: University of Texas Press, 2017), 150. If this is the case, then Diodotus was part of the body count that Xenophon describes as being buried at Notium rather than being sent back to Athens: see section 6.1.2.

98 Lys. 32.8.

99 For the fear of rumour bringing home false news see Aesch. *Ag.* 620–33.

100 Such as that described in Isae. 9.4.

101 Although it is certainly not unique. A similar case is described in Isae. 9, but describes a non-family member laying claim to the inheritance of a dead warrior based on an alleged adoption.

102 Lys. 32.21.

103 Diod. 13.101; Xen. *Hell.* 1.7.1–6. For a discussion on the different accounts see A Andrewes, 'The Arginousai Trial', *Phoenix* 28, 1 (1974): 112–2; Luca Asmonti, 'The Arginusae Trial, The Changing Role of Strategoi and the Relationship Between Demos and Military Leadership in Late-Fifth Century Athens', *Bulletin of the Institute of Classical Studies* 49, (2006): 1–3.

104 Eur. *Hel.* 1250–300

105 Stella Georgoudi, 'La Mer, la Mort et le Discours des Épigrammes Funéraires', *AION* 10, (1988): 53–61.

106 There is no evidence to explore the logistics behind the sending of messengers to inform hundreds of families, dispersed throughout Attica. Plausibly, one messenger was sent to each relevant *deme*, to inform the families. Another possibility is that returning slaves could have been the ones to report the message, but our only evidence for this is Menander's *Aspis*, the date for which is too late and the slave in question is unusually loyal. Furthermore, the master Kleostratos was not actually part of an Athenian army, but was a mercenary so the comparisons here are very limited.

107 Thuc. 2.44.1.

108 Hyp. 6.27.

109 Lys. 2.71–5; Dem. 60.36.

110 Plat. *Menex.* 247c.

111 There is a potential fourth category, siblings of the deceased, but these are only briefly addressed in Hyp. 6.27, and Thuc. 2.45, where the brothers are addressed with the sons of the dead. Brothers are also briefly mentioned on a list of mourners: Lys. 2.71.

112 Plat. *Menex.* 247d; Lys. 2.72-3; Thuc. 2.44.2.

113 Plat. *Menex.* 247e, 248b–c.

114 Plat. *Menex.* 247e.

115 Hyp. 6.41.

116 Lys. 2.73.

117 Lys. 2.72.

118 What is not made clear in any of the sources is what this meant for those parents who had surviving male heirs. Presumably they did not qualify for any support of this ilk.

119 Plat. *Menex.* 248e–f.

120 Loraux, *The Invention of Athens*, 54–56.

121 Lys. 2.72.

122 Of courageous stock: Plat. *Menex.* 246d, see also Dem. 60.32. War orphans' state provisions: Thuc. 2.46.1; Lys. 2.75; Plato. Menex. 248e–249a; Dem. 60.32; Arist. [*Ath. Pol.*] 24.3; Diog. Laert. *Vit.* 1.7.55.

123 Johannes Thiel, *Xenophōntos Poroi: specimen litterarium inaugurale* (Vienna: Österreichische Staatsdr, 1922), 46-7; Ronald Stroud, 'Greek Inscriptions

Theozotides and the Athenian Orphans', *Hesperia: The Journal of the American School of Classical Studies at Athens* 40, 3 (1971): 289–90; Richard Cudjoe, *The Social and Legal Position of Widows and Orphans in Classical Athens* (PhD diss., Glasgow: University of Glasgow (2000: 358–60)

124 *P. Hib.* I.14.

125 Stroud, 'Greek Inscriptions', 291–2.

126 Stroud, 'Greek Inscriptions', 290.

127 Loraux, *The Invention of Athens*, 56.

128 Plat. *Menex.* 249a; Aesch. 154.

129 The decree is clearly demonstrating that only sons should receive payment for those who died during the civil war of 404/3. Stroud, 'Greek Inscriptions', 291; K.R. Walters, 'Perikles' Citizenship Law'. *Classical Antiquity* 2, 2 (1983), 318; Todd, *Lysias*, 383.

130 Todd, *Lysias*, 383.

131 Thuc. 2.45.1 This is confirmed by Pericles' address to female excellence at the end of the section (Thuc. 2.45.2), suggesting that the prior section was aimed at male excellence.

132 Hyp. 6.27.

133 Plat. *Menex.* 247b.

134 Dem. 60.37.

135 Thuc. 2.45.1

136 Plat. *Menex.* 247b.

137 Plat. *Menex.* 248e.

138 Thuc. 2.45.2; Lys. 2.75, 73; Plat. *Menex.* 248c.

139 Hardwick, 'Philomel and Pericles', 147.

140 For an overview of these interpretive issues see Hardwick, 'Philomel and Pericles' and Tyrrell and Bennett, 'Pericles' Muting'.

141 Lys. 2.71.

142 Lys. 2.75.

143 Lys. 2.75. Trans. Todd (2000 [adapted]): οἵοίπερ ἐκεῖνοι ζῶντες ἦσαν.

144 Plat. *Menex.* 248c.

145 Plat. *Menex.* 236e.

146 Arrington, *Ashes, Images and Memories*, 208.

Bibliography

Austen, Jane. *Sense and Sensibility.* 1814. Reprinted with notes and introduction. Oxford: Oxford University Press, 2012.

Kinnes, Ian. 'The Cattleship Potemkin: Reflections on the First Neolithic in Britain'. In *The Archaeology of Context*, edited by John Barrett and Ian Kinnes, 308–11. Sheffield: University of Sheffield, 1988.

Roese, Horst. 'Some Aspects of Topographical Locations of Neolithic and Bronze Age Monuments in Wales'. *Bulletin of the Board of Celtic Studies* 29, no. 1 (1982): 763–5.

Schieffelin, Egon and John F. Riebow. The Sorrow of the Lonely and the Burning of the Dancers. New York: St Martin's Press, 1976.

Strunk, William, Jr and E. B. White. *The Elements of Style.* 4th edn. New York: Allyn and Bacon, 2000.

Editions of primary sources

Arnaoutoglou, I. (1998) *Ancient Greek Laws: A Sourcebook.* London: Routledge.

Austin, C. (ed.) (1968) *Nova fragmenta Euripidea in papyris reperta.* Berlin: Walter De Gruyter.

Bond, G.W. (1981) *Euripides' Heracles. With Introduction and Commentary.* Oxford: Clarendon Press.

Brownson, C.L. (trans.) (1918) *Xenophon, vols 1 and 2.* Cambridge MA: Harvard University Press.

Carey, C. (1989) *Lysias: Selected Speeches.* Cambridge: Cambridge University Press.

Carey, C. (2007) *Lysiae Orationes cum Fragmentis.* Oxford: Oxford University Press.

Collard, C. (1975) *Euripides, 'Supplices'.* Groningen: Bouma's Boekhuis.

Crawley, R. (1910) *Thucydides. History of the Peloponnesian War.* London: J.M. Dent.

DeWitt, N.J. (trans.) (1949) *Demosthenes, vol. 7.* Cambridge, MA: Harvard University Press.

Edwards, M. (trans.) (2007) *Isaeus.* Austin: Texas University Press.

Garvie, A.F. (1986), *Aeschylus' Choephori.* Oxford: Oxford University Press.

Herrman, J. (2004) *Athenian Funeral Orations.* Newburyport: Focus Publishing.

Kovacs, D. (1998) *Euripides: Suppliant Women, Electra, Heracles.* Cambridge, MA: Harvard University Press.

Lamb, W. R. M. (1930) *Lysias.* Cambridge, MA: Harvard University Press.

Lattimore, R. (trans.) (1951) *The Iliad of Homer.* Chicago: University of Chicago Press.

Lipka, M. (2002) *Xenophon's Spartan Constitution: Introduction. Text. Commentary.* Berlin: Walter De Gruyter.

Luschnig, C. E. and Woodruff, P. (trans.) (2011) *Euripides: Electra, Phoenician Women, Bacchae, & Iphigenia at Aulis.* Indianapolis: Hackett Publishing Company.

Maidment, K. J. (1968) *Minor Attic Orators in two volumes: vol. 1, Antiphon Andocides, with an English translation.* Cambridge, MA: Harvard University Press.

Miller, W. (trans.) 1914. *Xenophon: Xenophon in Seven Volumes, 5 and 6.* Cambridge, MA: Harvard University Press.

Oates, W. and O'Neil Jr., E. (eds) (1938) *The Complete Greek Drama: All the Extant Tragedies of Aeschylus, Sophocles and Euripides, and the Comedies of Aristophanes and Menander, in a Variety of Translations, vol. 2.* New York: Random House.

Perrin, B. (trans.) (1916) *Plutarch's Lives, vol. 4.* Cambridge, MA: Harvard University Press.

Rhodes, P. J., (ed. and trans.) (1988) *Thucydides: History II.* Warminster: Aris & Philips.

Rhodes, P. J. and Osborne, R. (2003) *Greek Historical Inscriptions: 404–323 BC.* Oxford: Oxford University Press.

Smyth, H. W. (trans.) *Aeschylus, vol. 2.* Cambridge MA: Harvard University Press.

Sommerstein, A. H. (trans.) (2008) *Aeschylus: Persians, Seven against Thebes, Suppliants, Prometheus Bound.* Cambridge, MA: Harvard University Press.

Strassler, R. (ed.) (2008) *The Landmark Thucydides: A Comprehensive Guide to the Peloponnesian War.* Trans. R. Crawley. New York: Free Press.

Svarlien, D. A. (ed. and trans.) (1991) *Odes.* Perseus Digital Library. [Online] Available at: www.perseus.tufts.edu/hopper/text?doc=Perseus:text:1999.01.0064.

Tichener, J. B. and Pease, A. S. (1928) 'Onasander'. In Henderson, J. (ed.) *Aeneas Tacticus, Asclepiodotus, Onasander.* Cambridge, MA: Harvard University Press.

Todd, S. (2000) *Lysias.* Austin: University of Texas Press.

Worthington, I., Cooper, C. and Harris, E. (2001) *Dinarchus, Hyperides, and Lycurgus.* Austin: University of Texas Press.

Wyse, W. (1904) *The Speeches of Isaeus.* Cambridge: Cambridge University Press.

Secondary sources

Abdul-Hamid, Walid Khalid and Jamie Hacker Hughes. 'Nothing New under the Sun: Post-Traumatic Stress Disorders in the Ancient World'. *Early Science and Medicine* 19, (2014): 1–9.

Alexiou, Margaret. *The Ritual Lament in Greek Tradition.* 2nd edn. Lanham, MD: Rowman & Littlefield Publishers, 1974/2002.

Alexopoulou, Marigo. *The Homecoming Pattern in Greek Tragedy.* PhD diss. Glasgow: University of Glasgow, 2003.

Alexopoulou, Marigo. *The Theme of Returning Home in Ancient Greek Literature: The Nostos of the Epic Heroes.* Lewiston: Edwin Mellen Press, 2009.

Anderson, Carl. 'Themistocles and Cleon in Aristophanes' Knights, 763ff'. *The American Journal of Philology*, 110(1) (1989): 10–16.

Andrewes, A. 'The Arginousai Trial', *Phoenix* 28, 1 (1974): 112–22.

Animal Health Australia. *Operational manual: Disposal (Version 3.1). Australian Veterinary Emergency Plan (AUSVETPLAN)*. ed. 3. Canberra, ACT: National Biosecurity Committee, 2015.

Arias, Paolo. *History of Greek Vase Painting*. London: Harry N. Abrams, 1962.

Arnott, W. Geoffrey. 'Double the Vision: A Reading of Euripides' "Electra"'. *Greece & Rome* 28, 2 (1981): 179–92.

Arrington, Nathan. *Between Victory and Defeat: Framing the Fallen Warrior in Fifth-Century Athenian Art*. PhD. diss., University of California, Berkeley, 2010a.

Arrington, Nathan. 'Topographic Semantics: The Location of the Athenian Public Cemetery and Its Significance for the Nascent Democracy'. *Hesperia* 79, 4 (2010b): 499–539.

Arrington, Nathan. 'Inscribing Defeat: The Commemorative Dynamics of the Athenian Casualty Lists'. *Classical Antiquity* 30, 2 (2011): 179–212.

Arrington, Nathan. *Ashes, Images and Memories: The Presence of the War-Dead in Fifth-Century Athens*. Oxford: Oxford University Press, 2015.

Asmonti, Luca. 'The Arginusae Trial, The Changing Role of Strategoi and the Relationship Between Demos and Military Leadership in Late-Fifth Century Athens'. *Bulletin of the Institute of Classical Studies* 49, (2006): 1–21.

Avramidou, Amalia. *The Codrus Painter: Iconography and Reception of Athenian Vases in the Age of Pericles*. London: The University of Wisconsin Press, 2011.

Badge, Shilpa, A. Bhole and Prasad Kokil. 'Design and Analysis of Energy Efficient Crematorium for Eco Body Burning'. *International Journal on Emerging Trends in Technology* 3, 2 (2016): 4129–33.

Bakewell, Geoffrey. 'Written Lists of Military Personnel in Classical Athens'. In *Politics of Orality*, ed. Craig Cooper, 87–102. Leiden: Brill, 2007a.

Bakewell, Geoffrey. 'Agamemnon 437: Chrysamoibos Ares, Athens and Empire'. *The Journal of Hellenic Studies* 127, (2007b): 123–32.

Balot, Ryan. *Courage in the Democratic Polis*. Oxford: Oxford University Press, 2014.

Banwell, Elizabeth, N. Greenberg, P. Smith, N. Jones and M. Fertout. 'What Happens to the Mental Health of UK Service Personnel after they Return Home from Afghanistan?' *Journal of the Royal Army Medical Corps* 162, (2015): 115–19.

Bassi, Karen. 'Spatial Contingencies in Thucydides' History'. *Classical Antiquity* 26, 2 (2007): 171–218.

Beard, Mary 'Adopting an Approach II'. In *Looking at Greek Vases*. ed. Tom Rasmussen and Nigel Spivey, 12-35. Cambridge: Cambridge University Press, 1991.

Beck, M. 'Xenophon'. In *Time in Ancient Greek Literature: Studies in Ancient Greek Narrative, vol. 2*. ed. Irene De Jong and René Nünlist, 385–96. Leiden: Brill, 2007.

Belfiglio, Valentine. 'Post-traumatic Stress Disorder and Acute Stress Disorder in the Army'. *Balkan Military Medical Review* 18, 3 (2015): 65–71.

Bicknell, Peter. *Studies in Athenian Politics and Genealogy.* Wiesbaden: Franz Steiner Verlag, 1972.

Birmes, Philippe, Eric Bui, Rémy Klein, Julien Billard, Laurent Schmitt, Charlotte Allenou, Nicolas Job and Christophe Arbus. 'Psychotraumatology in Antiquity'. *Stress & Health* 26, 1 (2009): 21–31.

Birnbaum, Aiton. 'Collective Trauma and Post-traumatic Symptoms in the Biblical Narrative of Ancient Israel'. *Mental Health, Religion and Culture* 11, 5 (2008): 533–46.

Blackman, David, Julian Baker and Nicholas Hardwick. 'Archaeology in Greece 1997-98'. *Archaeological Reports* 44 (1997–1998): 1–136.

Blech, Michael. *Studien zum Kranz bei den Griechen.* Berlin: de Gruyter, 1982.

Blok, Josine. 'Solon's Funeral Laws: Questions of Authenticity and Function'. In *Solon of Athens: New Historical and Philological Approaches.* ed. Josine Block and André Lardinois, 197–247. Leiden: Brill, 2006.

Blok, Josine. *Citizenship in Classical Athens.* Cambridge: Cambridge University Press, 2017.

Bloedow, Edmund. *Alcibiades Reexamined.* Wiesbaden: Franz Steiner Verlag, 1973.

Blundell, Mary. *Helping Friends and Harming Enemies: A Study in Sophocles and Greek Ethics.* Cambridge: Cambridge University Press, 1991.

Blundell, Sue and Nancy Rabinowitz. 'Women's Bonds, Women's Pots: Adornment Scenes in Attic Vase-Painting'. *Phoenix* 62, 1/2 (2008): 115–44.

Boardman, John. *Athenian Red Figure Vases: The Archaic Period.* London: Thames & Hudson, 1975.

Boardman, John. *Athenian Black-Figure Vases.* 2nd edn, London: Thames & Hudson, 1991.

Boedeker, Deborah. 'Family Matters: Domestic Religion in Classical Greece'. In *Household and Family Religion in Antiquity.* ed. John Bodel and Saul Olyan, 229–47. Oxford: Blackwell Publishing, 2008.

Boehnlein, James and John Kinzie. 'Commentary. DSM Diagnosis of Posttraumatic Stress Disorder and Cultural Sensitivity: A Response'. *Journal of Nervous and Mental Disease* 180, 9 (1992): 597–99.

Borza, Eugene. 'Timber and Politics in the Ancient World: Macedon and the Greeks'. *Proceedings of the American Philosophical Society* 131, 1 (1987): 32–52.

Bosworth, A. B. 'The Historical Context of Thucydides' Funeral Oration'. *The Journal of Hellenic Studies* 120 (2000): 1–16.

Bowes, Kimberly. 'At Home'. In *A Companion to the Archaeology of Religion in the Ancient World.* ed. Rubina Raja and Jörg Rüpke, 209–19. Oxford: Wiley Blackwell, 2015.

Bradeen, Donald. 'Athenian Casualty Lists'. *Hesperia: The Journal of the American School of Classical Studies at Athens* 33, 1 (1964): 16–62.

Bradeen, Donald. 'The Athenian Casualty Lists'. *The Classical Quarterly* 19, 1 (1969): 145–59.

Bron, Christiane and François Lissarrague. 'Looking at the Vase'. In *A City of Images: Iconography and Society in Ancient Greece.* ed. Claude Bérard, Christiane Bron, Jean-Louis Durand, Françoise Frontisi-Ducroux, François Lissarrague, Alain

Schnapp and Jean-Pierre Vernant. Translated by Deborah Lyons, 11–21. Princeton: Princeton University Press, 1989.

Brulé, Pierre. 'La mortalité de guerre en Grèce classique. L'exemple d'Athènes de 490 à 322' In *Armées et sociétés de la Grèce classique. Aspects sociaux et politiques de la guerre aux Ve et IVes. av. J.-C.* ed. Francis Prost, 51–68, Paris: Errances, 1999.

Bugh, Glenn. 'Introduction of the Katalogeis of the Athenian Cavalry'. *Transactions of the American Philological Association* 112 (1982): 23–32.

Bugh, Glenn. *The Horsemen of Athens.* Princeton: Princeton University Press, 1988.

Burgess, Theodore. *Epideictic Literature.* Chicago: University of Chicago Press, 1902.

Burian, Peter. 'Zeus Swthr Tritos and Some Triads in Aeschylus' Oresteia'. *The American Journal of Philology* 107 (1986): 332–42.

Carey, Christopher. 'Epideictic Oratory'. In *A Companion to Greek Rhetoric.* ed. Ian Worthington, 236–52, Chichester: Wiley, 2010.

Chaniotis, Angelos. *War in the Hellenistic World: A Social and Cultural History.* Oxford: Blackwell Publishing, 2005.

Charlier, Philippe, Joël Poupon, Murielle Goubard and Sophie Descamps. '"In This Way They Held Funeral for Horse-Taming Hector": A Greek Cremation Reflects Homeric Ritual.' In *New Directions in the Skeletal Biology of Greece, Hesperia Supplements 43.* ed. Lynne Schepartz, Sherry Fox and Chrissy Bourbou, 49–56. Princeton: American School of Classical Studies at Athens, 2009.

Chaston, Colleen. *Tragic Props and Cognitive Function: Aspects of the Function of Images in Thinking.* Leiden: Brill, 2010.

Christ, Matthew. 'Conscription of Hoplites in Classical Athens', *Classical Quarterly* 51 (2001): 398–422.

Christ, Matthew. *The Bad Citizen in Classical Athens.* Cambridge: Cambridge University Press, 2006.

Christ, Matthew. 'Helping Behavior in Classical Athens'. *Phoenix* 64, 3/4 (2010): 254–90.

Christesen, Paul. 'Athletics and Social Order in Sparta in the Classical Period'. *Classical Antiquity* 31, 2 (2012): 193–255.

Christensen, Johnny and Mogens Hansen. 'What is *Syllogos* at Thukydides 2.22.1?' In *The Athenian Ecclesia II: A Collection of Articles, 1983–1989.* ed. Mogens Hansen, 195–211. Copenhagen: Museum Tusculanum Press, 1989.

Clairmont, Christoph. 'New Evidence for a Polyandrion in the Demosion Sema of Athens?' *The Journal of Hellenic Studies* 101 (1981): 132–34.

Clairmont, Christoph. *Patrios Nomos: Public Burial in Athens during the Fifth and Fourth Centuries BC: The Archaeological, Epigraphic-Literary, and Historical Evidence.* Oxford: BAR International Series 161, 1983.

Clairmont, Christoph. *Classical Attic Tombstones.* Kilchberg: Akanthus, 1993.

Cole, Susan. *Landscapes, Gender, and Ritual Space: The Ancient Greek Experience.* Berkeley: University of California Press, 2004.

Collins, Derek. 'Mapping the Entrails: The Practice of Greek Hepatoscopy'. *The American Journal of Philology* 129, 3 (2008): 319–45.

Connor, Peter and Heather Jackson. *A Catalogue of Greek Vases in the Collection of the University of Melbourne at the Ian Potter Museum of Art.* Victoria: Macmillan Art Publishing, 2000.

Connor, Walter. *Thucydides.* Princeton: Princeton University Press, 1984.

Connor, Walter. 'Early Greek Land Warfare as Symbolic Expression'. In *Studies in Ancient Greek and Roman Society.* ed. Robin Osborne, 12–37. Cambridge: Cambridge University Press, 2004.

Cook, Arthur. *Zeus: A Study in Ancient Religion, vol. 2, part 2.* Rev. ed. Cambridge: Cambridge University Press, 1925/2010.

Cornell, Tim. 'On War and Games in the Ancient World'. In *The Global Nexus Engaged: Past, Present, Future Interdisciplinary Olympic Studies. Sixth International Symposium for Olympic Research.* ed. Kevin Wamsley, Scott Martyn and Kevin Wamsley, 29–40. London, Ontario: International Centre for Olympic Studies, 2002.

Couvenhes, Jean-Christophe. 'De Disciplina Graecorum: Les Relations de Violence entre les Chefs Militaire Grecs et leur Soldats'. In *La Violence dans les Mondes Grec et Romain.* ed. Jean-Marie Bertrand, 431–54. Paris: Publications de la Sorbonne, 2005.

Cox, Cheryl Anne. *Household Interests: Property, Marriage Strategies, and Family Dynamics in Ancient Athens.* Princeton: Princeton University Press, 1998.

Crowley, Jason. *Psychology of a Hoplite: The Culture of Combat in Classical Athens.* Cambridge: Cambridge University Press, 2012.

Crowley, Jason. 'Beyond the Universal Soldier: Combat Trauma in Classical Antiquity'. In *Combat Trauma and the Ancient Greeks.* ed. Peter Meineck and David Konstan, 105–30. New York: Palgrave Macmillan, 2014.

Crowley, Jason. 'Surviving Defeat: Battlefield Surrender in Classical Greece'. *Journal of Ancient History* 8, 1 (2020): 1–25.

Cudjoe, Richard. *The Social and Legal Position of Widows and Orphans in Classical Athens.* PhD diss., Glasgow: University of Glasgow, 2000.

Culler, Jonathan. *Structuralist Poetics. Structuralism, Linguistics, and the Study of Literature.* Routledge: London, 1975.

Currie, Shannon, Arla Day and Kevin Kelloway. 'Bringing the Troops Back Home: Modelling the Postdeployment Reintegration Experience'. *Journal of Occupational Health Psychology* 16, 1 (2011): 38–47.

Czech-Schneider, Raphaela. 'Das Demosion Sema und die Mentalität der Athener: Einige Überlegungen zur Einrichtung des athenischen Staatsfriedhofes'. *Laverna* 5 (1994): 3–37.

Day, Gregory, David F. Tang-Wai and Michel C. F. Shamy. 'A Case Study in the History of Neurology'. *The Neurohospitalist* 6, 4 (2016): 181–4.

Derderlan, Katharine. *Leaving Words to Remember: Greek Mourning and the Advent of Literacy.* Leiden: Brill, 2001.

Dillery, John. *Xenophon and the History of his Times.* London: Routledge, 1995.

Dillon, Matthew. *Girls and Women in Classical Greek Religion.* London: Routledge, 2002.

Dillon, Matthew, Christopher Matthew and Michael Schmitz, ed. *Religion & Classical Warfare: Archaic and Classical Greece.* Barnsley: Pen & Sword, 2020

Dinsmoor, William. 'Attic Building Accounts. I V. The Statue of Athena Promachos'. *American Journal of Archaeology* 25, 2 (1921): 118–29.

Dover, Kenneth. 'Aristophanes, Knights 11–20', *The Classical Review*, 9, 3 (1959): 196–9.

Dow, Sterling. 'Thucydides and the Number of Acharnian Hoplitai'. *Transactions and Proceedings of the American Philological Association* 92 (1961): 66–80.

Doyle, Andrea. 'Cassandra – Feminine Corrective in Aeschylus's "Agamemnon"'. *Acta Classica* 51 (2008): 57–75.

Ducrey, Pierre. *Le Traitement des Prisonniers de Guerre dans la Grèce Antique, des Origines à la Conquête Romaine.* Paris: E. De Boccard, 1968.

Durand, Jean-Louis. 'Greek Animals: Toward a Typology of Edible Bodies'. In *The Cuisine of Sacrifice Among the Greeks.* ed. Marcel Detienne and Jean-Pierre Vernant. Translated by Paula Wissing, 89–120. Chicago: University of Chicago Press, 1979/1990.

Eck, Bernard. *La mort rouge. Homicide, guerre et souillure en Grèce ancienne.* Paris: Les belles lettres, 2012.

Edwards, Michael. 'Lysias'. In *Time in Ancient Greek Literature: Studies in Ancient Greek Narrative, vol. 2.* ed. Irene de Jong and René Nünlist, 321–8. Leiden: Brill, 2007.

Ekroth, Gunnel. 'Theseus and the Stone. The Iconographic and Ritual Contexts of a Greek Votive Relief in the Louvre'. In *Divine Images and Human Imaginations in Ancient Greece and Rome,* ed. Ioannis Mylonopoulos, 143–70. Leiden: Brill, 2010.

Engels, Johannes. *Funerum sepulcrorumque magnficentia: Begräbnis- und Grabluxusgesetze in der griechisch-römischen Welt mit einigen Ausblicken auf Einschränkungen des funeralen und sepulkralen Luxus im Mittelalter und in der Neuzeit.* Stuttgart: Franz Steiner Verlag, 1998.

Fagan, Garrett and Trundle, Matthew, eds. *New Perspectives on Ancient Warfare.* Leiden: Brill, 2010.

Faraone, Christopher. *Talismans and Trojan Horses: Guardian Statues in Ancient Greek Myth and Ritual.* Oxford: Oxford University Press, 1992.

Faraone, Christopher. 'Molten Wax, Spilt Wine and Mutilated Animals: Sympathetic Magic in near Eastern and Early Greek Oath Ceremonies'. *The Journal of Hellenic Studies* 113 (1993): 60–80.

Faraone, Christopher. 'Household Religion in Ancient Greece'. In *Household and Family Religion in Antiquity,* ed. John Bodel and Saul Olyan, 210–28. Oxford: Blackwell Publishing, 2008.

Farrell, Alan. 'A Purple Heart and a Dime . . .' *Arion* 12, 1 (2004): 129–38.

Feaver, Douglas. 'The Historical Development in the Priesthoods of Athens'. *Yale Classical Studies* 15 (1957): 123–58.

Fenton, Norman. *Shell Shock and its Aftermath.* St Louis: CV Mosby Company, 1926.

Ferrajão, Paulo Correia and Rui Aragão Oliveira. 'Portuguese War Veterans: Moral Injury and Factors Related to Recovery From PTSD'. *Qualitative Health Research* 26, 2 (2016): 1–11.

Figley, Charles. *Encyclopedia of Trauma*. Los Angeles: Sage Publications, 2012.

Finley, Moses. *The World of Odysseus*. 2nd edn. London: Penguin, 1978.

Flower, Michael. *The Seer in Ancient Greece*. Berkeley: University of California Press, 2008.

Flower, Michael. *Xenophon's Anabasis, or The Expedition of Cyrus*. Oxford: Oxford University Press, 2012.

Foley, Helene. 'The Politics of Tragic Lamentation'. In *Tragedy, Comedy and the Polis*. ed. Alan Sommerstein, S. Halliwell, J. Henderson and B. Zimmerman, 101–43. (Bari: Levante Editori, 1993).

Foley, Helene. *Female Acts in Greek Tragedy*. Princeton: Princeton University Press, 2001.

Fontana, Alan and Robert Rosenheck. 'Posttraumatic Stress Disorder among Vietnam Theater Veterans: A Causal Model of Etiology in a Community Sample'. *The Journal of Nervous and Mental Disease* 182, 12 (1994): 677–84.

Forcen, Fernando and Arlenne Shapov. 'PTSD: A Recent Name for an Ancient Syndrome'. *The American Journal of Psychiatry Residents' Journal* 7, 2 (2012): 4–6.

Forsdyke, Sara. 'Street Theatre and Popular Justice in Ancient Greece: Shaming, Stoning and Starving Offenders Inside and Outside the Courts'. *Past & Present*, 201 (2008): 3–50.

Foxhall, Lin. 'House Clearance: Unpacking the "Kitchen" in Classical Greece'. *British School at Athens Studies*, 15, *Building Communities: House, Settlement and Society in the Aegean and Beyond*, (2007): 233–42.

Franchi, Elena and Giorgia Proietti. 'Commemorating War Dead and Inventing Battle Heroes: Heroic Paradigms and Discursive Strategies in Ancient Athens and Phocis'. In *Ancient Warfare: Introducing Current Research Vol. 1*. ed. Geoff Lee, Helene Whittaker and Graham Wrightson, 229–51. Newcastle-upon-Tyne: Cambridge Scholars Press, 2015.

Frangeskou, Vassiliki. 'Tradition and Originality in Some Attic Funeral Orations'. *The Classical World* 92, 4 (1999): 315–36.

Frisone, Flavia. 'Construction of Consensus: Norms and Change in Greek Funerary Rituals'. In *Ritual Dynamics in the Ancient Mediterranean: Agency, Emotion, Gender, Reception*. ed. Angelos Chaniotis, 179–201. Stuttgart: Steiner Verlag, 2011.

Gabriel, Richard. *The Madness of Alexander the Great: And the Myth of Military Genius*. Barnsley: Pen & Sword, 2015.

Gabrielsen, Vincent. 'The Impact of Armed Forces on Government and Politics in Archaic and Classical Greek Poleis: A Response to Hans van Wees'. In *Army and Power in the Ancient World*. ed. Angelos Chaniotis and Pierre Ducrey, 83–98. Stuttgart: Franz Steiner Verlag, 2002.

Garland, Robert. *The Greek Way of Death*. 2nd edn. Ithaca, NY: Cornell University Press, 1985/2001.

Garland, Robert. 'The Well-Ordered Corpse: An Investigation into the Motives behind Greek Funerary Legislation'. *Bulletin of the Institute of Classical Studies* 36 (1989): 1–15.

Gauer, Werner. 'Das Athenerschatzhaus und die marathonischen Akrothinia in Delphi'. In *Forschungen und Funde. Festschrift für Bernhard Neutsch*. ed. Bernhard Neutsch,

Friedrich Krinzinger, Fritz Krinzinger, Brinna Otto, Elisabeth Walde, 127–37. Innsbruck: Verlag des Instituts für Sprachwissenschaft der Universität Innsbruck, 1980.

Georgoudi, Stella. 'La Mer, la Mort et le Discours des Epigrammes Funéraires.' *AION* 10 (1988): 53–61.

Georgoulaki, Eleni. 'Religious and Socio-Political Implications of Mortuary Evidence: Case Studies in Ancient Greece.' *Kernos*, 9 (1996): 95–120.

Gera, Deborah. *Xenophon's* Cyropaedia: *Style, Genre, and Literary Technique.* Oxford: Oxford University Press, 1993.

Gernet, Louis and André Boulanger. *Le génie grec dans la religion.* Paris: La Renaissance du Livre, 1932.

Goette, Hans Rupprecht. 'Images in the Athenian 'Demosion Sema''. In *Art in Athens During the Peloponnesian War.* ed. Olga Palaiga, 188–206. Cambridge: Cambridge University Press, 2009.

Goff, Barbara. *Citizen Bacchae: Women's Ritual Practice in Ancient Greece.* Berkeley: University of California Press, 2004.

Goldhill, Simon. 'The Great Dionysia and Civic Ideology'. In *Nothing to Do with Dionysos?: Athenian Drama in Its Social Context.* ed. John Winkler and Froma Zeitlin, 97–129. Princeton: Princeton University Press, 1990.

Gomme, Arnold. *A Historical Commentary on Thucydides: I–V.* Oxford: Clarendon Press, 1945–81.

Gygax, Marc. 'Plutarch on Alcibiades' Return to Athens'. *Mnemosyne* 59, 4 (2006): 481–500.

Hall, Edith. *Greek Tragedy: Suffering under the Sun.* Oxford: Oxford University Press, 2010.

Hame, Kerri J. 'All in the Family: Funeral Rites and the Health of the Oikos in Aischylos' Oresteia'. *The American Journal of Philology* 125, 4 (2004): 513–38.

Hame, Kerri J. 'Female Control of Funeral Rites in Greek Tragedy: Klytaimestra, Medea, and Antigone'. *Classical Philology* 103, 1 (2008): 1–15.

Hamel, Debra. *Athenian Generals: Military Authority in the Classical Period.* Leiden: Brill, 1998.

Hamel, Debra. *The Battle of Arginusae: Victory at Sea and Its Tragic Aftermath in the Final Years of the Peloponnesian War.* Baltimore: Johns Hopkins University Press, 2015.

Hamilton, Richard. 'Sources for the Athenian Amphidromia'. *Greek, Roman and Byzantine Studies*, 25 (1984): 243–51.

Hamilton, Richard. 'Slings and Arrows: The Debate with Lycus in the Heracles'. *Transactions of the American Philological Association*, 115 (1985): 19–25.

Hannah, Patricia. 'The Warrior Loutrophoroi of Fifth-Century Athens'. In *War, Democracy and Culture in Classical Athens.* ed. David Pritchard, 266–303. Cambridge: Cambridge University Press, 2010.

Hansen, Morgens. 'The Number of Athenian Hoplites in 431 B.C.' *Symbolae Osloenses*, 56 (1981): 19–32.

Hansen, Morgens. *Three Studies in Athenian Demography*. Copenhagen: Det Kongelige Danske Videnskabernes Selskab, 1988.

Hansen, Morgens. *The Athenian Ecclesia II: A Collection of Articles, 1983–1989*. Copenhagen: Museum Tusculanum Press, 1989.

Hansen, Morgens. 'Introduction: The Polis as a Citizen-State'. In *The Ancient Greek City-State: Symposium on the Occasion of the 250th Anniversary of The Royal Danish Academy of Sciences and Letters July, 1–4 1992*. ed. Mogens Hansen, 7–29. Copenhagen: Munksgaard, 1993.

Hansen, Todd, ed. *The Alamo Reader: A Study in History*. Mechanicsburg: Stackpole Books, 2003.

Hanson, Victor Davis, ed. *Hoplites: The Classical Greek Battle Experience*. London: Routledge, 1991.

Hanson, Victor Davis, ed. *The Western Way of War: Infantry Battle in Classical Greece*. Berkeley: University of California Press, 1994/2009.

Hanson, Victor Davis, ed. *The Wars of the Ancient Greeks and Their Invention of Western Military Culture*. London: Cassell, 1999.

Hardwick, Lorna. 'Philomel and Pericles: Silence in the Funeral Speech'. *Greece & Rome* 40, 2 (1993): 147–62.

Harrison, Evelyn. *Athenian Agora XI: Archaic and Archaistic Sculpture*. Princeton: The American School of Classical Studies at Athens, 1965.

Harvey, Samuel, Stephani Hatch, Margaret Jones, Lisa Hull, Norman Jones, Neil Greenberg, Christopher Dandeker, Nicola Fear and Simon Wessely. 'Coming Home: Social Functioning and the Mental Health of UK Reservists on Return from Deployment to Iraq or Afghanistan'. *Annals of Epidemiology*, 21 (2011): 666–72.

Hatch, Thom. *Encyclopedia of the Alamo and the Texas Revolution*. Jefferson: MacFarland & Co, 1999.

Hau, Lisa. 'Nothing to Celebrate? The Lack or Disparagement of Victory Celebrations in the Greek Historians'. In *Rituals in Triumph in the Mediterranean World*. ed. Anthony Spalinger and Jeremy Armstrong, 57–74. Leiden: Brill, 2013.

Herman, Gabriel. *Ritualised Friendship and the Greek City*. Cambridge: Cambridge University Press, 1987.

Henry, Alan. *Honours and Privileges in Athenian Decrees*. Hildesheim: George Olms, 1983.

Hewitt, Joseph. 'The Necessity of Ritual Purification after Justifiable Homicide'. *Transactions and Proceedings of the American Philological Association*, 41 (1910): 99–113.

Hilton, John. 'War and Peace in the Ancient Greek Novel'. *Acta Classica*, 48 (2005): 57–85.

Hodkinson, Stephen. *Property and Wealth in Classical Sparta*. Swansea: The Classical Press of Wales, 2000/2009.

Hoepfner, Wolfram and Ernst-Ludwig Schwandner. *Haus und Stadt im klassischen Griechenland. Wohnen in der klassischen Polis I*. 2nd edn, Munich: Deutscher Kunstverlag, 1994.

Hoffman, Herbert. 'Why Did the Greeks Need Imagery? An Anthropological Approach to the Study of Greek Vase-Painting'. *Hephaistos*, 9 (1988): 143–62.

Hoffman, Herbert. *Sotades: Symbols of Immortality on Greek Vases*. Oxford: Oxford University Press, 1997.

Holck, Per. *Cremated Bones: A Medical-Anthropological Study of an Archaeological Material on Cremation Burials*. Oslo: Universitetet i Oslo, Antropologiske skrifter 1, 1987.

Hölscher, Tonio. 'Image and Political Identity: The Case of Athens'. In *Democracy, Empire, and the Arts in Fifth-century Athens*. ed. Deborah Boedeker and Kurt Raaflaub, 152–83. Cambridge, MA: Harvard University Press, 1998.

Hölscher, Tonio. 'Images of War in Greece and Rome: Between Military Practice, Public Memory, and Cultural Symbolism'. *The Journal of Roman Studies*, 93 (2003): 1–17.

Holst-Warhaft, Gail. *Dangerous Voices: Women's Laments and Greek Literature*. London: Routledge, 1992.

Honig, Bonnie. *Antigone, Interrupted*. Cambridge: Cambridge University Press, 2013.

Hornblower, Simon. *A Commentary on Thucydides, vols I–III*. Oxford: Oxford University Press, 1991–2008.

Hornblower, Simon. *Thucydides and Pindar: Historical Narrative and the World of Epinikian Poetry*. Oxford: Oxford University Press, 2004.

Hornblower, Simon. 'Sticks, Stones and Spartans: The Sociology of Spartan Violence'. In *War and Violence in Ancient Greece*. ed. Hans van Wees, 57–82. Oxford: Classical Press of Wales, 2009.

Hornum, Michael. *Nemesis, the Roman State and the Games*. Leiden: Brill, 1993.

Humphreys, Sally C. 'From a Grin to a Death: The Body in the Greek Discovery of Politics'. In *Constructions of the Classical Body*, ed. James Porter, 126–46. Ann Arbor: The University of Michigan Press, 1999.

Hunter, Virginia. 'The Prison of Athens: A Comparative Perspective'. *Phoenix* 51, 3/4 (1997): 296–326.

Huntsman, Theresa and Marshall Becker. 'An Analysis of the Cremated Human Remains in a Terracotta Cinerary Urn of the Third-Second Century BCE from Chiusi, now in the Metropolitan Museum of Art in New York'. *Etruscan Studies* 16, 2 (2013): 153–64.

Hurwit, Jeffrey. 'Reading the Chigi Vase'. *Hesperia* 71, 1 (2002): 1–22.

Hyland, John. 'The Desertion of Nicarchus the Arcadian in Xenophon's "Anabasis"'. *Phoenix* 64, 3/4 (2010): 238–53.

Immerwahr, Henry. 'Ergon: History as a Monument in Herodotus and Thucydides'. *The American Journal of Philology* 81, 3 (1960): 261–90.

Isler-Kerényi, Cornelia. 'Iconographical and Iconological Approaches'. In *The Oxford Handbook of Greek and Roman Art and Architecture*. ed. Clemente Marconi, 557–78. Oxford: Oxford University Press, 2015.

Jacoby, Felix. 'Patrios Nomos: State Burial in Athens and the Public Cemetery in the Kerameikos'. *The Journal of Hellenic Studies* 64, (1944): 37–66.

Jæger, Jonas and Veronica Johansen. 'The Cremation of Infants/Small Children: An Archaeological Experiment Concerning the Effects of Fire on Bone Weight'. *Cadernos do GEEvH* 2, 2 (2013): 13–26.

Jameson, Michael. 'Domestic Space in the Greek City-State'. In *Domestic Architecture and the Use of Space: An Interdisciplinary Cross-Cultural Study*. ed. Susan Kent, 92–113. Cambridge: Cambridge University Press, 1990a.

Jameson, Michael. 'Domestic Space and the Greek City'. In *The Greek City: From Homer to Alexander*. ed. Oswyn Murray and Simon Price, 171–96. Oxford: Oxford University Press, 1990b.

Jameson, Michael. 'Sacrifice Before Battle'. In *Hoplites: The Classical Greek Battle Experience*. ed. Victor David Hanson, 197–227. London: Routledge, 1991.

Jameson, Michael. *Cults and Rites in Ancient Greece Essays on Religion and Society*. ed. A. B. Stallsmith. Cambridge: Cambridge University Press, 2014.

Jameson, Michael H. 'The Provisions for Mobilization in the Decree of Themistokles'. *Historia: Zeitschrift für Alte Geschichte* 12, 4 (1963): 385–404.

Jim, Theodora. *Sharing with the Gods: Aparchai and Dekatai in Ancient Greece*. Oxford: Oxford University Press, 2014.

Johnson, David, H. Lubin, R. Rosenheck, A. Fontana, S. Southwick and D Charney. 'The Impact of the Homecoming Reception on the Development of Posttraumatic Stress Disorder: The West Haven Homecoming Stress Scale (WHHSS)'. *Journal of Traumatic Stress* 10, 2 (1997): 259–77.

Johansson, Mikael. 'The Inscription from Troizen: A Decree of Themistocles?' *Zeitschrift für Papyrologie und Epigraphik* 137 (2001): 69–92.

Johnstone, Sarah. *Restless Dead: Encounters Between the Living and the Dead in Ancient Greece*. Berkeley: University of California Press, 1999.

Jones, Nicholas. 'The Athenian Phylai as Associations: Disposition, Function and Purpose'. *Hesperia*, 64 (1995): 503–42.

Jones, Nicholas. *The Associations of Classical Athens: The Response to Democracy*. Oxford: Oxford University Press, 1999.

Kallet, Lisa. *Money and the Corrosion of Power in Thucydides: The Sicilian Expedition and its Aftermath*. Berkeley: University of California Press, 2001.

Kaltsas, Nikolaos. *Sculpture in the National Archaeological Museum, Athens*. Athens: Kapon Editions, 2002.

Kamieński, Łukasz. 'Helping the Postmodern Ajax: Is Managing Combat Trauma through Pharmacology a Faustian Bargain?' *Armed Forces & Society* 39, 3 (2012): 395–414.

Karner, Tracy. 'Fathers, Sons, and Vietnam: Masculinity and Betrayal in the Life Narratives of Vietnam Veterans with Post Traumatic Stress Disorder'. *American Studies* 37, 1 (1996): 63–94.

Kavoulaki, Athena. 'Processional Performance and the Democratic Polis'. In *Performance Culture and Athenian Democracy*. ed. Simon Goldhill and Robin Osbourne, 293–320. Cambridge: Cambridge University Press, 1999.

Keane, Terence, W. O. Scott, G. A. Chavoya, D. M. Lamparski and J. A. Fairbank. 'Social Support in Vietnam Veterans with Posttraumatic Stress Disorder: A Comparative Analysis'. *Journal of Consulting and Clinical Psychology* 53, 1 (1985): 95–102.

Keegan, John. *The Face of Battle: A Study of Agincourt, Waterloo and the Somme*. Guildford, Book Club Associates, 1978.

Keesling, Catherine. *The Votive Statues of the Athenian Acropolis*. Cambridge: Cambridge University Press, 2003.

Keesling, Catherine. 'The Callimachus monument on the Athenian Acropolis (*CEG* 256) and Athenian commemoration of the Persian Wars'. In *Archaic and Classical Greek Epigram*. ed. Manuel Baumbach, Andrej Petrovic and Ivana Petrovic, 100–30. Cambridge: Cambridge University Press, 2010.

Keesling, Catherine. *Early Greek Portraiture: Monuments and Histories*. Cambridge: Cambridge University Press, 2017.

Kennell, Nigel. *Spartans: A New History*. Chichester: Wiley-Blackwell, 2010.

Keuls, Eva. *Painter and Poet in Ancient Greece: Iconography and the Literary Arts* (Beitrage zur Altertumskunde, 87). Stuttgart-Leipzig: BG Teubner, 1997.

Kindt, Julia. 'Polis Religion – A Critical Appreciation'. *Kernos: Revue Internationale et Pluridisciplinaire de Religion Grecque Antique* 22 (2009): 9–34.

King, Helen. 'Recovering Hysteria from History: Herodotus and "The First Case of Shell Shock"'. In *Contemporary Approaches to the Science of Hysteria: Clinical and Theoretical Perspectives*. ed. Peter Halligan, Christopher Bass and John Marshall, 36–48. Oxford: Oxford University Press, 2001.

Knigge, Ursula. 'Die Ausgrabungen im Kerameikos 1970–2'. *Archäologischer Anzeiger*, (1974): 182–94.

Knigge, Ursula. 'Aison, der Meidiasmaler? Zu einer rotfigurigen Oionchoe aus dem Kerameikos'. *Mitteilungen Des Deutschen Archäologischen Instituts (Athenische Abteilung)* 90 (1975): 123–43.

Konstan, David. 'Introduction. Combat Trauma: The Missing Diagnosis in Ancient Greece?' In *Combat Trauma and the Ancient Greeks*. ed. Peter Meineck and David Konstan, 1–14. New York: Palgrave Macmillan, 2014.

Korres, S. G. 'Οἱ ἐπιτάφιοι λόγοι.' *Platon* 5 (1953): 120–5.

Krentz, Peter. 'Casualties in Hoplite Battle'. *Greek, Roman and Byzantine Studies* 26, 1 (1985): 13–20.

Krentz, Peter. 'The Salpinx in Greek Battle'. In *Hoplites: The Classical Greek Battle Experience*. ed. Victor Davis Hanson, 110–20. London: Routledge, 1991.

Krentz, Peter. 'War'. In *The Cambridge History of Greek and Roman Warfare, vol. 1: Greece, The Hellenistic World and the Rise of Rome*. ed. Philip Sabin, Hans van Wees, Michael Whitby, 147–85. Cambridge: Cambridge University Press, 2007.

Kucewicz, Cezary. *The Treatment of the War Dead in Archaic Athens: An Ancestral Custom*. London: Bloomsbury, 2021.

Kurtz, Donna and John Boardman. *Greek Burial Customs*. London: Thames and Hudson, 1971.

Lacey, William. 'The Family of Euxitheus (Demosthenes LVII).' *The Classical Quarterly* 30, 1 (1980): 57–61.

Lambert, Stephen. 'Dedications and Decrees Commemorating Military Action in 339–8 B.C.' In *Axon: Studies in Honor of Ronald S. Stroud.* ed. Angelos Matthaiou and Nikolaos Papazarkadas, 233–46. Athens: Greek Epigraphical Society, 2015.

Larson, Jennifer. *Ancient Greek Cults: A Guide.* New York: Routledge, 2007.

Lawler, Lillian. 'Orchêsis Kallinikos.' *Transactions and Proceedings of the American Philological Association* 79 (1948): 254–67.

Lee, John W. 'The Classical Greek Experience.' In *The Oxford Handbook of Warfare in the Classical World.* ed. Brian Campbell and Lawrence Tritle, 143–61. Oxford: Oxford University Press, 2013.

Lefkowitz, Mary. *Euripides and the Gods.* Oxford: Oxford University Press, 2016.

Lewis, D. M. 'Review: Die Trittyen Attikas und die Heeresreform des Kleisthenes.' *Gnomon* 55, 5 (1983): 431–36.

Lewis, Sian. *The Athenian Woman: An Iconographic Handbook.* London: Routledge, 2002.

Liddel, Peter. *Civic Obligation and Individual Liberty in Ancient Athens.* Oxford: Oxford University Press, 2007.

Lissarrague, François. 'The World of the Warrior.' In *A City of Images: Iconography and Society in Ancient Greece.* ed. Claude Bérard, Christiane Bron, Jean-Louis Durand, Françoise Frontisi-Ducroux, François Lissarrague, Alain Schnapp and Jean-Pierre Vernant. Translated by Deborah Lyons, 39–51. Princeton: Princeton University Press, 1989.

Lissarrague, François. *L'autre Guerrier: Archers, peltastes, cavaliers dans l'imagerie attique.* Paris: La Decouverte- École française de Rome, 1990.

Lonis, Raoul. *Guerre et religion en Grèce à l'époque classique. Recherches sur les rites, les dieux, l'idéologie de la victoire.* Besançon: Université de Franche-Comté, 1979.

Loraux, Nicole. *The Invention of Athens: The Funeral Oration in the Classical City.* Translated by Alan Sheridan. Cambridge, MA: Harvard University Press, 1986/2006.

Loraux, Nicole. *The Children of Athena: Athenian Ideas about Citizenship and the Division between the Sexes.* Translated by Caroline Levine. Princeton: Princeton University Press, 1993.

Loraux, Nicole. *The Experiences of Tiresias: The Feminine and the Greek Man.* Translated by Paula Wissing. Princeton: Princeton University Press, 1995.

Loraux, Nicole. *Mothers in Mourning: With the Essay, Of Amnesty and Its Opposite.* Translated by Corinne Pache. Ithaca: Cornell University Press, 1998.

Loraux, Nicole. *The Divided City: On Memory and Forgetting in Ancient Athens.* Translated by Corinne Pache and Jeff Fort. New York: Zone Books, 2001.

Low, Polly. 'Remembering War in Fifth-Century Greece: Ideologies, Societies, and Commemoration beyond Democratic Athens.' *World Archaeology* 35, 1 (2003): 98–111.

Low, Polly. 'Commemorating the War Dead in Classical Athens: Remembering Defeat and Victory'. In *War, Democracy and Culture in Classical Athens.* ed. David Pritchard, 341–58. Cambridge: Cambridge University Press, 2010.

Lucas, D. W. 'Epispendein nekroi: Agamemnon 1393–98'. *Proceedings of the Cambridge Philological Society* 15 (1969): 60–8.

Luce, Torrey. *The Greek Historians*. London: Routledge, 1997.

Lush, Brian. 'Combat Trauma and Psychological Injury in Euripides' Medea'. *Helios* 41, 1 (2014): 25–57.

MacDowell, Douglas M. *The Law in Classical Athens*. Ithaca, NY: Cornell University Press, 1978.

MacDowell, Douglas M. 'The Case of the Rude Soldier (Lysias 9)'. In *Symposion 1993. Vorträge zur griechischen und hellenistischen Rechtsgeschichte*. ed. Gerhard Thür, 153–64. Cologne: Böhlau, 1994.

MacDowell, Douglas M. 'Hereditary "Sitesis" in Fourth-Century Athens'. *Zeitschrift für Papyrologie und Epigraphik* 162 (2007): 111–13.

Manganaro, Giacomo. 'L'Elaphos Di Oro Dedicato Dai Selinuntini Nell' Apollonion (*IG* XIV, NR. 268)'. *Zeitschrift für Papyrologie und Epigraphik* 106 (1995): 162–4

Mannack, Thomas. *The Late Mannerists in Athenian Vase-painting*. Oxford: Oxford University Press, 2001.

Marconi, Clemente. 'Images for a Warrior. On a Group of Athenian Vases and their Public'. In *Greek Vases: Images, Contexts and Controversies*, ed. Clemente Marconi, 27–40. Leiden: Brill, 2004.

Matovina, Timothy. *The Alamo Remembered: Tejano Accounts and Perspectives*. Austin: Texas University Press, 1995.

Matthaiou, Angelos. 'Ἀθηναίοισι δὲ τεταγμένοισι ἐν τεμένεϊ Ἡρακλέος (Hdt. 6.108.1)'. In *Herodotus and His World: Essays from a Conference in Memory of George Forrest*. ed. Peter Derow and Robert Parker, 190–202. Oxford: Oxford University Press, 2003.

Matheson, Susan. *Polygnotos and Vase Painting in Classical Athens*. Madison: University of Wisconsin Press, 1995.

Matheson, Susan. 'A Farewell with Arms: Departing Warriors on Athenian Vases'. In *Periklean Athens and Its Legacy: Problems and Perspectives*, ed. Judith Barringer and Jeffrey Hurwit, 23–35. Austin: University of Texas Press, 2005.

Matheson, Susan. 'Farewells by the Achilles Painter'. In *On the Fascination of Objects: Greek and Etruscan Art in the Shefton Collection*. ed. John Boardman, Andrew Parkin and Sally Waite, 63–75. Oxford: Oxbow Books, 2016.

McKinley, Jacqueline. 'Cremations: Expectations, Methodologies and Realities'. In *Burial Archaeology: Current Research, Methods and Developments*, ed. Charlotte Roberts, Frances Lee and John Bintliff, 67–76. Oxford: British Archaeological Report S211, 1989.

McKinley, Jacqueline. 'Bone Fragment Size and Weights of Bone from Modern British Cremations and Its Implications for the Interpretation of Archaeological Cremations'. *International Journal of Osteoarchaeology* 3 (1993): 283–7.

McKinley, Jacqueline. 'Bone Fragment Size in British Cremation Burials and Its Implications for Pyre Technology and Ritual'. *Journal of Archaeological Science* 21, 3 (1994): 339–42.

McKinley, Jacqueline. 'Bronze Age "Barrows" and Funerary Rites and Rituals of Cremation'. *Proceedings of the Prehistoric Society* 63 (1997): 129–45.

McKinley, Jacqueline. 'In the Heat of the Pyre'. In *The Analysis of Burned Human Remains*. ed. Christopher Schmidt and Steven Symes, 181–202. London: Academic Press, 2008.

McNeil, Lynda. 'Bridal Cloths, Cover-ups, and Kharis: The "Carpet Scene" in Aeschylus' "Agamemnon"'. *Greece & Rome* 52, 1 (2005): 1–17.

McNiven, Tim. *Gestures in Attic Vase Painting: Their Use and Meaning, 550–450 B.C.* PhD diss. Ann Arbor: University of Michigan, 1982.

Meiggs, Russell. *Trees and Timber in the Ancient Mediterranean World*. Oxford: Clarendon Press, 1982.

Meineck, Peter. 'Combat Trauma and the Tragic Stage: Ancient Culture and Modern Catharsis?' In *Our Ancient Wars: Rethinking War Through the Classics*. ed. Victor Caston and Silke-Maria Weineck, 184–223. Ann Arbour: University of Michigan Press, 2016.

Melchior, Aislinn. 'Caesar in Vietnam: Did Roman Soldiers Suffer from Post-Traumatic Stress Disorder?' *Greece & Rome* 58, 2 (2011): 209–23.

Miles, Margaret. 'A Reconstruction of the Temple of Nemesis at Rhamnous', *Hesperia* 58 (1989): 131–249.

Mills, Sophie. *Theseus, Tragedy, and the Athenian Empire*. Oxford: Clarendon Press, 1997.

Monoson, Sara S. 'Socrates in Combat: Trauma and Resilience in Plato's Political Theory'. In *Combat Trauma and the Ancient Greeks*. ed. Peter Meineck and David Konstan, 131–62. New York: Palgrave Macmillan, 2014.

Monoson, Sara S. 'Socrates' Military Service'. In *Our Ancient Wars: Rethinking War Through the Classics*. ed. Victor Caston and Silke-Maria Weineck, 96–118. Ann Arbour: University of Michigan Press, 2016.

Morgan, Janett. *The Greek Classical House*. Exeter: Bristol Phoenix Press, 2010.

Morris, Ian. *Burial and Ancient Society: The Rise of the Greek City-State*. Cambridge: Cambridge University Press, 1987.

Morris, Ian. *Death-Ritual and Social Structure in Classical Antiquity*. Cambridge: Cambridge University Press, 1992.

Morrison, John, J. E. Coates and N. B. Rankov. *The Athenian Trireme: The History and Reconstruction of an Ancient Greek Warship*. 2nd edn. Cambridge: Cambridge University Press, 2000.

Moulinier, Louis. *Le Pur et l'impur dans la pensée des Grecs d'Homère à Aristote*. Paris: Librairie C. Klineksieck, 1952.

Musgrave, Jonathan. 'Dust and Damn'd Oblivion: A Study of Cremation in Ancient Greece'. *The Annual of the British School at Athens* 85, (1990): 271–99.

Nadon, Christopher. *Xenophon's Prince: Republic and Empire in the* Cyropaedia. Berkeley: University of California Press, 2001.

Neils, Jenifer. 'Hera, Paestum, and the Cleveland Painter'. In *Greek Vases: Images, Contexts and Controversies*. ed. Clemente Marconi, 73–84. Leiden: Brill, 2004.

Nevin, Sonya. 'Animating Ancient Warfare: The Spectacle of War in the Panoply Project Vase Animations'. In *War as Spectacle: Ancient and Modern Perspectives on the Display of Armed Conflict*. ed. Anastasia Bakogianni and Valerie Hope, 335–52. London: Bloomsbury Academic, 2015.

Neer, Richard. *Style and Politics in Athenian Vase-Painting: The Craft of Democracy, ca. 530–460 BCE*. Cambridge: Cambridge University Press, 2002.

Nilsson, Martin. *Greek Folk Religion*. New York: Harper Torchbooks, 1940.

Noy, David. '"Half-Burnt on an Emergency Pyre": Roman Cremations Which Went Wrong'. *Greece & Rome* 47, 2 (2000): 186–96.

Oakley, John and Rebecca Sinos. *The Wedding in Ancient Athens*. Madison: University of Wisconsin Press, 1993.

Ober, Josiah. 'Tyrant Killing as Therapeutic *Stasis*: A Political Debate in Images and Texts'. In *Popular Tyranny: Sovereignty and Its Discontents in Ancient Greece*. ed. Kathryn Morgan, 215–50. Austin: University of Texas Press, 2003.

Ober, Josiah. *Athenian Legacies: Essays on the Politics of Going on Together*. Princeton: Princeton University Press, 2005.

O'Connell, Peter. *The Rhetoric of Seeing in Attic Forensic Oratory*. Austin: University of Texas Press, 2017.

O'Donnell, Karen. 'Help for Heroes: PTSD, Warrior Recovery, and the Liturgy'. *Journal of Religion and Health* 54 (2015): 2389–97.

Oost, Stewart. 'Xenophon's Attitude toward Women'. *The Classical World* 71, 4 (1977): 225–36.

Osborne, Michael. 'Entertainment in the Prytaneion at Athens', *Zeitschrift für Papyrologie und Epigraphik* 41 (1981): 153–70.

Osborne, Robin. 'The Erection and Mutilation of the Hermai'. *Proceedings of the Cambridge Philological Society* 25 (1985): 45–73.

Osborne, Robin. 'Images of a Warrior. On a Group of Athenian Vases and their Public'. In *Greek Vases: Images, Contexts and Controversies*. ed. Clemente Marconi, 41–54. Leiden: Brill, 2004.

Osborne, Robin. 'Democratic Ideology, the Events of War and the Iconography of Attic Funerary Sculpture', In *War, Democracy and Culture in Classical Athens*. ed. David Pritchard, 245–65. Cambridge: Cambridge University Press, 2010.

Osborne, Robin. *The History Written on the Classical Greek Body*. Cambridge: Cambridge University Press, 2011.

Ozer, Emily, Suzanne Best, Tami Lipsey and Daniel Weiss. 'Predictors of Posttraumatic Stress Disorder and Symptoms in Adults: A Meta-Analysis'. *Psychological Bulletin Copyright* 129, 1 (2003): 52–73.

Panofsky, Erwin. *Meaning in the Visual Arts*. London: University of Michigan Press, 1955.

Panofsky, Erwin. *Tomb Sculpture: Four Lectures on its Changing Aspects from Ancient Egypt to Bernini*. New York: Harry N. Abrams, Inc, 1964.

Papadopolou, Thalia. *Euripides: Phoenician Women*. London: Bloomsbury Academic, 2008.

Papazarkadas, Nikolaos and Dimitris Sourlas. 'The Funerary Monument for the Argives who fell at Tanagra (*IG* I³ 1149): A New Fragment'. *Hesperia* 81, 4 (2012): 585–617.

Parker, Robert. *Miasma: Pollution and Purification in Early Greek Religion*. Oxford: Clarendon Press, 1983/1996.

Parker, Robert. *Athenian Religion: A History*. Oxford: Clarendon Press, 1996.

Parker, Robert. 'Sacrifice and Battle'. In *War and Violence in Ancient Greece*. ed. Hans van Wees, 299–314. Oxford: Classical Press of Wales, 2009.

Parker, Robert. 'War and Religion in Ancient Greece'. In *The Religious Aspects of War in the Ancient Near East, Greece, and Rome*. ed. Krzysztof Ulanowski, 123–32. Leiden: Brill, 2016.

Parry, Hugh. 'The Second Stasimon of Euripides' Heracles (637–700)'. *The American Journal of Philology* 86, 4 (1965): 363–74.

Patterson, Cynthia. *The Family in Greek History*. Cambridge, MA: Harvard University Press, 1998.

Patterson, Cynthia. '"Citizen Cemeteries" in Classical Athens?' *The Classical Quarterly* 56, 1 (2006): 48–56.

Patton, Kimberley. *Religion of the Gods: Ritual, Paradox, and Reflexivity*. Oxford: Oxford University Press, 2009.

Pelling, Chrisopher. 'Bringing Autochthony Up-to-Date: Herodotus and Thucydides'. *The Classical World* 102, 4 (2009): 471–83.

Pemberton, Elizabeth. 'The Name Vase of the Peleus Painter'. *The Journal of the Walters Art Gallery* 36 (1977): 62–72.

Petrakos, Vasileios. *Rhamnous*. Athens: Ministry of Culture, 1991.

Petrakos, Vasileios. Ὁ δῆμος τοῦ Ραμνοῦντος. *vols 1–2*. Athens: Ἡ ἐν Ἀθήναις Ἀρχαιολογικὴ Ἑταιρεία (Βιβλιοθήκη τῆς ἐν Ἀθήναις Ἀρχαιολογικῆς Ἑταιρείας), 1999.

Phang, Sara, Iain Spence, Douglas Kelly and Peter Londey. *Conflict in Ancient Greece and Rome: The Definitive Political, Social, and Military Encyclopedia, vol. 1*. Santa Barbara: ABC-CLIO, 2016.

Piontek, Janusz. 'Proces kremacji i jego wpływ na morfologię kości w świetle wyników badań eksperymentalnych'. *Archeologia Polski* 21, 2 (1976): 247–80.

Pohlenz, Max. 'Zu den attischen Reden auf die Gefallenen'. *Symbolae Osloenses* 26 (1948): 46–74.

Poliakoff, Michael. *Combat Sports in the Ancient World: Competition, Violence, and Culture*. New Haven: Yale University Press, 1987.

Pouilloux, Jean. *Recherches sur l'Histoire et les cultes de Thasos. Études thasiennes 3*. Paris: E. De Boccard, 1954.

Pritchard, David. 'Thetes, Hoplites and the Athenian Imaginary'. In *Ancient History in a Modern University, vol. 1: The Ancient Near East, Greece and Rome*. ed. Tom Hillard, 121–7. Cambridge: Eerdmans Publishing, 1998.

Pritchard, David. 'Sport, War and Democracy in Classical Athens'. *The International Journal of the History of Sport* 26, 2 (2009): 212–45.

Pritchard, David. 'The Symbiosis between Democracy and War: The Case of Ancient Athens.' In *War, Democracy and Culture in Classical Athens*. ed. David Pritchard, 1–62. Cambridge: Cambridge University Press, 2010.

Pritchard, David. 'Public Honours for Panhellenic Sporting Victors in Democratic Athens'. *Nikephoros* 25 (2012): 209–20.

Pritchard, David. *Sport, Democracy and War in Classical Athens*. Cambridge: Cambridge University Press, 2013.

Pritchett, William K. *The Greek State at War, vols 1–5*. Berkeley: University of California Press, 1979–1991.

Pucci, Pietro. *Euripides' Revolution under Cover: An Essay*. Ithaca: Cornell University Press, 2016.

Quinn, Colin, Lynne Goldstein, Babriel Cooney and Ian Kuijt. 'Perspectives—Complexities of Terminologies and Intellectual Frameworks in Cremation Studies'. In *Transformation by Fire: The Archaeology of Cremation in Cultural Context*, ed. Ian Kuijt, Colin P. Quinn and Gabriel Cooney, 25–32. Tuscan: University of Arizona Press, 2014.

Quinn, Josephine. 'Herms, Kouroi and the Political Anatomy of Athens'. *Greece & Rome* 54, 1 (2007): 82–105.

Raaflaub, Kurt. 'Father of All, Destroyer of All: War in Late Fifth-Century Athenian Discourse and Ideology'. In *War and Democracy: A Comparative Study of the Korean War and the Peloponnesian War*. ed. David McCann and Barry Strauss, 307–56. Armonk, NY: M.E. Sharpe, Inc, 2001.

Raaflaub, Kurt. 'Lysistrata and War's Impact on the Home Front'. In *Our Ancient Wars: Rethinking War Through the Classics*. ed. Victor Caston and Silke-Maria Weineck, 38–74. Ann Arbour: University of Michigan Press, 2016.

Rabinowitz, Nancy. *Greek Tragedy*. Malden, MA: Blackwell Publishing, 2008.

Rausch, Mario. 'Miltiades, Athen und "die Rhamnusier auf Lemnos" (*IG* I3 522bis)'. *Klio* 81, 1 (1999): 7–17.

Rawlings, Louis. *The Ancient Greeks at War*. Manchester: Manchester University Press, 2007.

Rees, Owen. 'Picking over the Bones: The Practicalities of Processing the Athenian War Dead'. *Journal of Ancient History* 6, 2 (2018): 167–84.

Rees, Owen. 'We Need to Talk about Epizelus: 'PTSD' and the Ancient World'. *Medical Humanities* 46 (2020): 46–54.

Rehm, Rush. *Marriage to Death: The Conflation of Wedding and Funeral Rituals in Greek Tragedy*. Princeton: Princeton University Press, 1994.

Rehm, Rush. *The Play of Space: Spatial Transformation in Greek Tragedy*. Princeton: Princeton University Press, 2002.

Reisman, Miriam. 'PTSD Treatment for Veterans: What's Working, What's New, and What's Next'. *Pharmacy and Therapeutics* 41, 10 (2016): 632–34.

Retief, François and Louise Cilliers. 'The Army of Alexander the Great and Combat Stress Syndrome (326 BC)'. *Acta Theologica* 26, 2 (2005): 29–43.

Reverdin, Olivier. *La Religion de la Cité Platonicienne*. Paris: E. de Boccard, 1945.

Rich, John and Graham Shipley, ed. *War and Society in the Greek World*. London: Routledge, 1993.

Ridley, Ronald. 'The Hoplite as Citizen: Athenian Military Institutions in their Social Context'. *L'antiquité classique* 48, 2 (1979): 508–48.

Riley, Kathleen. *The Reception and Performance of Euripides' Herakles: Reasoning Madness*. Oxford: Oxford University Press, 2008.

Robertson, Noel. 'The Collective Burial of Fallen Soldiers at Athens, Sparta and Elsewhere: "Ancestral Custom" and Modern Misunderstandings'. *Echoes du Monde Classique/Classical Views* 27 (1983): 78–92.

Rosivach, Vincent J. 'Execution by Stoning in Athens'. *Classical Antiquity* 6, 2 (1987a): 232–48.

Rosivach, Vincent J. 'Autochthony and the Athenians'. *The Classical Quarterly* 37, 2 (1987b): 294–306.

Rosivach, Vincent J. 'Zeugitai and Hoplites'. *Ancient History Bulletin* 16, 1 (2002): 33–43.

Rosivach, Vincent J. 'Notes on the Pentakosiomedimnos' Five Hundred Medimnoi'. *The Classical Quarterly* 55, 2 (2005): 597–601.

Roth, Paul. 'The Theme of Corrupted Xenia in Aeschylus' "Oresteia"'. *Mnemosyne* 46, 1 (1993): 1–17.

Rouse, William. *Greek Votive Offerings*. Cambridge: Cambridge University Press, 1902.

Ruano, Paloma. '*IG* VII 53, An Epigraphicrara Avis in the Corpus of Greek Metrical Inscriptions'. *Mare Nostrum* 7 (2016): 35–55.

Rudhardt, Jean. *Notions fondamentales de la pensée religieuse et actes constitutifs du culte dans la Grèce classique*. Geneva: Librairie Droz, 1958.

Runciman, Walter G. 'Doomed to Extinction: The Polis as an Evolutionary Dead-End'. In *The Greek City: From Homer to Alexander*. ed. Oswyn Murray and Simon Price, 347–68. Oxford: Oxford University Press, 1990.

Sage, Michael. *Warfare in Ancient Greece: A Sourcebook*. London: Routledge, 1996.

Santoni, Anna. 'Figure femminili nell'opera di Senofonte: il caso di Pantea'. In *Donne Che Contano Nella Storia Greca*. ed. Umberto Bultrighini and Elisabetta Dimauro, 345–72. Lanciano: Carabba, 2014.

Schmidt, Stefan. *Rhetorische Bilder auf attischen Vasen: Visuelle Kommunikation im 5. Jahrhundert v. Chr.* Berlin: Dietrich Reimer, 2005.

Seaford, Richard. 'Homeric and Tragic Sacrifice'. *Transactions of the American Philological Association* 119 (1989): 87–95.

Seifert, Martina. 'Oikos and Hetairoi: Black Figure Departure Scenes Reconsidered'. In *Athenian Potters and Painters, vol III*. ed. John Oakley, 215–20. Oxford: Oxbow Books, 2014.

Sekunda, Nicholas. 'Athenian Demography and Military Strength 338–322 BC'. *The Annual of the British School at Athens* 87 (1992): 311–55.

Shapiro, H. Alan. 'Comings and Goings: The Iconography of Departure and Arrival on Attic Vases'. *Mètis* 5 (1990): 113–26.

Shapiro, H. Alan. 'The Iconography of Mourning in Athenian Art'. *American Journal of Archaeology* 95, 4 (1991): 629–56.

Shapiro, H. Alan. 'Correlating Shape and Subject: The Case of the Archaic Pelike'. In *Athenian Potters and Painters: The Conference Proceedings*. Oxbow Monographs 67. ed. John Oakley, 63–70. Oxford: Oxbow Books, 1997.

Shay, Jonathan. *Achilles in Vietnam: Combat Trauma and the Undoing of Character*. New York: Atheneum, 1994.

Shay, Jonathan. 'The Birth of Tragedy – Out of the Needs of Democracy'. *Didaskalia* 2, 2 (1995) [Online] (Accessed 4 February 2018). Available at: www.didaskalia.net/issues/vol2no2/shay.html.

Shay, Jonathan. *Odysseus in America: Combat Trauma and the Trials of Homecoming*. New York: Scribner, 2002.

Shear, Julia L. *Polis and Revolution: Responding to Oligarchy in Classical Athens*. Cambridge: Cambridge University Press, 2011.

Shear, Julia L. '"Their Memories Will Never Grow Old': The Politics of Remembrance in the Athenian Funeral Orations'. *The Classical Quarterly* 63, 2 (2013): 511–36.

Shear Jr, T. Leslie. 'The Monument of the Eponymous Heroes in the Athenian Agora'. *Hesperia* 39, 3 (1970): 145–222.

Sherman, Nancy. '"He Gave me His Hand but Took My Bow": Trust and Trustworthiness in the *Philoctetes* and Our Wars'. In *Combat Trauma and the Ancient Greeks*. ed. Peter Meineck and David Konstan, 207–24. New York: Palgrave Macmillan, 2014.

Sheth, Hitesh, Zindadil Gandhi and G. K. Vankar. 'Anxiety Disorders in Ancient Indian Literature'. *Indian Journal of Psychiatry* 52, 3 (2010): 289–91.

Sidwell, Keith. *Aristophanes the Democrat: The Politics of Satirical Comedy During the Peloponnesian War*. Cambridge: Cambridge University Press, 2009.

Siewert, Peter. *Die Trittyen Attikas und die Heeresreform des Kleisthenes*. Munich: Beck, 1982.

Sikes, E. E. 'Nike and Athena Nike'. *The Classical Review* 9, 5 (1895): 280–3.

Sissa, Guilia and Marcel Detienne. *La Vie Quotidienne des Dieux Grecs*. Paris: Hachette, 1989.

Siurla-Theodoridou, Vasiliki. *Die Familie in der griechischen Kunst und Literatur Des 8. Bis 6. Jahrhunderts V. Chr*. Munich: V. Florentz, 1989

Small, Jocelyn. 'Time in Space: Narrative in Classical Art'. *The Art Bulletin* 81, 4 (1999): 562–75.

Smith, Gertrude. 'Athenian Casualty Lists'. *Classical Philology* 14, 4 (1919): 351–64.

Solomon, Zahava, Mario Mikulincer and Hanoch Flum. 'The Implications of Life Events and Social Integration in the Course of Combat-related Post-traumatic Stress Disorder'. *Social Psychiatry and Psychiatry Epidemiology* 24 (1989): 41–8.

Sourvinou-Inwood, Christiane. 'Altars with Palm-Trees, Palm-Trees and Parthenoi'. *Bulletin of the Institute of Classical Studies* 32 (1985): 125–46.

Sourvinou-Inwood, Christiane. *'Reading' Greek Death: To the End of the Classical Period.* Oxford: Clarendon Press, 1995.

Sourvinou-Inwood, Christiane. 'Further Aspects of Polis Religion'. In *Oxford Readings in Greek Religion*. ed. Richard Buston, 38–55. Oxford: Oxford University Press, 2000.

Sparkes, Brian. *The Red and the Black: Studies in Greek Pottery.* London: Routledge, 1996.

Spieß, Angela B. *Der Kriegerabschied auf attischen Vasen der archaischen Zeit.* Frankfurt: Peter Lang, 1992.

Spivey, Nigel. *The Ancient Olympics: A History.* Oxford: Oxford University Press, 2004.

Stadter, Philip. 'Fictional Narrative in the *Cyropaideia*'. *The American Journal of Philology* 112, 4 (1991): 461–91.

Stafford, Emma. *Greek Cults of Deified Abstractions.* PhD diss. London: University College London, 1998.

Stafford, Emma. *Heracles.* London: Routledge, 2012.

Stansbury-O'Donnell, Mark. *Pictorial Narrative in Ancient Greek Art.* Cambridge: Cambridge University Press, 1999.

Stanton, G. R. 'The Tribal Reforms of Kleisthenes the Alkmeonid'. *Chiron* 14 (1984): 1–41.

Steenkamp, Maria, W. E. Schlenger, N. Corry, C. Henn-Haase, M. Qian, M. Li, D. Horesh, K-L. Karstoft, C. Williams, C-L. Ho, A. Shalev, R. Kulka and C. Marmar. 'Predictors of PTSD 40 years After Combat: Findings from the National Vietnam Veterans Longitudinal Study'. *Depression and Anxiety* 34 (2017): 711–22.

Steinbock, Bernd. *Social Memory in Athenian Public Discourse: Uses and Meanings of the Past.* Ann Arbor: University of Michigan Press, 2013.

Steiner, Deborah. 'The Immeasures of Praise: The Epinician Celebration of Agamemnon's Return'. *Hermes* 138, 1 (2010): 22–37.

Stewart, Andrew. 'Stesichoros and the François Vase'. In *Ancient Greek Art and Iconography*, ed. Warren Moon, 53–74. Madison: University of Wisconsin Press, 1983.

Stewart, Andrew. *History, Myth, and Allegory in the Program of the Temple of Athena Nike, Athens.* Washington DC: National Gallery of Art, 1985.

Storey, Ian. *Euripides: Suppliant Women.* London: Bloomsbury Academic, 2008.

Stoupa, Charis. 'Γ' Εφορεία Προϊστορικών και Κλασικών Αρχαιοτήτων, ανασκαφικές εργασίες: Οδός Σαλαμίνος 35'. *ArchDelt* 52, *Chronika*, Β'1 (1997): 52–56.

Strauss, Barry. 'Ritual, Social Drama, and Politics in Classical Athens'. *American Journal of Ancient History* 10, 1 (1985): 67–83.

Strauss, Barry. *Athens after the Peloponnesian War: Class, Faction and Policy 403–386 B.C.* Abingdon: Routledge, 1986.

Strauss, Barry. *Salamis: The Greatest Naval Battle of the Ancient World.* London: Arrow Books, 2005.

Strauss, Barry. 'Perspectives on the Death of the Fifth Century Athenian Seaman'. In *War and Violence in Ancient Greece*. ed. Hans van Wees, 261–84. Oxford: Classical Press of Wales, 2009.

Stroud, Ronald S. 'Greek Inscriptions Theozotides and the Athenian Orphans'. *Hesperia: The Journal of the American School of Classical Studies at Athens* 40, 3 (1971): 280–301.

Stroud, Ronald S. *Athenian Empire on Stone*. Athens: Hellēnikē epigraphikē hetaireia, 2006.

Stupperich, Reinhard. *Staatsbegräbnis und Privatgrabmal im klassischen Athen*. PhD diss. Münster: Universität Münster, 1977.

Stupperich, Reinhard. (1994) 'The Iconography of Athenian State Burials in the Classical Period'. In *The Archaeology of Athens and Attica under the Democracy*. ed. William Coulson, Olga Palaiga and H. Alan Shapiro, 93–103. Oxford: Oxbow Books, 1994.

Sutton, Robert F. 'Family Portraits: Recognizing the "Oikos" on Attic Red-Figure Pottery'. *XAPIΣ: Essays in Honor of Sara A. Immerwahr. Hesperia Supplements* 33 (2004): 327–50.

Svoronos-Hadjimichalis, Vanna. 'L'Evacuation de la fumée dans les maisons grecques des Ve et IVe siècles'. *Bulletin de Correspondance Hellénique* 80, 1 (1956): 483–506.

Swift, Laura. *The Hidden Chorus: Echoes of Genre in Tragic Lyric*. Oxford: Oxford University Press, 2010.

Tataki, Argyro. 'Nemesis, Nemeseis, and the Gladiatorial Games at Smyrna'. *Mnemosyne* 62, 4 (2009): 639–48.

Tatum, James. *Xenophon's Imperial Fiction: On the Education of Cyrus*. Princeton: Princeton University Press, 1989.

Tetlow, Elisabeth. *Women, Crime and Punishment in Ancient Law and Society: Volume 2: Ancient Greece*. New York: Continuum International Publishing Group, 2005.

Thiel, Johannes H. *Xenophōntos Poroi: specimen litterarium inaugurale*. Vienna: Österreichische Staatsdr, 1922.

Thompson, Homer. 'Excavations in the Athenian Agora: Buildings on the West Side of the Agora'. *Hesperia* 6 (1937): 1–226.

Toher, Mark. 'On "Thucydides' Blunder": 2.34.5'. *Hermes* 127, 4 (1999): 497–501.

Toher, Mark. 'Euripides' "Supplices" and the Social Function of Funeral Ritual'. *Hermes* 129, 3 (2001): 332–43.

Toohey, Peter. '(Review) Achilles in Vietnam. Combat Trauma and the Undoing of Character by Jonathan Shay'. *Phoenix* 50, 2 (1996): 162–63.

Touchais, Gilles. 'Chronique des fouilles et découvertes archéologiques en Grèce en 1996 et 1997'. *Bulletin de Correspondance Hellénique* 122, (1998): 705–988.

Trembinski, Donna. 'Comparing Premodern Melancholy/Mania and Modern Trauma: An Argument in Favor of Historical Experiences of Trauma'. *History of Psychology* 14, 1 (2011): 80–99.

Trenkner, Sophie. *The Greek Novella in the Classical Period*. Cambridge: Cambridge University Press, 1958.

Treves, P. 'Apocrifi demostenici: L' Epitafio'. *Athenaeum* 14 (1936): 153–74.

Tritle, Lawrence. *Melos to My Lai: War and Survival*. London: Routledge, 2000.

Tritle, Lawrence. 'Gorgias, the Encomium of Helen, and the Trauma of War'. *Clio's Psyche* 16, 2 (2009): 195–99.

Tritle, Lawrence. *A New History of the Peloponnesian War*. Oxford: Wiley-Blackwell, 2010.

Tritle, Lawrence. 'Men at War'. In *The Oxford Handbook of Warfare in the Classical World*. ed. Brian Campbell and Lawrence Tritle, 279–93. Oxford: Oxford University Press, 2013.

Tritle, Lawrence. '"Ravished Minds" in the Ancient World'. In *Combat Trauma and the Ancient Greeks*. ed. Peter Meineck and David Konstan, 87–104. New York: Palgrave Macmillan, 2014.

Trivigno, Franco. 'The Rhetoric of Parody in Plato's Menexenus'. *Philosophy and Rhetoric* 42, 1 (2009): 29–58.

Trundle, Matthew. 'Light Troops in Classical Athens'. In *War, Democracy and Culture in Classical Athens*. ed. David Pritchard, 139–60. Cambridge: Cambridge University Press, 2010.

Trundle, Matthew. 'Commemorating Victory in Classical Greece: Why Greek Tropaia?' In *Rituals in Triumph in the Mediterranean World*, ed. Anthony Spalinger and Jeremy Armstrong, 95–122. Leiden: Brill, 2013.

Tsagalis, Christos. '*CEG* 594 and Euripides' *Erechtheus*'. *Zeitschrift für Papyrologie und Epigraphik* 162 (2007): 9–13.

Tucker, Philip. *Exodus from the Alamo: The Anatomy of the Last Stand Myth*. Havertown: Casemates Publishers, 2009.

Tucker, Thomas. *The Seven Against Thebes of Aeschylus*. Cambridge: Cambridge University Press, 1908.

Tyrrell, William and Larry Bennett. *Recapturing Sophocles' Antigone*. London: Rowman & Littlefield Publishers, 1998.

Tyrrell, William and Larry Bennett. 'Pericles' Muting of Women's Voices in Thuc. 2.45.2'. *The Classical Journal* 95, 1 (1999): 37–51.

Ulanowski, Krzysztof, ed. *The Religious Aspects of War in the Ancient Near East, Greece, and Rome*. Leiden: Brill, 2016.

Ustinova, Yulia. *Caves and the Ancient Greek Mind: Descending Underground in the Search for Ultimate Truth*. Oxford: Oxford University Press, 2009.

Ustinova, Yulia and Etzel Cardeña. 'Combat Stress Disorders and Their Treatment in Ancient Greece'. *Psychological Trauma: Theory, Research, Practice, and Policy* 6, 6 (2014): 739–48.

Valdés Guía, Miriam and Julián Gallego. 'Athenian "Zeugitai" and the Solonian Census Classes: New Reflections and Perspectives'. *Historia: Zeitschrift für Alte Geschichte* 59, 3 (2010): 257–81.

Valla, D. 'Il Mito di Pantea'. *Atene e Roma* 3 (1922): 119–24.

van Lommel, Korneel. 'The Recognition of Roman Soldiers' Mental Impairment'. *Acta Classica* LVI (2013): 155–84.

van Wees, Hans. 'Greeks Bearing Arms: The State, the Leisure Class, and the Display of Weapons in Archaic Greece'. In *Archaic Greece: New Approaches and New Evidence*. ed. Nick Fisher and Hans van Wees, 333–78. London: Duckworth, 1998a.

van Wees, Hans. 'A Brief History of Tears: Gender Differentiation in Archaic Greece'. In *When Men Were Men: Masculinity, Power and Identity in Classical Antiquity*. ed. Lin Foxhall and John Salmon, 10–53. London: Routledge, 1998b.

van Wees, Hans. *Greek Warfare: Myths and Realities*. London: Duckworth, 2004.

van Wees, Hans. 'Rivalry in History: An Introduction'. In *Competition in the Ancient World*. ed. Nick Fisher and Hans van Wees, 1–33. Swansea: Classical Press of Wales, 2011.

van Wees, Hans. 'Farmers and Hoplites: Models of Historical Development'. In *Men of Bronze: Hoplite Warfare in Ancient Greece*, ed. Donald Kagan and Gregory Viggiano, 222–55. Princeton: Princeton University Press, 2013.

Vanderpool, Eugene. 'The State Prison of Athens'. In *From Athens to Gordion: The Papers of a Memorial Symposium for Rodney S. Young*. ed. Keith DeVries, 17–31. Philadelphia: The University Museum, 1980.

Vaughn, Pamela. 'The Identification and Retrieval of the Hoplite Battle-Dead'. In *Hoplites: The Classical Greek Battle Experience*, ed. Victor Davis Hanson, 38–62. London: Routledge, 1991.

Vermeule, Emily. 'Five Vases from the Grave Precinct of Dexileos'. *Jahrbuch des Deutschen Archäeologischen Instituts* 85 (1970): 94–111.

Vernant, Jean-Pierre. 'Hestia - Hermes: The Religious Expression of Space and Movement among the Greeks'. *Social Science Information* 8, 4 (1969): 131–68.

Vernant, Jean-Pierre. 'Preface'. In *A City of Images: Iconography and Society in Ancient Greece*. ed. Claude Bérard, Christiane Bron, Jean-Louis Durand, Françoise Frontisi-Ducroux, François Lissarrague, Alain Schnapp and Jean-Pierre Vernant. Translated by Deborah Lyons, 7–11. Princeton: Princeton University Press, 1989.

Verrall, Arthur. *The 'Seven Against Thebes' of Aeschylus*. London: Macmillan and Co, 1887.

Von Bothmer, Dietrich. 'Greek Vases from the Hearst Collection'. *The Metropolitan Museum of Art Bulletin* 13 (1957): 165–80.

Walters, K. R. 'Rhetoric as Ritual: The Semiotics of the Attic Funeral Oration'. *Florilegium* 2 (1980): 1–27.

Walters, K. R. '"We Fought Alone at Marathon": Historical Falsification in the Attic Funeral Oration'. *Rheinisches Museum für Philologie, Neue Folge* 124, 3/4 (1981): 204–11.

Walters, K. R. 'Perikles' Citizenship Law'. *Classical Antiquity* 2, 2 (1983): 314–36.

Wassermann, Felix. 'Serenity and Repose: Life and Death on Attic Tombstones'. *The Classical Journal* 64, 5 (1969): 193–202.

Wheeler, Everitt and Barry Strauss. 'Battle'. In *The Cambridge History of Greek and Roman Warfare, vol. 1: Greece, the Hellenistic World and the Rise of Rome*. ed. Philip Sabin, Hans van Wees and Michael Whitby, 186–247. Cambridge: Cambridge University Press, 2007.

Whitehead, David. *The Demes of Attica, 508/7-ca. 250 B.C.: A Political and Social Study*. Princeton: Princeton University Press, 1986.

Wickkiser, Bronwen L. 'Speech in Context: Plato's "Menexenus" and the Ritual of Athenian Public Burial'. *Rhetoric Society Quarterly* 29, 2 (1999): 65–74.

Winkler, John. 'Phallos Politikos: Representing the Body Politic in Athens'. *Differences* 2, 1 (1990): 29–45.

Wolpert, Andrew. *Remembering Defeat: Civil War and Civic Memory in Ancient Athens.*
  Baltimore, Johns Hopkins University Press, 2002.

Worcester, Dean. 'Shell-Shock in the Battle of Marathon.' *Science* 50, 1288 (1919): 230.

Worthington, Ian. 'The Authorship of the Demosthenic "Epitaphios".' *Museum*
  Helveticum 60, 3 (2003): 152–57.

Wrede, Walther. 'Kriegers Ausfahrt in der archaisch-griechischen Kunst'. *Athenische*
  Mitteilungen 41 (1916): 221–374.

Yalouri, Athanasia. 'A Hero's Departure'. *American Journal of Archaeology* 75, 3 (1971):
  269–75.

Young, Allan. *The Harmony of Illusions: Inventing Post-Traumatic Stress Disorder.*
  Princeton: Princeton University Press, 1995.

Zaccarini, Matteo. 'Thucydides' Narrative on Naval Warfare: Epibatai, Military Theory,
  Ideology'. In *Ancient Warfare: Introducing Current Research Vol. 1.* ed. Geoff Lee,
  Helene Whittaker and Graham Wrightson, 210–28. Newcastle-upon-Tyne:
  Cambridge Scholars Press, 2015.

Zeitlin, Froma I. 'The Motif of the Corrupted Sacrifice in Aeschylus' Oresteia'.
  Transactions and Proceedings of the American Philological Association 96 (1965):
  463–508.

Zeitlin, Froma I. 'Postscript to Sacrificial Imagery in the Oresteia (Ag. 1235–37)'.
  Transactions and Proceedings of the American Philological Association 97 (1966):
  645–53.

Ziolkowski, John E. *Thucydides and the Tradition of Funeral Speeches at Athens.*
  New York: Arno Press, 1981.

Index

The letter *f* following an entry indicates a page that includes a figure.
The letter *m* following an entry indicates a page that includes a map.
The letter *t* following an entry indicates a page that includes a table.

Abradatas 30–1
Acharnians (Aristophanes) 55
Achilles painter
 Red figure *stamnos* 21*f*
Aeschines 72
Aeschylus
 Agamemnon. See *Agamemnon*
 Seven Against Thebes 55, 101, 131
Against Agoratus (Lysias) 69–70
Against Eubulides (Demosthenes) 79
Against Leocrates (Lycurgus) 29
Agamemnon (Aeschylus)
 cremation 108
 domestic religion 95, 96
 hearths 11, 12, 93–4, 95
 homecomings 88, 90, 91, 93–4
 hospitality 100
 ritual 97, 99
 sacrifice 97
 Zeus Ctesius, cult of 88, 94–5
Agesilaus 76
Agora, Athens 44–5
Agoratus 69, 70
Ajax (Sophocles) 11
Alamo, battle of the 108
Alcestis (Euripides) 11
Alcibiades 65–7, 75
Altamura Painter
 red-figure *pelike* 85*f*–7
American Psychiatric Association
 Diagnostic and Statistical Manual of
  Mental Disorders (DSM-V) 2
Amphiaraos 22, 23*f*
Anabasis (Xenophon) 57
Andocides 47, 48
Andromache 29–30, 31
Antiphon 88
Apollo Lykeios 47

archers 92, 93
Arginusae, battle of 109
Aristophanes 45
 Acharnians 55
 Clouds 39
 Knights 74
 Peace 39
armour 6, 76–7, 79, 84
army. *See* Athenian army
Art 17–18
ashes (cremation) 108–10 *see also*
  cremains
aspis 84 *see also* shields
Athena 23–5
Athenian army *see also* musters
 battle figures 43*t*
 honours/rewards 72–6
 military dedications 75–80
 military identity 76
 transport 64–8
 victory parades 69–72
Athenian hoplites 6, 9–10, 60
 agency 26–7
 bravery 193 n. 50
 ceramics, depicted on 18, 19, 20,
  21*f*–3*f*, i26
 class system 36–8
 collective identity 27, 123
 Crowley, Jason 6–7
 dedications 75–80
 individualism 27–8, 123–4
 legal challenges to 72, 75–6
 mustering. *See* musters
 number of 36–7, 41–4
 oikos 28, 36–7
 polis 13
 pollution 101–2
 ritual 26–7, 59, 102

Sicilian expedition 52–5
tithes 79
wealth 50–1
working-class 37
Athens/Athenians, the 9, 14, 88
  archaeology 131–2
  army, the 64–80, 43t see also musters
  Assembly 72
  as *autochthones* 117
  casualty lists 127–9, 132–3, 141
  demosion sema 105
  hoplites. See Athenian hoplites
  Kerameikos 132
  military homecomings 63–80 see also
    warrior homecomings
  mustering points 44–9
  navy, the 52–5, 65–8, 135–6
  tribes 38–9, 114, 115, 128
  Zeus Ctesius, cult of 88, 94–5, 96
Athens painter 22
  white-ground *lekythos* 22–3f
athletes 73–5, 92, 93

Bachhylides
  Ode to Theseus 39–40
battle figures 43t
birds 163 n. 30
bodies, touching 126
bone (cremation) 108–10 see also
    cremains
boundaries 10, 12
Brasidas 74
burial 105, 111–12, 116–18

casualty lists 127–9, 132–3, 141 see also
    stelae
cavalry 49, 133–4
cenotaphs 131–5
ceramics 17–19 see also red-figure pottery
  iconography 20–7
  loss 22
  red-figure amphora (attrib. Niomid
    Painter) 97f–9
  red-figure amphora (attrib. painter of
    the Berlin Hydria) 25f
  red-figure *hydria* (attrib. 'Dwarf'
    painter) 22, 23f
  red-figure *lekythos* (attrib. Oionokles
    Painter) 131

red-figure *pelike* (attrib. Altamura
    Painter) 85f–7
red-figure *pelike* (unattrib.) 83f–5
red figure *stamnos* (attrib. Achilles
    Painter) 21f–2
  space 22
  white ground *lekythos* (attrib. Vouni
    Painter) 129–30f
  white-ground *lekythos* (attrib. Athens
    painter) 22–3f
children 126, 143–5
Christ, Matthew 39–40
class system 36–8, 134
Clearchus 4
Clouds (Aristophanes) 39
collective dedications 77–9
collective identity 27, 77–9, 118–19, 128
commemorations 75–80
conscription. See musters
Constitution of the Spartans (Xenophon)
    58
Corinthian army 7
Corinthian-style helmets 76–7
cremains 110–13, 114–15
cremation 105–13
Crowley, Jason 5–7, 9
Cyropaedia (Xenophon) 28, 29, 30–1, 57,
    59, 60–1

De Gloria Atheniensium (Plutarch)
    109–10
de-individuation 14, 15, 27, 124, 129, 137,
    150–1
death see also funerals *and*
    memorialisation *and* war-dead
  bodies, touching 126
  burial 105, 111–12, 116–18
  ceramics 22
  cremation 105–13
  notification 138–42
decree of Themistocles 59
dedications 75–80
deme 38, 50–1, 77, 128
Demokleides grave relief 135f–7
demosion sema, the 105
Demosthenes 65, 74
  Against Eubulides 79
  war-dead 117, 118, 119, 120, 142,
    144–5

departures 52, 59–60 *see also* warrior
        departures
    divine support 55–61
    ritual 52–7
    Sicilian expedition 52–5
Derkylidas 70–1
deuteropotmos 139
Dexileos 132–5
διαβατήρια 58, 59
*Diagnostic and Statistical Manual of
    Mental Disorders* (DSM-V)
    (American Psychiatric Association)
    2
Diodorus 43*t*, 68–9, 140–1
Diodotus 139–40
Diogeiton 139–40, 142
dogs 20–2
domestic sphere 10–13, 60, 81 *see also*
        oikos
    death notification 138–42
    funeral orations 142–6
    funerals 124
    funerals of the war-dead 123–46
    hearths 11–12, 93–4, 95, 96
    libation 99
    memorialisation 129–37
    war-dead, return of the 146–8
    Zeus Ctesius, cult of 88, 94–5, 96
DSM-V (*Diagnostic and Statistical Manual
    of Mental Disorders*) (American
    Psychiatric Association) 2
'Dwarf' painter
    Red-figure *hydria* 22, 23*f*

Eck, Bernard 101
ekphora 124, 125
Electra (Euripides) 74–5, 93
emotion 28–32, 90, 103 *see also* mourning
    envy 142, 143–4
    Sicilian expedition 53
    war-dead 142, 143–4
empty hearths 11
Encyclopedia of Trauma (Figley, Charles)
    4–5
enlistment 27 *see also* mobilisation
envy 142, 144–4
Ephesus, battle of 110–12
epic imagery 20
epitaphioi logoi 116–21, 127, 142–6

Epizelus 3, 4
Eponymoi monument 39, 60
Erechtheus (Euripides) 28–9, 32–3
Euripides 55
    Alcestis 11
    Electra 74–5, 93
    Erechtheus 28–9, 32–3
    Helen 141
    Heracles. See *Heracles*
    Medea 126
    Suppliant Women 125–6, 130

Face of Battle, The (Keegan, John) 3
families 142–3 *see also* domestic sphere
    children 126, 143–5
    death notification 138–42
    envy of 142
    funeral orations 142–6, 147
    parents 32–3, 125–6, 142–3
    state support 142–3, 145–6
    war-dead, funerals of the 123–46
    war-dead, return of the 146–8
    widows 145–6
    wives 31–2, 91
fathers 126, 143
For Mantitheus (Lysias) 50
For Polystratus (Lysias) 37
From Melos to My Lai (Tritle, Lawrence) 3
funerals
    bodies, touching 126
    burial 105, 111–12, 116–18
    cremation 105–13
    epitaphioi logoi 116–21, 127 142–6
    families and 123–46
    funeral norms 124
    funerary materials 19
    orations 116–21, 127, 142–6, 147
    patrios nomos 113–21

garlands 131
gods, support of the 55–61
Gorgias 3–4, 120

hair 130–1
Hamel, Debra 109
Harmodius 134
Hau, Lisa 63
hearths 11–12, 93–4, 95, 96, 100
Hector 29–30

Hegelochus 79–80
Helen (Euripides) 141
Hellenica (Xenophon) 58, 111
helmets 76–7
Heracles (Euripides) 90, 91–3
    hearths 94, 95, 96, 100
    purification 100–1, 102
    Zeus Ctesius, altar of 95
heralds 39, 40
Hermes 10
herms 10
Herodotus 4, 57
hieroscopy 26–7, 97
hippeis 36
Holck, Per 109
Hölscher, Tonio 18
homecomings. *See* military homecomings
    and warrior homecomings
Homer
    Iliad. See *Iliad*
    Odyssey 2, 8–9
honour 30–1, 32
honours/rewards 72–6
hoplites. *See* Athenian hoplites
hospitality 99–100
households 10–11, 13, 96 *see also*
    oikos
    hearths 11–12, 93–4, 95, 96, 100
Hyperides 118, 119, 120, 142, 143,
    144

identity 118–19 *see also* individuation/
    de-individuation
    collective 27, 77–9, 118–19, 128
    Dexileos 134–5
    heroic identity 117–18, 119, 121, 135
    military identity 76, 79
Iliad (Homer) 2, 26
    emotion 28, 29–30, 31
immortality 119–20
individuation/de-individuation 114, 15,
    27, 124, 129, 137, 150–1
Inscriptions Graecae
    I³ 138 45–6
    I³ 1147 115
    I³ 1162 128–9
    II² 1155 77–8
    13 522*bis* 77
Iris 25*f*–6, 27

Isaeus 88, 139, 141
Izumi Tōru 112–13

Jameson, Michael 47, 59
Japan 112–13
Justin 56

kallinikos 92
Kamieński, Łukasz 8
katalogoi 27, 60
    muster, the 36, 38–40, 49
    war-dead 106
Keegan, John 3
    Face of Battle, The 3
Kekropis 77–8
klinē 115–16
Knights (Aristophanes) 74
kyrios 142

larnakes 114–15
Laws (Plato) 11
lekythoi 22
lexiarchikon grammateion 38, 51
libation 27, 53, 56, 96
    red-figure pottery 25*f*–6, 83*f*, 84,
        85*f*–6*f*, 87–9, 97*f*–9
    shields 84
    variations 87–9
Lissarrague, François 19–20, 23–4
literary evidence
    departures 28–33
    homecomings 90–7, 99–103
    themes 91–3
lochos 50
Low, Polly 127
Lyceum, Athens 44, 45–7, 48
Lycurgus 33
    Against Leocrates 29
Lysias 51
    Against Agoratus 69–70
    For Mantitheus 50
    For Polystratus 37
    war-dead 117, 119, 120
    war-dead, family of 139–40, 142,
        143–4, 145–6

mantis/eis 57, 59, 60, 149
mass levy 36
Matheson, Susan 25

Medea (Euripides) 126
Melchior, Aislinn 5
memorialisation 147–8
  cenotaphs 131–5
  Demokleides grave relief 135*f*–7
  Dexileos monument 132–5
  garlands 131
  hair 130–1
  private 129–37
  public 126–9
memory 120 *see also* memorialisation
  collective 118, 119, 120
  immortality of 120
methodology 14, 17–19
miasma 10–11, 101
military, the 13
military dedications 75–80
military homecomings 63–4 *see also*
    warrior homecomings
  Athens 64–75
  dedications 75–80
  honours/rewards 72–6
  military *pompe* 68–72
  war-dead. *See* war-dead
military honours/rewards 72–6
military identity 76, 79
military *pompe* 68–72
military transitions 10
military victory celebrations 63–4,
    68–74
missing in action 141
mobilisation 35–44 *see also* musters
  selection 36
mourning 123, 124, 130, 131, 142–3
  bodies, touching 126
  immortality 120
  white-ground *lekythos* 22, 23*f*
musters 19, 35–6, 59–60
  Athenian mustering figures 42*f*–3*f*
  cavalry 49
  locations 44–9
  map 48*m*
  mechanism of 38–41
  mobilisation 35–8
  rolling muster, the 49–51
  Sicilian expedition 52–5
  size 41–4
  terms 41
  transportation 64–8

names 127–8, 147
navy, the 52–5, 65–8, 135–6
New History of the Peloponnesian War, A
    (Tritle, Lawrence) 3
Nike 24–6
Niomid Painter
  red-figure amphora 97*f*–9

Ode to Theseus (Bachhylides)
    39–40
O'Donnell, Karen 8–9
Odyssey (Homer) 2, 8–9
oikos 10, 11–13, 195 n. 84 *see also*
    households
  ceramics 18–21*f*, 22–3*f*
  death notification 138–42
  departure from 19–33
  farms 36–7
  funeral orations 142–6
  funerals 124
  funerals of the war-dead 123–46
  hearths 11–12, 93–4, 95, 96, 100
  memorialisation 129–37
  rituals 88–9, 103
omens 57–61
Onasander 57, 59
Orestes 75

painter of the Berlin Hydria
  red-figure amphora 25*f*
pandemei/panstratia 36, 44
Panthea 30–2, 60–1
parents 32–3, 125–6, 142–3
Parker, Robert 100, 101, 102, 118
paternal hearths 11
patrios nomos 113–21
Pausanias 57
Peace (Aristophanes) 39
Peloponnesian War 7
pentacosiomedimnoi 36
Pericles 73
  war-dead 117–18, 119, 120,
  war-dead, family of 142, 143, 145
  war widows 145
personal dedications 79–80
phyle 77, 78
Piraeus 65, 71
Plato 142–3, 144, 146
  Laws 11

Plutarch 39, 58
    Alcibiades 65–7, 75
    De Gloria Atheniensium 109–10
    Pericles 73
polis 10, 12–13, 23–8
pollution 12, 101–2, 139
polyandria 105, 116
pompe 68–72
post-traumatic stress disorder (PTSD).
        See PTSD
pottery. *See* ceramics
πομπή 69
Praxithea 32–3
Pritchard, David 73–5
Pritchett, William 76–7, 101
private sphere *see also* domestic sphere
    memorialisation 129–37
prizes 27
prosthesis 114, 124
PTSD (post-traumatic stress disorder) 2
    Heracles (Euripides) 92
    in history 2 –10
    military homecomings 7–10
    relativist approach 5–7
    universalist approach 2–5
public sphere 10, 12–13
    memorialisation 126–30
purification ceremonies 8, 9, 12
pyres 107–10, 132

reading of the liver and entrails, the 26 *see
        also* hieroscopy
red-figure amphora (attrib. Niomid
        Painter) 97*f*–9
red-figure amphora (attrib. painter of the
        Berlin Hydria) 25*f*
red-figure *hydria* (attrib. 'Dwarf' painter)
        22, 23*f*
red-figure *lekythos* (attrib. Oionokles
        Painter) 131
red-figure *pelike* (attrib. Altamura Painter)
        85*f*–7
red-figure *pelike* (unattrib.) 83*f*–5
red-figure pottery
    ambiguity 89–90, 103
    departure scenes 17–28, 81–90, 95–6,
        97*f*–9, 103
    homecoming scenes 81–90, 97*f*–9, 103
    parallel scenes 82 –7

participants 95–6, 103
    variation 87–9
    women 89
red figure *stamnos* (attrib. Achilles
        Painter) 21*f*–2
reintegration 9
religion 13, 95
    ceramics 18
    dedications 76, 79–80
    victory processions 69–72
    Zeus Ctesius, cult of 88, 94–5, 96
Rhamnous 77
ritual 55–61, 95–100 *see also* libation *and*
        sacrifice
    aspis 84
    border 58, 59
    community 54–7
    death. *See* death
    διαβατήρια 58, 59
    hearths 11–12, 93–4, 95, 96
    hieroscopy 26–7, 97
    missing in action 141
    navy, the 53–5
    patrios nomos 113–21
    purification 8, 9, 12, 95, 100–2
    reading of the liver and entrails, the
        26
    Sicilian expedition departure 52–5
    Zeus Ctesius, cult of 88, 94–5, 96
rolling muster, the 49–51
Runciman, Walter 13

sacrifice 54, 57, 96, 97*f*–9 *see also*
        hieroscopy
    aspides 84
    διαβατήρια 58, 59
    Erechtheus (Euripides) 32, 33
    hieroscopy 26–7, 97
    omens 57–61
    purification 100
    Zeus Ctesius, cult of 88, 95
salpinx 39–40
Second World War 112–13
Seven Against Thebes (Aeschylus) 55, 101,
        131
shame 6
    Corinthian army 7
Shapiro, Alan 82
Shay, Jonathan 2–3, 4

shields 84
  discarding 6
Sicilian expedition 52–5, 57, 107, 108, 138
Siewert, Peter 49–50
social support 7–8
Solygeia, battle of 106
Sophocles
  Ajax 11
Spartans, the 58–9
  captives 68
  war-dead 138
state support 142–3, 145–6
stelae 28, 127–30*f see also* casualty lists
strategoi 38, 54, 59–60, 72–3, 79, 149–50
Suppliant Women (Euripides) 125–6, 130
symbolic dedications 79

taxiarchoi 38, 60
taxes 45–7, 51 *see also* tithes
Theopompus 58
thetes 36, 37
Thrasyllus 67–8
Thucydides 48, 64
  Brasidas 74
  musters 42*t*
  patrios nomos 113–15
  pyres 107, 108
  Sicilian expedition 52–5, 57, 107, 108, 138
  war widows 145
  war-dead 138, 142, 143 144
tithes 76, 79 *see also* taxes
token cremation burials 112–13
tombs 118
θρίαμβος 68–9
tribes 38–9, 114, 115, 128
trierarchos 36, 139
Tritle, Lawrence 3–4
  From Melos to My Lai 3
  New History of the Peloponnesian War, A 3
trittyes 38, 42–3, 44, 49, 50
Trundle, Matthew 63–4

Valla, D. 31
van Lommel, Korneel 5
van Wees, Hans 36–7

vases 18–19 20–1
  Athena 24–5
  departure scenes 17–28, 81–90, 95–6, 97*f*–9
  homecoming scenes 81–90, 97*f*–9
  Nike 24–5
  participants 95–6
  red-figure amphora (attrib. Niomid Painter) 97*f*–9
  red-figure amphora (attrib. painter of the Berlin Hydria) 25*f*
  red-figure *hydria* (attrib. 'Dwarf' painter) 22, 23*f*
  red-figure *lekythos* (attrib. Oionokles Painter) 131
  red-figure *pelike* (attrib. Altamura Painter) 85*f*–7
  red-figure *pelike* (unattrib.) 83*f*–5
  red figure *stamnos* (attrib. Achilles Painter) 21*f*–2
  white ground *lekythos* (attrib. Vouni Painter) 129–30*f*
  white-ground *lekythos* (attrib. Athens painter) 22–3*f*
Vaughn, Pamela 106
victory celebrations 63–4, 68–74
Vietnam War 7, 156 n. 46
Vouni Painter
  white ground *lekythos* 129–30*f*
vows 56–7

war
  affect on society 8
  Athenian preparation for 9
  pollution 101–2
  spoils 76
war captives 68
war-dead 105–6
  battlefield burial 105
  battlefield cremation 105–13
  casualty lists 127–9, 132–3, 141
  collecting 102
  collective identity 118–19, 128
  epitaphioi logoi 117–21, 127 142–6
  families of the 123–46
  funeral orations 117–21, 127, 142–6
  heroic identity 117–18, 119, 121, 135
  identification 106, 141
  immortality 119–20

left behind 110–13, 115–16, 141
memorialisation 126–37
naming of 278
notification 138–42
oikos 137–46
patrios nomos 113–21
return of the 146–8
war orphans 143–5
warrior departures 17
  literary evidence 28–33
  methodology 17–19
  oikos, departure from 19–33
  red-figure pottery 17–28, 81–90, 95–6,
    97*f*–9, 103
warrior homecomings 81 *see also* military
    homecomings
  epitaphioi logoi 117
  literary evidence 90–7, 99–103
  location 93–4
  pollution 101
  red-figure pottery 81–90, 97*f*–9, 103
wealth 50–1, 76
  Sicilian expedition 52–3
white-ground *lekythos* (attrib. Athens
    painter) 22–3*f*
white ground *lekythos* (attrib. Vouni
    Painter) 129–30*f*
women 19–20
  ceramic iconography 23–6

emotion 29–33
female orphans 144
funerals 123, 124, 125–6, 137
ideal wives 31–2, 91
mothers 32–3, 125–6
red-figure pottery 89
Spartan 168 n. 104
widows 145–6
winged 24–6
Worcester, Dean A. 4

Xenophon 4, 11, 47, 48, 59
  Agesilaus 76
  Alcibiades 65–7
  Anabasis 57
  Constitution of the Spartans 58, 59
  Cyropaedia 28, 29, 30–1, 57, 59, 60–1
  Hellenica 58, 111
  musters 42*t*
  purification 101
  sacrifice 57
  Thrasyllus 67–8
  victory parades 69, 70–1
  war-dead 110–11, 138, 141, 144

Young, Allen 5

zeugitai 36–7
Zeus Ctesius, cult of 88, 94–5, 96